COMPANY LAW AND SUSTAINABILITY

This investigation of the barriers to and opportunities for promoting environmental sustainability in company law provides an in-depth comparative analysis of company law regimes across the world. The social norm of shareholder primacy is the greatest barrier to progress, and this recognition also helps explain why voluntary action by companies and investors alone is insufficient. By deconstructing the myth that shareholder primacy has a legal basis and challenging the economic postulates on which the mainstream corporate governance debate is based, *Company Law and Sustainability* reveals the surprisingly large unexplored potential in current company law regimes for companies to reorient themselves towards sustainability. It also suggests possible methods of reforming the existing legal infrastructure for companies and makes an important contribution to the wider debate on how to achieve sustainability.

BEATE SJÅFJELL heads the international network of scholars in the Sustainable Companies Project, on which much of the ground-breaking research in this book is based. Professor Sjåfjell is also the head of the University of Oslo's research group, Companies, Markets, Society and the Environment (jus.uio.no/companies), as well as of its European Law Network.

BENJAMIN J. RICHARDSON is Professor of Environmental Law at the Faculty of Law and Institute for Marine and Antarctic Studies, University of Tasmania, Australia. His teaching and scholarship cover climate change law, socially responsible investment, corporate social responsibility, and Aboriginal legal issues.

COMPANY LAW AND SUSTAINABILITY

Legal Barriers and Opportunities

Edited by
BEATE SJÅFJELL
BENJAMIN J. RICHARDSON

CAMBRIDGE
UNIVERSITY PRESS

University Printing House, Cambridge CB2 8BS, United Kingdom

Cambridge University Press is part of the University of Cambridge.

It furthers the University's mission by disseminating knowledge in the pursuit of education, learning and research at the highest international levels of excellence.

www.cambridge.org
Information on this title: www.cambridge.org/9781107043275

© Cambridge University Press 2015

This publication is in copyright. Subject to statutory exception and to the provisions of relevant collective licensing agreements, no reproduction of any part may take place without the written permission of Cambridge University Press.

First published 2015

A catalogue record for this publication is available from the British Library

Library of Congress Cataloging in Publication data
Company law and sustainability : legal barriers and opportunities / edited by Beate Sjåfjell, Benjamin J. Richardson.
pages   cm
Includes bibliographical references and index.
ISBN 978-1-107-04327-5 (hardback)
1. Corporate governance – Law and legislation.   2. Sustainable development – Law and legislation.   3. Corporation law.   I. Sjåfjell, Beate, editor.   II. Richardson, Benjamin J., editor.
K1315.C65   2015
346'.066 – dc23   2015005503

ISBN 978-1-107-04327-5 Hardback

Cambridge University Press has no responsibility for the persistence or accuracy of URLs for external or third-party internet websites referred to in this publication, and does not guarantee that any content on such websites is, or will remain, accurate or appropriate.

In memory of my deeply beloved daughter,
Aleksandra (1997–2014)

Beate Sjåfjell

CONTENTS

List of contributors   *page* ix
Foreword   xii
Preface   xv

1 Capitalism, the sustainability crisis, and the limitations of current business governance   1

BENJAMIN J. RICHARDSON AND BEATE SJÅFJELL

2 Corporate social responsibility and environmental sustainability   35

DAVID MILLON

3 Shareholder primacy: the main barrier to sustainable companies   79

BEATE SJÅFJELL, ANDREW JOHNSTON, LINN ANKER-SØRENSEN, AND DAVID MILLON

4 The role of board directors in promoting environmental sustainability   148

BLANAID CLARKE

5 Accounting, auditing, and reporting: supporting or obstructing the sustainable companies objective?   175

CHARLOTTE VILLIERS AND JUKKA MÄHÖNEN

6 Financial markets and socially responsible investing   226

BENJAMIN J. RICHARDSON

7 Limits to corporate reform and alternative legal structures   274

CAROL LIAO

vii

8 The future of company law and sustainability 312
BEATE SJÅFJELL AND BENJAMIN J. RICHARDSON

Index 341

CONTRIBUTORS

LINN ANKER-SØRENSEN is a research assistant in the Faculty of Law of the University of Oslo, Norway, and her work focuses on corporate law, international law, and comparative law.

BLANAID CLARKE holds the McCann FitzGerald Chair in Corporate Law at Trinity College Dublin. Her research interests include company law, corporate governance, banking law, and takeover law, and she has published extensively in these areas. She was previously a member of the European Commission's Reflection Group on the Future of EU Company Law and is currently a member of the European Commission's Informal European Company Law Expert Group. Blanaid is a member of the OECD Corporate Governance Committee, the EU's European Securities and Markets Authority Takeover Bids Network, and the European Corporate Governance Institute. She works with the Irish Takeover Panel, and in October 2010, she was appointed to the board of the Irish Central Bank Commission.

ANDREW JOHNSTON is Professor in Company Law and Corporate Governance at the School of Law at the University of Sheffield, UK, a member of the Sustainable Companies Project at the University of Oslo, and a research associate at the University of Cambridge Centre for Business Research. He has also taught at the Universities of Queensland, Cambridge, and Warsaw. In 2009, he published a monograph with Cambridge University Press entitled, *EC Regulation of Corporate Governance*. His current research interests lie in the intersection of corporate governance, law, and heterodox and institutional economics. Recent papers have examined regulatory responses to the financial crisis, including the cap on pay in financial institutions, the European Regulation on Credit Rating Agencies, and the legality of Quantitative Easing, and offered a critical appraisal of corporate social responsibility initiatives from both economic and sustainability perspectives.

CAROL LIAO is an Assistant Professor in the Faculty of Law at the University of Victoria, Canada. She is an advisor to the Philippe Kirsch Institute and Canadian Centre for International Justice, and a member of the University of Toronto Responsible Investment Committee. Previously, she practised as a senior associate in the Mergers & Acquisitions Group of Shearman & Sterling LLP (New York). She has also served as the Director of Corporate Innovation at a Canadian technology company, where she led a project to design the legal infrastructure to support the company's dual mandate of creating economic and social value. She is a Liu Scholar at the Liu Institute for Global Issues, and winner of the 2012 Robert Bertram Award, issued by the Canadian Foundation for Governance Research and Institute of Corporate Directors. Her research has been published in several journals, including *European Company Law* and the *Canadian Review of Social Policy*.

JUKKA MÄHÖNEN is Professor of Civil Law and Dean at the University of Turku Faculty of Law, Finland. He was educated in Finland (LL.B., LL.Lic, and LL.D. from the University of Turku, and M.Sc. (Econ.) from the Turku School of Economics) and the United States (LL.M. from the University of California, Berkeley). He has written numerous monographs and articles in Finnish, Swedish, and English on company, securities, accounting, and auditing law as well as legal theory and the economic analysis of law. He is the principal investigator in the Academy of Finland-funded research project, eCoherence – Reconciling Economic and Non-Economic Values in a Multi-Polar Society, and a member of the Sustainable Companies Project. In addition to his academic activities, he is the chair of the Auditing Board of the State of Finland and regularly acts as a consultant for Finnish governmental ministries and the authorities.

DAVID MILLON is the J.B. Stombock Professor of Law at Washington and Lee University in Lexington, Virginia, USA, where he has been a member of the law faculty since 1986. He teaches contracts and corporate law and has published numerous articles on corporate social responsibility and corporate governance. He also holds a PhD in medieval English legal history and has published a book on church–state legal relations.

BENJAMIN J. RICHARDSON is a scholar of environmental law at the University of Tasmania, Australia, where he holds a joint professorial appointment with the Faculty of Law and the Institute for Marine and Antarctic Studies. He previously held academic posts in the law faculties of the University of Auckland, the University of Manchester, and Osgoode Hall Law School of York University, and, most recently before his return to Australia, he was at the University of British Columbia, where he held the Canada Research Chair in Environmental Law and Sustainability. Professor Richardson's expertise includes climate change law, socially responsible investment, corporate social responsibility, and Aboriginal legal issues.

BEATE SJÅFJELL is Professor dr. juris at the University of Oslo, Faculty of Law, Department of Private Law, in Norway. Her fields of interest include company and securities law, corporate governance and corporate social responsibility, EU law, environmental law, and law and economics. She is the head of the Sustainable Companies Project and of the Faculty's Research Group, Companies, Markets, Society and the Environment (jus.uio.no/companies), as well as of its European Law Network. In addition to her monograph, *Towards a Sustainable European Company Law* (Kluwer, 2009), and the edited volume, *The Greening of European Business Under EU Law* (Routledge, 2014, co-editor Anja Wiesbrock), Beate has published extensively on EU company law and the integration of sustainable development. Many of her papers are available at ssrn.com/author=375947.

CHARLOTTE VILLIERS is Professor of Company Law at the University of Bristol, UK. She is a qualified solicitor, and she has also worked at the Universities of Sheffield, Glasgow, and Oviedo in Spain. Her teaching and research expertise cover the broad areas of company law, corporate governance, and labour and employment law. She is interested in corporate social responsibility and sustainability issues. She is the author of several books and articles, and currently she is writing on boardroom diversity, disclosure, executive pay, and workers' participation.

FOREWORD

Company law has typically been seen as a dry and technical subject principally of interest only to the community of lawyers. Traditionally, its aim has been to create legal certainty for companies themselves in their relations with each other in the marketplace, and to define and combat corrupt, fraudulent, or other criminal acts by individuals using company structures to shield their behaviour. This book takes a completely different perspective, analysing how company law is being and can be used as a vital tool to combat new collective threats in the world, including climate change, social disintegration, and conflict. It is partly a response to the successes, but also the limitations, of movements towards corporate social and environmental responsibility in the past 20 years that have largely been pursued through a range of voluntary, soft law, and other initiatives kept strictly separate from those of corporate governance.

A number of factors make this new approach timely and relevant to decision-makers:

The financial crisis of 2008 threw a new focus on issues of integrity and short-termism which have demanded responses that go far beyond simply narrow financial transparency for companies.

Delays and failures in global climate change and trade talks have highlighted the weakness of relying on inter-governmental processes alone, and placed new emphasis on what companies can and should do directly to meet global challenges.

Widespread business support for the UN Guiding Principles on Business and Human Rights also saw a subtle shift away from a simplistic anti-regulation, voluntary-only approach to corporate responsibility from business lobbyists, to an acceptance of the concept of a 'smart mix' that both regulatory as well as voluntary initiatives are needed in order to promote responsible corporate behaviour.

Meanwhile, many in the investment community, from pension funds to insurance companies, have come to the growing realisation that the risks due to climate change and other societal challenges pose a level of potential cost to their business activities, that represents not just a generic threat to the sustainability of the planet but also a very direct threat to the sustainability of the company itself.

Many of those who have worked on issues of corporate responsibility and accountability, including myself, have not come to these issues of company law with any great expertise or previous experience of the subject. What brought us to it was a new understanding of how company law was actually acting as a barrier to companies adopting more sustainable practices, as well as having the potential to create frameworks which can assist rather than hinder this process. The analysis in this book emanating from the Sustainable Companies Project provides a fresh perspective and challenges old assumptions in this respect.

Concepts of 'shareholder primacy' and 'fiduciary duty' which have acted as a straitjacket restricting responsible business are shown to be greatly over-stated, and largely based on societal rather than legal norms.

The authors in this volume demonstrate that current approaches, however worthy, are grossly inadequate to address the scale of change required to achieve the necessary transition to low-carbon growth.

There is a critique of the traditional 'business case' for corporate social responsibility, with its assumption that corporate behaviour will be modified simply by increased understanding of the cost and opportunities created by unsustainable business practices.

Such arguments have already contributed to a political climate where it has been possible to reach agreement on new reporting requirements on the environmental, social, and human rights impacts of the company in the European Union – new legal requirements that I personally have long advocated and am proud to have helped deliver.

Reporting is perhaps the easiest aspect of corporate governance with which to address issues of corporate responsibility because it involves no specific new obligations on the company, except for that of transparency itself. It can be seen as an approach which is primarily of benefit as a management tool within the company, and one which externally utilises market-based rather than regulatory forces to foster changes in behaviour.

However, the EU law is only one example of a company law approach to corporate sustainability analysed in this volume and one which I would be the first to say was preceded by non-financial reporting requirements in individual European countries, including France, Belgium, and Denmark. Indeed, it can be argued that the leading global example was found, not in

Europe, but from the King III Report on Corporate Governance in South Africa.

Nevertheless, the debate in Europe is now moving on to include questions such as whether corporate sustainability reports should be debated and voted at company Annual General Meetings, how far management remuneration could be linked to environmental, social, and governance issues, and whether directors' duties should be changed to embrace wider sustainability objectives.

Indeed, at the time of writing, company law responses in new or developing instruments of global governance are being debated, including a through revision of the OECD Corporate Governance Code and proposals to incorporate corporate sustainability reporting in a new Sustainable Development Goal as part of the UN post-2015 Development Agenda.

The analysis that follows in this volume represents a much-needed contribution to current public policy discourse and is truly global in character. It sounds trite to say that this debate affects the future of the planet as the enormity of the issues involved often makes this so difficult to comprehend.

However, the concept of 'climate justice' which has now entered the debate emphasises that the challenge of global warming can only be met by addressing issues of law and of rights. For the company lawyers who have been used to the more conventional debates of the past, this is a language which they will swiftly understand.

What we will all have to understand, including those who start off primarily from the social and environmental perspective, is that the challenges we identify can actually be met, not only by setting limits in mega-tonnes of carbon emissions, but also by addressing the sphere of corporate governance and coming to new definitions of what is the very purpose of the company.

I very much welcome this understanding in what follows.

Richard Howitt, MEP
European Parliament Rapporteur on Corporate Social Responsibility
Opinion Rapporteur, EU Non-Financial Reporting Directive
Cambridge, United Kingdom
October 2014

PREFACE

This book originates from the Sustainable Companies Project (2010–2014),[1] an international scholarly network whose principal aim has been to deepen our understanding of how company law hinders or facilitates corporate environmental responsibility. In an innovative stance, this project has sought to shift the dominant focus beyond environmental law to the role of company law and related areas of business regulation in promoting sustainable development. Our vision has been to contribute to the conceptual framework and tools to realise the potential of some companies to make independent, creative, and significant contributions to mitigate climate change and other global environmental problems. Climate change provides a powerful example illustrating the broader challenges in promoting corporate environmental and social responsibility through company law reform.

The Sustainable Companies Project has received invaluable funding from the Research Council of Norway, under its programme 'Norwegian Environmental Research towards 2015'. The Project's broad international scope was made possible through the academic contributions of a team of scholars from all continents. While only a few team members were directly involved in the writing of this book, the analysis, especially in the chapters on comparative company law (Chapter 3, 'Shareholder primacy: the main barrier to sustainable companies' by Sjåfjell and others) and accounting law (Chapter 5, 'Accounting, auditing, and reporting: supporting or obstructing the sustainable companies objective?' by Villiers and Mähönen), draws on the original research of the Project's many scholars. We thank them all for their fine contributions, constructive feedback, and unwavering enthusiasm for the project and this book.[2] For the book

---

[1] See jus.uio.no/companies under Projects.

[2] A list of team members may be found on the Sustainable Companies Project's website (see note 1). We also acknowledge the contribution of other scholars, including that of Dr Andreas Rühmkorf, Sheffield University, UK, for his help in explaining German company law.

xvi   PREFACE

manuscript itself, we express our gratitude not only, of course, to the chapters' authors, but also to the University of Oslo research assistants, Linn Anker-Sørensen and Elisabeth Hvaal Lingaas, for their technical support.

The subject matter of this book is timely and significant. We need bold new approaches to curb environmentally unsustainable trends. Some 50 years of environmental legislation in the modern era hardly seem to have made a difference in the bigger picture of the biosphere's increasing degradation and decay. The time is right to discuss how to promote sustainable business by reforming corporate governance and the related legal rules for commerce. In other words, we need to consider how the imperative of sustainability can be embedded within the very core of business decision-making, so that economic enterprise, from the outset, is pursued within nature's parameters. Mere tinkering with 'business as usual', as is presently the case with most corporate social responsibility codes and practice, is not good enough. It is our hope that this book's analysis of the legal barriers to sustainability and the possibilities of changes within business law will help policy-makers move from incremental to fundamental reform.

Beate Sjåfjell and Benjamin J. Richardson
January 2015

1

Capitalism, the sustainability crisis, and the limitations of current business governance

BENJAMIN J. RICHARDSON AND BEATE SJÅFJELL

1 Impetus for a new direction

This book investigates the limitations of corporate governance and some related business laws, and their potential reform in furthering environmentally sustainable development, or 'sustainability', as this term is more conveniently known. The central idea is that promoting sustainability cannot be left solely to corporate volunteerism, but also requires enabling legal frameworks that go beyond conventional environmental regulation to ensconce within company law the necessary standards and procedures. While the book is strongly motivated by the threat of global climate change, which challenges the traditional assumptions and purpose of business enterprise over the long term, along with many other domains of human endeavour, a range of other environmental problems such as the loss of biodiversity also suggests that a different approach to business activity is needed. Arising from the work of the Sustainable Companies Project, led by Professor Beate Sjåfjell at the University of Oslo,[1] this volume offers multi-jurisdictional perspectives from scholars of business and environmental law. Over eight chapters, a mosaic of analyses, spanning company law, accounting standards, and financial markets regulation, identify both the barriers to and the opportunities to promote sustainability in the context of corporations and their financial investors. The book concludes with some ideas to further 'sustainable companies', a phrase intended to capture the ideal of corporations and other business entities acting within environmentally sustainable parameters. The focus of the book is to deepen our understanding of the barriers to creating sustainable companies, rather than outlining a blueprint for reform. The

---

[1] See jus.uio.no/companies under Projects. The project received funding from the Research Council of Norway. The project's broad international scope was made possible through the academic contributions of the large team of scholars from all around the world, to whom we express our gratitude and whose work we hereby recognise.

path to reform largely hinges on better understanding of the source and nature of the problems, and recognition that the tools and strategies for such reform will vary somewhat across societies and jurisdictions.

Creating sustainable companies has never been more urgent in a world beset by the intertwined crises afflicting global financial markets and the planetary environment. The Global Financial Crisis (GFC) that erupted in 2008 revealed profound weaknesses in the conventional paradigm of market finance, and the need to rethink its fundamental tenets and purpose. Another emerging crisis stems from humankind's degradation of life-sustaining natural resources with an intensity and speed that threaten the livelihoods and prosperity not only of future generations, but also of those alive today. Climate change looms large as the most ominous such threat. The GFC and environmental crises stem from a different aetiology but they also share the problem of how short-sighted economic activity can lead to dangerous long-term problems.

To promote sustainability, it is not sufficient simply to have more environmentally efficient businesses, in the sense that companies use fewer natural resources or emit less pollution relative to their economic activity. An efficiency standard fails to ensure sustainability when the economy continues to grow and the human population is increasing. The 'efficiency' paradigm also avoids addressing the significant social injustices in contemporary environmental decision-making. Putting the economy on a sustainable path requires a more comprehensive and fundamental strategy that includes rethinking the very purpose and nature of economic activity, including that of the dominant business organisation: the corporation.

This book proceeds from the position that sustainable business should not be a discretionary preference, to follow only if corporate leaders perceive an economic benefit for their company. All economic activity must avoid depleting non-substitutable natural capital or creating environmental externalities. It must invest more in clean, low-carbon technologies, climate adaptation projects, ecosystem rehabilitation and improvement, and other ways to build sustainability.[2] Economic activity that has public costs should be accountable for such impacts.

Presently, business enterprise and the wider capitalist system in which it functions still have a long way to go before it might fulfil this vision. The movement for corporate social responsibility (CSR) and its offshoot,

---

[2] T. Jackson, *Prosperity Without Growth: Economics for a Finite Planet* (Earthscan, 2009), 138–9.

CAPITALISM, SUSTAINABILITY, BUSINESS GOVERNANCE 3

socially responsible investing (SRI), have captured only a relatively small group of committed converts. CSR has a long history in the context of industrial capitalism, dating back to the nineteenth century in the first movement for improved labour conditions.[3] Its influence has generally been episodic and fleeting. It has more recently regained prominence as modernist economic virtues such as efficiency, profits, and maximum growth have waned in an increasingly cynical world plagued by social and environmental problems.[4] Rejecting the unbridled free market doctrines of previous years,[5] the World Business Council for Sustainable Development (WBCSD) explains: 'Corporate social responsibility is the continuing commitment by business to behave ethically and contribute to economic development while improving the quality of life of the workforce and their families as well as of the local community and society at large.'[6]

However, while many investors and business leaders today distance themselves from the hyperbole of Milton Friedman, who once admonished CSR as one of the '[f]ew trends [that] could so thoroughly undermine the very foundations of our free society',[7] most are unwilling to sacrifice profits for environmental gains. The minority of firms and investors that have embraced CSR have tended to recast it in a new business paradigm that views environmental and social issues instrumentally for potential financial advantage.[8] But even this restrictive version of business responsibility has struggled to attract many followers, partly because of problems in organisational cultures and difficulties in financially quantifying the business value of improved environmental performance. Rather

---

[3] J.J. Asongu, 'The history of corporate social responsibility' (2007) 1(2) *Journal of Business and Public Policy* 1.

[4] E. Garriga and D. Mele, 'Corporate social responsibility theories: mapping the territory' (2004) 53 *Journal of Business Ethics* 51. D. Birch, 'Corporate social responsibility: some key theoretical issues and concepts for new ways of doing business' (2003) 1(1) *Journal of New Business Ideas and Trends* 1.

[5] On financial and corporate management attitudes in the 1980s, see A. Smith, *The Roaring '80s* (Viking Press, 1988).

[6] WBCSD, *Corporate Social Responsibility: Meeting Changing Expectations* (WBCSD, 1999), 3. Among important CSR literature of recent years, see D. Crowther and L. Rayman-Bacchus (eds.), *Perspectives on Corporate Social Responsibility* (Ashgate, 2004); D. Vogel, *The Market for Virtue: The Potential and Limits of Corporate Social Responsibility* (Brookings Institution Press, 2005).

[7] M. Friedman, *Capitalism and Freedom* (University of Chicago Press, 1962), 133–4.

[8] H. Jemel-Fornetty, C. Louche, and D. Bourghelle, 'Changing the dominant convention: the role of emerging initiatives in mainstreaming ESG', in W. Sun, C. Louche, and R. Pérez (eds.), *Finance and Sustainability: Towards a New Paradigm? A Post-Crisis Agenda* (Emerald Group, 2011), 85.

than ask how business might contribute to sustainability, today's corporate managers are more likely to self-servingly question how sustainability might contribute to their firms' profitability. There is nothing intrinsically objectionable from benefitting financially from sustainable business practices; the problem arises when the financial rationale becomes the only rationale for acting, given that this logic can also work the other way to encourage environmentally unscrupulous development.

The prevalence of a myopic, single-value approach to commerce and investment may thus marginalise CSR strategies that cannot be commuted into the language of financial risk or profitability. The prevailing belief in the CSR movement that companies' ability to manage environmental risks and opportunities is increasingly relevant to business competitiveness, profitability, and organisational competence, while valid, does not provide a comprehensive framework for sustainable business. Missing from this perspective is acceptance of an ethical responsibility to act for environmental well-being, regardless of immediate financial returns. Dominant global CSR and SRI standards, such as the United Nations Principles for Responsible Investment (UNPRI)[9] and the UN Global Compact (UNGC),[10] lack explicit sustainability performance benchmarks. If fund managers or business leaders rely only on narrow grounds to act responsibly, then by their own reasoning they would be justified in making an exception if ignoring those 'extraneous' values would be more profitable. Any commitment to CSR thus remains fragile.

Unsustainable business practices are also attributable to failures of the legal system. Corporate law is an obstacle, especially its problematic tendency to view business enterprises as private institutions despite their often public-like characteristics and social impacts. Under prevailing legal understandings, this book reveals in Chapter 2 by Millon, and Chapter 3 by Sjåfjell and others, that business managers cannot easily accommodate sustainability considerations if they lack economic benefits for the firm or its shareholders, unless the firm is explicitly established as a non-profit or mixed-purpose corporation. The legal duties of senior managers and directors of companies to act to benefit their company's economic prosperity are perceived to exclude consideration of social and environmental issues unless they can offer financial benefits to the business. There is a cognate assumption that environmental standards are preferably quarantined in separate external regulation as opposed to being incorporated

---

[9] See www.unpri.org.   [10] See www.unglobalcompact.org.

into corporate governance. But as will be explained shortly, modern environmental law has had limited success, despite the sincere efforts of many regulators, judges, and other actors dedicated to the long-term well-being of the planet.[11]

While smarter and more discrete 'external' environmental regulation of companies and financial institutions may help promote sustainability, we also need to incorporate such legal measures into economic institutions. We need to embed environmental standards in the governance of economic institutions in order to minimise the tensions their managers face between reconciling expectations that they act in the public interest while serving their private constituencies. Fund managers, business managers, and other economic decision-makers are expected to prioritise profits or maximise returns to shareholders – goals that create powerful incentives to avoid paying for environmental externalities. Conversely, environmental regulation seeks to communicate responsibility for such externalities and thereby constrain profit-making. By reconciling such mixed messages, environmental protection could be internalised as a fundamental norm for investment and business. It should also thereby help improve compliance with external environmental regulation.

The following section examines the global economic and ecological predicaments that require that this challenge be addressed urgently.

2   The global economic and ecological crises

Politicians and corporate executives frequently remind us that our well-being depends on growing the economy.[12] Despite its unsustainable burden on the biosphere, economic growth remains the foremost goal of nations worldwide. The historic economic trends are truly staggering. Worldwide consumer expenditure during the last century rose from US$1.5 trillion in 1900 to US$24 trillion in 1998.[13] Likewise, international trade in goods and services soared from US$50 billion in 1870 to US$8043

---

[11] For example, S. Wood, G. Tanner, and B.J. Richardson, 'Whatever happened to Canadian environmental law?' (2011) 37(4) *Ecology Law Quarterly* 981.

[12] For example, 'Flaherty raises economic growth forecast', *CBC News*, 2 February 2010, www.cbc.ca/news/business/flaherty-raises-economic-growth-forecast-1.954083; L.P. Bloomfield Jr, 'Corporate investments can help accelerate economic growth in the developing world', *International Business Times*, 19 November 2013, www.ibtimes.com.

[13] United Nations Development Programme (UNDP), *Human Development Report 1998* (UNDP, 1998), 1.

billion in 2005.[14] Both trends vastly outstripped even the extraordinary surge in human population from some 1.6 billion in 1900 to 7 billion in 2011. In recent decades, a further economic impetus has come from the financial sector. The assets of the world's 1000 largest banks surged from US$23 trillion in 1990 to approximately US$101 trillion by mid-2010, despite the headwinds from the GFC.[15] In late 2010, the global financial economy was valued at approximately US$212 trillion.[16] Such majestic statistics suggest we live in an age of great prosperity that has raised living standards and lifted billions out of poverty.

Apart from the rising economic and social inequalities for some people that have accompanied such growth, one uncomfortable consequence is that the global economy has become very large compared to the ecosystems that sustain it. Natural systems provide innumerable economic and life-support benefits,[17] yet humanity acts brazenly as though Earth's natural bounty is infinitely abundant and free.[18] In *The Cancer Stage of Capitalism*, John McMurtry metaphorically depicts this economic plundering as a malignant tumour.[19] As ecological economists have more academically put it, infinite economic and population growth in a physically finite world is impossible.[20] The debate about such 'limits' is not recent; Thomas Malthus raised it in his influential *Essay on Population*, published in 1778, and since the early 1970s, numerous scientists have warned against rampant growth that devours nature.[21] Resource scarcities

---

[14] *World Trade Organization (WTO)*, World Trade Report 2007 (WTO, 2007), 244 (expressed in constant 1990 dollar values); see also W. Bernstein, *A Splendid Exchange: How Trade Shaped the World* (Atlantic Monthly Press, 2008).

[15] International Financial Services London (IFSL, now known as TheCityUK), 'Worldwide assets of the banking industry', see also TheCityUK 'Banking: May 2012, financial markets series', available at: www.thecityuk.com/research/our-work/reports-list/.

[16] C. Boxburgh, S. Lund, and J. Piotrowski, *Mapping Global Capital Markets 2011* (McKinsey Global Institute, 2011), 2.

[17] See G.C. Daily, *Nature's Services: Societal Dependence on Natural Ecosystems* (Island Press, 1997); Y. Baskin and P.R. Ehrlich, *The Work of Nature: How the Diversity of Life Sustains Us* (Island Press, 1998); T. Prugh, *et al.*, *Natural Capital and Human Economic Survival* (CRC Press, 1999).

[18] Its economic value is undoubtedly staggering, and was quantified by one notorious study in 1997 at somewhere between US$16–54 trillion annually, dwarfing a then annual global gross economic product of about US$18 trillion: R. Costanza, *et al.*, 'The value of the world's ecosystem services and natural capital' (1997) 389 *Nature* 253.

[19] J. McMurtry, *The Cancer Stage of Capitalism* (Pluto Press, 1999).

[20] H. Daly and J.B. Cobb, Jr., *For the Common Good* (Beacon Press, 1989); H. Daly, *Ecological Economics and the Ecology of Economics* (Edward Elgar, 1999); P. Victor, *Managing Without Growth* (Edward Elgar, 2008).

[21] D.H. Meadows, *et al.*, *The Limits to Growth* (Universe Books, 1972).

are only part of the problem. There are also limits to the capacity of environmental 'sinks', which serve to assimilate the pollution and other by-products of economic activity. Climate change is the most severe of these emerging sink problems.

Soaring ecological problems provoked the UN's Millennium Ecosystem Assessment in 2005 to warn that 'human activity is putting such strain on the natural functions of the Earth that the ability of the planet's ecosystems to sustain future generations can no longer be taken for granted'.[22] Many other international studies echo this view.[23] In 2012, scientists spoke of the risk of 'threshold-induced state shifts' in the Earth's biosphere that could trigger myriad, unforeseen, devastating consequences for all life.[24] With emerging economies such as China and India rapidly industrialising, and thereby intensifying the global environmental burden, grave ecological tipping points may be irreparably passed soon.

These trends are not simply an expression of some carnal human urge for greater material prosperity – though they do have deep cultural and biological roots[25] – but substantially reflect prevailing economic and political systems. The market economy is particularly influential. Some economists laud the market as crucial to human welfare and a tool to solve our environmental problems, such as by unleashing competitive pressures to pioneer innovative green technologies, efficiently using scarce resources, and pricing pollution risks.[26] Geoffrey Heal optimistically contends, 'This poor [environmental] record is not intrinsic to markets. They can be reoriented in a positive direction, in which case their potential for good is immense.'[27] Similarly, through dematerialisation, new technologies, better management systems, and investment in a knowledge-based economy, Paul Hawken and others champion a benevolent 'natural

---

[22] Millennium Ecosystem Assessment, *Living Beyond Our Means: Natural Assets and Human Well-Being, Statement from the Board* (Millennium Ecosystem Assessment, 2005) at 5.

[23] United Nations Environment Programme (UNEP), *Global Environment Outlook GEO-5* (UNEP, 2012); Worldwatch Institute, *State of the World 2012: Moving Toward Sustainable Prosperity* (Island Press, 2012).

[24] A.D. Barnosky, *et al.*, 'Approaching a state shift in Earth's biosphere' (2012) 486 *Nature*, 52 at 52.

[25] S. Boyden, *Western Civilization in Biological Perspective: Patterns in Biohistory* (Oxford University Press, 1987).

[26] See generally K. Midgley and R. Burns, *The Capital Market: Its Nature and Significance* (Macmillan, 1977).

[27] G. Heal, 'Markets and sustainability', in R.L. Revesz, P. Sands, and R.B. Stewart (eds.), *Environmental Law, the Economy and Sustainable Development* (Cambridge University Press, 2000), 410 at 427.

capitalism' that respects the critical interdependency between the economy and nature.[28] Ecological economists recommend more fundamental changes that go beyond improved 'efficiency' of resource use to actually limit economic growth.[29] They highlight how the market suffers from several environmental blind-spots, including fugitive pollution 'externalities',[30] degradation of 'public goods' such as the atmosphere and oceans,[31] undervaluation of ecological services and amenities such as biodiversity,[32] and myopic decision-making that ignores posterity's interests.[33]

Equally troubling, the cornucopia of material wealth gained from this growth binge does not necessarily equate with heightened prosperity. Empirical research suggests that once basic human needs are satiated, further economic growth yields a diminishing marginal return to human happiness.[34] Economic indicators such as Gross Domestic Product (GDP) undervalue the contribution of nature to overall well-being.[35] Moreover, much of this growth has delivered uneven benefits, with just a fifth of humanity earning about 2 per cent of global wealth.[36] Some economists have pioneered alternative measures of economic vitality and satisfaction, suggesting that the seemingly most prosperous nations do not necessarily enjoy the highest contentment.[37]

---

[28] P. Hawken, L.H. Lovins, and A. Lovins, *Natural Capitalism: Creating the Next Industrial Revolution* (Earthscan, 2000).

[29] See, e.g. M. Common and C. Perrings, 'Towards an ecological economics of sustainability' (1991) 6 *Ecological Economics* 7; A.M. Jansson, *et al.* (eds.), *Investing in Natural Capital: The Ecological Economics Approach to Sustainability* (Island Press, 1994); Jackson, *Prosperity Without Growth*, 5.

[30] A.A. John and R A. Pecchenino, 'International and intergenerational environmental externalities' (1997) 99(3) *Scandinavian Journal of Economics* 371.

[31] T. Cowen, *Public Goods and Market Failures: A Critical Examination* (Transaction Publishers, 1991).

[32] M. Common, *Environmental and Resource Economics: An Introduction* (2nd edn, Longman, 1996), 330–5.

[33] Common, *Environmental and Resource Economics*.

[34] William Rees documents that recent increases in per capital expenditures on US healthcare have not improved the overall health of its population: W.E. Rees, 'The end (of growth) is nigh', paper presented at Ecological Integrity and Sustainable Society Conference (Dalhousie University, 23–7 June 2007).

[35] R. Eisler, *The Real Wealth of Nations: Creating a Caring Economics* (Berrett-Koehler Publishers, 2007).

[36] Jackson, *Prosperity Without Growth*, 5.

[37] H. Henderson, *Ethical Markets; Growing the Green Economy* (Chelsea Green Publishing, 2007). Consider alternative measures of prosperity, such as the 'Index of Sustainable Economic Welfare', www.neweconomics.org, or the 'Happy Planet Index', www.happyplanetindex.org.

CAPITALISM, SUSTAINABILITY, BUSINESS GOVERNANCE 9

Another crisis, in global financial markets, has recently attracted greater attention from policy-makers and business leaders, yet its causes are partly associated with the same processes fuelling the planetary ecological crisis – namely, excessive risk-taking, failure to incorporate all social costs in the pricing of financial assets, and the short-term orientation of the market. Although some commentators believe '[t]here is nothing inherent in the structure of the financial system which necessarily leads to environmental destruction',[38] such an assumption is largely only plausible at a theoretical level because it ignores problems such as imperfect information, the culture of financial organisations, and collective action problems in the financial industry. The fall-out from the GFC that began in 2008 illustrates how excessive risk-taking by financiers can precipitate wide-ranging economic and social devastation. We are tied to an interconnected global financial system 'in which money traverses national capital markets with dramatic speed and callous scrutiny, bringing with it both the ability to enhance local economic opportunities or break an economy at its very core'.[39] These impacts are also the product of governance gaps and weaknesses, as a growing preference since the 1970s for market deregulation has led to diminished state oversight and control of the financial economy.

The separation of capital and the control of business, the hallmark of corporate capitalism, has also leveraged the separation between investment and social responsibility.[40] Ease of access to capital through financial markets removes corporate financing constraints that might otherwise curb economic growth and thus its environmental consequences. Passive investors also tend to be physically distant from the activities that directly impact the environment, thus weakening their sense of responsibility for taking corrective action. Further fraying the ties between those who manage companies and those who contribute capital, investors tend to own tiny fractional stakes in a multitude of companies in their portfolio, and the ease of selling corporate securities helps diminish the perceived importance of being a shareholder or creditor to the company. The result of so many intermediaries is the diminution of the sense of moral agency of investors for the activities of the companies they fund.

---

[38] M.A. White, 'Environmental finance: value and risk in an age of ecology' (1996) 5 *Business Strategy and the Environment* 198, at 200.

[39] C.J. Mailander, 'Financial innovation, domestic regulation and the international marketplace' (1997–98) 31(3) *George Washington Journal of International Law and Economics* 341, at 378.

[40] See B.J. Richardson, 'Putting ethics into environmental law: fiduciary duties for ethical investment' (2008) 46(2) *Osgoode Hall Law Journal* 243.

Whatever environmental sensitivities investors may have, they function within a financial system whose aim is to mobilise capital through loans and investments in order for it to deliver a profit (or 'return' as investors call it). Such returns are unlikely to accrue from investing in firms that do not expand or innovate. Shareholders' and financiers' desire for returns in turn creates pressure on corporations to be profitable in order to repay creditors or generate returns for shareholders. The recent rise in financial capital and the decline in natural capital are thus surely not merely coincidental.

In addition to squandering natural capital, the markets' contribution to material prosperity is reproachable. Although investing has the generic purpose of sacrificing current value and use of existing capital in order to obtain greater future benefit, the financial system is prone to speculative, ephemeral, and short-term tactics that can undermine long-term social and economic well-being.[41] The dominant paradigm of the finance system that arose after the 1950s is grounded on several models, particularly the efficient market hypothesis, the capital asset pricing model for the trade-off between risk and return, the modern portfolio theory of diversification of investment, and arbitrage pricing theory.[42] Over-reliance on these models, which suffer from some unrealistically simple assumptions about financial risk and investor behaviour, coupled with regulatory lacunae and lax market supervision, has created vulnerabilities in the financial economy that metamorphosed into the GFC in 2008. Financial crises are not new, however: a World Bank study identified 112 systemic financial crises in 93 countries between the late 1970s and 2000.[43] The 2008 crisis, however, was of historic breadth and depth, partly because financial markets have become much more integrated than was the case in earlier decades. The crisis led to financial bailouts of US$4.89 trillion between 2007 and 2009 in the United States and the European Union (EU), equivalent to 6 per cent of GDP in each country/region.[44] By contrast, no commensurate sense of urgency and commitment of financial resources have been offered to address global ecological problems.

---

[41] F. Jameson, 'Culture and finance capitalism' (1997) 24(1) *Critical Inquiry* 246, at 247; A. Harmes, *Unseen Power: How Mutual Funds Threaten the Political and Economic Wealth of Nations* (Stoddard, 2001) at 76.

[42] C.F. Lee and A.C. Lee (eds.), *Encyclopedia of Finance* (Springer, 2006).

[43] World Bank, *Finance for Growth: Policy Choices in a Volatile World* (World Bank, 2001).

[44] J. Black, *Restructuring Global and EU Financial Regulation: Capacities, Coordination and Learning*, Law, Society and Economy Working Paper 18/2010 (London School of Economics, 2010), 8.

Other commentators are hopeful that markets can sort themselves out. Gordon Clark and Dariusz Wójcik praise global finance for reshaping the economic landscape of twenty-first-century capitalism by facilitating corporate restructuring, technological innovation, and economic development.[45] They see the growing presence of institutional investors as a generally positive phenomenon that can help align corporate behaviour with social norms. Clark and Tessa Hebb, whose writings focus on pension funds, contend these actors have helped re-group dispersed shareholders with unprecedented concentrations of ownership that enable them to pressure corporations into raising their business practices and standards on a range of issues, including transparency, and improving their social and environmental performance.[46] Relatedly, other commentators such as Robert Monks have observed a willingness of institutional investors to collaborate in order to amplify their influence over the governance of their investee firms.[47] The voices of institutional funds, whose beneficiaries are millions of ordinary workers and households, are promoting CSR not only in response to broad societal demands, but also because they believe improved social and environmental performance may lower financial risks over the long term.

The capacity and willingness of enlightened investors to nudge the economy towards sustainability are examined later in this book, in Richardson's Chapter 6. Suffice to say at this point that institutional funds and the SRI movement largely failed to predict the 2008 financial crisis, let alone do anything to prevent it. Many in the SRI sector have been preoccupied with ad hoc or specific issues of corporate conduct, while giving insufficient attention to the structural and systemic dimensions of the financial economy that are also determinative of progress towards sustainability. Similarly, as David Millon discusses in Chapter 2, the CSR movement that focuses on companies in the productive or 'real' economy has struggled to leverage positive change in the environmental behaviour of companies through voluntary or discretionary initiatives such as CSR reporting.

Before examining further the barriers and opportunities in corporate and business law to address these economic and environmental challenges,

---

[45] G.L. Clark and D. Wójcik, *The Geography of Finance: Corporate Governance in the Global Marketplace* (Oxford University Press, 2007).

[46] G.L. Clark and T. Hebb, 'Pension fund corporate engagement: the fifth stage of capitalism' (2004) 59(1) *Relations Industrielles/Industrial Relations* 141.

[47] R.A.G. Monks, *The New Global Investors: How Shareowners Can Unlock Sustainable Prosperity Worldwide* (Capstone, 2001).

it is important to pause and consider the limitations of conventional environmental regulation. Why can we not just rely on such regulation to discipline environmentally irresponsible companies?

3   Environmental law in the dyadic state

The assumption that the environmental activities and impacts of business can be successfully improved through external regulation rather than through company law or other areas of business law is doubtful. Ostensibly, environmental law has blossomed in many countries over the past half-century as governments have legislated to curb pollutants, protect endangered species, and restrict the exploitation of nature's scarce or finite resources. However, all states have struggled to discipline humankind's environmentally wanton behaviours because those behaviours, especially through industry and the marketplace, also deliver material prosperity and sustain the states themselves. This is the outcome even when we increasingly recognise that plundering nature's capital will eventually deprive business of the capacity to create new, economic capital. These contradictory tendencies between the need for environmental protection (in the long term) and allowing its exploitation for economic development (in the short term) are central to understanding the dyadic or conflictual character of the modern state charged with regulating business. The following pages thus delve into the limitations of environmental law in order to help us understand this book's agenda about the imperative for a supplementary means of governing the source of our most serious environmental pressures: the business sector.

Depressingly, global environmental conditions have generally deteriorated despite the vast swathe of environmental regulations enacted in many nations in recent decades. We continue to edge closer to the precipice of an anthropogenic collapse in planetary ecological systems. Species are disappearing at unprecedented rates and the planet's sixth mass extinction is forecast,[48] while atmospheric carbon dioxide is at its highest level in some 800,000 years, and is rising rapidly.[49] We should not be misled by the law's occasional triumphs, such as the phasing out of atmospheric

---

[48]   A.D. Barnosky, et al., 'Has the Earth's sixth mass extinction already arrived?' (2011) 471 *Nature* 51.

[49]   'First time in 800,000 years: April's CO_2 levels above 400 ppm'. *CBS News*, 6 May 2014, www.cbsnews.com/news/first-time-in-800000-years-aprils-co2-levels-above-400-ppm.

CAPITALISM, SUSTAINABILITY, BUSINESS GOVERNANCE 13

ozone-depleting chemicals[50] or the rescue of iconic species from the brink of extinction.[51] At most, we can concede that environmental law is modestly mitigating what would be a more dire situation.

While the subject of environmental law deserves much more comprehensive treatment and we should be mindful of differences in its design and impact among jurisdictions, especially between the rich developed countries and the poorer nations of the Global South, some general trends can be observed here. Until now, environmental law has tended to function as external controls on economic activity rather than as norms embedded within the inner institutional structure of companies, financiers, and other economic agents. These entities have had to obtain licences or other approvals to harvest resources, pollute, or commit other environmental impacts, overseen by a labyrinth of administrative agencies and procedures. The function of environmental law, therefore, remains limited to mitigating the worst excesses of the dominant model of economic development rather than fundamentally challenging or transforming it. It is rare for a major project, especially one that promises jobs and other economic benefits, to be vetoed in the name of protecting nature.

The efficacy of environmental law has been undermined by the convergence of several negative factors, including its political-economic context and its methods of governance,[52] in addition to more fundamental characteristics of humankind's evolutionary disposition.[53] The modern environmental administrative state is structured largely to legalise environmental damage, for under most legislation, the governing agency has the authority – or discretion – to permit the very pollution or resource destruction that the regulations were drafted to prevent or reduce. Further, within this context, government agencies often confront and succumb to political pressure and lobbying by vested interest groups, especially the corporations they are supposed to police, in order to issue permits

---

[50] Montreal Protocol on Substances That Deplete the Ozone Layer, ILM 28, 1989, 649.

[51] A notable example is the American Bald Eagle (*Haliaeetus leucocephalus*), the national symbol of the United States, which was saved by the Endangered Species Preservation Act, Pub. L. 89–669, 1966.

[52] See e.g. D. Boyd, *Unnatural Law: Rethinking Canadian Environmental Law and Policy* (UBC Press, 2003); B.A. Ackerman and R.B. Stewart, 'Reforming environmental law: the democratic case for market incentives' (1985) 37 *Stanford Law Review* 1333; A. Gillespie, *The Illusion of Progress: Unsustainable Development in International Law* (Earthscan, 2001).

[53] B.J. Richardson, 'A damp squib: environmental law from a human evolutionary perspective' (2011) 3 *Law and Prosociality eJournal*.

and sanction other harmful actions.[54] Areas set aside for strict nature conservation, such as national parks, usually reflect such areas' perceived weaker economic value for mining, forestry, human settlement, or other developments, rather than any unadulterated ethical commitment to nature's sanctity.

The target of environmental regulation can also be misguided. It tends to focus on the 'front-line' companies (e.g. manufacturing firms or mining companies) that most visibly pollute or exploit natural resources, rather than their financial sponsors, such as global banks or multinational companies shielded behind subsidiaries that become the 'fall guy' for any environmental problems. The latter have been viewed as systemically remote from these environmental and social consequences,[55] despite the capital they provide and their ability as shareholders or creditors to voice concerns to the firms they aid. Causal relationships between finance and environmental impacts are separated widely across time and space, frequently obscuring holistic responsibility for the degradation.

States tend not to favour stringent environmental regulation because their political fortunes hinge more on their success as economic managers than as environmental stewards, despite a growing environmental movement in many countries. Driven by the imperatives of national housekeeping, the state acts as the *'parens patriae'* with responsibility to sustain economic growth.[56] Yet, because economic activity can also produce politically contentious environmental impacts, the state must reconcile the antagonistic imperatives of curbing the worst pollution while allowing market actors enough freedom to grow the economy.[57] Unresolved contradictions between these imperatives have prompted major disputes over forestry, nuclear power, mining, and other resource issues in recent decades.[58] Governments have sought to manage their conflicted

---

[54] One notorious example is the Gunns' pulp mill proposal in northern Tasmania, Australia, a development allegedly approved by state and federal governments because of the political influence of Gunns, a major forestry company: Q. Beresford, 'Corporations, government and development: the case of institutional corruption in Tasmania' (2010) 45(2) *Australian Journal of Political Science* 209.

[55] J. Rada and A. Trisoglio, 'Capital markets and sustainable development' (1992) 27 *Columbia Journal of World Business* 42; W. Thomas, 'The green nexus: financiers and sustainable development' (2001) 13 *Georgetown International Environmental Law Review* 899.

[56] See H. Arendt, *The Human Condition* (University of Chicago Press, 1957).

[57] See K. Walker, 'The state in environmental management: the ecological dimension' (1989) 37(1) *Political Studies* 25.

[58] For example, R. Falkner, *Business Power and Conflict in International Environmental Politics* (Palgrave Macmillan, 2007); I. Watson, *Fighting Over the Forests* (Allen and Unwin, 1990).

CAPITALISM, SUSTAINABILITY, BUSINESS GOVERNANCE 15

roles and the attendant challenges to their legitimacy by devolving more authority to market actors.[59] Particularly since the 1980s, states have increasingly privatised public services and assets and liberalised market controls in the hope of reducing the regulatory burden on industry and creating more opportunities to harness market efficiencies.[60] This strategy, however, carries its own risks. The GFC of 2008–2009 led governments worldwide to intervene to restore market stability in a way not seen since the Great Depression.[61] By contrast, the looming crisis of climate change prompted only a lukewarm political accord in Copenhagen in 2009.[62]

The effectiveness of environmental law is blunted not only by its political and economic context, but also its *methods*. The rise of modern environmental regulation in the countries of the West was closely associated with the norms and institutions of the welfare state, including reliance on instruments of public ownership and prescriptive standards.[63] While these techniques helped mitigate such acute pollution problems as water pollution and lead in petrol, their ability to solve complex environmental issues is increasingly in doubt.[64] The main elements of the critique are now quite familiar:[65] the conventional techniques of 'command and control' regulation were too rigid, complex, burdensome, costly, inefficient, adversarial, and ineffective; they stifled entrepreneurial innovation, eliminated jobs, and hindered competitiveness in return for diminishing environmental benefits; and they were prone to industry capture. Their proliferation resulted in a dense maze of legal controls, the effectiveness of which was increasingly outweighed by their administrative costs and economic burden, threatening finally to collapse under their own weight

---

[59] D. Boaz and E. Crane (eds.), *Market Liberalism: A Paradigm for the 21st Century* (Cato Institute, 1993).

[60] B. Bortolotti and D. Siniscalco, *The Challenges of Privatization: An International Analysis* (Oxford University Press, 2004).

[61] 'Adding up the government's total bailout tab', *New York Times*, 4 February 2009, available at: www.nytimes.com/interactive/2009/02/04/business/20090205-bailout-totals-graphic .html.

[62] 'Copenhagen Accord climate pledges too weak: UN' (31 March 2010) *Reuters*, available at: www.reuters.com/article/idUSTRE62U13M20100331.

[63] C. Sunstein, 'Paradoxes of the regulatory state' (1990) 57 *University of Chicago Law Review* 407; M. Moran, 'Understanding the regulatory state' (2002) 32 *British Journal of Political Science* 391.

[64] See e.g. P. Yeager, *The Limits of Law: The Public Regulation of Private Pollution* (Cambridge University Press, 1991).

[65] See e.g. C. Abbott, 'Environmental command regulation', in B.J. Richardson and S. Wood (eds.), *Environmental Law for Sustainability* (Hart Publishing, 2006), 61.

or to seize up in a process of 'juridification'.[66] According to one influential account, 'The present regulatory system wastes tens of billions of dollars every year, misdirects resources, stifles innovation, and spawns massive and often counterproductive litigation.'[67] While this is not an accurate depiction of *all* environmental regulation, which sometimes has been characterised by a consultative style in which environmental rules were negotiated and enforced in a largely non-coercive way via closed-door, bilateral deals between government and industry,[68] it does reflect much of the history of modern environmental law.

In recent decades, criticisms of the efficacy of the regulatory state and its reliance on coercive prescriptive regulation have fostered experimentation with alternate approaches that cede some responsibility for environmental governance to the market or civil society. These realignments have been described by commentators using various terms, such as 'mutual regulation',[69] 'self-organisation',[70] 'responsive regulation',[71] 'smart regulation',[72] and 'post-regulatory governance'.[73] Among the common elements of these so-called 'decentred' forms of regulation are the preference for legal systems that are 'less heavy-handed, and more responsive to the demands and possibilities of their context',[74] and also, the

---

[66] G. Teubner, 'Juridification: concepts, aspects, limits, solutions', in R. Baldwin, C. Scott, and C. Hood (eds.), *A Reader on Regulation* (Oxford University Press, 1998), 389 at 398.

[67] Ackerman and Stewart, 'Reforming environmental law', 1333.

[68] M. Howlett, 'Policy instruments and implementation styles: the evolution of instrument choice', in D. Van Nijnatten and R. Boardman (eds.), *Canadian Environmental Policy: Context and Cases* (Oxford University Press, 2002), 25.

[69] See P. Simmons and B. Wynne, *State, Market and Mutual Regulation? Socioeconomic Dimensions of the Environmental Regulation of Business* (Lancaster University, 1994).

[70] G. Teubner, L. Farner, and D. Murphy (eds.), *Environmental Law and Ecological Responsibility: The Concept and Practice of Ecological Self-Organisation* (John Wiley & Sons Ltd, 1994).

[71] I. Ayres and J. Braithwaite, *Responsive Regulation: Transcending the Deregulation Debate* (Oxford University Press, 1992).

[72] N. Gunningham and P. Grabosky, *Smart Regulation: Designing Environmental Policy* (Oxford University Press, 1998).

[73] C. Scott, 'Regulation in the age of governance: the rise of the post regulatory state', in J. Jordana and D. Levi-Faur (eds.), *The Politics of Regulation: Institutions and Regulatory Reforms for the Age of Governance* (Edward Elgar, 2004), 145.

[74] J. Steele and T. Jewell, 'Law in environmental decision-making', in T. Jewell and J. Steele (eds.), *Law in Environmental Decision-Making. National, European and International Perspectives* (Clarendon Press, 1998), 1 at 14; see further, D. Osborne and T. Gaebler, *Reinventing Government: How the Entrepreneurial Spirit Is Transforming the Public Sector* (Addison-Wesley Publishing, 1992); J. Black, 'Decentring regulation: understanding the role of regulation and self-regulation in a "post-regulatory world"' (2001) 54 *Current Legal Problems* 103.

CAPITALISM, SUSTAINABILITY, BUSINESS GOVERNANCE 17

enlistment of non-state actors in regulatory governance. Gunther Teubner describes reflexive law as one of these approaches – a system of regulation that does not seek coercive policy direction but confines itself to the 'regulation of organization, procedures and the redistribution of competences'.[75] With the vision that governance should no longer arise out of external regulation but should occur through the internal reconfiguration of decision-making within corporations, detailed regulatory prescription is thus replaced by mechanisms encouraging internal reflection, learning, and behavioural changes. Thus, the function of law is recast from direct control to 'procedural' control.[76] For environmental policy, Eric Orts describes reflexive law as seeking 'to encourage internal self-critical reflection within institutions about their environmental performance . . . to set up processes that encourage institutional self-reflective thinking and learning about environmental effects'.[77] Similar reflexive law approaches have been used in business law, with regard to CSR reporting, for instance. Thus, many jurisdictions are increasingly relying on informational policy instruments, norms of self-governance, economic incentives, and contractual agreements to govern markets.[78]

But their effectiveness in promoting sustainability has not yet been demonstrated. Instead, they have served to reduce pressure on the regulatory system by offering a more efficient and cost-effective environmental governance. These mechanisms leave unaltered the basic assumptions about the purpose and value of economic development, fail to provide tools to steer the economy towards long-term horizons, and fail to provide a mechanism to scale the economy within biosphere limits. They can nudge change and deliver incremental improvements, as evident in gradual improvements in corporate environmental accounting and reporting (discussed in Chapter 5 by Villiers and Mähönen in this book),

---

[75] G. Teubner, 'Social order from legislative noise? Autopoietic closure as a problem for legal regulation', in G. Teubner (ed.), *State, Law, Economy as Autopoietic Systems: Regulation and Autonomy in a New Perspective* (Giuffrè, 1992); G. Teubner, 'After legal instrumentalism?' in G. Teubner (ed.), *Dilemmas of Law in the Welfare State* (Walter de Gruyter, 1986), 222.

[76] J. Black, 'Proceduralising regulation: Part I' (2000) 20 *Oxford Journal of Legal Studies* 597.

[77] E.W. Orts, 'Reflexive environmental law' (1995) 89(4) *Northwestern University Law Review* 1227, at 1254.

[78] See D.A. Farber, 'Taking slippage seriously: noncompliance and creative compliance in environmental law' (1999) 23 *Harvard Environmental Law Review* 297; A. Iles, 'Adaptive management: making environmental law and policy more dynamic, experimentalist and learning' (1996) 13 *Environmental and Planning Law Journal* 288; E.W. Orts and K. Deketelaere (eds.), *Environmental Contracts: Comparative Approaches to Regulatory Innovation in the United States and Europe* (Kluwer Law, 2000).

but do not engender the kind of comprehensive change that is urgently needed.

Other regulatory failures and gaps that contribute to unsustainability inhere in business law, including companies legislation, securities regulation, and financial markets controls, whose effects are critiqued later in this book. In these domains, the primary problem is the general lack of environmental standards, rather than misguided standards or insufficient enforcement. The deregulation of financial markets since the 1980s has generally aimed to lighten legislative restrictions to be replaced by disclosure standards and self-regulation under government supervision.[79] The expansion of the CSR and SRI movements in recent years may charitably be viewed as a surrogate governance strategy to compensate for deficiencies in official business regulation in these domains.[80] However, we can also view these movements less charitably as attempts to thwart stricter regulatory standards through pre-emptive action by market actors.[81]

Transnationally, an even larger regulatory lacuna exists. Global environmental rules are typically quarantined within designated 'environmental treaties', such as those governing biodiversity conservation or transboundary pollution, and their implementation has tended to be poor.[82] Conversely, treaties governing investment and other economic activities are largely devoid of sustainability considerations. Market liberalisation and technological advances have greatly accelerated the mobility and liquidity of financial capital across national borders, and consequently the capacity for more unsustainable development.[83] Largely missing from these policy prescriptions are mechanisms to ensure that transnational firms and their investors who benefit from the liberal economic framework adhere to high standards of corporate governance and environmental responsibility. While globalisation has helped disseminate and universalise voluntary standards for CSR and business ethics, 'hard' regulation of foreign investment, banking, and capital markets at an international

---

[79] On Canadian reforms, see A.M. Abdalyan, 'The Porter Commission Report revisited' (1995) 11 *Banking and Finance Law Review* 57, at 64.

[80] R. Aguilera, *et al.*, 'Corporate governance and social responsibility: a comparative analysis of the UK and the US' (2006) 14(3) *Corporate Governance and Social Responsibility* 147.

[81] B. Sjåfjell, 'Report from Norway: another CSR victory for the business lobbyists', available at: SSRN: http://ssrn.com/abstract=1413388.

[82] Gillespie, *The Illusion of Progress*.

[83] C. Williams, 'Corporate social responsibility in an era of economic globalization' (2002) 35 *University of California Davis Law Review* 705, at 731.

CAPITALISM, SUSTAINABILITY, BUSINESS GOVERNANCE 19

level remains sparse and deeply fragmented.[84] The corporate hostility to the relatively stringent proposed UN Norms on the Responsibilities of Transnational Corporations in 2003 illustrates how many business actors view credible regulation of their social and environmental activities.[85] The human rights standards subsequently adopted by the UN in 2011 from the Ruggie process are comparatively much milder for business.[86]

The GFC has provoked much debate among policy-makers, academics, and other observers about the future governance of the global economy, but so far politicians have struggled to agree to long-term solutions. Mainly ad hoc, expedient, or temporary measures have been adopted, such as controls on short-selling, tighter regulation of financial derivatives, closer scrutiny of lending conditions, and bail-outs and partial nationalisations of insolvent financial institutions.[87] The measures have tended to serve restoration of business-as-usual rather than engineering fundamental, structural reforms. The environmental sustainability agenda has hardly featured in these policy-making discussions, with the UN initiative, the 'Global Green New Deal', quickly fizzling out.[88]

In conclusion, around the world, the environmental law for the frontline companies in the productive economy has generally been of limited success, and environmental standards have hardly extended to the financial economy or corporate governance. Serious deficiencies in the capacity and willingness of states to regulate the market for sustainability exist. In developing an alternative governance model, to mitigate the deficiencies of external environmental regulation and the limitations of business voluntarism, it is important to clarify the meaning of sustainability and

---

[84] See generally, K. Alexander, R. Dhumale, and J. Eatwell, *Global Governance of Financial Systems* (Oxford University Press, 2006).

[85] UN Economic and Social Council (ECOSOC), Sub-Commission on Promotion and Protection of Human Rights, Norms on the Responsibilities of Transnational Corporations and Other Business Enterprises with Regard to Human Rights (ECOSOC, 2003).

[86] J. Ruggie, *Guiding Principles on Business and Human Rights: Implementing the United Nations 'Protect, Respect and Remedy' Framework*, HRC 17th Session, UN Doc A/HRC/17/31 (2011).

[87] K. Davis, *Regulatory Reform post the Global Financial Crisis: An Overview* (Australian Centre for Financial Studies, 2011).

[88] UN Environmental Programme (UNEP), 'Global Green New Deal – Environmentally-Focused Investment Historic Opportunity for 21st Century Prosperity and Job Generation', Press release, 22 October 2008; available at www.unep.org/Documents.Multilingual/Default.asp?DocumentID=548&ArticleID=5957; E. B. Barbier , 'Green stimulus is not sufficient for a global green recovery', *Vox*, 3 June 2010, available at: www.voxeu.org/index.php?q=node/5134. For more about UNEP's recent green economy efforts, see www.unep.org/greeneconomy.

20 BENJAMIN J. RICHARDSON AND BEATE SJÅFJELL

its manifestation in the notion of the 'sustainable company', which is discussed in Section 4.

4 Sustainability and the 'sustainable company'

The concept of 'sustainability' emerged in the late twentieth century as the Zeitgeist of environmental policy and law. In its most prevalent formulation, 'sustainable development', it has been widely endorsed as the goal of states, international bodies, non-governmental organisations (NGOs), and the business community itself. Sustainability has been enshrined in the European Union's Treaty as a core objective,[89] and it features in many international environmental conventions, multilateral development policies, national environmental strategies, and legislation.[90] In the context of business enterprise, sustainability has been incarnated in the motifs of 'sustainable companies', 'sustainable finance', and similar phrases that imply economic activity within acceptable environmental parameters.[91] The CSR movement, as discussed in Millon's Chapter 2, is also now deeply infused with the rhetoric of sustainability.

In contrast to the older terminology of environmentalists who spoke of 'nature conservation', the sustainability discourse seeks to integrate the environmental, social, and economic agendas. It advocates a responsible balance between the otherwise incongruous imperatives of unfettered economic exploitation of natural resources and the dependence of all life on healthy ecosystems. A stronger version of the concept would prioritise the maintenance of ecological integrity as a precondition to economic and social development.[92] Sustainability is supported by several specific

---

[89] Treaty on European Union (1992), last amended by the Treaty of Lisbon, OJ 2008 C115 (consolidated version), Art. 3; B. Sjåfjell, 'Quo vadis, Europe? The significance of sustainable development as objective, principle and rule of EU law', in C. Bailliet (ed.), *Non State Actors, Soft Law and Protective Regimes* (Cambridge University Press, 2012), 254.

[90] C. Voigt, *Sustainable Development as a Principle of International Law: Resolving Conflicts Between Climate Measures and WTO Law* (Martinus Nijhoff, 2009); M.C. Cordonier Segger and A. Khalfan, *Sustainable Development Law: Principles, Practices, and Prospects* (Oxford University Press, 2005); S.A. Atapattu, *Emerging Principles of International Environmental Law* (Transnational Publishers, 2006); R.L. Revesz, P. Sands, and R.B. Stewart (eds.), *Environmental Law, the Economy and Sustainable Development: The United States, the European Union and the International Community* (Cambridge University Press, 2000).

[91] M. Jeucken, *Sustainable Finance and Banking: The Financial Sector and the Future of the Planet* (Earthscan, 2001).

[92] E. Neumayer, *Weak Versus Strong Sustainability* (4th edn, Edward Elgar Publishing, 2013).

policy principles that give it some operational traction. The 'polluter pays' principle expects polluters to bear the expenses of pollution prevention and remediation.[93] The precautionary principle addresses acting in situations of uncertainty regarding the environmental risks of development choices.[94] Sustainability also adheres to principles of social justice by requiring the fair distribution of the benefits and burdens of environmental policy, as reflected in the cognate principles of inter- and intra-generational equity.[95]

Sustainability concepts have ostensibly informed vast swathes of modern environmental governance and policy.[96] These efforts include strategic environmental plans, framework laws, and reconfigured regulatory agencies, policy tools such as pollution taxation and environmental liability, as well as democratic reforms widening participation in environmental decision-making.[97] Many environmental statutes and codes explicitly proclaim sustainability as their purpose, such as Nova Scotia's Environmental Goals and Sustainable Prosperity Act 2007 and the German Sustainability Code, 2011. New Zealand's pioneering Resource Management Act 1992 was perhaps the first such example, declaring that 'the purpose of this Act is to promote the sustainable management of natural and physical resources'.[98] Considerable effort since has been expended devising tools to implement such aspirations, and setting 'sustainability indicators' to measure progress.[99] Overall, the sustainability paradigm supports a more principled and strategic approach to environmental policy in contrast to earlier more fragmented efforts.

---

[93] OECD, *The Polluter Pays Principle: OECD Analyses and Recommendations* (OECD, 1992).

[94] N. de Sadeleer (ed.), *Implementing the Precautionary Principles: Approaches from the Nordic Countries, the EU and USA* (Earthscan, 2007).

[95] I. Voinovic, 'Intergenerational and intragenerational equity requirements for sustainability' (1995) 22(3) *Environmental Conservation* 223; J.E. Roemer, *Intergenerational Equity and Sustainability* (Palgrave Macmillan, 2007).

[96] See K. Bosselmann, *The Principle of Sustainability: Transforming Law and Governance* (Ashgate, 2008).

[97] J.C. Dembach, 'Sustainable development as a framework for national governance' (1998) 49(1) *Case Western Reserve Law Review* 1; K. Ginther, *et al.* (eds.), *Sustainable Development and Good Governance* (Graham and Trotman; Martinus Nijhoff, 1995); G.C. Bryner, 'Policy devolution and environmental law: exploring the transition to sustainable development' (2002) 26 *Environs: Environmental Law and Policy Journal* 1.

[98] Section 5(1).

[99] S. Bell and S. Morse, *Sustainability Indicators: Measuring the Immeasurable* (Earthscan, 1999).

Part of sustainability's appeal is its ambiguity and open-endedness, enabling numerous actors with divergent objectives to commonly embrace it.[100] The success of the sustainability ideal also derives from how the business and political elites have tamed its broad possible implications to avoid radical economic changes. The prevailing rhetoric seeks to reassure us that environmental protection and economic growth can mutually reinforce each other.[101] Sustainability is presented as supporting the means to gain competitive advantages and to build new markets and improve production efficiency, rather than imposing rigid ecological limits on business activity.[102] It also implies soft business advantages, such as improved relations with employees and local communities, and therefore fewer costly disputes.[103]

Also in this business context, the sustainability paradigm has been closely associated with the philosophy of 'ecological modernisation', a potent influence on environmental law and policy.[104] Ecological modernisation accepts environmental degradation as a by-product of our modern industrial 'risk' society,[105] but believes that degradation can be mitigated through rational and technocratic methods. Ecological modernisation therefore does not renounce capitalism. Rather, it promises more efficient and careful husbandry of environmental resources, implemented through a framework of industrial modernity that harnesses innovative technologies, business acumen, and managerial professionalism.[106]

---

[100] A.D. Basiago, 'Methods of defining sustainability' (1995) 3 *Sustainable Development* 109; K. Pezzoli, 'Sustainable development: a transdisciplinary overview of the literature' (1997) 40(5) *Journal of Environmental Planning and Management* 549.

[101] On the potential symbiosis of environmental and economic concerns, see M.E. Porter and V. der Linde, 'Green and competitive: ending the stalemate' (1995) 73(5) *Harvard Business Review* 120.

[102] For example, WBCSD and UNEP, *Cleaner Production and Eco-Efficiency: Complementary Approaches to Sustainable Development* (WBCSD, 1998).

[103] M. Grieg-Gran, *Financial Incentives for Improved Sustainability Performance: The Business Case and the Sustainability Dividend* (Institute for the Environment and Development, WBCSD, 2002), 5–6.

[104] For a discussion of the central tenets of ecological modernization, see M.S. Andersen and I. Massa, 'Ecological modernization: origins, dilemmas and future directions' (2000) 2 *Journal of Environmental Policy and Planning* 337; M. Hajer, *The Politics of Environmental Discourse: Ecological Modernisation and the Policy Process* (Oxford University Press, 1995); S. Young (ed.), *The Emergence of Ecological Modernisation: Integrating the Environment and the Economy?* (Routledge, 2000).

[105] U. Beck, *Ecological Politics in an Age of Risk*, trans. A. Weisz (Polity Press, 1995).

[106] See especially J. Huber, *Die verlorene Unschuld der Okologie* (Fischer Verlag, 1982); M. Jänicke, *Staatsversagen. Die Ohnmacht der Politik in der Industriegesellschaft* (Piper, 1986).

CAPITALISM, SUSTAINABILITY, BUSINESS GOVERNANCE 23

Thus, pollution prevention and sustainable practices can yield competitive advantages for companies.[107] This outlook also informs the business case model of CSR, which depicts environmental constraints as opportunities for higher profitability through more frugal use of resources or less costly pollution. Therefore, ecological modernisation, like many understandings of sustainability, deftly reframes the ethical and political dilemmas of industrialisation as primarily technical and entrepreneurial challenges.[108] Legally, this stance also supports changes in environmental governance towards 'smart regulation',[109] whereby the state partners the market through negotiated agreements, economic instruments, auditing, reporting, and management systems rather than seeking change through inflexible regulatory prescriptions.

This incremental and reformist approach to sustainable development has not gone uncontested. The anti-globalisation movement represents the most visible form of resistance.[110] Diverse campaigns by civil society advocacy networks have exposed the environmental and social impacts of firms and investors, keeping their influence on the sustainable development discourse somewhat in check.[111] The post-GFC 'Occupy Movement' has extended this discontent to the sustainability of the financial economy and its crippling social and economic impacts.[112] Activists in the Global South also have censured some of the Western proponents of sustainability for glossing over the social justice dimensions of the environmental agenda, such as more equitable global trade and poverty alleviation.[113]

Likewise, this book's advocacy of 'sustainable companies' is informed by a critical stance that views the planetary environmental crisis as requiring fundamental changes in the governance and purpose of business

---

[107] See further, J. Elkington, 'Towards the sustainable corporation: win-win-win business strategies for sustainable development' (1994) 36(2) *California Management Review* 90.

[108] S. Baker, 'The evolution of European Union environmental policy', in S. Baker, *et al.* (eds.), *The Politics of Sustainable Development: Theory, Policy and Practice within the European Union* (Routledge, 1997), 91 at 96.

[109] Gunningham and Grabosky, *Smart Regulation*; J. Elias and R. Lee, 'Ecological modernisation and environmental regulation: corporate compliance and accountability', in S. MacLeod (ed.), *Global Governance and the Quest for Justice. Volume 2: Corporate Governance* (Hart Publishing, 2006), 163.

[110] N. Klein, *No Logo: Taking Aim at the Brand Bullies* (Vintage Canada, 2000).

[111] D. Szablowski, *Transnational Law and Local Struggles: Mining, Communities and the World Bank* (Hart Publishing, 2007) at 64.

[112] Writers for the 99%, *Occupying Wall Street: The Inside Story of an Action That Changed America* (OR Books, 2011).

[113] V. Shiva, *Earth Democracy: Justice, Sustainability and Peace* (Southend Press, 2005).

enterprise. The hallmarks of a sustainable company are that it is procedurally managed in a more transparent and democratic manner, and substantively it is accountable to robust environmental performance standards. A sustainable company also functions within a market system that likewise is restructured along these principles.

Of course, sustainability is not simply a matter of environmental protection and improvement. It has important social justice dimensions, such as respect for basic human rights and social justice. Environmental management is not just about humankind's relationship with nature but also involves the relations among stakeholders over access to scarce resources and the distribution of environmental benefits and burdens. For example, the livelihood of indigenous peoples and their land rights and other legal claims are often closely intertwined with environmental protection.[114] The principle of intra-generational equity most directly engages with sustainability's social dimensions.

However, the analysis and reforms proposed by this book focus on sustainability's environmental side for several reasons. Notably, social concerns such as the abuse of human rights will sometimes motivate stakeholders to be more willing to speak out, protest, or initiate legal action, because those stakeholders' personal well-being is directly affected or because other people's suffering is easier to empathise with than nature's voiceless distress. By contrast, the environment, especially its long-term integrity, indeed tends to be a mute stakeholder, unable to represent itself except indirectly through environmental NGOs who advocate on its behalf. While some environmental problems directly threaten individuals, such as pollution of one's property or person, and often disproportionately bring suffering to the poorest and vulnerable,[115] in many cases, the impacts are so widely dispersed across space or time that they lack sufficient proximity to motivate people to take costly action. In particular, the long-term interests of future generations in environmental well-being are less likely to be represented in public policy debates or business decision-making than the immediate interests of people alive. Because many environmental impacts are irreversible, such as climate change or species extinction, it would not be possible for future generations to obtain justice retroactively. Thus, there is a strong moral imperative to

---

[114] B.J. Richardson, 'The ties that bind: indigenous peoples and environmental governance', in B.J. Richardson, S. Imai, and K. McNeil (eds.), *Indigenous Peoples and the Law: Comparative and Critical Perspectives* (Hart Publishing, 2009), 337.

[115] R. Nixon, *Slow Violence and the Environmentalism of the Poor* (MIT Press, 2011).

address sustainability's environmental dimensions at their inception in business and economic decision-making.

Legally incorporating environmental sustainability into the purpose and decision-making of companies, however, is not without some serious challenges. Sustainability is neither a blueprint nor a manual to apply mechanically – rather, it is malleable because its parameters and application require further reflection on each specific context. Asking whether a specific activity is environmentally sustainable will yield different answers depending on the time and place. One might condemn as utterly unsustainable a polluting factory sited adjacent to a biologically diverse wetland, while the same facility placed in a remote desert largely devoid of life might evoke less concern. Another way to understand the importance of context is that an environmentally problematic activity practised by 100 companies might be of some concern, but their impact is dramatically amplified when in a growing economy 1000 companies are culprits. We thus often cannot measure the sustainability of corporate behaviour without a flexible, case-by-case approach. Additionally, obliging corporate managers to be more responsive to their environmental performance may pose cognitively challenging problems of reconciling seeming incommensurables. The incommensurability issue refers to the difficulty of comparing and synthesising different values into business decision-making. If a corporate manager is obliged both to seek profitability for shareholders while taking into account environmental costs, how can those dissimilar values be understood in a common metric to enable coherent, integrated decision-making?

In meeting these challenges, business law needs to promote decision-making approaches that are sufficiently flexible and adaptable, yet not so unbounded as to leave corporations and their investors unaccountable or unable to reconcile seemingly competing economic and environmental considerations. We need processes that neither privilege morally absolutist judgements about environmental protection nor leave decision-makers with open-ended discretion. Rigid, absolutist stances about appropriate corporate environmental conduct are rarely useful except in relation to prohibiting intrinsically dangerous environmental practices such as manufacturing certain toxic chemicals. Simplistic moral slogans such as 'respect the intrinsic value of nature'[116] tend to hinder 'genuine

---

[116] J. Pietarinen, 'The principal attitudes of humanity towards nature', in H.O. Okura (ed.), *Philosophy, Humanity and Ecology* (African Centre for Technology Studies Press, 1994), 290 at 293.

and enlightening debate about complex and nuanced real-world ethical issues'.[117] Alternatively, leaving the environmental conduct of businesses to managers' discretionary judgement would likely not make companies measurably accountable for their conduct.

While we should recognise a variety of values may inform sustainable companies' decision-making, they should be considered in a manner that allows us to ethically reason, critique, and choose the best justified values. Defensible positions on sustainability emanate from decision-making processes and forums that foster well-informed and nuanced evaluation of the specific circumstances and rival values. The governance of companies should open a space for such dialogue, for otherwise any sustainability standards might be construed as simply imposed, extraneous prescriptions. But it would also be naïve to expect that more transparent, democratic, and consultative decision-making in companies alone would be transformative, given the power dynamics in business organisations and market pressures. Thus, such decision-making must be bounded within certain fundamental environmental performance standards. Furthermore, beyond the level of individual businesses, processes to improve consultation and transparency might be successfully embedded in governance frameworks that are pitched at entire industries or markets.

A 'sustainable company' therefore is one that not only respects national and international environmental laws, but is also informed by a different model of corporate and related business law that embeds within the corporation the fundamental aim of respecting ecological constraints and opportunities for its development. This sustainability envelope may take the form of a number of legal mechanisms, including an overarching duty to avoid environmental harm and the requirement to make corporate governance more transparent and democratic with regard to consideration of a firm's environmental activities and impacts. A sustainable company is also embedded within a sustainable market system, in which the investors and banks that fund business enterprise themselves function under sustainability standards.

5   The Sustainable Companies Project

As mentioned at the outset of this chapter, this book reflects the work of the Sustainable Companies Project, the name for a global research

---

[117] W. Ransome and C. Sampford, *Ethics and Socially Responsible Investment: A Philosophical Approach* (Ashgate, 2010), 54.

CAPITALISM, SUSTAINABILITY, BUSINESS GOVERNANCE

network of scholars based at the University of Oslo that was launched in 2009 to improve our understanding of the intersection between business and environmental law, notably through an analysis of company law to identify barriers to and possibilities for the promotion of environmental sustainability. The work of the Sustainable Companies Project is based, as is this book, on three key assumptions.

First, while the exact impact of looming climate change, continued biodiversity depletion, and unchecked social decay from the economic challenges we face are hard to fully quantify and understand,[118] we know one thing for certain: *business as usual is not an alternative*. Enough has already been said in this opening chapter about these environmental threats and impacts. Suffice it to say here that incremental tinkering with the governance of business and markets, while seemingly politically attractive, will not stave off more serious ecological trauma and social upheaval this century.

Second, to change to a sustainable path, we *need business to contribute*.[119] Clearly, our governments, even if they were brave and progressive enough, cannot single-handedly adopt sustainability. The contribution of business is needed, as a source of innovation and financial resources. As Carol Liao's penultimate Chapter 7 in this book conveys, some companies are taking advantage of new legal templates to redesign their business models to focus on contributing to the community. And if business changes in the right direction, customers, employees, and, indeed, whole societies may shift with them. As recognised by the seminal 1992 Earth Summit's leading manual for sustainability – *Agenda 21* – our task requires multi-stakeholder collaboration with business playing an especially prominent role in proportion to its environmental impacts and the resources and expertise it can offer to forge solutions.[120]

The third key assumption that informs this book is that a *voluntary business response is not sufficient*, and indeed it is anathema if voluntarism is manipulated to avoid accountability or to deflect attention from serious action. CSR and SRI initiatives generally are insufficient to leverage positive change, as David Millon in Chapter 2 and Benjamin Richardson in Chapter 6 explain. Even worse, well-intended CSR or SRI initiatives

---

[118] And there always will be, until we can describe the impact in retrospect, questions as to the various prognoses: see e.g. 'A sensitive matter', *The Economist* (30 March 2013), available at: www.economist.com.

[119] As the European Commission also states: 'Enterprises can significantly contribute to the European Union's treaty objectives of sustainable development and a highly competitive social market economy', COM (2011) 681 final, s. 1.2.

[120] United Nations, *Agenda 21* (3 vols), E. 92–38352, A/CONF. 151/26, 1992.

can have the problematic effect of supporting the shareholder focus of the mainstream corporate governance debate. CSR and SRI proponents often direct arguments towards the shareholders and the management and board of the company. This inevitably – albeit unwillingly – supports a definition of the company as consisting of only shareholders, the board, and management, which, in turn, through the influence of the corporate governance debate, are seen as principals (shareholders) and agents (the board and, by extension, management), respectively. This observation is not meant to trivialise how the CSR and SRI movements have significantly contributed to bringing important issues on the impact of the companies to the forefront of public discussion and the business agenda. However, in spite of some convergence between mainstream corporate governance thinking and the more critical CSR and SRI discourses, the dominant perspective remains that companies' and investors' consideration of societal interests, outside of enforceable legal standards, is limited mainly to discretionary business case considerations.

While the company as a legal form may be said to be one of the most ingenious inventions of humanity, as a means for people to invest resources and build wealth,[121] the Sustainable Companies Project set out to investigate whether there is something in the legal infrastructure of this institution that contributes significantly to environmental degradation, especially to dangerous climate change (impacts, which of course, in the long run would undermine business success). The Project has focused on analysing the barriers to and possibilities for enhanced environmental protection and mitigation of climate change within the legal infrastructure for corporate decision-making. The corporate form dominates the business world, not only in rich developed countries but also in emerging economies. The aim of the analysis is to contribute to identifying what prevents attention to climate change and other environmental issues in corporate decision-making, and what might increase it. The hypothesis informing the work of the Sustainable Companies Project is that regulation of decision-making in business should be an indelible part of the governance framework for sustainability. This emphasis is consistent with the early conceptualisation of sustainability, such as at the seminal 1992

---

[121] Whereas the enforceable contract may be the most innovative contribution of Roman law, see A. Watson, 'The evolution of law: the Roman system of contracts' (1984) 2 *Law and History Review* 1, company law may be said to have made a similar contribution to the contemporary economy, see R.G. Rajan and L. Zingales, *Saving Capitalism from the Capitalists: Unleashing the Power of Financial Markets to Create Wealth and Spread Opportunity* (Crown Business, 2003).

Earth Summit, which stressed the need to *integrate* environmental and economic considerations into holistic decision-making.[122]

The work of the Sustainable Companies Project, which concluded in 2014, delved into the hitherto generally ignored area of company law to ascertain the barriers to and possibilities for environmentally sustainable companies. On a comparative law basis, this involved a number of well-documented methodological challenges.[123] One issue is choice of terminology. As explained in the comparative company law chapter by Beate Sjåfjell and others (Chapter 3), there is no common understanding across jurisdictions of core company law concepts such as the purpose of the company or the interests of the company. Often these concepts are not expressly addressed in preparatory works, legislation, case law, or legal doctrine. This makes in-depth analysis within each jurisdiction, and especially comparative analysis across nations, difficult. The authors of this chapter also found that there is a general lack of clarity and distinction with regard to other fundamental concepts such as shareholder value and shareholder primacy; the former used by the authors to denote a legal duty and the latter a social norm. Company law in general appears to be characterised by a discrepancy in terms of the relationship between law in practice and law on the books. When academic commentators are not always clear on whether they refer to the former or the latter, to corporate practice or to the results of legal analysis, and when the underlying value choices seem to be ignored, comparative analysis is extra challenging.

The working method of the Sustainable Companies Project has served to mitigate some of these challenges. Team members from the various jurisdictions have read and commented on each other's work in order to clarify concepts or terminology and share news of recent legal developments. A number of workshops and seminars were held where tentative results were presented and discussed. Nevertheless, as with all work of this kind, the comparative chapters of this book must be read with all the caveats that this type of analysis involves.

Similarly, when it comes to recommending governance reforms to move the business world closer to sustainability, members of the Sustainable Companies Project appreciate that sweeping, universal blueprints for change are problematic. There are some guiding norms of collective

---

[122] F. Dodds and M. Strauss, *Only One Earth: The Long Road via Rio to Sustainable Development* (Earthscan, 2012), passim.

[123] For example, M. Reimann and R. Zimmermann (eds.), *The Oxford Handbook of Comparative Law* (Oxford University Press, 2006).

importance regarding the need to embed sustainability thinking in the kernel of financial investing and corporate decision-making, but such 'embedding' can take a variety of permutations in different times and places. A host of factors – political, cultural, and economic – as well as local geographies and historical legacies, will require some accommodation. Thus, the methods of designing reforms (such as processes for dialogue and engagement with stakeholders) as well as the substantive reform agenda (whether it be fiduciary law or corporate reporting, among many issues) must be sensitive to the local context. A legal innovation in one jurisdiction will not necessarily thrive in another, operating under different circumstances and constraints. Yet, the Sustainable Companies Project also has a great deal of faith in the value of transnational sharing of experiences and ideas to help stimulate positive change in any part of the world.

6 Synopsis of the book

This book comprises eight chapters that take the reader on a journey of understanding of the barriers to and possibilities for sustainable companies. The journey begins with an analysis of the limitations of current governance approaches in the business world and then moves to a critique of some recent solutions, such as social investing and corporate hybrid structures, and concludes with a distillation of the main challenges and the paths ahead. The book's nine contributors offer diverse expertise on business and environmental law, as well as insights from the variety of jurisdictions that they represent: Australia (Richardson), Canada (Liao), Finland (Mähönen), Norway (Anker-Sørensen and Sjåfjell), the United Kingdom (Johnston and Villiers), Ireland (Clarke), and the United States (Millon). In addition, through their consideration of the numerous 'mapping papers' of corporate law and sustainability authored by the many other international participants to the Sustainable Companies Project, these contributors present insights from a wider array of jurisdictions, such as South Africa, India, Germany, and many more.

David Millon's Chapter 2, 'Corporate social responsibility and environmental sustainability', evaluates the potential for CSR to stimulate commitment to environmental sustainability. Because domestic environmental laws and regulations generally are inadequate for this task, CSR offers the possibility of voluntary action to reduce the negative effects of corporate activity on the environment and to invest in the development of 'green' products and services. Millon distinguishes between two models that have dominated the CSR agenda: the 'ethical' and the 'strategic'. The former evokes the notion that companies ought in some circumstances to promote the interests of their non-shareholder stakeholders, even if that detracts from financial returns to the company and its shareholders. According to this view, this should be an ethical imperative rather than a matter of discretionary philanthropy. Millon argues that the prospects for ethical CSR depend greatly on the institutional context. In countries where shareholder primacy is strongly embedded in company law or extra-legal social norms or where institutional investors are able to insist on short-term financial returns, ethical CSR struggles to gain much traction. Where, however, a stakeholder orientation is more established in corporate governance, the prospects are more promising. Millon surveys three institutional contexts – Continental Europe, the United States, and the United Kingdom – offering differing perspectives on this issue.

In contrast to ethical CSR, strategic CSR leads to investment in stakeholder well-being in order to promote the company's long-run economic viability. Both shareholders and non-shareholders stand to gain, so this version of CSR has the potential to overcome objections based on shareholder primacy. Two caveats are made. First, shareholders may still object if they are unwilling to tolerate the near-term costs of investment in stakeholder well-being in return for financial benefits that will materialise, if at all, only in the long run. Additionally, because the costs of strategic CSR are justified by financial benefits, there is a built-in limit; companies will invest in environmental sustainability and other stakeholder benefits only if they perceive that they stand to profit. Corporate (and shareholder) financial return is the relevant criterion, not aggregate social welfare, so companies will probably not go far enough in meeting social needs. Until law reform effectively addresses sustainability, the need to cultivate an ethics-based model of CSR persists.

Chapter 3, 'Shareholder primacy: the main barrier to sustainable companies', by Sjåfjell *et al.*, builds on the hypothesis informing the work of the Sustainable Companies Project, that environmental sustainability should be incorporated into the core regulation of business decision-making. Beate Sjåfjell, Andrew Johnston, Linn Anker-Sørensen, and David Millon provide a comparative analysis of core features of company law – the rules regulating the duties and purpose of corporate decision-makers – in evaluating the existing scope for integrating sustainable development, especially in its environmental dimension, into corporate decision-making. Their analysis reveals much unexplored potential in current company law regimes for companies to change from 'business as usual'. No company law system mandates the fundamentalist narrow version of shareholder profit maximisation that we see expressed in the social norm of 'shareholder primacy'. That social norm is the most formidable barrier to core company law furthering sustainability. This norm is falsely perceived as supported by company law because that area of law focuses on the position of shareholders. Shareholder primacy has been allowed to develop in the absence of an explicit legal statement setting out the purpose of companies and delineating the company interest, leaving the competence and duty of the company organs, notably of the governing board, rather vague. 'Business as usual' is driven by shareholder primacy, but is actually detrimental to any shareholder with more than a very short-term perspective on their investment, including institutional investors such as pension funds. The shareholder primacy drive keeps mainstream legal reform on a narrow, path-dependent track. In concluding that corporate law reform is necessary, the authors acknowledge that on its own it cannot engender revolutionary change; rather, it must be nested within a wider mosaic of sustainability governance initiatives. Such reform should include an express redefinition of the purpose of companies and its implications for the role, duties, and liability of the board. This has the potential to make more effective the external regulation of companies and realise the potential within each company to make its own independent, creative, and active contribution to society's transformation to sustainability.

The analysis of corporate boards of directors is continued in Blanaid Clarke's more specialised Chapter 4, 'The role of board directors in promoting environmental sustainability'. She discusses the role that boards and individual directors can play in ensuring that their companies act in a manner that promotes sustainability. Clarke considers how this role has developed in recent times with a view to what is expected of boards and what discretion is afforded to them in this respect. She describes the manner in which corporate boards are regulated, with particular emphasis on UK and EU-level regulation. The chapter examines the evolution of the role of non-executive directors and considers their role in embedding sustainability within the business organisational framework. Clarke considers the necessary attributes and skills of non-executive directors that may allow them to fulfil this role (such as independence, diversity, expertise and personal integrity, and character).

In Chapter 5, 'Accounting, auditing and reporting: supporting or obstructing the sustainable companies objective?', Charlotte Villiers and Jukka Mähönen discuss whether and how corporate reporting and auditing requirements encompass the environmental performance of business activity. If we expect companies to be more mindful of their environmental impact, they and their stakeholders must be able to understand the environmental performance and impacts of business. There is a strong

CAPITALISM, SUSTAINABILITY, BUSINESS GOVERNANCE   33

and well-established corporate financial accounting culture worldwide, but few jurisdictions appear to have developed robust accounting for environmental performance. While the authors acknowledge the potential of accounting and reporting to improve corporate environmental performance, they find that these mechanisms, if poorly designed, can hinder such improvements. The chapter explores the barriers and possibilities for improved sustainability through accounting and reporting as well as related audit and other quality assurance processes. Through its cross-jurisdictional analysis, with particular reference to EU Member States, Villiers and Mähönen identify a more progressive role for sustainability-focused reporting and auditing.

The book's next two chapters examine the impact and potential of some recent innovations in the business world that purport to offer new pathways to sustainability: the movement for socially responsible or ethical investing (SRI) and its accompanying legal reforms, and the development of new legal templates for corporate 'hybrids' that mandate community contributions in addition to profit-making goals.

In Chapter 6, 'Financial markets and socially responsible investing', Benjamin Richardson extends the analysis beyond regular companies in the productive economy, which the other chapters in this book discuss, to these companies' investors or financiers. Richardson investigates how the financial sector shapes the environmental performance of the economy, and assesses whether the rising global movement for SRI can foster sustainable companies in the absence of credible governmental regulation. The chapter closely examines five areas of potential SRI influence: (1) changing the cost of capital to companies; (2) making SRI financially advantageous to investors; (3) engaging with companies through dialogue and shareholder activism; (4) enacting voluntary SRI codes; and (5) leveraging change through public policy and legal reform. The principal argument is that the financial sector continues to cast a mostly negative environmental impact, and SRI so far has had a rather muted remedial influence. SRI will likely only acquire greater significance through a more enabling regulatory and public policy framework, and existing efforts of social investors to collaborate with governments appear to be the most promising pathway for this movement to engender change.

A similarly cautious tone is evident in Carol Liao's perspicacious analysis of the 'Limits to corporate reform and alternative legal structures' (Chapter 7). She explores the potential of a new wave of legal reforms in North America and the UK to establish corporate 'hybrids' that combine the goals of business profits and community contributions. These reforms build on the cooperative model, the oldest corporate structure in history.

While the cooperative has been recognised by the UN as playing a critical role in economic development and social innovation throughout the world,[124] it has, for several reasons, not had the success its model might seem to warrant. The new breed of alternative legal structures – called corporate 'hybrids' – not only enable, but require, CSR concepts to be embodied within corporate practices. However, there is no legal obligation on any company to transform itself into a corporate hybrid – thus the potential for this model to nudge companies towards sustainability is highly debatable when the option of remaining a for-profit business persists. Nonetheless, Liao argues that corporate hybrids may help stimulate positive change despite the onerous barriers facing reformation of the shareholder primacy model. These barriers identified by her include entrenched ideological beliefs that have permeated the psyche of corporate governance practices in global capital markets, and path dependence in narrowing legal reform. Liao's analysis of corporate hybrid reforms in Canada, the United States, and the United Kingdom explores some of the main types of hybrids, their governance features that attempt to accommodate and unite both the for-profit and non-profit agendas, the reasons behind these features, the main challenges that implementation of these models face, and their overall potential impact.

The book concludes with a pithy Chapter 8, 'The future of company law and sustainability', in which Beate Sjåfjell and Benjamin Richardson distil the principal findings of the book, place them in the broader context of the sustainability discourse, and outline priority policy goals and governance reforms that states and non-state actors should embrace so that the business community can make a more positive contribution to the shared task of seeking environmental sustainability. The kernel of such reform rests on redefining the fundamental purpose of the company and the duties of those who manage and supervise it. The core challenge of climbing the sustainability mountain is to inculcate in the decision-making of economic and other societal actors the imperative to act for the long term.

---

[124] United Nations, 'International year of cooperatives', available at: http://social.un.org/coopsyear.

2

Corporate social responsibility and environmental sustainability

DAVID MILLON

1 The sustainability challenge

Large multinational corporations can inflict heavy damage on the environment – highly publicised catastrophes like the *Exxon Valdez* or BP Deepwater oil spills are obvious and dramatic examples – but businesses also interact with the environment in countless ways as part of their day-to-day operations. Continuation of business as usual endangers the future of human existence. Irreversible climate change, resource depletion, accumulation of nonbiodegradable waste, and loss of biodiversity will continue and will increasingly threaten the quality of all human life.[1] To stop this momentum, a commitment to environmental sustainability is required. Although the parameters of 'environmental sustainability' are contested among policy-makers and scholars, at a minimum, this requires that renewable resources should not be consumed in quantities greater than the rate of regeneration; pollution should not exceed the environment's assimilative capacity; and depletion of nonrenewable resources should be accompanied by the development of renewable alternatives.[2] In other words, we must redesign the way we live so that we meet our needs today without compromising the ability of future generations to meet theirs.[3]

Inasmuch as corporations are now major contributors to this looming environmental crisis, they also have a potentially hugely important role

---

[1] See e.g. Millennium Ecosystem Assessment (MEA), *Living Beyond Our Means: Natural Assets and Human Well-Being, Statement from the Board* (MEA, 2005); United Nations Environment Programme (UNEP), *Global Environment Outlook GEO-5* (UNEP, 2012).

[2] H.E. Daly, 'Toward some operational principles of sustainable development' (1990) 2(1) *Ecological Economics* 1.

[3] World Commission on Environment and Development, *Our Common Future* (Oxford University Press, 1987), commonly referred to as the Brundtland Report.

to play in contributing to sustainability. Many companies are already working to reduce their harmful effects on the environment. They are finding ways to use scarce resources more efficiently. They are developing innovative 'green' products and industrial processes as well as products that will help society adjust to the physical effects of climate change that cannot be reversed. Important as they are, however, these activities also remind us how much more corporations can and must do.

Existing domestic laws – particularly in the United States (the USA) and China – do not do nearly enough to require corporations to contribute to environmental sustainability.[4] As yet, most countries have not enacted stringent regulations on greenhouse gas (GHG) emissions and other impediments to sustainability. The USA has pursued a largely voluntary agenda in recent years, after the wave of ambitious environmental law-making in the late 1960s and 1970s.[5] Even if a company is incorporated in a jurisdiction with relatively strict environmental laws, extraterritoriality limitations may mean that a corporation's operations in another country will be governed by local environmental laws that may be lax or unenforced. Developing countries may be especially reluctant to enact tough regulations for fear of discouraging badly needed foreign investment.[6] To date, international law and institutions have been largely ineffective.[7]

Despite the frightening prospects of continued climate change and other environmental calamities, there is no reason to assume that coordinated domestic environmental regulation or international legal initiatives that boldly address the role of corporations – both as threats to environmental preservation and potential contributors to sustainability – are likely to emerge in the near future. Powerful corporations can often thwart credible environmental regulation that impinges on their

---

[4] B. Sjåfjell, 'Regulating companies as if the world matters: reflections from the ongoing Sustainable Companies Project' (2012) 47(1) *Wake Forest Law Review* 121.

[5] K. Southworth, 'Corporate voluntary action: a valuable but incomplete solution to climate change and energy security challenges' (2009) 27(4) *Policy and Society* 329; Z.J.B. Plater, 'From the beginning, a fundamental shift of paradigms: a theory and short history of environmental law' (1994) 27 *Loyola of Los Angeles Law Review* 981.

[6] B.J. Richardson, 'Is East Asia industrialising too quickly? Environmental regulation in its special economic zones' (2005) 22 *UCLA Pacific Basin Law Journal* 150.

[7] D. Levy and R. Kaplan, 'Corporate social responsibility and theories of global governance: strategic contestation in global issue arenas', in A. Crane, *et al.* (eds.), *The Oxford Handbook of Corporate Social Responsibility* (Oxford University Press, 2008), 432 at 434–5; A. Gillespie, *The Illusion of Progress: Unsustainable Development in International Law and Policy* (Earthscan, 2001).

profitability.[8] Nor can it be assumed that domestic company laws will fill this void on a scale anywhere near what is needed. For the time being, therefore, further progress is likely to depend on voluntary corporate initiatives.

The need for such action to protect the environment suggests a potential role for corporate social responsibility (CSR). This chapter explores the prospects for CSR as a partial solution. (CSR, when understood as voluntary behaviour, can be only a partial solution because law is needed as well.) Section 2 discusses the contested meanings of CSR and how it might be relevant to the sustainability challenge. Section 3 presents one widely held conception of CSR, which I term the 'ethical' model. This conceives of the corporation as an aggregation of stakeholders whose interests often conflict with each other's. Corporate managers should under certain circumstances favour nonshareholders, even where doing so may be at the shareholders' expense. There is an ethical or normative dimension to the allocation question; it is not purely a matter of management discretion and philanthropy.

The prospects for ethical CSR depend very much on the institutional context within which a particular corporation is embedded. Where shareholder primacy is the basic value, ethical CSR confronts a formidable obstacle if it is seen to detract from short-term profitability. Where, instead, stakeholder value dominates, ethical CSR is more likely to gain traction. Section 4 therefore surveys three institutional contexts – continental Europe, the USA, and the United Kingdom (UK) – in order to obtain institutionally grounded perspectives on the likelihood of success for environmental sustainability initiatives justified by ethical CSR. Different answers are suggested in each case.

Because of shareholder primacy's strong presence in the USA and, to a lesser extent, in the UK, the prospects for ethical CSR – with its built-in trade-off or zero-sum assumption – are problematic. Section 5 therefore presents a different theory of CSR, the 'strategic' model. Here the corporation spends money on nonshareholders' well-being (this is the CSR benefit), but the purpose and the expectation are that the corporation and its shareholders will, in the long run, earn a sufficient return on those investments. In other words, shareholders gain rather than lose from CSR in this model. This idea has the potential to overcome objections to CSR based on shareholder primacy values. As such, it is a 'business case' for

---

[8] S. Beder, *Global Spin: The Corporate Assault on Environmentalism* (Green Books, 2002).

CSR, so Section 5 also considers evidence bearing on the validity of the positive cost–benefit assumption.

Lest strategic CSR be assumed to be a 'win–win' scenario for all concerned, Section 6 concludes this chapter with some critical reflections. First, resistance from shareholders can still arise if they are unwilling to accept the short-term costs of CSR investments in return for benefits that will materialise, if at all, only in the long run. To the extent this is so, the promise of strategic CSR will fall on deaf ears, together with the ethical model. Second, because strategic CSR rests on cost–benefit analysis, there is a built-in limit on the extent of its CSR benefits. Corporations will only invest in environmental sustainability if and to the extent that they stand to benefit financially because the touchstone is corporate (and shareholder) financial interest, not aggregate social benefit. There is a significant likelihood, therefore, that corporations will not go far enough to satisfy social needs because doing so will often not be cost effective. If CSR is to be part of the solution, the need for an ethics-based model of CSR therefore persists.

2 The potential importance of CSR

There is no single, widely accepted definition of CSR. It is a contentious subject that has attracted increased academic attention since the 1990s.[9] Even among sympathetic analysts, key questions generate controversy. There is disagreement about the role of business in society, the scope of its responsibilities, what responsibility entails, and the relationship between CSR and law.

My attempt to specify the meaning of CSR begins with its 'social' element. The idea is simply that corporations have responsibilities to the broader society. One part of this may be the generation of financial returns for investors, but this alone cannot be the extent of CSR because it is too narrow a conception of what counts as society. Especially when one sees that corporations affect the well-being – for good or ill – of many people besides shareholders in direct and potentially very important ways, it becomes apparent that the social dimension of business activity extends to a broad array of stakeholders, such as workers, creditors, local communities, suppliers, and consumers.

---

[9] Two important general studies of CSR are A. Crane, *et al.* (eds.), *The Oxford Handbook of Corporate Social Responsibility* (Oxford University Press, 2008); and T. Lambooy, *Corporate Social Responsibility: Legal and Semi-Legal Frameworks Supporting CSR* (Kluwer, 2010).

CSR AND ENVIRONMENTAL SUSTAINABILITY

Some claim that corporations best serve their stakeholders and the broader society by maximising financial returns for shareholders.[10] A moment's reflection reveals the error in that claim. Many of the costs that flow from profit generation are inflicted on others. Pollution is the classic example. Because compensation is not required in many cases, there is no reason why corporations seeking to maximise profits should seek to minimise those third-party effects. This is what Bakan has in mind when he calls the corporation the 'externalising machine'.[11]

One can consider the content of the corporation's responsibilities to its stakeholders in various ways. For example, one might assert a duty not to harm, with a corresponding duty to rectify harm that is inflicted.[12] In the language of economics, this can be referred to as a duty to internalise the corporation's externalities.[13] More ambitiously, one could argue that corporations have an affirmative duty to contribute in some way to its stakeholders' quality of life or, more broadly still, 'to further some social good'.[14]

How one defines the breadth of corporate obligation and what that obligation entails are difficult and controversial questions that need not occupy us here. For the purposes of this chapter, it is enough to claim that CSR implies an obligation to take reasonable steps to refrain from damaging the environment and, where possible, to assist others in doing the same. CSR may also extend to a positive duty to improve environmental conditions. Reasonableness depends on the idiosyncratic characteristics of the particular firm, including its capabilities and limitations, its financial condition, and the constraints inherent in the industry in which it operates. Reasonableness is also complicated by the cumulative and incremental nature of much environmental harm; as Lichtenberg explains, harm is 'essentially aggregative: there is nothing intrinsically

---

[10] M. Friedman, 'The social responsibility of business is to increase profits', *New York Times Magazine*, 13 September 1970, 32.

[11] J. Bakan, *The Corporation: Pathological Pursuit of Profit and Power* (Simon & Schuster, 2005), Chapter 3.

[12] J. Campbell, 'Why would corporations behave in socially responsible ways? An institutional theory of corporate social responsibility' (2007) 32 (3) *Academy of Management Review* 951.

[13] A. Johnston, 'Facing up to social cost: the real meaning of corporate social responsibility' (2011) 20(1) *Griffith Law Review* 221; B. Sjåfjell, 'Internalizing externalities in EU Law: why neither corporate governance nor corporate social responsibility provides the answers' (2009) 40(4) *George Washington International Law Review* 977.

[14] A. McWilliams and D. Siegel, 'Corporate social responsibility: a theory of the firm perspective' (2001) 26 (1) *Academy of Management Review* 117.

harmful to the environment or other people in burning fossil fuels; the harms depend on the joint effects of many people's action'.[15]

The other element of my definition of CSR turns on the distinction between legal obligation and voluntarily chosen conduct. There is a sense in which simply obeying the law amounts to socially responsible behaviour. However, where the law is inadequate to address a particular social need – as is the case in the area of environmental sustainability – this notion of CSR offers little of value, if that is all it has to say. To make a significantly positive impact on the environment, corporations need to do more than simply comply with legal requirements. Indeed, scholars of environmental law conceive of a new style of regulation that can harness CSR imperatives to stimulate companies to 'go beyond compliance' to achieve truly beneficial outcomes.[16] Further, even those, like Milton Friedman, who insist that business's sole obligation is to generate profits for corporate shareholders, acknowledge that corporations should comply with applicable laws and regulations and honour contractual obligations.[17] Normatively, therefore, a notion of CSR limited to legal compliance would add little to the debate, though where legal standards and rules leave companies with discretion, CSR may be relevant to expectations that companies seek the most exemplary performance where feasible.

The concept of voluntariness can get slippery if one recognises that actors are embedded within institutional frameworks that strongly influence their sense of what counts as appropriate or inappropriate behaviour.[18] Beyond legal obligation, there are widely shared assumptions and values that structure perceptions of right and wrong. These 'social norms' can be powerful enough to motivate behaviour just as much as law does.[19] Even so, the distinction between legally required conduct and conduct that goes beyond that minimum still seems relevant and useful if the goal is for companies to commit resources to sustainability where the law does not require it. The extent to which such choices are truly 'voluntary' would seem to be beside the point.

---

[15] J. Lichtenberg, 'Negative duties, positive duties, and the "new harms"' (2010) 120(3) *Ethics* 568.

[16] N. Gunningham, 'Beyond compliance: management of environmental risk', in B. Boer, R. Fowler and N. Gunningham (eds.), *Environmental Outlook: Law and Policy* (Federation Press, 1994), 254.

[17] Friedman, 'The social responsibility of business is to increase its profits.'

[18] S. Brammer, G. Jackson, and D. Matten, 'Corporate Social Responsibility and institutional theory: new perspectives on private governance' (2012) 10 (1) *Socio-Economic Review* 3.

[19] See E.A. Posner, *Law and Social Norms* (Harvard University Press, 2002).

Critics have expressed legitimate misgivings about the value of CSR, pointing out that at least some of what claims the mantle of CSR amounts to little more than public relations manoeuvres – 'greenwashing'[20] – designed to deflect pressures from nongovernmental organisations (NGOs) and consumers. Corporations may also see these voluntary initiatives as ways proactively to reduce the threat of governmental regulation. While recognising that greenwashing does occur and provides little social value, it is also important to see that corporations have the capacity to do much more than that. Ideally, company law and international regulation would impose legal requirements supporting sustainability, but for now that seems to be happening piecemeal and too slowly.[21] Meanwhile, some corporations, without legal obligation, are making genuine and effective voluntary efforts to report on and reduce GHG emissions, pollution, and waste.[22] Others are developing products, such as hybrid automobiles, that will allow consumers to reduce their environmental burden. Others still are joining with firms in their industry to develop codes of conduct on environmental and human rights matters, such as Responsible Care governing the chemical industry.[23] My view of CSR has these kinds of meaningful activities in mind, without claiming that all that passes for CSR is significant or that even effective CSR could be a complete solution to the sustainability challenge.

3 The 'ethical' model of CSR

3.1 Balancing stakeholder interests

Given the lack of an agreed definition of CSR, it comes as no surprise that there are several different models or theories of CSR.[24] They are in

---

[20] The term seems to have been coined in 1986 by an environmental activist named Jay Westerveld. See J. Motavalli, 'A history of greenwashing: how dirty towels impacted the green movement' (12 February 2011), available at: www.dailyfinance.com/2011/02/12/the-history-of-greenwashing-how-dirty-towels-impacted-the-green.

[21] B. Sjåfjell, 'Why law matters: corporate social irresponsibility and the futility of voluntary climate change mitigation' (2010) 8(2–3) *European Company Law* 56.

[22] Southworth, 'Corporate voluntary action'.

[23] See www.icca-chem.org/en/Home/Responsible-care; and also D. Vogel, *The Market for Virtue: The Potential and Limits of Corporate Social Responsibility* (Brookings Institution Press, 2005), 82–101.

[24] D. Melé, 'Corporate social responsibility theories', in A. Crane, *et al.* (eds.), *The Oxford Handbook of Corporate Social Responsibility* (Oxford University Press, 2008). For alternative views, see A. Geva, 'Three models of corporate social responsibility: interrelationships between theory, research, and practice' (2008) 113(1) *Business and Society Review* 1; M.D.P.

turn derived from among a range of different normative imperatives.[25] At a general level, one approach is to distinguish between CSR theories that conceive of the corporation as a discrete entity and others that see it instead as an aggregation of stakeholder constituencies.[26] Entity-based theories rely on the idea of corporate personality, characterising the corporate person in a certain way and then, from that descriptive assertion, deriving normative conclusions about the relation between the corporation and society. So, for example, the corporation can be described as a citizen, analogous to a natural person.[27] The political implications of the citizenship idea can then form the basis for a theory of the corporation's social responsibilities.[28] It is also possible to describe the corporate person with reference to the great power it wields and argue that from this power comes the duty to exercise it responsibly.[29]

One shortcoming of entity-based CSR theories is the problematic nature of attempting to derive concrete normative implications from metaphorical, fictitious attributions of personality. One response to such claims is to deny the assertion of personhood. Conceptions of the person are also normatively ambiguous, and it can be difficult to determine to whom the corporate entity is supposed to be responsible. For these reasons, an aggregate theory of the corporation, which sees the firm as an aggregation of its various stakeholder constituencies, is appealing conceptually as well as practically.[30]

To be sure, specifying the class of relevant stakeholders has been controversial,[31] but Freeman's pragmatic definition has intuitive appeal,

Lee, 'A review of the theories of corporate social responsibility: its evolutionary path and the road ahead' (2008) 10(1) *International Journal of Management Reviews* 53.

[25] One analysis identifies four: instrumental, political, integrative, and ethical. E. Garriga and D. Melé, 'Corporate social responsibility theories: mapping the territory' (2004) 53(1–2) *Journal of Business Ethics* 51.

[26] For discussion, see D. Millon, 'Corporate theory and CSR' (unpublished paper).

[27] Melé, 'Corporate social responsibility theories', 68–75.

[28] E. Dodd, 'For whom are corporate managers trustees?' (1932) 45(7) *Harvard Law Review* 1145; J.B. White, 'How should we talk about corporations? The languages of economics and of citizenship' (1985) 94 *Yale Law Journal* 1416.

[29] Garriga and Melé, 'Corporate social responsibility theories', 56; S. Wood, 'The case for leverage-based corporate human rights responsibility' (2012) 22(1) *Business Ethics Quarterly* 63.

[30] See D. Millon, 'Two models of corporate social responsibility' (2011) 46 *Wake Forest Law Review* 523, in which I use the term 'constituency model'.

[31] T.W. Dunfee, 'Stakeholder theory: managing corporate social responsibility in a multiple actor context', in Crane, *et al.* (eds.), *The Oxford Handbook of Corporate Social Responsibility*, 353.

is reasonably workable, and has proved to be durable: anyone who 'can affect or is affected by the achievement of the organisation's objectives'.[32] Here one avoids metaphysical assertions by thinking of the corporation as an organisation of people who fall into categories of common interest. Having identified the possible beneficiaries, stakeholder theory focuses attention on what must be the relevant question, namely, to whom should we deem the fictitious corporate person to be responsible? The various stakeholder constituencies typically include – in addition to shareholders – employees, creditors, consumers, local communities in which the company has a presence, and those individuals who are affected by the company's impact on the environment.

Thinking of CSR in terms of duties owed to stakeholder constituencies is often assumed to necessitate 'trade-offs' or 'zero-sum' choices. It is generally taken for granted – often, though not necessarily, with justification – that the interests of nonshareholders conflict with those of shareholders. So, if management acts in the interest of some nonshareholder constituency, it is assumed that corporate profits are reduced accordingly and shareholders' wealth is thereby diminished. For example, management may decide to install expensive new equipment to decrease air pollution even though it is not legally required to do so. The public stands to benefit, but the added expense will reduce shareholders' profits, at least in the near term. Certainly one hears this complaint from partisans of shareholders, who insist that CSR comes at their expense and is illegitimate for that reason.[33]

The flip side of this coin is that acting in the interests of shareholders by seeking to maximise profits will often come at the expense of nonshareholders. Faced with a plant that is producing insufficient revenue, for instance, management may have to decide between closing it, which would be bad for workers, suppliers, and the local community, or keeping it going, which would be bad for shareholders. A decision in favour of the shareholders will have a negative impact on nonshareholding stakeholders.

CSR rejects the idea that such trade-offs should necessarily be decided in the interests of the shareholders, but complex allocation questions are embedded here. Under what circumstances might management of the corporation legitimately prefer shareholders' interests over those of

---

[32] R.E. Freeman, *Strategic Management: A Stakeholder Approach* (Pittman, 1984), 46.
[33] The classic statement of this position is by Friedman, 'The social responsibility of business is to increase its profits.'

other stakeholders? Shareholders being stakeholders as well, it is surely unsatisfactory to claim that shareholders must always lose. And what about cases in which there are conflicts of interest among nonshareholder constituencies? How are choices to be made? Stakeholder theory does not offer clear answers to these questions and might be criticised on that ground, but this is a complex and controversial problem that is not readily amenable to specific, generalisable, rule-like prescriptions about appropriate conduct.[34]

From the shareholders' perspective, the idea of CSR as requiring a balancing of stakeholder interests might be thought of as philanthropy. It is as if management has made a gift of the corporation's assets; the value of the shareholders' equity declines and they receive nothing in return. Shareholders might therefore call this approach to CSR the 'philanthropic' model. Other stakeholders would see the matter differently. For them, these benefits are not gratuitous acts of charity. The question instead is whether there is an obligation to favour nonshareholders' interests in appropriate cases. Scholars primarily in the field of business ethics have developed a number of normative theories that can ground such obligations.[35] I therefore prefer to use the term 'ethical' CSR[36] to refer to stakeholder theories that argue for a balancing of shareholders' and nonshareholders' interests.

Finally, it should be noted that CSR does not necessarily entail zero-sum choices between conflicting shareholders' and nonshareholders' interests. At times, investments in the well-being of nonshareholders can generate shareholder value, at least in the long run. In such cases, regard for nonshareholders' well-being need not be grounded in an ethics-based notion of obligation. Rather, it can be justified in instrumental terms, as part of a business strategy designed to enhance shareholders' wealth.[37] The distinction can be important because some objections to 'ethical' CSR might not apply to 'strategic' CSR. The strategic model of CSR will be discussed in Section 5, after the prospects for the potentially more controversial ethical theory have been explored in Section 4.

---

[34] Dunfee, 'Stakeholder theory'.

[35] For a brief summary with references, see S. Benn and D. Bolton, *Key Concepts in Corporate Social Responsibility* (Sage, 2011), 13–17.

[36] For a discussion of various versions of ethical CSR and their normative foundations, see Garriga and Melé, 'Corporate social responsibility theories', 60–2.

[37] Garriga and Melé, 'Corporate social responsibility theories', 53–5.

3.2 *Corporate governance, corporate purpose, and the prospects for ethical CSR*

Understood as described above, CSR has the potential to contribute to environmental sustainability to the extent that corporations choose to alter existing business practices and relationships, and make investments in new processes and products. A salient determinant of whether such activities are likely to be undertaken is the extent to which such expenditures are tolerated or even encouraged. This is not a question that yields a single answer. Many variables determine how individual companies approach these questions, including the attitudes, motivations, and actions of individual employees and managers, shareholders, outsiders such as consumers and NGOs who may be capable of exerting pressure on the corporation, national governments, and intergovernmental organisations.[38]

To appreciate the complexity of the question of individual companies' propensities for or against CSR and the variability of actual behaviour is not to suggest that this is an entirely idiosyncratic phenomenon. Institutional theory helps to explain general tendencies that are related to the ways in which states differ with respect to the formal and informal structures that shape economic and social governance.[39] These structures consist not just of law and legal institutions, but also of a broad array of social norms, expectations, and practices that shape thinking and behaviour with respect to the appropriate role of business in society. These institutional structures can in turn be grouped into general types, according to the ways in which markets are defined and regulated, the role of the state, and the more general values or normative traditions that inform understandings of the role of business in society.

An institutional theory perspective makes it possible to offer some generalisations about the likelihood that companies will choose voluntarily to promote environmental sustainability in the absence of legal duress. Kang and Moon have recently argued for a complementarity between different forms of corporate governance and different approaches to CSR.[40] This

---

[38] R.V. Aguilera, *et al.*, 'Putting the "s" back in corporate social responsibility: a multi-level theory of social change in organizations' (2007) 32(3) *Academy of Management Review* 836.

[39] Brammer, *et al.*, 'Corporate social responsibility and institutional theory'.

[40] N. Kang and J. Moon, 'Institutional complementarity between corporate governance and corporate social responsibility: a comparative institutional analysis of three capitalisms' (2012) 10(1) *Socio-Economic Review* 85.

46   DAVID MILLON

approach makes intuitive sense because corporate governance, properly understood, influences the extent to which companies will pursue CSR and the forms that such pursuits are likely to take. Section 4 therefore examines differences in institutional context with respect to corporate governance.

Before proceeding to that inquiry, it is first necessary to articulate an appropriate understanding of what 'corporate governance' should mean in this context. The term may refer simply to the idea that corporate management is supposed to act as the shareholders' agent, and corporate governance is better or worse depending on the extent to which management promotes shareholders' financial interests.[41] A more useful notion of corporate governance broadens the perspective to incorporate the other principal contributor to corporate activity, namely, labour (employees).[42] Together, management, shareholders, labour, and also lenders are the principal investors in the firm, contributing either human or financial capital. Corporate governance therefore can be understood as the set of arrangements and ideas that structures the balance of power among these constituencies and defines the mechanisms by which they interact with each other in order to pursue their own interests, the interests of the corporation as a whole, and the relationship between the corporation and the broader society.

The concept of corporate governance should also be expanded to include recognition of differing conceptions of corporate purpose.[43] In addition to differences in governance arrangements and practices, company law and social norms also present divergent understandings of the ultimate purpose of the corporation. Generally speaking, some traditions emphasise shareholders' wealth maximisation while others conceive of the company's purpose more broadly, in terms of the maximisation of stakeholder or social wealth. Differences in corporate governance understood in the broader manner described here can influence the ways in

---

[41] For example, H. Hansmann and R. Kraakman, 'The end of history for corporate law' (2001) 89(2) *Georgetown Law Journal* 439; R. La Porta, *et al.*, 'Investor protection and corporate governance' (2000) 58(1–2) *Journal of Financial Economics* 1. For a critical perspective on the agency idea and explanation of its recent origins, see D. Millon, 'Radical shareholder primacy' (2014) 10(4) *University of St Thomas Law Journal* 1013.

[42] Kang and Moon, 'Institutional complementarity', 89.

[43] Differences exist even as to for-profit firms, which are the focus of this chapter. In addition, other forms of business entity – including, in the USA, non-profit and benefit corporations – also conceive of corporate purpose in different ways.

CSR AND ENVIRONMENTAL SUSTAINABILITY 47

which firms approach decisions about whether and how to engage in ethical CSR.

4 CSR and institutional context

As a potential, albeit only partial, solution to the problem of environmental sustainability, CSR practices cannot be viewed as a unitary, cross-national phenomenon. Countries vary widely in their institutional frameworks, and these contexts influence corporate behaviour. In this section, I address some of these differences at a general level. I begin with a broad-brush look at continental Europe as representing a single tradition or system, necessarily overlooking significant country-specific variations for the sake of generalisation.[44] I then turn to the USA and the UK, two institutional contexts that are often assumed to be one, standing in contrast to the European model, but that in fact diverge from each other in significant ways.

4.1   Continental Europe: stakeholder-oriented traditions

In a seminal paper in the emerging field of comparative CSR, Matten and Moon point to unique features of European and American political and institutional cultures as explanations for the explicit commitment to CSR expressed by many US companies and the corresponding relative silence on this issue by European companies.[45] Their core insight is that institutional differences structure companies' attitudes towards CSR, differences not just in legal regimes, but also in informal but nonetheless powerful social norms and values. The European institutional context includes traditions of strong government authority, combined with greater willingness to address economic and social issues through regulation. Some countries have publicly managed health[46] and pension[47] programmes,

---

[44] For more specific treatment of differences among specific countries, see other chapters in this book.

[45] D. Matten and J. Moon, ' "Implicit" and "explicit" CSR: a conceptual framework for a comparative understanding of corporate social responsibility' (2008) 33(2) *Academy of Management Review* 404. See also G. Jackson and A. Apostolakou, 'Corporate social responsibility in Western Europe: an institutional mirror or substitute?' (2010) 94(3) *Journal of Business Ethics* 371.

[46] For example, Italy, Spain, Sweden, and Norway.

[47] For example, Denmark, France, Germany, and the Netherlands among continental European countries.

48 DAVID MILLON

while others impose these responsibilities on corporations as employers. Extra-legal norms may also encourage companies to address social needs. Explicitly articulated CSR policies may seem less necessary as long as formal and informal institutions impose expectations of social responsibility on corporations that are implicit in the normal ways business leaders conceive of their roles.[48] In contrast to the Anglo-American conception of corporate purpose, which is said to be based on shareholder primacy, continental European company law and social norms tend to expect the corporation and its management to attend to the well-being not just of shareholders but also of workers and the broader society. One survey found that nearly 83 per cent of German senior managers believed that the company belonged to all the stakeholders. In France, the number was 78 per cent. By way of contrast, in the USA (76 per cent) and the UK (71 per cent), managers overwhelmingly said the company belongs to the shareholders.[49] Although published in 2000, these data indicate a profound difference in outlook about the purpose of the company.

The European commitment to a pluralistic conception of corporate purpose is most evident in formal governance structures that provide workers with a voice in the boardroom.[50] The best-known of these is German co-determination. In companies with over 2,000 German-based employees, workers elect one-half of the membership of the supervisory board, which appoints the managing board, monitors its performance, and approves major corporate decisions. In other countries, including Austria, Denmark, Luxembourg, Hungary, the Netherlands, Slovenia, and the Czech Republic, workers elect or nominate one-third of the board, while in still others, including France, some board seats are reserved for labour representatives.[51]

---

[48] J.R. Macey, *Corporate Governance: Promises Kept, Promises Broken* (Princeton University Press, 2008), 11; A.N. Licht, 'The maximands of corporate governance: a theory of values and cognitive style' (2004) 29(3) *Delaware Journal of Corporate Law* 649, at 732–5. Japan is typically thought to reflect the European approach, rather than the Anglo-American one; Macey, *Corporate Governance*, 35. Observers have noted evidence of movement in the direction of a shareholder value orientation in continental Europe, but these developments have been 'layered' onto the existing stakeholder value institutional framework rather than 'displacing' it. Kang and Moon, 'Institutional complementarity between corporate governance and corporate social responsibility', 97.

[49] Macey, *Corporate Governance*, 35 (citing F. Allen and D. Gale, *Comparing Financial Systems* (MIT Press, 2000)).

[50] R. Kraakman, *et al.*, *The Anatomy of Corporate Law: A Comparative and Functional Approach* (2nd edn, Oxford University Press, 2009), 100–1.

[51] The only EU states without some formal structure for worker representation are Belgium, Italy, Portugal, and the UK. Kraakman, *et al.*, *The Anatomy of Corporate Law*, 100 at n. 47.

Even given this stakeholder orientation, the implications for environmental sustainability are not obvious. By rejecting shareholder primacy, continental European states avoid one potentially important objection to corporate policies designed to protect the environment. But governance regimes that add workers' voices to those of shareholders could amplify tendencies to object to expenditures of money on the environment; those funds might otherwise go to workers (in the form of higher salaries) or to shareholders (in the form of higher dividends or increases in shareholders' equity). Whether a social conception of the corporation extends beyond workers' concerns about the environment presumably depends on historically conditioned cultural assumptions parallel to those that have produced pro-worker governance arrangements. A stakeholder tradition that emphasises workers' interests will not necessary promote environmental sustainability.

Looking more closely at Germany for insight on this issue, a general recognition of the responsibility of business towards the environment is evident in recent developments, even if there is as yet limited progress towards the enactment of formal legal requirements.[52] In October 2011, the German Council for Sustainable Development – established by the federal government in 2001 and consisting of public and private sector representatives – adopted a voluntary German Sustainability Code.[53] In the wake of the 2008 financial crisis, an amendment to the Corporate Governance Code company law states that management board directors have a duty to consider the interests of the corporation's stakeholders, 'with the objective of sustainable creation of value'.[54] In a similar vein, the Stock Corporation Act now requires that compensation of management board members be geared towards 'sustainable development of the company'.[55] Deipenbrock argues that the statutory concept of 'sustainable development' embraces regard for the environment, even though there is no express statutory language to that effect.[56] Initiatives

---

[52] G. Deipenbrock, *Sustainable Development, the Interest(s) of the Company and the Role of the Board from the Perspective of a German Aktiengesellschaft*, Research Paper No. 2010–02 (University of Oslo, Faculty of Law, 2010).

[53] German Sustainability Code, *Recommendations of the German Council for Sustainable Development* (January 2012); available at: www.nachhaltigkeitsrat.de/.

[54] German Corporate Governance Code, s. 4.1.1 (as amended 26 May 2010). The Code uses a 'comply-or-explain' framework of compliance.

[55] German Stock Corporation Act, s. 87, para. 1 (effective 5 August 2009).

[56] Deipenbrock, *Sustainable Development, the Interest(s) of the Company and the Role of the Board from the Perspective of a German Aktiengesellschaft*.

like these imply a significant commitment at the federal level towards a broad notion of corporate purpose that may well embrace environmental sustainability.

Evidence of corporations' own interpretation of their social responsibilities may be found in voluntary undertakings. Many of Germany's largest corporations disclose extensive information about environmental and social matters, often using the template created by the Global Reporting Initiative, a non-profit organisation that seeks to promote sustainability through transparency and accountability.[57] It is also notable that 29 German corporations have already agreed to comply with the Sustainability Code.[58] The combination of public and private initiatives suggests the possibility of collaborative governance arrangements not necessarily requiring formal legal mandate.[59]

The institutional landscape in the Netherlands is different, but the idea of the social responsibility of business appears to be well established, perhaps even more so than in Germany.[60] The Dutch Corporate Governance Code refers expressly to CSR in its provisions governing both the management and supervisory boards.[61] The supervisory board has a statutory duty to promote 'the best interests of the company and the enterprise' and to 'take into account the relevant interests of the company's stakeholders'. The reference to stakeholders reflects the Code's conception of the corporation as 'a long-term alliance between the various parties involved in the company'. As a practical matter, Lambooy observes that 'CSR has become an important theme for Dutch companies.'[62] Some corporations have dedicated CSR departments and others have created CSR councils that include board members, managers, and representatives of other departments within the firm.

---

[57] See www.globalreporting.org.

[58] See www.nachhaltigkeitsrat.de/en/projects/projects-of-the-council/deutscher-nachhaltig keitskodex/?subid=6690&cHash=3de02e04e7.

[59] 'New governance' theory emphasises the dynamic, interactive character of regulatory processes involving private parties as well as governmental entities. See I. Ayres and J. Braithwaite, *Responsive Regulation: Transcending the Deregulation Debate* (Oxford University Press, 1992); G. Teubner, L. Farmer, and D. Murphy (eds.), *Environmental Law and Ecological Responsibility: The Concept and Practice of Ecological Self-Organization* (John Wiley & Sons, 1994); G. de Búrca and J. Scott (eds.), *Law and New Governance in the EU and the US* (Hart Publishing, 2006).

[60] T. Lambooy, 'A model code on co-determination and CSR, the Netherlands: a bottom-up approach' (2001) 8(2–3) *European Company Law* 74.

[61] Sections II.1 and III.1. See www.ecgi.org/codes/documents/cg_code_netherlands_dec 2008_en.pdf.

[62] Lambooy, 'A model code on co-determination and CSR', 78.

CSR AND ENVIRONMENTAL SUSTAINABILITY 51

At the supranational level of European Union (EU) law, a commitment to environmental sustainability is found in the EU Treaties, in the statement of general objectives,[63] and in the environmental integration rule setting out that '[e]nvironmental protection requirements must be integrated into the definition and implementation of the Union policies and activities, in particular with a view to promoting sustainable development'.[64] EU regulations impose some environmental obligations on corporations, including the GHG emission trading system.[65] To date, however, the EU has not regulated the company law of its Member States in the area of environmental sustainability except to require reporting on environmental (and employee) matters.[66] Nevertheless, general expressions of commitment to the environment contained in treaties may reflect the basic values of the Member States.

The European Commission's new policy on CSR and corporate governance may also be relevant in this regard. Corporations 'should have in place a process to integrate social, environmental, ethical and human rights concerns into their business operations and core strategy in close collaboration with their stakeholders'.[67] One of the Commission's objectives in this initiative is to better align the EU's understanding of CSR with internationally recognised CSR statements of principle, including the OECD Guidelines for Multinational Enterprises[68] and the recently

---

[63] Until 1 Dec. 2009 the objectives were expressed particularly in Article 2 of the former Treaty establishing the European Community (1957), last amended (and name changed to Treaty on the Functioning of the European Union, TFEU) by the Treaty of Lisbon, OJ 2008 C115 (consolidated version); as well as the former Art. 2 and Art. 6 of the Treaty on European Union, TEU (1992), last amended by the Treaty of Lisbon, OJ 2008 C115 (consolidated version), now notably in the new Art. 3 TEU.

[64] The Treaty on the functioning of the European Union, last amended by the Treaty of Lisbon, OJ 2008 C115 (consolidated version), Art. 11. For an analysis of the importance of this development, see B. Sjåfjell 'Quo vadis, Europe? The significance of sustainable development as objective, principle and rule of EU law', in C. Bailliet (ed.), *Non State Actors, Soft Law and Protective Regimes* (Cambridge University Press, 2012).

[65] Directive 2003/87/EC of the European Parliament and of the Council establishing a scheme for greenhouse gas emission allowance trading within the Community and amending Council Directive 96/61/EC, O.J. 2003 (L 275/32–46), and most recently Directive 2009/29/EC of the European Parliament and of the Council of 23 April 2009 amending Directive 2003/87/EC so as to improve and extend the greenhouse gas emission allowance trading scheme of the Community, O.J. 2009, (L 140/63–87).

[66] See Chapter 5 by Villiers and Mähönen in this book.

[67] European Commission, A Renewed EU Strategy 2011–14 for Corporate Social Responsibility, COM(2011) 681 final.

[68] OECD, *Guidelines for Multinational Enterprises* (2011), available at: www.oecd.org/investment/guidelinesformultinationalenterprises/1922428.pdf.

endorsed UN Guiding Principles on Business and Human Rights.[69] The OECD Guidelines include an express reference to corporate responsibility to contribute to environmental sustainability: 'Enterprises should... take due account of the need to protect the environment, public health and safety, and generally to conduct their activities in a manner contributing to the wider goal of sustainable development.'[70] The European Commission's (2012) *Action Plan on European Company Law and Corporate Governance* emphasises enhancing transparency and engagement with stakeholders, and envisions future legislative measures to achieve these goals, but lacks explicit discussion of environmental sustainability as a performance goal.[71]

Clearly, neither the EU nor other proponents of CSR codes are attempting to impose legal obligations on corporations that would radically depart from corporate governance traditions, but they are seeking to articulate an emerging normative consensus on the obligations of business with respect to the environment, human rights, and other social imperatives. Encouragement from the EU, though still essentially hortatory, parallels traditions of the relatively robust and ambitious top-down exercise of state authority addressing a broad range of social problems. Seen as part of the larger institutional framework within which European companies operate, emerging norms of environmental sustainability expressed at the EU level may influence corporations to act responsibly in this area.[72] Among continental European states, there is no widely shared indigenous tradition of shareholder primacy to stand in the way.

To be clear, the point here is not a simplistic prediction that continental European corporations will voluntarily address environmental

---

[69] Report of the Special Representative of the Secretary-General on the issue of human rights and transnational corporations and other business enterprises, J. Ruggie, *Guiding Principles on Business and Human Rights: Implementing the United Nations "Protect, Respect and Remedy" Framework* (Council of Foreign Relations, 2011).

[70] OECD, *Guidelines*, no. VI.

[71] European Commission, 'Action Plan: European Company Law and Corporate Governance: A Modern Legal Framework for More Engaged Shareholders and Sustainable Companies', COM(2012) 740/2; B. Sjåfjell and L. Anker-Sørensen, 'Directors' duties and corporate social responsibilities (CSR)', in H. Birkmose, M. Neville, and K. Engsig Sørensen (eds.), *Boards of Directors in European Companies: Reshaping and Harmonising Their Organisation and Duties* (Kluwer Law International, 2013).

[72] Note, however, that features of EU law do support shareholder interests and as such, potentially at least, work at cross-purposes to sustainability and CSR more generally to the extent that they are seen as inimical to shareholder financial interests. For a thorough analysis of the relevant directives in the context of sustainability, see B. Sjåfjell, *Towards a Sustainable European Company Law: A Normative Analysis of the Objectives of EU Law, with the Takeover Directive as a Test Case* (Kluwer Law International, 2009).

sustainability aggressively and successfully. Rather, the question is whether existing institutional frameworks, which include social norms and traditions in addition to legal rules, establish a context within which significant commitments to ethical CSR seem to be a plausible possibility. Country-specific institutional variations (for example, with respect to the role of institutional shareholders) make uniform outcomes unlikely. Even so, especially when compared to the USA and the UK, the traditional continental European commitment to a pluralistic conception of CSR and more recent expressions of concern for sustainability could encourage greater attention to environmental values. Attempts to promote a narrow-minded focus on shareholders' wealth maximisation would seem to be a hard sell in this institutional context. Nevertheless, the traditional focus on the interests of employees, when combined with pressures from shareholders for financial returns, could still present an obstacle to ambitious efforts to promote sustainability, especially in times of economic hardship.

4.2 The United States: shareholder primacy

It is widely assumed that in the USA shareholder primacy is the dominant conception of the purpose of the company.[73] According to this idea, the company exists first and foremost to maximise the value of the shareholders' investments. From this, it follows that corporate management's primary responsibility is to maximise the company's profits. As residual claimants last in line after the fixed claims of employees, lenders, and other creditors have been paid, shareholders enjoy fully the benefits of increases in net income and net worth. Management therefore should limit its regard for nonshareholders to respect for their contractual rights, which should be based on market prices, and for any other rights or entitlements mandated by relevant regulatory regimes. Anything beyond these limits would come at the expense of the shareholders and therefore could only be justified by a net financial benefit to them.

American company law does not mandate shareholder primacy. No statute specifies that shareholders' interests must take priority over competing nonshareholder considerations. To the contrary, 41 states have

---

[73] L. Stout, *The Shareholder Value Myth* (Berrett-Koehler Publishers, 2012), 4. Stout writes: 'By the turn of the millennium ... [b]usiness and policy elites in the United States and much of the rest of the world as well accepted as truth that should not be questioned that corporations exist to maximize shareholder value.'

54 DAVID MILLON

enacted 'constituency' (or 'stakeholder') statutes that expressly authorise management to consider nonshareholders' as well as shareholders'
interests.[74] There is variation from state to state, but typically they list a
number of stakeholder constituencies and authorise the board of directors
and senior officers to take their interests into account while discharging
their managerial responsibilities. With one exception (Connecticut), the
statutes are permissive rather than mandatory. The Pennsylvania statute
is typical:

(a) General rule. – In discharging the duties of their respective positions, the board of directors, committees of the board and individual
directors of a domestic corporation may, in considering the best interests of the corporation, consider to the extent they deem appropriate:
  (1) The effects of any action upon any or all groups affected by such
  action, including shareholders, members, employees, suppliers,
  customers and creditors of the corporation, and upon communities in which offices or other establishments of the corporation
  are located . . .
(b) Consideration of interests and factors. – The board of directors, committees of the board and individual directors shall not be required,
in considering the best interests of the corporation or the effects of
any action, to regard any corporate interest or the interests of any
particular group affected by such action as a dominant or controlling
interest or factor.[75]

Implicit in subsection (b) is the idea that shareholder interests enjoy
no special privilege. Other statutes convey this explicitly. By enunciating
that the board of directors is not required to prioritise shareholders, the
US constituency statutes amount to a clear repudiation of shareholder
primacy.

Delaware, the leading US company law jurisdiction, has not enacted
a constituency statute. Nonetheless, its judicial decisions define management's discretion in a way that reaches essentially the same result. The
basic premise of Delaware law is that management has broad discretion to
chart the course for 'the corporate enterprise'.[76] Fiduciary duties of care

---

[74] K. Hale, 'Corporate law and stakeholders: moving beyond stakeholder statutes' (2003)
45(3) *Arizona Law Review* 823. For further discussion, see D. Millon, 'Redefining corporate
law' (1991) 24(2) *Indiana Law Review* 223.
[75] Pennsylvania Consolidated Statutes, Title 15, s. 515.
[76] *Unocal Corp. v. Mesa Petroleum Co.*, 493 A 2d 946 (Del. 1985).

and loyalty are owed to 'the corporation and its shareholders'[77] rather than to the shareholders alone. Delaware courts have done little to explicate the implications of this distinction, but at the very least we know that shareholders are not the sole beneficiaries of fiduciary duties and that the corporation cannot be equated simply with its shareholders. Presumably the point is that management must attend to the interests of the company as a whole, whether one conceives of it as a distinct entity or as an aggregation of shareholder and nonshareholder stakeholders. In either event, this must mean that management is not committed to maximising profits for the benefit of the shareholders where that might compromise the corporation's well-being.

The Delaware Supreme Court explained the nature of management's primary responsibility to the company in a series of important cases involving attempted hostile takeovers by means of tender offer. Early on, the court stated that the management of a takeover target had the authority to block offers that threatened 'the corporate enterprise'. The board was authorised to consider 'the impact on "constituencies" other than shareholders (i.e. creditors, customers, employees, and perhaps even the community generally)'.[78] Then, shortly after, in the *Time/Warner* case,[79] the court rejected the idea that shareholders possess the right to determine business policy. Denying management the power to block a hostile takeover would in effect allow the shareholders to determine the corporation's future. That would offend the basic premise of Delaware company law, which authorises the management of the company to determine the best interests of the corporate enterprise, including 'the selection of a time frame for the achievement of corporate goals'.[80] Consistent with this idea, the business judgment rule accords broad deference to managerial prerogative at the expense of shareholder power. As long as management can say plausibly that a decision was believed to be in the long-term best interests of the corporation and was based on reasonable information, and untainted by conflict of interest, courts will usually defer to such determinations.[81]

Even though the law accords management broad discretion to pursue business policies that are not clearly motivated by profit maximisation,

---

[77] To illustrate, see *Loft, Inc. v. Guth*, 2 A 2d 225, 238 (Del. Ch. 1938), aff'd sub nom. *Guth v. Loft*, 5 A 2d 503 (Del. 1939).

[78] *Unocal*, 955.

[79] *Paramount Communications, Inc. v. Time Inc.*, 571 A 2d 1140 (Del. 1989).

[80] *Paramount Communications, Inc. v. Time Inc.*, 571 A 2d 1140 (Del. 1989).

[81] *Aronson v. Lewis*, 373 A2d 805 (Del. 1984).

56   DAVID MILLON

the shareholder primacy idea nevertheless has strong normative force in shaping management practices. Business leaders typically assume that this is what they are supposed to do.[82] Leading business schools lend their imprimatur to this view of management's responsibility.[83] Prominent company law academics, including several writing from a law-and-economics perspective, assume that shareholder primacy is the law and favour it as a matter of policy.[84] There are some highly regarded dissenters, but they are the minority position within the academy.[85] The business press has likewise tended to take it for granted that shareholder primacy is the appropriate role for corporate management,[86] though this may be changing.[87]

Not surprisingly, institutional shareholders typically (though not always[88]) operate on the assumption that management's responsibility is to pursue share price maximisation. Certain classes of institutional investor are especially likely to prefer short-term profit over long-term value.[89] Managers of these institutions – termed by Bushee 'transient' investors[90] – focus on quarter-to-quarter performance and high portfolio

---

[82] For example, Business Roundtable, *Principles of Corporate Governance 2012* (2012), 30.

[83] R. Khurana, *From Higher Aims to Hired Hands: The Social Transformation of American Business Schools and the Unfulfilled Promise of Management as a Profession* (Princeton University Press, 2007), 364.

[84] S.M. Bainbridge, *Corporation Law and Economics* (Foundation Press, 2002), 419–21; R.C. Clark, *Corporate Law* (Little, Brown & Co., 1986), 17–19, 677–81; Hansmann and Kraakman, 'The end of history for corporate law', 440–1; J.R. Macey, 'An economic analysis of the various rationales for making shareholders the exclusive beneficiaries of corporate fiduciary duties' (1991) 21 *Stetson Law Review* 23.

[85] K. Greenfield, *The Failure of Corporate Law: Fundamental Flaws and Progressive Possibilities* (University of Chicago Press, 2010); L.E. Mitchell, *Corporate Irresponsibility: America's Newest Export* (Yale University Press, 2001); Stout, *The Shareholder Value Myth*.

[86] A. Karnani, 'The case against corporate social responsibility' *Wall Street Journal*, 23 August 2010, 1: 'The movement for corporate social responsibility is in direct opposition . . . to the movement for better corporate governance, which demands that managers fulfill their fiduciary duty to act in the shareholders' interest.'

[87] J. Fox, 'What we've learned from the financial crisis', *Harvard Business Review* (Nov. 2013): 94–101.

[88] B.J. Richardson, *Socially Responsible Investment Law: Regulating the Unseen Polluters* (Oxford University Press, 2008); B.J. Richardson, *Fiduciary Law and Responsible Investing: In Nature's Trust* (Routledge, 2013).

[89] For a discussion of this phenomenon and its implications for CSR, see D. Millon, 'Shareholder social responsibility' (2010) 36 *Seattle University Law Review* 911.

[90] B.J. Bushee, 'Do institutional investors prefer near-term earnings over long-run value?' (2001) 18(2) *Contemporary Accounting Research* 207. In contrast to transient shareholders are institutions termed by Bushee 'dedicated' and 'quasi-indexers'.

turnover in order to maximise current returns.[91] Public pension funds such as the California Public Employees Retirement System (CalPERS) have tended to be relatively longer-term investors.[92] However, even this sector faces pressures to act in the near term; CalPERS historically has been expected to achieve an 8 per cent annual return on its portfolios in order to meet commitments to its members.[93] Bank trust departments are subject to fiduciary obligations that courts have interpreted as requiring prudent investments.[94] In practice, this leads to a strong preference for investments in companies that generate superior short-term earnings and against those whose value includes a significant long-term component.[95] Some investment managers compete aggressively for client funds on the basis of short-term portfolio performance.[96] The threat of replacement motivates mutual fund managers to meet or beat performance benchmarks. In the case of 'aggressive growth' mutual funds that seek rapid increase in value, this means high rates of portfolio turnover and prioritisation of short-term returns.[97]

Even if they were inclined to act otherwise, senior management officials at many major companies are subject to powerful positive and negative incentives to privilege short-term returns over longer-term value or CSR objectives. Equity-based compensation – stock grants and options – are typically the most important component of Chief Executive Officer (CEO) compensation packages, giving executives a direct stake in share price movements.[98] CEOs must also be wary of the consequences of

[91] Aspen Institute, *Overcoming Short-termism: A Call for a More Responsible Approach to Investment and Business Management* (Aspen Institute, 2009).

[92] T. Hebb, *No Small Change, Pension Funds and Corporate Engagement* (Cornell University Press, 2008).

[93] R. Lowenstein, 'The next crisis: public pension funds', *New York Times Magazine*, 27 June 2010, MM9. For a positive view of CalPERS as an active shareholder on sustainability issues, see J. Cook, 'Political action through environmental shareholder resolution filing: applicability to Canadian Oil Sands?' (2012) 2(1) *Journal of Sustainable Finance and Investment* 26.

[94] D. Del Guercio, 'The distorting effect of the prudent-man laws on institutional equity investments' (1996) 40(1) *Journal of Financial Economics* 31.

[95] Bushee, 'Do institutional investors prefer near-term earnings?', 229.

[96] S.B. Graves and S.A. Waddock, 'Institutional ownership and control: implications for long-term corporate strategy' (1990) 4(1) *Academy of Management Executive* 1034.

[97] A. Khorana, 'Top management turnover: an empirical investigation of mutual fund managers' (1996) 40(3) *Journal of Financial Economics* 403.

[98] A. Lund and G.D. Polsky, 'The diminishing returns of incentive pay in executive compensation contracts' (2011) 87(2) *Notre Dame Law Review* 698.

58 DAVID MILLON

poor short-term performance. Failure to meet quarterly earning targets typically results in an immediate, even if only temporary, share price decline. For CEOs facing strong pressures from boards of directors to generate acceptable financial performance, weak share price results can cost them their jobs. The increasing rate of CEO turnover appears to be related to increasing sensitivity by boards of directors to stock performance.[99] Transient institutional shareholders may also encourage short-termism. One study shows that managers of companies whose shares are held in significant proportion by transient institutional investors tend to focus on short-term performance at the expense of long-term value,[100] presumably because these shareholders are more likely to respond to disappointing earnings news by large-scale selling, resulting in stock price decline. Another study finds that companies that prioritise short-term results tend to attract higher percentages of transient shareholder ownership than do those that pursue longer-term strategies.[101]

As far as environmental sustainability is concerned, the widespread acceptance of shareholder primacy – despite the absence of an explicit legal mandate – and the prevalence of short-term time horizons on the part of managers and investors encourage a general reluctance to pursue policies that have the effect of reducing short-term profits. Management typically seeks to avoid environmentally destructive practices that will result in potentially massive clean-up, litigation, or reputational costs. This stance is part of its risk management responsibility. It will also have an incentive to adopt eco-friendly policies – such as waste reduction and enhanced energy efficiency – that result in immediate net cost savings. However, for many companies, proactive policies that go further may be harder to justify. Even if long-term economic benefits are achievable, the immediate negative impact on earnings and potentially on share prices may discourage management from moving forward. As long as the shareholder primacy social norm persists and institutional shareholders insist on short-term share price maximisation, the ethical model of CSR is not likely to provide much traction for proponents of sustainability where it is assumed to come at the expense of shareholders' profits.

---

[99] S.N. Kaplan and B.A. Minton, 'How has CEO turnover changed?' (2012) 12(1) *International Review of Finance* 57.

[100] Bushee, 'Do institutional investors prefer near-term earnings?'

[101] F. Brochet, M. Loumioti, and G. Serafeim, *Short-Termism, Investor Clientele, and Firm Risk*, HBS Working Paper Number: 12–072 (HBS, February 2012).

CSR AND ENVIRONMENTAL SUSTAINABILITY

4.3 The United Kingdom: enlightened shareholder value

It is often stated that there exists a unique 'Anglo-American' approach to corporate governance that privileges shareholders' interests and, as such, stands in contrast to stakeholder-oriented perspectives that are embraced in continental Europe and Japan.[102] As we have just seen, US law is in fact a good deal less shareholder-centric than is broadly assumed, though in practice the idea of shareholder primacy is widely accepted by business leaders, institutional investors, prominent legal and business academics, and the business press. A closer look at UK law and practice similarly reveals the inaccuracy of simplistic assertions of the dominance of the shareholder primacy model, though for different reasons.

UK company law has traditionally embraced the shareholder primacy conception of corporate purpose. Fiduciary duties were said to be owed to 'the company' but this was interpreted to mean a duty to the shareholders. Nonshareholders' interests might be considered, but only to the extent that shareholders would benefit.[103] Two widely discussed provisions of the Companies Act 2006 appear, at least at first glance, to signal a move away from strict shareholder primacy towards the stakeholder model of corporate governance. The key language of Section 172(1) reads as follows:

> A director of a company must act in the way he considers, in good faith, would be most likely to promote the success of the company for the benefit of its members as a whole, and in doing so have regard (amongst other matters) to –
>
> (a) the likely consequences of any decision in the long term,
> (b) the interests of the company's employees,
> (c) the need to foster the company's business relationships with suppliers, customers and others,
> (d) the impact of the company's operations on the community and the environment,
> (e) the desirability of the company maintaining a reputation for high standards of business conduct, and
> (f) the need to act fairly as between members of the company.[104]

The Companies Act 2006 also includes reporting requirements relating to the company's relations with its stakeholders. Section 417 requires that

---

[102] J. Armour, S. Deakin, and S. Konzelmann, 'Shareholder primacy and the trajectory of UK corporate governance' (2003) 41(3) *British Journal of Industrial Relations* 531.

[103] *Hutton v. West Cork Railway Co* (1883) 23 Ch. D. 654.

[104] Companies Act 2006, s. 172(1).

large companies produce a 'business review' designed to allow shareholders to assess the efficacy of directors' efforts 'to promote the success of the company'.[105] Beyond this mandate, which could be read as referring solely to financial performance metrics, the statute requires disclosure of information about impact on the environment and about the corporation's employees and 'social and community issues', 'to the extent necessary for an understanding of the development, performance or position of the company's business'. If the review does not include information on these matters, 'it must state which of those kinds of information it does not contain'.[106] Where appropriate, the review must include 'analysis using financial key performance indicators, and . . . other key performance indicators, including information relating to environmental matters and employee matters'.[107]

Focusing only on the statutory language, it is apparent that Section 172 does not endorse a stakeholder vision of corporate governance comparable to the constituency statutes enacted in the USA. It states expressly that the overarching responsibility of the company's directors is to 'promote the success of the company' for the benefit of its shareholders ('members'), which is essentially a restatement of traditional common law doctrine. The statute itself, in Section 170, states that the general duties specified in Section 172 are 'based on certain common law rules and equitable principles'[108] and that the specified general duties 'shall be interpreted and applied in the same way as common law rules or equitable principles'.[109] Directors are supposed to 'have regard to' the interests of other stakeholders and to environmental effects, but it is unclear whether directors must simply refer to these considerations or whether they must actually take them into account, and it is also unclear whether they must do so only to the extent that the shareholders are benefited. There is certainly no suggestion that stakeholders' interests might deserve priority where that would work to the detriment of shareholders' interests.

---

[105] Companies Act 2006, s. 417. This provision replaced a more extensive Operating and Financial Review (OFR) disclosure regime recommended by the Company Law Review Steering Group, whose work laid the foundation for the Companies Act 2006. The OFR would have mandated significantly broader disclosure regarding stakeholder issues but it was withdrawn by the government in 2005.

[106] Companies Act 2006, s. 417(5).   [107] Companies Act 2006, s. 417(6).

[108] Companies Act 2006, s. 170(3).

[109] Companies Act 2006, s. 170(4). See G. Deipenbrock and M. Andenæs, 'Directors' duties to promote the success of the company and "enlightened shareholder value": comparing English and German company law' (2010) 7 *International and Comparative Corporate Law Journal* 1.

By its terms, Section 417 requires disclosure of material information regarding the corporation's relations with its employees and relevant communities and also its effects on the environment, if deemed necessary by the board for an understanding of the corporation's business. However, the provision acknowledges that directors may omit this information and, if they do, the only consequence is a requirement that they disclose that they have done so. Aside from this, Section 417 says nothing about whether or the extent to which directors are obliged to consider stakeholder interests or the environment in their management of the corporation.[110]

Although neither provision specifically mandates deviation from shareholder primacy, Sections 172 and 417 taken together are said to reflect an 'enlightened shareholder value' conception of corporate purpose. The Company Law Review Steering Group, whose deliberations laid the foundation for these provisions of the statute, expressly endorsed the shareholder primacy idea.[111] However, the Steering Group also advocated that regard for shareholders should be 'enlightened' by due regard also for stakeholders' interests.[112] According to this view, directors should not focus exclusively on short-term profit maximisation. Rather, they should take a long-run approach towards the production of shareholder value, building long-term relationships with key stakeholders and paying attention to environmental considerations where appropriate.[113]

A lively debate has ensued as to whether the statute actually amounts to something more than traditional shareholder primacy. Keay early pointed out the vagueness inherent in Section 172's 'have regard to' phrase, and characterised the board's discretion as appearing to be 'completely

---

[110] Some argue that the provision was enacted primarily to facilitate investors' interest in accurate stock pricing, while at the same time attempting to give limited expression to EU pressures for non-financial, social, and environmental disclosure: G.L. Clark and E. Knight, 'Implications of the UK Companies Act 2006 for institutional investors and the market for corporate social responsibility' (2009) 11(2) *University of Pennsylvania Journal of Business Law* 259.

[111] Company Law Review Steering Group, *Modern Company Law for a Competitive Economy: Final Report* (Department of Trade and Industry, 1999), 41. For a thorough analysis of this process, see D. Collison, *et al.*, *Shareholder Primacy in UK Corporate Law: An Exploration of the Rationale and the Evidence* (Association of Chartered Certified Accountants, 2011), 20–4.

[112] Company Law Review Steering Group, *Modern Company Law for a Competitive Economy*, para. 5.1.12.

[113] For a discussion of the Company Law Review Steering Group's conception of 'enlightened shareholder value', see A. Keay and H. Zhang, 'An analysis of enlightened shareholder value in light of ex post opportunism and incomplete law' (2011) 8(4) *European Company and Financial Law Review* 445.

62   DAVID MILLON

unfettered'. Further, the opening clause of Section 172 suggests a personal and subjective judgment, despite the confusing reference to the seemingly more objective 'good faith' standard. Both *Re Southern Counties Fresh Foods Ltd*[114] and *People & Planet v. HM Treasury*[115] emphasise this subjective test, and thus frame the question as whether the directors acted in a manner they believed would promote the company's success. Also, in *Iesini v. Westrip Holdings*, it was noted that courts were not in the best position to weigh the relevant considerations under Section 172, except in unambiguous cases, as those judgments are essentially of a commercial nature and therefore are best made by directors.[116] Such determinations would presumably enjoy the protection of the business judgment principle, which under UK law focuses on the directors' subjective state of mind.[117] Keay also pointed out the absence of any enforcement mechanism available to nonshareholder stakeholders when claiming that the directors have failed to pay appropriate attention to their interests.[118]

The statute does not seem to have had much actual impact. The UK Department for Business, Innovation and Skills in late 2009 commissioned a study to evaluate the awareness of and compliance with the Companies Act, and found that the new directors' duty was not well understood and had not resulted in significant behavioural changes among company directors.[119] A 2011 study for the Association of Chartered Certified Accountants also concluded that Section 172 has had minimal effect.[120]

Even so, some commentators suggest that the statute's 'enlightened shareholder value' idea represents a compromise[121] or a 'third way'[122]

---

[114] [2008] EWHC 2810.   [115] [2009] EWHC 3020.

[116] [2009] EWHC 2526; [2010] BCC 420.

[117] S. Wen and J. Zhao, 'Exploring the rationale of enlightened shareholder value in the realm of UK company law: the path dependence perspective' (2011) 14 *International Trade and Business Law Review* 153, 157–9.

[118] A. Keay, 'Enlightened shareholder value, the reform of the duties of company directors and the corporate objective' (2006) part 3, *Lloyd's Maritime and Commercial Law Quarterly* 356.

[119] ORC International, *Evaluation of the Companies Act 2006*, vol. 1 (ORC International, 2010), 67–72.

[120] D. Collison, *et al.*, *Shareholder Primacy in UK Corporate Law: An Exploration of the Rationale and Evidence* (Association of Chartered Certified Accountants, 2011).

[121] C. Villiers, 'Directors' duties and the company's internal structures under the UK Companies Act 2006: obstacles for sustainable development' (2011) 8 *International and Comparative Corporate Law Journal* 47.

[122] C.A. Williams and J.M. Conley, 'An emerging third way? The erosion of the Anglo-American shareholder value construct' (2005) 38 *Cornell International Law Journal* 493; see also S. Kiarie, 'At crossroads: shareholder value, stakeholder value and enlightened shareholder value; which road should the United Kingdom take?' (2006) 17 *International Corporation and Commercial Law Review* 329; A. Mickels, 'Beyond corporate social

between shareholder primacy and the stakeholder model. Focusing solely on statutory language, which does not clearly mandate a new direction, may miss the point if political and social movements within which the enlightened shareholder value concept arose have produced a significant institutional commitment to CSR. Today, UK companies are thought to be among the leaders worldwide with respect to CSR.[123] Kinderman argues that this development began during the deregulation and privatisation reforms of the 1970s and 1980s.[124] Partly this was a matter of legitimating business's standing in society and staving off the possibility of new government regulation, but it was more fundamentally a concerted effort to redefine the role of business in the new political and economic environment. Voluntarism and private discretion have been the hallmarks of this approach to CSR. One study suggests that many large corporations do not see shareholders' wealth maximisation as their primary mission. Analysing annual reports and other public documents recently issued by 50 of the UK's largest companies, the authors found that only slightly over a third explicitly articulated shareholder value as their primary focus, while 20 per cent identified stakeholder benefits (such as customers or employees) as of primary importance.[125] The authors, aware of the possible shortcomings of reliance on these kinds of data, conclude that shareholder value 'is not as strong an influence as many have said'.[126] Deakin and Hobbs, however, argue that UK corporations, despite CSR rhetoric, have done little to improve working conditions for British workers, even though the ethical argument for a lighter work load is bolstered by a business case justification as well.[127] Others have criticised corporate social performance in stronger terms.[128]

responsibility: reconciling the ideals of a for-benefit corporation with director fiduciary duties in the U.S. and Europe' (2009) 32 *Hastings International and Comparative Law Review* 271; V. Harper Ho, ' "Enlightened shareholder value": corporate governance beyond the shareholder-stakeholder divide' (2010) 36(1) *Journal of Corporation Law* 59.

[123] D. Kinderman, ' "Free us up so we can be responsible!" The co-evolution of corporate social responsibility and neo-liberalism in the UK, 1977–2010' (2012) 10(1) *Socio-Economic Review* 32; Jackson and Apostolakou, 'Corporate social responsibility in Western Europe', 388. Vogel says that the 'center of gravity' for CSR is the UK: Vogel, *The Market for Virtue*, 7.

[124] Kinderman, ' "Free us up so we can be responsible!" '

[125] A. Keay and R. Adamopoulou, 'Shareholder value and UK companies: a positivist inquiry' (2012) 13(1) *European Business Organization Law Review* 1. The remaining 44 per cent did not specify either a shareholder value or a stakeholder emphasis.

[126] Keay and Adamopoulou, 'Shareholder value and UK companies', 25.

[127] S. Deakin and R. Hobbs, 'False dawn for CSR? Shifts in regulatory policy and the response of the corporate and financial sectors in Britain' (2007) 15(1) *Corporate Governance: An International Review* 68.

[128] Kinderman, ' "Free us up so we can be responsible!" ', 51.

One indication of a potentially significant effort to incorporate social considerations into company law may be the 2011 revision to the City Code on Takeovers and Mergers.[129] In the wake of Kraft Foods' controversial takeover of Cadbury PLC, there was a widespread outcry over the likely negative effects of the change of control on Cadbury's extensive CSR policies. Some advocated express harmonisation of the Takeover Code with Section 172 but, in the event, a more oblique reform resulted. The new edition of the Code states expressly that the target company board, when giving its opinion on the offer to the shareholders as required by the Code, is not limited solely to offer price considerations and may 'tak[e] into account any other factors which it considers relevant'.[130] Nevertheless, the board's inability to block hostile bids probably contributes to a short-term outlook that is at odds with enlightened shareholder value because of the belief that keeping share prices high will discourage takeover attempts. In this important respect at least, UK law continues to be even more shareholder-centric than does US law, which gives target boards broad power to block hostile bids despite their appeal to target shareholders.

4.4 Summary

As discussed in Section 3, ethical CSR asserts that corporations are responsible to their stakeholders without reference to whether financial performance of the firm is thereby enhanced. In appropriate cases, corporations should attend to the needs of nonshareholder stakeholders even if that risks diminution in the value of shareholders' investments. Seen in this light, the prospects for this kind of CSR may vary, depending on where companies are incorporated. The stakeholder-oriented tradition that is characteristic of continental Europe is more likely to expect or even encourage CSR activities than is the institutional framework found in the USA, where ethical CSR runs up against the shareholder primacy objection. The UK may be an intermediate case. Company law purports to

---

[129] G. Tsagas, 'Reflecting on the value of socially responsible practices post takeover of Cadbury Plc by Kraft Foods Inc: implications for the revision of the EU Takeover Directive' (2012) 9(2) *European Company Law* 70.

[130] The *City Code on Takeovers and Mergers* (10th edn, 2011), notes on rule 25.2. The Panel on Takeovers and Mergers issues and administers the City Code. It has been designated as the supervisory authority pursuant to the EU Directive on Takeover Bids (2004/25/EC) and its statutory functions are set out in Chapter 1 of Part 28, Chapter 1 of the Companies Act 2006.

endorse shareholder primacy, but it does so in a way that at least acknowledges the existence and potential relevance of stakeholder interests, and business leaders profess a commitment to CSR. Ethical CSR may fare somewhat better in that climate.

The analysis offered above ignores Japan, emerging economies, and the developing world, but the analytical approach may provide a way to evaluate the prospects for ethical CSR in those regions as well. The focus should be on the rules, norms, and values, both formal and informal, that structure attitudes and behaviour regarding the relative importance of the interests of shareholders and to those of other corporate stakeholders. Depending on the institutional context, the viability of ethics-based arguments for environmental sustainability may be more or less plausible.

5   Strategic CSR

5.1   The long-term perspective and CSR benefits

We have seen that the prospects for ethical CSR are likely to be problematic in institutional contexts that are committed to or lean in the direction of shareholder primacy. A different perspective on CSR has the potential to overcome this obstacle, which is based on presumed trade-offs between shareholder and nonshareholder interests. This alternative is the 'strategic' model.[131] The core idea is that CSR policies – business decisions that confer benefits on nonshareholder constituencies – can under certain circumstances enhance shareholder wealth. Strategic CSR is therefore instrumental, in the sense that it is undertaken to promote the interests of shareholders rather than out of a sense of ethical obligation.[132] This is therefore an instance of the 'business case' for CSR.

Crucial to this concept of CSR is the problem of time. The costs and benefits of particular corporate decisions need not and often do not occur simultaneously. So, for example, a decision to invest corporate funds in the development of a new eco-friendly product requires an immediate

---

[131]   M.E. Porter and M.R. Kramer, 'Strategy and society: the link between competitive advantage and corporate social responsibility' (December 2006) *Harvard Business Review* 88. In Millon, 'Two models of CSR', I term this the 'sustainability' model because an important aspect is the long-run sustainability of the corporation. Because that term can also refer to environmental sustainability, I here use the term 'strategic' instead in order to avoid ambiguity.

[132]   Garriga and Melé, 'Corporate social responsibility theories', 53–5.

66   DAVID MILLON

expenditure that will reduce corporate profits in the accounting period in which it is made. Shareholders therefore are less wealthy than they would have been if this money had not been spent. However, if the result is a new product, the financial payoff to the corporation and therefore to the shareholders may eventually exceed the cost. In such cases, stakeholder benefits can be justified in terms of long-run financial gains, without resort to claims of ethical obligation.[133]

Strategic CSR starts from the premise that management's duty is to promote the long-range sustainability of the corporate entity, rather than simply focusing on the interests of particular constituencies such as shareholders' desire for quarter-to-quarter profit maximisation or workers' desire for job security. This orientation requires that management nurture its relationships with key stakeholders, including workers, customers, suppliers, and the communities in which production is located. The corporation's future depends on the long-range welfare of these people and the durability of its relationships with them.

Porter and Kramer provide illustrations of companies that have invested heavily in stakeholder relationships in order to strengthen the company's future prospects.[134] For example, Yara International is a Norwegian multinational corporation that is the world's largest producer of chemical fertiliser. Yara has invested $60 million in transportation, storage, and port infra-structure in a region in Africa. These commitments are designed to increase agricultural production by facilitating lower-cost access to markets. The result will be increased demand for Yara's fertiliser products over a long-term time horizon, as well as higher incomes for farmers. In a similar vein, Nestlé, the Swiss global food products company, sought to develop milk production in a poor region in India. It therefore made substantial investments in well-drilling and irrigation, refrigeration, veterinary medicine, and training in animal husbandry. Significant increases in output and product quality have resulted, as has enhancement of the local population's quality of life. In the USA, Johnson & Johnson, the major healthcare products company, has spent heavily on improving employee health through lifestyle training and anti-smoking

---

[133] Sometimes cost to the corporation and environmental benefit can coincide. An example is investment in new equipment that immediately reduces resource consumption. Here the case for CSR is unproblematic because shareholders do not have to wait for future financial benefits.

[134] For these and other examples, see M.E. Porter and M.R. Kramer, 'Creating shared value: how to reinvent capitalism – and unleash a wave of innovation and growth' (January–February 2011) *Harvard Business Review* 1.

programmes. The company has realised large savings in health care costs, and employee loyalty and productivity have increased. Employees benefit from better health; for example, the number of smokers has declined by over two-thirds. In each of these cases, corporations are producing significant social benefits, while furthering their own long-range business strategies. Another instance would be a pharmaceutical company's multi-million dollar investment in the search for a cancer cure, which stands to produce massive social benefits if successful, as well as substantial corporate profits.

The standard objection to ethical CSR (that it is bad for shareholders) should not apply to these kinds of business policies. Corporations are not making these very large expenditures, thereby reducing current profits, out of a sense of ethical obligation, or at least that is not their primary motivation. Rather, these investments are designed to generate future returns and thereby promote the corporation's financial interests. In the short run, profits are reduced, but adding the long-run perspective changes the analysis because it is expected that the return on these investments will eventually result in net gains for the corporation and its shareholders, while also contributing to the company's continued existence and profitability decades into the future.

5.2 Strategic CSR and the environment

Expenditures on environmental sustainability are problematic under the ethical model of CSR because of the assumed negative effects on shareholder wealth. In contrast, a strategic perspective on CSR has the potential to justify significant expenditures. This is because a proactive commitment to environmental sustainability (rather than a minimalist, reactive one) can create value for the corporation as well as for the larger society. All corporations concerned about the long-term future of their business must attend to the impact of their activities on the environment, because large-scale environmental destruction could threaten the future of all business. Corporations must also pay attention to the long-term availability of reliable sources of raw materials. Some industries, like tourism and agriculture, may be especially threatened by environmental degradation. Corporations that sell directly to consumers must be wary of the potentially long-lasting negative reputational effects resulting from disregard for environmental values. A strategic approach to waste reduction and energy efficiency can reduce costs, and the development of new eco-friendly products and services can enhance future revenues.

68   DAVID MILLON

A meaningful commitment to environmental sustainability encompasses several kinds of initiative. González-Benito and González-Benito present a functional classification of practices necessary for a proactive approach.[135] Planning and organisational practices involve the creation of management systems and structures to develop strategies and objectives and to assess outcomes. Communications practices inform relevant constituencies about the corporation's environmental performance. Operational practices include process and product design. The former include efforts to reduce waste and pollution, decrease the use of nonrenewable resources such as fossil fuels, and increase energy efficiency more generally. They can also include attention to environmental effects in supply and distribution chains. Product design includes the development of green goods and services. These have been defined as products 'designed to minimise [their] environmental impacts during [their] whole life-cycle'.[136] They are devised so as to reduce negative environmental effects through the manufacturing process and also when they are used and disposed of by consumers.

Nidumolu, Prahalad, and Rangaswami offer several examples of companies that have used process and product design innovations effectively to reduce costs while also contributing to environmental sustainability.[137] FedEx, for example, has invested heavily in new aircraft and hybrid motor vehicles in order to reduce fuel consumption substantially and has developed computer software to improve the efficiency of transportation scheduling. Cisco Systems, the computer networking company, has found new, internal uses for out-of-date or no longer needed equipment returned to the company. As reuse of equipment rose from 5 to 45 per cent, recycling expenses declined by 40 per cent, saving millions of dollars. Procter & Gamble's development of cold water laundry detergent offers the prospect of substantial reduction in energy consumption used for heating water. Clorox has spent $20 million to develop a new line of nonsynthetic home cleaning products and now has a 40 per cent share of a

---

[135] J. González-Benito and Ó. González-Benito, 'A review of determinant factors of environmental proactivity' (2006) 15(2) *Business Strategy and the Environment* 87.

[136] V. Albino, A. Balice, and R.M. Dangelico, 'Environmental strategies and green product development: an overview on sustainability-driven companies' (2009) 18(2) *Business Strategy and the Environment* 86.

[137] R. Nidumolu, C.K. Prahalad, and M.R. Rangaswami, 'Why sustainability is now the key driver of innovation' (September 2009) *Harvard Business Review* 3. See also M.E. Porter and C. van der Linde, 'Green and competitive: ending the stalemate' (September–October. 1995) *Harvard Business Review* 120.

$200 million market. Toyota's creation of the first hybrid electric/gasoline automobile, which emits as little as 10 per cent of the pollution produced by conventional vehicles and uses only half the gasoline, has yielded a competitive advantage so great that Ford and other companies are looking to license its technology.[138]

These are cases of companies that have moved forward proactively to identify ways to reduce expenses and increase revenues while contributing to environmental sustainability. Although they must spend money on research and development, marketing, and new processes and equipment, companies like these expect eventually to increase their profits and enhance their prospects for long-term success. At the same time, they reduce their own negative effects on the environment or make it possible for consumers to do so as well.

5.3   The case for the business case

Since the 1970s, many researchers have attempted to determine whether in fact corporations can 'do well by doing good'.[139] The question is whether shareholders do in fact derive long-run financial gains that offset CSR investments in nonshareholder stakeholders of the kind discussed above. Aggregate social benefits are irrelevant here because the claim is that shareholders can benefit from CSR expenditures that undoubtedly benefit others as well. Are such claims credible? Are corporations mistaken in their belief that CSR investments are worth the cost? The question is inherently difficult because, even if costs can be identified, gains that occur only in the long run may be hard to measure and it may be very difficult to allocate them to particular CSR investments.

Orlitzky's meta-analysis critically evaluates existing studies and seeks to correct statistical and research design inaccuracies.[140] In contrast to earlier literature reviews that have tended to be inconclusive, he finds that primary studies in the aggregate indicate a positive correlation between financial and social performance. Reputational benefits, improved management learning, and internal efficiencies are identified as causal

---

[138]   Porter and Kramer, 'Strategy and society', 88–9.
[139]   For a critical analysis of this literature, see M. Orlitzky, 'Corporate social performance and financial performance: a research synthesis', in Crane, *et al.* (eds.), *The Oxford Handbook of Corporate Social Responsibility*, 113.
[140]   Orlitzky, 'Corporate social performance and financial performance'.

70   DAVID MILLON

linkages. It goes without saying, of course, that these conclusions do
not imply that adoption of CSR strategies will always yield net benefits
for all corporations. As discussed later in this chapter, Vogel has argued
persuasively that often the 'market for virtue' is quite limited.[141]

One carefully constructed recent study provides particularly intriguing
evidence of the financial benefits of CSR policies and practices. This study
is important not only for that reason but also because it supports the idea
that strategic CSR may be the source of a competitive market advantage. Eccles, Ioannou, and Serafeim examined 90 companies that began
to adopt environmental and social policies during the early 1990s.[142] This
set of companies – labelled by the authors the 'high sustainability' group –
chose to develop 'a culture of sustainability by adopting a coherent set
of corporate policies related to the environment, employees, community,
products, and customers'.[143] These policies resulted in changes in corporate governance and stakeholder engagement and commitment to a
long-term performance time horizon. In contrast, a set of 90 'low sustainability' firms did not adopt such policies. The members of this group
were matched with their high-sustainability counterparts with respect to
industry sector, size, capital structure, performance, and growth opportunities. Using both stock market results and accounting measures, the
authors find that the companies in the high-sustainability group significantly outperformed their low-sustainability counterparts over an 18-year
period. Coinciding with Orlitzky's conclusion, the findings of Eccles and
his co-authors imply that firms committed to sustainability 'generate
significantly higher profits and stock returns, suggesting that developing a corporate culture of sustainability may be a source of competitive
advantage for a company in the long-run'.[144]

---

[141] Vogel, *The Market for Virtue.*

[142] R.G. Eccles, I. Ioannou, and G. Serafeim, 'The impact of a corporate culture of sustainability on corporate behavior and performance' (Harvard Business School Working
Paper 12–035 (Harvard Business School, 2012).

[143] Eccles, *et al.,* The impact of a corporate culture of sustainability on corporate behavior
and performance, 8. High sustainability companies were identified by their performance
on over two dozen specific metrics, including emissions and waste reduction policies,
water and energy efficiency policies, use of environmental criteria in selection of supply
chain partners, employee well-being policies, and human rights and corporate citizenship
policies.

[144] Eccles, *et al.,* 'The impact of a corporate culture of sustainability on corporate behavior
and performance', 30.

5.4 Summary

'Strategic' CSR is the idea that regard for nonshareholders' interests can be justified if it promotes shareholders' financial interests. This model contrasts with the ethical version of CSR discussed in Section 3, which grounds responsibility to stakeholders on ethical norms and finds obligation to exist in appropriate cases even if there is no benefit (or if there is cost) to shareholders. There is evidence that strategic CSR may indeed yield financial benefits for the corporations that adopt it and that it may also generate competitive advantages vis-à-vis corporations that do not. The potential appeal of this version of CSR is that it answers objections that are based on an assumed trade-off or zero-sum relationship between shareholders' and nonshareholders' benefits. That can be important for corporations operating in institutional frameworks that prioritise shareholder interests over those of other stakeholders.

6 Critical reflections

6.1 Strategic CSR and short-termism

While strategic CSR has enthusiastic supporters,[145] this way of thinking about the problem may not be as compelling as it might first appear to be. For one thing, a business case for CSR may not do enough to make corporations accountable for their impact on the environment, a point discussed below. It should be noted that in some institutional contexts, important norms and practices are at odds with the long-term perspective on shareholder value on which strategic CSR depends. In particular, many corporations, especially in the USA and the UK, embrace a short-term approach to management.[146]

As explained above in Section 4, many US companies are committed to a short-term business strategy to maximise current earnings and share price, which may be at the expense of the firm's long-run value. Some UK companies may behave this way as well, despite an institutional milieu that seems to be more receptive to CSR. Companies that seek to maximise

---

[145] For example, Nidumolu, *et al.*, 'Why sustainability is now the key driver of innovation'; Porter and Kramer, 'Creating shared value'; Porter and Kramer, 'Strategy and society'.

[146] We should recognise that there is no agreement about the actual temporal distinction between 'long term' from 'short term' in evaluating a company's business model and commitment to CSR; the answer likely depends on the specific context.

quarter-to-quarter profits will tend to be reluctant to spend money today for the sake of future benefits because of the negative impact on current net income. A short-term orientation generally results in lower levels of R&D, advertising, and capital investment than would be observed in corporations pursuing long-term strategies.[147] Investments in environmental sustainability are similarly problematic. The development of new eco-friendly processes and products costs money. In the short run, this can result in lower profits because most such expenditures must be accounted for as current expenses that reduce net income. Even though these kinds of expenditures might be considered analogous to capital investments because they are intended to create future value, US accounting rules do not allow amortisation and they cannot be listed as assets on the balance sheet.[148]

Even managers who do consider long-term value as well as immediate cost are likely to have trouble evaluating the potential benefits of investments in environmentally responsible processes and products because their future value may be impossible to monetise with any degree of confidence. In such cases, it may be difficult to communicate the expected benefits to board members and investors in a convincing manner. Climate change is a dramatic example.[149] On a macro level, concentrations of GHGs will increase but the actual magnitude of these effects is unknown as scientists debate the long-term effects of carbon emissions, the levels of which will depend on a number of sociological, economic, technological, and natural variables. Even if the actual risks were well understood, pricing would still be controversial. Further, the magnitude of the future benefit to an individual company from current investments in cleaner production is hard to evaluate because the impact on the environment may depend on how other corporations facing similar decisions behave. Even in the more mundane case of the long-term value of a newly developed green product, projections of future sales can depend on numerous

---

[147] B.J. Bushee, 'The influence of institutional investors on myopic R&D investment behavior' (1998) 73(3) *The Accounting Review* 305.

[148] For the treatment of R&D under US accounting rules, see Financial Accounting Standards Board, *Statement of Financial Accounting Standards No. 2: Accounting for Research and Development Costs* (October 1974). In contrast, International Accounting Standard No. 38 allows partial capitalisation of R&D expenditures. For a comparative perspective on accounting rules and principles, see Chapter 5 by Villiers and Mähönen in this book.

[149] R. Litterman, 'Pricing climate change risk appropriately' (2011) 67(5) *Financial Analysts Journal* 4.

variables, including the development of consumer preferences, the impact of possible regulatory incentives or mandates, cost and pricing issues, and the prospect of competing products. Thus, the benefit side of long-term investments in sustainability is much harder to measure than are the costs, and this reduces the likelihood that managers and investors concerned about current expenses and lower earnings might be willing to accept those costs for the sake of future gains.

Not all firms are fixated on the short term. As discussed above, Eccles and his colleagues have shown that companies differ with respect to their commitment to sustainability strategies.[150] Some do little in this regard, and are more likely to maintain a short-term time horizon and to attract transient as opposed to dedicated, patient investors. For these companies, the business case for environmental sustainability and strategic CSR more generally is apparently unconvincing. Other corporations, however, embrace the idea that there is long-run economic value to be derived from a commitment to proactive environmental and social policies. Some examples have been mentioned above. These companies are more likely to adopt corporate governance structures that focus on sustainability, to link executive compensation to defined environmental and social outcomes, to pursue high levels of stakeholder engagement, and to emphasise long-run economic objectives in communications with investors. Their investor base is likely to include more patient, long-term-oriented institutional shareholders. These corporations in effect reject the assumption that investment in the environment and other CSR values necessarily reduces shareholder wealth. If other companies can be persuaded to accept the business case for sustainability, further progress may be possible.

The reasons why some corporations have chosen not to pursue sustainability are no doubt complex and specific to each company or market. The influence of transient shareholders may be part of the story, but the causal connection is unclear: impatient investors pursuing their own investment objectives may be drawn to these companies precisely because their management has chosen not to sacrifice short-term profits for long-term value. In any event, for companies like these, thinking about environmental sustainability in terms of CSR automatically implies scepticism and reluctance. In a business environment in which a large number of corporations take this view, investment in environmental sustainability will continue to encounter resistance.

---

[150] Eccles, *et al.*, 'The impact of a corporate culture of sustainability'.

6.2 The limits of the business case for sustainability

The business case for environmental sustainability – and for strategic CSR more generally – is of limited value for another reason. Even a corporation that has embraced sustainability as part of its mission will only go as far as the business justification will take it, if that is the basis for its commitment. Companies that think about their impact on the environment solely in self-interested economic terms are likely to reject some environmentally beneficial policies and initiatives even when it is within their capability to make a positive difference. Where the present value of future financial gains to the corporation and its shareholders does not exceed the costs of an investment in the environment, the corporation will not spend the money. Even if the social benefits of the expenditure, when added to shareholder profits, would be enough to tip the scales, this makes no difference because the business case is about shareholder value, not aggregate social value. Advocates for environmental sustainability are therefore likely to find that strategic CSR does not take corporations far enough.

Strategic CSR's sole focus on corporate costs and corporate benefits is a conceptual limitation that is built into the model. There are practical limitations as well. For one thing, the business case for CSR is stronger in some industries than in others. Large, visible, global companies that sell to consumers must be attentive to reputational concerns, as BP belatedly discovered in the wake of the Deepwater Horizon oil spill disaster in 2010. NGOs, the news media, and activists pay attention to these companies' behaviour and publicise their findings. Consumers may react to negative information by withholding their money and taking their shopping elsewhere. The response to Nike's reliance on child labour in its supply chain is a classic example.[151] When the issue was brought to light, retail sales fell, leading Nike eventually to adopt a code of conduct applicable to its suppliers. Compare, though, a corporation that conducts its operations in remote locations, has a low-profile brand name, and does not sell directly to consumers. For example, a large mining company might do serious damage to the environment while extracting a commodity like coal that will itself cause further environmental degradation when it is consumed by the company's industrial clients. Unless its activities attract the attention of someone with the ability to publicise them effectively, they will escape notice. Even if they do not, possible consumer boycotts

---

[151] Vogel, *The Market for Virtue*, 77–82.

present no threat to sales. In a case like this, there is no economic reason for this corporation to change its behaviour.

Related to this practical limit on the efficacy of strategically motivated CSR is the problem of greenwashing.[152] If reputation and a positive image are the real concern, spending money on skilful public relations might be as effective as investment in tangible improvements in environmental performance. If the corporation believes that millions spent on burnishing its reputation are likely to be more effective than spending those funds on actual changes in its processes or products, a purely economic calculation will justify the cosmetic strategy.

The business case approach to CSR can also present difficult practical challenges of application that may limit its reach. Sometimes the cost–benefit calculation will be relatively straightforward. For example, a company considering an investment in a new fleet of energy-efficient delivery vehicles can calculate the future savings in lower fuel costs, reduced maintenance expenses, new tax benefits, and the like with a reasonable degree of precision and compare them to the purchase price. The exercise gets harder if the corporation is considering a project for which the immediate cost can only be justified by longer-term gains in the form of reduced expense or increased revenue. Consider a decision whether to develop a new green product. This will require current expenditures on research and development and new production processes, followed by marketing and distribution expenses. The offsetting benefits, if they are realised at all, may not materialise until many years later and, as discussed above, they are hard to predict. Companies that evaluate pro-environmental choices solely in cost–benefit terms may be more reluctant to embark on projects like these than would a company that views commitment to sustainability as something more than a purely economic proposition.

The business case may collapse altogether when it comes to decisions that are not readily amenable to cost–benefit analysis.[153] The climate change example discussed above is pertinent. There is scientific consensus on the causal connection between carbon emissions and climate change. Even among scientists, however, there is a range of informed opinion about the magnitude and time horizon of the risk, both of which depend

---

[152] See C.A. Ramus and I. Montiel, 'When are corporate environmental policies a form of greenwashing?' (2005) 44(4) *Business & Society* 377; W.S. Laufer, 'Social accountability and corporate greenwashing' (2003) 43 *Journal of Business Ethics* 253.

[153] For a critique of reliance on cost–benefit analysis in environmental regulation, see D.A. Kysar, *Regulating from Nowhere: Environmental Law and the Search for Objectivity* (Yale University Press, 2010).

76   DAVID MILLON

on several assumptions not just about scientific processes and techno-logical innovations but also about human behaviour in future years. A company that is attempting to decide whether to invest in new processes and equipment designed to reduce its emissions will find it difficult to justify that decision in terms of economic benefit because it cannot con-fidently predict or monetise the magnitude of the benefit.

Yet another practical limitation on the social value of strategic CSR is the problems of scale and scope. There are typically significant limits on how much money corporations are willing to spend on environmental improvements in comparison to investment in the growth of their core businesses. For most companies, attention to the environment will be only a small part of what they do, and thus constrain the potential of strategic CSR to make large-scale differences. As Vogel writes, 'In most cases, CSR only makes business sense if the costs of more virtuous behavior remain modest.'[154] Vogel also points out the related problem of scope. Despite the urgent environmental problems faced by developing countries, most NGO attention and corporate attention have resulted in improvements that benefit citizens of the developed countries.[155]

Though self-limited, the business case for sustainability does embrace a broad range of significant eco-friendly policy choices. Even traditionally minded companies appreciate the importance of enhanced energy effi-ciency, waste reduction, and decreased reliance on nonrenewable natural resources. Spending money on initiatives in areas like these can yield mea-sureable short-term savings. Furthermore, the desire to avoid the costs of lawsuits or bad publicity can prod some corporations into being good environmental citizens. Ultimately, however, many will argue that the appropriate measure of large corporations' responsibility for sustainabil-ity lies beyond the conceptual and practical limits of the business case. As with human rights, companies arguably have a responsibility to 'do the right thing' even if doing so will not be profitable. The strategic model of CSR, built on the possibility of long-term economic benefits, may not go far enough in satisfying society's demands for environmentally responsible corporate behaviour.

7   Conclusion

Global society is facing an environmental crisis. Irreversible climate change, loss of biodiversity, waste and pollution, and depletion of nonrenewable natural resources have occurred on a large scale and there

---

[154] Vogel, *The Market for Virtue*, 4.   [155] Vogel, *The Market for Virtue*, 111.

is more to come unless there are fundamental behavioural changes. Large corporations are major contributors to these problems but also have a significant role to play as problem solvers.

Current domestic and international legal regimes do not do nearly enough to mandate responsible environmental management, partly because these regimes have been weakened as a result of lobbying from business interests hostile to measures that diminish their profitability, such as has occurred with the fossil fuel industry's reaction to proposals to mitigate climate change. Important as they are, effective legal initiatives should not be expected in the near future.[156] For the time being, therefore, voluntary undertakings by enlightened business will continue to be a useful supplement. This is where CSR can help, especially if the definition of CSR encompasses the attitudes companies take to public policy reform, as Vogel has argued it should.[157]

The prospects for CSR thus depend both on the way it is conceived and justified, and also on the institutional contexts within which companies operate. Ethical CSR asserts that corporations should act responsibly towards all their stakeholders. Allocation of costs and benefits can present difficult problems but no one stakeholder group – such as the shareholders – has a right to claim ex ante priority in the decision process. In many cases, conflicting interests mean that trade-off, zero-sum choices must be made. Expenditures on the environment or on working conditions, for example, may mean lower net income and therefore reduction in shareholders' wealth.

In a country like the USA, where strong social norms encourage an emphasis on short-term share price maximisation, ethical CSR encounters an immediate and formidable obstacle. This predicament is not necessarily the case in countries with different normative traditions and conceptions of the proper relationship between business and society. In continental Europe, CSR does not happen automatically, but a built-in, indigenous commitment to shareholder primacy is not the problem. The UK presents yet another case, and there are signs that CSR may fare better there as well.

One response to institutional contexts like that of the USA, which tend to be reflexively hostile to ethics-based CSR claims because of the commitment to shareholder primacy, is the strategic model of CSR that

---

[156] N. Bakker and B.J. Richardson, 'Breaching the Maginot Line: the frailty of environmental law in Europe and North America', in P. Taylor (ed.), *Environmental Law for a Sustainable Society* (New Zealand Centre for Environmental Law, 2013), 51.

[157] Vogel, *The Market for Virtue*, passim.

holds out the promise of shareholder gains from investment in stakeholder well-being. There is reason to believe that this business case justification for CSR can be valid at least under certain circumstances, but in business cultures like those in the USA which are committed to short-termism, the necessary patience needed to see long-term returns on short-term costs is often lacking. Even when patience is present, because strategic CSR is a matter of cost–benefit analysis, environmentally friendly policies may not be adopted unless there is a persuasive likelihood of a net benefit to shareholders. Shareholder benefits, rather than aggregate social wealth, are the relevant criterion, making it highly likely that corporations will decline to make choices in favour of sustainability that could generate significant social value. In the final analysis, CSR – in the sense of voluntary corporate behaviour designed to enhance environmental sustainability – may seem to be the best currently available option for moving forward, but we should not expect that it will be sufficient to produce progress on a large scale. The gravity of our looming ecological crisis is such that more profound and radical changes, including a reassertion of public responsibility for legislative solutions, may be necessary. For now, the prognosis is generally bleak, even in those countries with the most advanced CSR practices and sophisticated environmental legal regimes.

3

Shareholder primacy: the main barrier to sustainable companies

BEATE SJÅFJELL, ANDREW JOHNSTON, LINN ANKER-SØRENSEN, AND DAVID MILLON

1 The significance of companies and company law

1.1 'Business as usual' is not an option

While we may well agree that the company is an ingenious invention, we also know that 'business as usual' is not viable if we wish to preserve the very basis of our existence. Our own well-being and that of future generations depend on companies, the dominant form of business, contributing to the transformation towards sustainability. As explained in the Introduction to this book, the hypothesis informing the work of the Sustainable Companies Project is that regulation or governance of business decision-making should be included in the toolbox for sustainability. A comparative analysis of core company law – the rules regulating the identity of corporate decision-makers, and the aims of, and any limitations on, those decisions – is essential to evaluate whether there is a realistic prospect of integrating sustainable development, and especially its environmental dimensions, into corporate decision-making.

The historically contingent coupling of a legal entity with limited liability for those holding shares in it has become the hallmark of the capitalist economy.[1] Society has gradually accepted and even promoted the rise to dominance of this business form on the assumption that it contributes significantly to the overarching goal of society – that is, to increasing societal welfare, especially as measured in greater material wealth. Although the concept of societal welfare has deep historical and philosophical roots, the interesting point for our analysis is the way this societal goal has, in

---

[1] See M-L. Djelic, 'When limited liability was (still) an issue: mobilization and politics of signification in 19th-century England' (2013) 34 *Organization Studies* 595.

the mainstream law-and-economics literature, become an argument for giving shareholders priority over other interests as the way to ensure that companies contribute to increasing societal welfare.

While the purpose of the company[2] and its role in society have been a topic of intellectually stimulating and heated discussions since the nineteenth century, recent decades have witnessed a narrowing of the debate, increasingly dominated by the law-and-economics-inspired view of the company, first, as the shareholders' property, and latterly as a 'nexus of contracts' in which only the shareholders require protection. This view effectively equates 'the interests of the company' with those of the shareholders. This chapter will show that a broader view of the corporate purpose and 'the interests of the company' has a more convincing normative basis; is more in line with the reality in which companies operate; and also has support in company law across jurisdictions.

This section of the chapter introduces the legal architecture of the company, the economic organisation of many companies into corporate groups, and the need to revisit conventional wisdom about the purpose of companies and how they should be managed. Thereafter, this chapter proceeds with a legal analysis of the purpose of the company (Section 2) and the interests of the company as the guideline for the board in discharging its duty to the company, touching also upon the possibilities of enforcing this duty (Section 3). Section 3 concludes with more discussion of the continued dominance of the social norm of shareholder primacy and its significance in our context. Section 4 follows up on this with a discussion of the role of the shareholder as a company law actor, including a discussion of the control rights of the shareholder, the extent of shareholder liability for abuse of those rights, and the role of the parent company in groups. Section 5 concludes by summarising the main barriers and possibilities and indicating possible ways forward as a prelude to the analysis in this book's final chapter, Chapter 8.

1.2   The company and the corporate group

The firm, through which business is conducted, may be described as a means of allocating resources to different uses.[3] A number of parties are involved, both within the firm (employees including managers, and arguably the board), and other interests outside the firm, whether in

---

[2] Discussed below in Section 2.
[3] R. Coase, 'The nature of the firm' (1937) 4 *Economica* 386.

SHAREHOLDER PRIMACY 81

contractual relations with the firm (suppliers, (other) creditors, investors including shareholders, consumers, and other customers) or without contractual relations but affected by its business and its decision-making (local communities, workers in suppliers' firms, subcontractors in supply chains, and the local and global environment).[4]

The firm may be – and is in our context – organised formally through the legal entity of the company, which is structured through company law. Organising the firm through a corporate legal structure has – or is meant to have – implications for the decision-making process in the firm. Those implications include constituting the shareholders as the general meeting within which certain important decisions are made; vesting in the board[5] a strategy-setting, supervisory, and in some jurisdictions executive role; protecting creditors; and, in some jurisdictions, also regulating employee participation through codetermination rules.[6] For historical reasons, the focus of company law is, as we shall return to below, mainly on relations between the majority and minority shareholders; the shareholders and the company; the company and its creditors; and the decision-making processes in the company. In general, company law itself does not regulate the relationship between the company and broader society.

The company may list its shares, or a class of its shares, on one or more stock exchanges.[7] While this is primarily intended to facilitate the financing of the company or one of its ventures, and to give shareholders a platform to buy and sell shares among themselves, listing potentially also impacts on the company itself, and therefore on the firm that it structures. Listing subjects the company to financial market law and the semi-regulatory (or 'soft law') regime of corporate governance codes.

---

[4] See B. Sjåfjell, *Towards a Sustainable European Company Law: A Normative Analysis of the Objectives of EU Law* (Kluwer Law International, 2009), Chapter 4.

[5] Or boards, as the case may be, depending on whether the company has a two-tier or one-tier structure. In our chapter we use the term 'the board' to refer to the one-tier board and generally to both boards in the two-tier system unless specific reference is made to one of the boards. References to the 'board' also include the board in the intermediate structure observed in the Nordic countries. We will generally use 'board of directors' when referring to UK, US, Australian, and Canadian law. The UK Companies Act 2006 removed all reference to 'boards of directors' replacing them with references to 'the directors'. References to 'boards (of directors)' in relation to the UK should be understood simply to refer to the directors collectively.

[6] Which may be in company law, as in Norway, or regulated through separate acts, as in Germany and the Netherlands.

[7] Listing is an option for the public limited liability company. When we use 'company' in this chapter, we include both the private and the public kind, unless otherwise stated.

82   B. SJÅFJELL, A. JOHNSTON, L. ANKER-SØRENSEN, D. MILLON

The company as a separate legal entity with limited liability for its share-holders, combined with the widespread legal acceptance that corporate entities may hold shares in other corporate entities, has allowed corporate groups to develop. In this popular business structure, one company can be at the top of an enormous network or pyramid consisting of dozens or even hundreds of subsidiaries, sub-subsidiaries, and related affiliates.

These structures bring to a head some of the issues we analyse in our chapter, notably the relationship between shareholders' pursuit of profit and the law's concession to them of limited liability, which protects their personal assets from creditors. The extension of the latter to groups (i.e. to companies as shareholders) may, on the one hand, as Philip Blumberg does, be denoted a 'historical accident'.[8] On the other hand, if legal entities were not permitted to be shareholders, this would deprive businesses of a means of diversification of investments and control of risk. The point is that the recognition of companies as shareholders has led to the development of complex structures that company law in many jurisdictions, being premised on a single entity with natural persons as shareholders, has struggled to come to terms with.

The corporate group may consist of a mix – and indeed typically does – of listed and unlisted, large and small companies (and other entities). In addition, each single entity within a group may, as may stand-alone companies, have branches (which do not involve the creation of a separate entity but allow a company to do business in a different jurisdiction) and agencies, as well as a complex set of contractual relationships with other entities (including lengthy, transnational supply chains). This is the broader picture within which our analysis is undertaken.

1.3   Shareholder primacy and conventional wisdom

Mainstream company law and corporate governance debates are dominated by law-and-economics thinking, which rests on simplified economic assumptions that can and have been questioned. This chapter is not the place for a deeper discussion and critique of this development – that has been sufficiently dealt with elsewhere.[9] Here we will just present

---

[8] P.I. Blumberg, *The Law of Corporate Groups. Tort, Contract and Other Common Law Problems in the Substantive Law of Parent and Subsidiary Corporations* (Aspen Law & Business, 1987 and 2000), 5; P.I. Blumberg, 'Accountability of multinational corporations: the barriers presented by concepts of the corporate juridical entity' (2001) 24 *Hastings International and Comparative Law Review* 303.

[9] For a more detailed discussion, see Sjåfjell, *Towards a Sustainable European Company Law*, Chapter 3; A. Johnston, *EC Regulation of Corporate Governance* (Cambridge University

SHAREHOLDER PRIMACY 83

briefly that which is necessary for our context. Much of the mainstream debate stems from premises drawn inter alia from economic agency theory, which focuses on board and management accountability to shareholders in order to achieve efficient resource allocation.[10] This is assumed to serve what may be seen as the normative purpose of company law, formulated by Reiner Kraakman and others as 'advancing social welfare' through enhancing the aggregate welfare of shareholders, employees, suppliers, and customers 'without undue sacrifice – and if possible with benefit – to third parties such as local communities and beneficiaries of the natural environment'.[11] The mainstream debate claims that the members of the board are 'agents' for the shareholders only, and then limits itself to trying to reduce the 'agency costs' that the board can impose on their principals.[12] The multifaceted purpose set out by Kraakman and others is quickly reduced to a simple assumption that prioritisation of shareholders will result in the achievement of all these goals, as is illustrated by Henry Hansmann and Reiner Kraakman's brazenly entitled paper 'The end of history for corporate law': 'as a consequence of both logic and experience, there is convergence on a consensus that the best means to ... the pursuit of aggregate social welfare is to make corporate managers strongly accountable to shareholder interests and, at least in direct terms, only to those interests'.[13]

Agency theory has contributed to the rise of shareholder primacy as a dominant social norm, as well as a number of changes in the financial sector, including the growth of equity-based institutional investing.[14]

In this chapter, we contrast this social norm of 'shareholder primacy', which insists that board and senior managers are the 'agents' of the

---

Press, 2009), Chapters 2 and 3; L. Talbot, *Progressive Corporate Governance for the 21st Century* (Routledge, 2013).

[10] A critique and an alternative approach are set out in B. Sjåfjell, 'More than meets the eye: law and economics in modern company law', in E. Røsæg, H.B. Schäfer, and E. Stavang (eds.), *Law and Economics. Essays in Honour of Erling Eide* (Cappelen Akademisk, 2010), 217–35.

[11] R. Kraakman, *et al.*, *The Anatomy of Corporate Law* (Oxford University Press, 2004), 18. We may note that the economic perspective is so overriding that the authors refer to 'beneficiaries of the natural environment', rather than preserving the environment itself.

[12] In spite of recognition of other issues right from the beginning: M.C. Jensen and W.H. Meckling 'Theory of the firm: managerial behaviour, agency costs and ownership structure' (1976) 3 *Journal of Financial Economics* 310.

[13] H. Hansman and R. Kraakman, 'The end of history for corporate law' (2000–2001) 89 *Georgetown Law Journal* 441.

[14] W. Lazonick and M. O'Sullivan 'Maximizing shareholder value: a new ideology for corporate governance' (2000) 29 *Economy and Society* 1, 15–16; K. Williams, 'From shareholder value to present-day capitalism' (2000) 29 *Economy and Society* 1.

shareholders and should maximise returns to shareholders as measured by the current share price, with 'shareholder value', which we use to label the legal requirement, in jurisdictions like the UK, that directors run the company for the collective benefit of its shareholders. Many other authors, particularly those influenced by law and economics, do not make this distinction, being content to assume that the law reflects their normative position, blurring the distinctions between ideology, corporate practice, and the strict legal position.

As a response to the agency issue between managers and particularly the dispersed shareholders, shareholder primacy aims to encourage managers to act in the interests of the shareholders by maximising their returns. This social norm, claim John Armour and Jeffrey Gordon, has acquired 'almost axiomatic status'.[15] Economic incentives, such as share options for executives, are premised on an assumption that incentivising management to focus on returns to shareholders enhances aggregate social wealth. A more critical approach, which rejects the existence of unquestionable axioms in social science, suggests that these economic incentives only serve to exacerbate the narrow, short-term focus of the shareholder primacy drive.

Shareholder primacy also draws normative support from the 'nexus of contracts' theory, though that theory actually demonstrates that shareholders are just one of several contracting parties.[16] The primacy accorded to shareholders on the basis of this contractual view is founded on an unconvincing belief that, alone among the contracting parties, shareholders have a distinct type of contractual relationship which makes them 'residual risk bearers'.[17] This belief then leads to the assumption that focusing on shareholders and maximising their profits will be for the greater good of all involved parties, and even of society in general. Although the caveat 'absent externalities' is sometimes made in more theoretical discussions, it is often forgotten in the mainstream corporate governance debate, or else externalities are assumed to be taken care of by other areas of law, or even the market

---

[15] J. Armour and J.N. Gordon, *Systemic Harms and Shareholder Value*, Law Working Paper No. 222 (European Corporate Governance Institute, 2013).

[16] See also W. Lazonick and M. O'Sullivan, 'Maximizing shareholder value: a new ideology for corporate governance' (2000) 29 *Economy and Society* 1, 15–16; K. Williams, 'From shareholder value to present-day capitalism' (2000) 29(1) *Economy and Society*, 1 explaining how the theory can equally support a 'stakeholder theory' of corporate governance.

[17] Discussed by A.A. Alchian and H. Demsetz, 'Production, information and economic organization' (1972) 62 *American Economic Review*, 777.

itself.[18] The main flaw in the argument is the idea that only the shareholders have a residual interest, with the implication being that shareholders benignly further all interests in furthering their own.[19]

These economic models of the firm as an agency relationship or a nexus of contracts are meant to be descriptive and explanatory, but are frequently used as a normative argument to guide regulation.[20] Often only the conclusions drawn from those models remain. Viewed in isolation from their simplifying assumptions, they become mere postulates and conventional wisdom, while their apparent theoretical rigour allows them to exercise a dominant influence on legislative discussions. Rather than witnessing an ever-evolving analysis and evaluation of assumptions, means, and goals in this area, public debates about company law in the past few decades have been dominated by unsubstantiated postulates and axioms that have been very difficult to question, even in the light of their apparent failure. Specifically, the rise to prominence in Anglo-American scholarship and public policy discourse of the social norm of shareholder primacy has dominated debates about company law reform across the world. This has sidelined the great tradition of lively debates in company law scholarship about the nature, purpose, and interests of the corporation, from the 1850s onwards, especially in Germany and in the United States (the USA).[21] Academic arguments, which uncritically adopt Anglo-American, law-and-economics assumptions, are beguilingly seen as 'modern' and 'efficient' calls for company law reform. The equation of increasing share prices and cash flow to shareholders with increased social welfare means that these phenomena become benchmarks of successful company law and corporate governance. Shareholder primacy becomes the goal, rather than one means among many by which companies might be governed so as to advance social welfare. This blurring of means and goals is a seminal finding in our work.

---

[18] Armour and Gordon recognise the problem of lack of internalisation for systemically important financial institutions, but are otherwise still enthusiastic about shareholder primacy as a positive driver: Armour and Gordon, *Systemic Harms and Shareholder Value*, 4.3.5.2.

[19] See e.g. Sjåfjell, *Towards a Sustainable European Company Law*, s. 4.3.5; Johnston, *EC Regulation of Corporate Governance*, Chapter 2; M. Aglietta and A. Rebérioux, *Corporate Governance Adrift* (Edward Elgar, 2005).

[20] See e.g. M.A. Eisenberg 'The conception that the corporation is a nexus of contracts, and the dual nature of the firm' (1999) 24 *Journal of Corporation Law* 836.

[21] Including the famous Berle and Dodd debate in the 1930s, see e.g. W.W. Bratton and M.L. Wachter, 'Shareholder primacy's corporatist origins: A. Berle and "the modern corporation"' (2008) 34 *Journal of Corporation Law* 99.

86   B. SJÅFJELL, A. JOHNSTON, L. ANKER-SØRENSEN, D. MILLON

In contrast to the reception of shareholder primacy arguments, the broader view of the company, where employees and other affected groups are taken into account or play a role in decision-making, is seen as inefficient and old-fashioned.[22] The financial crises of the last decade, together with the apparent convergence of crises – economic, environmental, and social – which confront us, are slowly leading to wider recognition that we need to revisit the conventional wisdom that shareholder primacy necessarily leads to greater social welfare.[23] Here we analyse these issues through the lens of comparative company law, in order to shed light on one of the pervasive questions of our time: how can the law contribute to moving companies away from 'business as usual' and onto an environmentally sustainable path, and thereby contribute to securing the very basis of our existence?

1.4   Sources, methodology, and starting points

As a starting point, companies are 'creatures of national law'.[24] Accordingly, that is the focal point of our legal analysis. The core area of national law examined is company law and other areas of law regulating decision-making in companies.[25]

National systems of company law, with their focus on the governance of the firm and the relationship between the company and its shareholders,

---

[22] Hansmann and Kraakman, 'End of history'; F.H. Easterbrook and D.R. Fischel, *The Economic Structure of Corporate Law* (Harvard University Press, 1991); Armour and Gordon, *Systemic Harms and Shareholder Value*. For the 'framing bias' shareholder primacy enjoys, see T. Belinfanti, 'Forget Roger Rabbit – is corporate purpose being framed?' (2013–2014) 58 *New York Law School Law Review* 675.

[23] See e.g. L. Stout, *The Shareholder Value Myth* (Berret-Koehlers Publishing, 2012), G. Serafeim, *The Role of the Corporation in Society: An Alternative View and Opportunities for Future Research*, Working Paper 14–110 (Harvard Business School, 2013); C.M. Christensen and D. van Bever, 'The capitalist's dilemma' (2014) *Harvard Business Review* 60; G.K. Wilson, 'The United States: the strange survival of (neo)liberalism', in W. Grant and G. K. Wilson (eds.), *The Consequences of the Global Financial Crisis: The Rhetoric of Reform and Regulation* (Oxford Scholarship Online, 2012), Chapter 4. However, see also C. Crouch, *The Strange Non-Death of Neoliberalism* (Polity, 2011); J. Quiggin, *Zombie Economics* (Princeton University Press, 2010).

[24] As stated repeatedly in the case law of the Court of Justice of the EU, see e.g. Case 81/87, Daily Mail Plc, para 19; Case C-210/06, Cartesio para 104.

[25] The USA is an important exception. State law is the primary source of company law, with Delaware by far the most important. Approximately two-thirds of the largest US companies are incorporated there. Federal law regulates publicly traded securities and affects core company law only in marginal and indirect ways.

SHAREHOLDER PRIMACY

do not in general regulate the company's impact on the environment.[26] However, obviously all jurisdictions have some laws aimed at regulating companies' environmental performance, and some have concrete initiatives to reduce greenhouse gas (GHG) emissions.[27] Indeed, a rising number of jurisdictions include in their constitution the right to a clean and healthy environment for current and future generations, with corresponding duties on the state and, exceptionally, directly on companies.[28] The actual environmental performance of companies depends on the interlinked issues of the quality and effectiveness of environmental law; the extent to which companies comply with environmental law; and the extent to which companies incorporate environmental considerations into their decision-making beyond the minimalist requirements of hard law.[29] The well-documented limitations of environmental law (which are not considered in this chapter) are a fundamental reason why we should focus on the hitherto mainly ignored area of company law. The aim is to contribute to finding out how legal compliance can be increased while also stimulating the innovative and creative potential within each company to contribute beyond what the law requires.

Obviously, company law of all jurisdictions assumes that companies will comply with 'external law'. No company law mandates the board to ignore environmental legal compliance in order to promote profit. Yet in practice this occurs, and we will return to the significance of this in our conclusion. Further, environmental law tends to consist of

---

[26] See the extremely limited findings in relation to Nordic companies acts in B. Sjåfjell, 'Towards a sustainable development: internalising externalities in Norwegian company law' (2008) 8(1) *International and Comparative Corporate Law Journal* 103.

[27] For the European Emission Trading Scheme, see http://ec.europa.eu/clima/policies/ets/index_en.htm.

[28] For just two examples, see the Constitution of the Republic of South Africa 1996, s. 24; J.J. Henning, *et al.*, *Sustainable Companies, Climate Change and Corporate Social Responsibility in South African Law*, mapping paper (Sustainable Companies Project, 2011); Polish Constitution, Article 5, in conjunction with Articles 74 and 86; A. Radwan and T. Regucki, *The Possibilities for and Barriers to Sustainable Companies in Polish Company Law*, Research Paper No. 2012–32 (University of Oslo Faculty of Law, 2012), available at: http://ssrn.com/abstract=2159217,1.4.

[29] N. Bakker and B.J. Richardson, 'Breaching the Maginot Line: the frailty of environmental law in Europe and North America', in P. Taylor (ed.), *Environmental Law for a Sustainable Society* (New Zealand Centre for Environmental Law, 2013), 51; B. Sjåfjell and L. Anker-Sørensen, 'Directors' duties and corporate social responsibility (CSR)', in H. Birkmose, M. Neville, and K. Engsig Sørensen (eds.), *Boards of Directors in European Companies: Reshaping and Harmonising Their Organisation and Duties* (Kluwer Law International, 2013), Chapter 7.

'command-and-control', anti-pollution law, while sustainable development requires more than that: it requires a new and holistic way of thinking for decision-makers in companies that embraces positive, green development. Through the comparative analysis in Section 2 and Section 3 we will see that company law provides very broad scope for companies to cut GHG emissions and integrate environmental protection into their decision-making as a way of pursuing profit. Augmented by the wide discretion given to boards in the shape of the business judgement rule, the 'business case' for running companies along environmentally friendly lines allows boards to do far more than they currently do. Looking beyond 'business case' scenarios to more 'pluralist' approaches, the picture is more mixed. The company law of several jurisdictions allows environmental protection to be prioritised, albeit within limits. However, this seldom or never comes to a head as, under pressure from the shareholder primacy drive, boards generally do not consider sacrificing profits in order to protect the environment. Indeed, in many cases, they do not even use the room given to them by law to choose the most environmentally friendly option among equally profitable alternatives. In the worst cases, they do not even ensure that their decisions comply with environmental law.

2 The purpose of the company

2.1 The interlinked issues of purpose and interests of the company

A crucial element in our research has been to identify the interlinked concepts of 'the purpose of the company' and 'the interests of the company'. Legally, these concepts should inform the contents and direction of corporate decision-making. However, despite their importance, these concepts and arguably especially the purpose of the company are difficult to deduce from the legal sources.[30] This does not mean that all national companies legislation is silent about corporate purpose. However, where something is said about purpose, it is open for discussion whether that refers to *the* purpose of the company, as in a legislative normative stance that this is the overarching purpose of companies, or whether it is rather a specific, historically-based stipulation of the purpose of the company in relation to a particular context or relationship. We can therefore imagine

---

[30] This is the case in most (if not all) jurisdictions, see e.g. Radwan and Regucki, *The Possibilities for and Barriers to Sustainable Companies in Polish Company Law*, s. 1.2.

three different concepts of the purpose of the company as a matter of law: (1) a specific purpose, in relation to a particular context or relationship, that the companies legislation expresses;[31] (2) an overarching purpose of the company as a matter of company law, which may or may not coincide with any specific purpose stipulated in companies legislation; and (3) the purpose of the company as a societal institution, the purpose for which society through law recognises the existence of companies as separate legal entities.

The concept of the interests of the company or, more simply, the company interest, as it is known in many jurisdictions,[32] is not an easy object of legal analysis either. It is at least a clearly recognised company law concept, albeit that discussion has often been on a superficial level.[33] The interests of the company may be said to form the core of the guidelines, according to which the company is to be operated, and is a crucial touchstone in many legal systems' framework of the duties and competence of corporate organs. The board has a duty to take decisions which they think will further the interests of the company. The interests of the company also inform the application of other company law rules; it can be decisive for whether a decision by the majority of the general assembly of shareholders is valid.[34] The key point is that the interests of the company are the means to the end of achieving the societal purpose of companies. Ideally, if the board of every company complies with and promotes the interests of the company, this should result in the achievement of the societal purpose of the company. As a matter of terminology, some scholars consider the interests of the company as synonymous with the purpose of the

---

[31] See, for example, the discussion of the Norwegian Companies Acts' expression of purpose in relation to the shareholders' expectations of profit, further in this chapter.

[32] To illustrate: *Unternehmensinteresse* in German, *vennootschappelijkbelang* in Dutch, *l'intérêt social* in French, and *selskapsinteresse* in Norwegian.

[33] As Blanaid Clarke notes, remarkably little serious judicial or legislative attention has been given in Ireland to whether the company should be run purely for the benefit of the shareholders or whether the company might have its own interests: B. Clarke, *Irish Company Law Mapping Paper*, Research Paper No. 2012–35 (University of Osloe Faculty of Law, 2012), available at: http://ssrn.com/abstract=2178420,s.2.1. See also J. Mukwiri, 'Myth of shareholder primacy in English law' (2013) 24(2) *European Business Law Review* 21. For a detailed theoretical discussion of this issue, see G. Teubner, 'Enterprise corporatism: new industrial-policy and the essence of the legal person' (1988) 36 *American Journal of Comparative Law* 130.

[34] On France: P.H. Conac, 'Corporate governance of France', in A.M. Fleckner and K. Hopt (eds.), *Comparative Company Law: The State of the Art and International Regulation* (Cambridge University Press, 2013), 475.

company, and indeed many discuss only the interests of the company. We maintain that we should distinguish between these two interlinked topics for reasons of analytical clarity.[35] The purpose of the company is the topic of the remainder of this section, while Section 3 covers the interests of the company.

2.2 The purpose of the company

We are looking for the concept of the purpose of the company as a societal institution; that is, the purpose for which society recognises the existence of companies as separate legal entities. Filling such a concept with content is fraught with philosophical and theoretical challenges, and has been the topic of much debate at least over the past 150 years.[36] Our aim is to discuss the concept through the lens of our cross-jurisdictional company law analysis.[37]

In the sense we are using the term, the purpose of the company differs both from the purpose of company law,[38] and from the purpose (or 'objects') of individual companies, as typically set out in their articles of association.[39] It should also be distinguished from the company's purpose in relation to any involved party, or, for that matter, any party's purpose with their investment in, or dealings with, companies. The purpose or reason for which a party invests in or deals with a company may coincide to some extent with the company's purpose as a matter of company law, but that is a matter that is subject to clarification and not an appropriate starting point for this analysis. The specific purposes of the various involved parties will be more or less related to the purpose

---

[35] See Sjåfjell, *Towards a Sustainable European Company Law*, s. 5.2; e.g. Radwan and Regucki, *The Possibilities for and Barriers to Sustainable Companies in Polish Company Law*, s. 1.2.

[36] G.M. Hayden and M.T. Bodie, 'One share, one vote and the false promise of shareholder homogeneity' (2008) 30 *Cardozo Law Review* 445; D. Millon, 'Theories of the corporation' (1999) *Duke Law Journal* 201; J. Dine and M. Koutsias, *The Nature of Corporate Governance* (Edward Elgar, 2013).

[37] In comparison, Andrew Keay's approach is an ideological stakeholder/shareholder discussion: A. Keay, *The Corporate Objective* (Edward Elgar, 2011).

[38] For the purpose of company (and securities) law in an EU perspective, see Sjåfjell, *Towards a Sustainable European Company Law*, Chapters 6 and 8–11.

[39] Namely, e.g. manufacturing furniture or selling clothing. Examples include jurisdictions requiring that the companies state the purpose of their business, e.g. in Australia, companies may choose to have an objects clause, and, if they do, company decision-makers will be in breach of duty if they ignore it, see S. Deva, *Sustainable Business and Australian Corporate Law: An Exploration*, Research Paper No. 2013-11 (University of Oslo Faculty of Law, 2013), available at: http://ssrn.com/abstract=2248621, s. II B.

of the individual company: the employees' purpose may be to contribute to the development of the company's production, as well as their individual purposes of a steady income and job satisfaction. Suppliers may have as their purpose the regular sale of goods and the earning of profits thereby, while the providers of debt capital, typically banks as lenders or investors as purchasers of debt securities, will desire to finance the expansion of productive enterprise and so to profit from their long-term relationship with the company. Shareholders will normally see their purpose in relation to the company as to make a profit, and may also have collateral purposes relating to the development of a meaningful business venture or an ethical investment (shareholders are not a homogeneous group).

As a result of their veneration of shareholder primacy, some scholars equate the purpose of the company with the assumed common purpose of one involved party, namely the shareholders, who are assumed to seek maximisation of their returns.[40] We reject this conclusion, and argue that the societal purpose of companies transcends the specific purpose of any single corporate constituency.

Company law tells us very little explicitly about the purpose of the company as a societal institution. Thus, unsurprisingly, many academic contributions in the field of company law focus only on the interests of the company, and not the overarching issue of the societal purpose of companies.[41] Discussion tends to focus, first, on which interests the board can legally take into account and, second, on whether the interests of the shareholders, as one of the stakeholders in the company, should be given priority, or whether the interests of other involved parties or interests may also take priority.[42] In such discussions, the purpose of the company as a matter of company law is then indirectly deduced from the way in which the concept of the interests of the company is understood.

---

[40] For example, M.C. Jensen, 'Value maximization, stakeholder theory, and the corporate objective function' in J. Andriof, *et al.* (eds.), *Unfolding Stakeholder Thinking: Theory, Responsibility and Engagement* (Greenleaf Publishing, 2002).

[41] An exception here is, e.g. E. Lauraitytė and P. Miliauskas, *Sustainable Companies Under the Lithuanian Company Law*, Research Paper No. 2013–10 (University of Oslo Faculty of Law, 2013), available at: http://ssrn.com/abstract=2248591, s. 2.1, which attempts to piece together the purpose of the company in Lithuanian law from a variety of legal sources.

[42] For example, in Germany, the purpose of the company is discussed under the heading 'company interest'; see G. Deipenbrock, *The Management Board of a German Aktienge-sellschaft, the Managing Directors of a German GmbH, the Unternehmensinteresse and the Goal of Sustainable Development of Companies – Some Fundamentals*, mapping paper (Sustainable Companies Project, 2010), at 11 f. and at 28.

92   B. SJÅFJELL, A. JOHNSTON, L. ANKER-SØRENSEN, D. MILLON

To the extent that national companies legislation uses the term 'purpose', it tends to be in relation to profit for shareholders.[43] For example, in the Nordic companies statutes, it is stipulated that the articles of association must specify if the company is not to have profit for its shareholders as its purpose. At first glance, this suggests that there is a default (but rebuttable) company law rule that the purpose of the company is shareholder profit. For example, the Norwegian Companies Acts require that companies that do not have as their purpose the making of a profit for the shareholders include provisions about the distribution of their profits (and their capital if the company is dissolved) in their articles of association.[44] These provisions arguably reflect the purpose of the shareholders as investors (which company law, for historical reasons, particularly aims to regulate). Delving deeper into case law and collateral legal materials shows that the company as a matter of company law has a broader purpose, with long-term value for the firm as the balancing point for a number of interests, among them shareholders' interest in profit, which is itself derived from the interest of the firm in making a profit.[45] In Finnish company law, on the other hand, the purpose of the company is understood as a long-term, inclusive shareholder value variant, inspired by the UK's legislated concept of 'enlightened shareholder value', though Finland's case law emphasises the secondary nature of shareholders' right to profit in relation to the interests of the company.[46]

To flesh out further the purpose of the company as a matter of company law, we find that we need to go to the stipulation of the interests of the company, which the board of the company has a duty to promote. As we will show in our analysis below, there is a wide spectrum of approaches here. At one end, there is the UK's enlightened shareholder value, where

---

[43] See e.g. Macedonia Company Act, Art. 19 (2), and J. Stamenkova van Rumpt, *Macedonia: Mapping Paper on the Company Law Barriers and Possibilities for Sustainable Companies*, mapping paper (Sustainable Companies Project, 2011), 2.1.

[44] *Allmennaksjeloven* [the Norwegian Public Companies Act] (13 June 1997, No. 45) § 2–2 (2) and the former Finnish ABL 12:1.2 and indirectly in the Finnish Act, *Aktiebolagslag* [the Finnish Companies Act] (21 July 2006, No. 624) s. 1:5.

[45] See B. Sjåfjell, *Sustainable Companies: Possibilities and Barriers in Norwegian Company Law*, Research Paper No. 2013–20 (University of Oslo Faculty of Law, 2013), available at: http://ssrn.com/abstract=2311433, s. 2.2, where Sjåfjell presents this argument based on an analysis of the companies acts, their preparatory works, and to a certain extent, case law, while conceding that other commentators may take a different view.

[46] This reading is supported by an analysis of preparatory works as well as of the case law, see Mähönen, *Sustainable Companies Mapping Paper on Company Law Issues: Finland*, ss. 2.1 and 2.2.

SHAREHOLDER PRIMACY 93

the collective shareholder interest is to take priority over a broad range of other interests, including the employees and the environment, but those interests are to be considered as a means to an end of shareholder value. At the other, there is the broader, Germanic-inspired concept of 'company interest', where the interest of the enterprise arguably is the balancing point around which a number of interests are to be considered.

An analysis of the purpose of the company as a matter of company law produces a wide variety of conclusions across jurisdictions, ranging from shareholder profit as a company purpose in itself to a balance of a much wider range of interests. While superficial discussion of the issue often leads to the conclusion that shareholder profit is the purpose, more in-depth analysis of the legal sources leads to this broader variety of conclusions, from shareholder profit being the purpose to a broader, pluralist purpose.[47]

However, when considering the purpose of the company as a societal institution, profit for shareholders is clearly but one function of companies. Even where, exceptionally, company law expressly turns this function into the primary goal by requiring the board to prioritise the shareholder interest,[48] it is still understood that this is merely a means to the end of increasing society's welfare through wealth production, including the provision of goods, services, jobs, and income.[49] Taking a step further

---

[47] Superficial conclusions may be based on textbook declarations of assumed purpose, without necessarily distinguishing between the business actors' typical intention with setting up a firm and the purpose of the company as we are discussing it here: see e.g. the discussion in Sjåfjell, *Sustainable Companies: Possibilities and Barriers in Norwegian Company Law*, s. 2.2; and in J. Andersson and F. Segenmark, *Mapping Paper on the Company Law Barriers and Possibilities for Sustainable Companies: Sweden*, Research Paper No. 2015–09 (University of Oslo Faculty of Law, 2013), available at: http://ssrn.com/abstract=2248584, s. 2.1. On the other hand, in Lithuania the shareholder profit conclusion is supported by proper analysis, namely of case law; shareholder profit is the aim of companies, according to company law in Lithuanian law: Lauraitytė and Miliauskas, *Sustainable Companies under the Lithuanian Company Law*, s. 2.1.

[48] As does the UK Companies Act, in spite of its broad inclusion of a number of interests, including the environment, that should be taken into account: C. Villiers, *Mapping Paper: Sustainable Companies UK Report*, Research Paper No. 2013–16, (University of Oslo Faculty of Law, 2013), available at: http://ssrn.com/abstract=2280350, s. 2.1.

[49] See e.g. the UK's Company Law Review, *Final Report* (June 2001) that stated at 1.12 that the main driver in drafting the reform proposals was 'to provide the means for effective collaborative business activity and in particular effective generation of wealth, in the broadest sense'. The summary at the beginning of the White Paper on *Modernising Company Law* (Cm 5553, July 2002) began with the statement that 'Company law is central to our prosperity'. The second White Paper on *Company Law Reform* (Cm 6456,

and considering the purpose of the company through the lens of our comparative company law analysis, we find it safe to say that no jurisdiction intends the maximisation of returns to shareholders to be the ultimate or only goal given to companies by the societies which through law recognise their existence.

The issue of the overarching purpose of the company of course is essentially a normative question. It must be determined based on a view of what the company is meant to do, on which interests are involved or affected and on how those various interests combine and relate to the common good. Political, cultural, and theoretical biases will influence our understanding of this concept. Our normative definition of the concept of the societal purpose of the company, inspired by our comparative analysis, is that it is to manage their businesses in a manner that creates benefits for investors, creditors, customers, employees, and local communities, in a way that contributes to or at least does not harm overarching societal goals such as sustainable development.

The core of the duty of the board across jurisdictions to promote and protect the interests of the company is somewhat easier to analyse on a comparative company law basis because it requires less extrapolation from company law to the broader societal context. In the analysis below, we concentrate on the interests of the company as the operational concept most directly relevant to the competence and duties of the company organs and thereby to the barriers and possibilities for sustainable companies. The significance of the ideologically-driven social norm of shareholder primacy will be a recurring topic.

3 The interests of the company, the business judgement rule, and shareholder primacy

3.1 Introduction

The concept of the interests of the company has traditionally been understood quite differently across jurisdictions, with continental European, civil law countries such as Germany, and Anglo-American, common law jurisdictions such as the USA and the UK, generally viewed as occupying opposite ends of a spectrum. That spectrum runs between pluralism,

---

March 2005) emphasised that the law should promote 'enterprise, growth and the right conditions for investment and employment'.

where a broader set of interests are encompassed by the interests of the company, and monism, which equates the interests of the company with the interests of the shareholders, denoted here as 'shareholder value'. In legal terms, this concept gives content to the core duty of the board, and so limits the discretion of the board in managing the company's business. While litigation to enforce the duty of promoting the interests of the company may face practically insurmountable hurdles, lack of enforcement does not in itself alter the nature of the legal obligation.[50] The few litigated cases, however, entail challenges in defining the boundaries of the interests of the company in terms of both what the board must do and what it may do.

The social norm of 'shareholder primacy', which insists that the board of directors and senior managers are the 'agents' of the shareholders and should maximise returns to shareholders as measured by the current share price, is not the legal position in any of the jurisdictions explored in this chapter. Even the apparently monistic common law jurisdictions that have an instrumental (or 'enlightened') shareholder value focus stop far short of requiring the board of directors to maximise returns to shareholders. We use 'shareholder value' as a label for the legal requirement in jurisdictions like the UK, and contrast it with 'shareholder primacy' as a social norm. As many other authors do not make this distinction, this makes a comparative legal analysis much more difficult, and our analysis should be read with this caveat.

A pluralist approach to the interests of the company either requires the board, or gives it discretion, to balance a variety of interests independent of the effect of this on shareholders.[51] Whichever approach is adopted, the legislator may or may not fix an order of priority between these different interests. In contrast, a monistic approach begins with this question of prioritisation, with priority obviously given to the one interest that the board is required to promote. As we can see from the UK's 'enlightened shareholder value' approach to the interests of the company, a monistic approach will, either explicitly or implicitly, include a variety of interests that must, should, or may be considered with the aim of promoting the

---

[50] See B. Sjåfjell, 'Quo vadis, Europe? The significance of sustainable development as objective, principle and rule of EU law', in C. Bailliet (ed.), *Non State Actors, Soft Law and Protective Regimes* (Cambridge University Press, 2012), s. 3.1.

[51] A pluralist and broad approach does not mean that the encompassed interests are easily identified. This may partly be explained by a fear of indicating a prioritisation where none is intended, and of delimiting against legitimate interests.

primary interest.[52] Where shareholder value remains implicit in case law rather than being explicitly stated in legislation, it is normally acceptable for boards to determine for themselves which interests to consider provided they can articulate a 'business case' for doing so. Accordingly, we can identify a spectrum of approaches from ultra-pluralist, which imposes an express duty to balance a range of interests, to ultra-monistic, where the identification and consideration of other interests are wholly left to the board's discretion. In Section 3.2 we will analyse the different approaches to the interests of the company that lie along this spectrum.

An important determinant of the extent to which the board's duty to act in the interests of the company can be enforced is the business judgement rule, which exists in stronger and weaker variants across the various jurisdictions we survey here. As our discussion in Section 3.3 shows, this legal concept, which was first explicitly formulated in the US state of Delaware, may be found in some form in most jurisdictions. Long implicit in case law in common law jurisdictions, it operates to encourage risk-taking by shielding the board against intrusive and retrospective review of its business decisions by the courts. Theoretically, a broad business judgement rule in monistic jurisdictions may give the board greater discretion to balance various interests than is apparent on the face of any legal statement of the board's duties. Thus, the scope of action for the board as a starting point may be quite similar in monistic and pluralist jurisdictions. Furthermore, where a board can plausibly argue that a particular course of action is likely to enhance returns to shareholders, this will in any jurisdiction increase their scope for taking account of other interests. However, it is commonly argued by advocates of shareholder primacy that, in order to ensure accountability, the board of directors should have only one master.[53] As we indicate in Section 3.4, the dominance of the ideology of shareholder primacy means that boards do not in the aggregate use the discretion they generally have across jurisdictions, or comply with the duty they have in some to promote and balance a plurality of interests. In Section 4, we therefore consider where shareholder primacy is leading us, taking account of the prospects for shareholder activism, both generally, and more specifically as regards environmental activism.

---

[52] UK Companies Act 2006 Section 172, criticised by E. Lynch, 'Section 172: a groundbreaking reform of director's duties, or the emperor's new clothes?' (2012) 33 (7) *Company Lawyer* 196.

[53] M. Jensen, *Value Maximization, Stakeholder Theory, and the Corporate Objective Function*, Working Paper 00–058 (Harvard Business School, 2011); J.F. Johnston, 'No man can serve two masters' (1998) *Social Affairs Unit Research Report* 25.

SHAREHOLDER PRIMACY 97

3.2 The board's duty or discretion to promote the interests of the company

3.2.1 Shareholder value

Traditionally, as Klaus Hopt points out, the UK and the USA are assumed to be the main bastions of shareholder value as a company law norm.[54] Shareholder value is also enshrined in company law in newer economies such as China,[55] Brazil,[56] Argentina,[57] and Taiwan,[58] in aspiring and relatively new EU Member States such as Turkey,[59] Poland,[60] and Lithuania,[61] and in common law countries like Ghana.[62] However, in, for example, China[63] and Brazil[64] there is a clear recognition that companies also have

---

[54] K. Hopt, 'Comparative corporate governance: the state of the art and international regulation', in Fleckner and Hopt, *Comparative Corporate Governance*, 10. See also Chapter 2 by David Millon in this book.

[55] J. Lou and L. Tian, *A Study on Sustainable Companies in the P.R. China*, Research Paper No. 2013–05 (University of Oslo Faculty of Law, 2013), available at: http://ssrn.com/abstract=2218284, ss. 2.1 and 2.1.3. See also J. Liu and K.B. Pissler, 'China: corporate governance of business organizations', in Fleckner and Hopt, *Comparative Corporate Governance*, 174–5.

[56] See N. Eizirik and A.C. Weber, 'Corporate governance of Brazil', in Fleckner and Hopt, *Comparative Corporate Governance*, 1021.

[57] R.A. Etcheverry and R.M. Manòvil, 'Corporate governance of Argentina', in Fleckner and Hopt, *Comparative Corporate Governance*, 975; D. Parravicini, *Sustainability and CSR in Argentina: An Analysis within Argentine Company Law*, Research Paper No. 2013–01 (University of Oslo Faculty of Law, 2013), available at: http://ssrn.com/abstract=2197774, s. 2.1

[58] See W.Y. Wang and W.R. Tseng, 'Corporate governance of Taiwan', in Fleckner and Hopt, *Comparative Corporate Governance*, 209 and 215.

[59] See M. Eroglu, *Obstacles and Possibilities for Sustainable Companies in Turkey*, Research Paper No. 2013–04 (University of Oslo Faculty of Law, 2013), available at: http://ssrn.com/abstract=2218220, 32.

[60] See K. Oplustil and A. Radwan, 'Company law in Poland: between autonomous development and legal transplants', in C. Jessel-Holst, R. Kulms, and A. Trunk (eds.), *Private Law in Eastern Europe: Autonomous Developments or Legal Transplants?* (Mohr Siebeck, 2011), 461.

[61] See Lauraitytè and Miliauskas, *Sustainable Companies under the Lithuanian Company Law*, s. 21.

[62] P. Schwartz, *Developing States and Climate Change: Solutions in Company Law?*, Research Paper No. 2013–15 (University of Oslo Faculty of Law, 2013), available at: http://ssrn.com/abstract=2275177, 11.

[63] Discussed further below; see text to note 83.

[64] Apparently quite similar also to the UK's 'enlightened shareholder value', Brazilian scholars argue that the board is to pursue the company's purpose of generating profits while taking into consideration the public at large and the company's social role. The social role is defined as, inter alia, environmental preservation: see Report of the Special Representative of the Secretary-General on the issue of human rights and transnational corporations and

a social role, and that shareholder value cannot be promoted exclusively. There is no jurisdiction of which the authors are aware that *requires* the board and senior managers to ignore other interests when running the company for the benefit of the shareholders. The monistic approach in common law jurisdictions is widely assumed to focus on the shareholders' interest, with the board of directors given discretion to take account of other interests only in so far as they hold out the prospect of enhancing returns to shareholders.[55] While Australia continues to use the original common law doctrine, and has explicitly rejected changes to the common law,[66] it has been supplemented, codified, or subtly altered in many other common law jurisdictions.[67]

Perhaps most famously, the majority of US states have, since the early 1980s, introduced provisions aiming to reinforce managerial discretion by allowing or requiring boards of directors to have regard to other concerns than the shareholder interest. While 41 states had enacted such a statute as of mid-2014, Delaware had not. Even so, there is virtually no legal authority for the proposition that directors must maximise shareholder wealth at the expense of competing nonshareholder considerations.[68] Writing extrajudicially, William Allen, formerly Chancellor of the Delaware Court of Chancery, has argued that the 'interests of the company as a whole' are better understood as distinct from the interests of the shareholders.[69] However, while directors owe their fiduciary duty of care and good faith

---

other business enterprises, John Ruggie, Addendum: Human rights and corporate law: trends and observations from a cross-national study conducted by the Special Representative (May 2011, A/HRC/17/31/Add.2), para. 72.

[65] See e.g. the English case of *Hutton v. West Cork Railway* (1883) 23 Ch D 654. For Australia, see Corporations and Market Advisory Committee (CAMAC), *The Social Responsibility of Corporations* (CAMAC, 2006), 92 and 103. For China, see M. Hansong, *Financial Enterprises Social Responsibility under the Perspective of Stakeholder Theory* (Morality and Civilization, 2010), 55, cited in Lou and Tian, *A Study on Sustainable Companies in the P. R. China*, s. 2.1.1.

[66] Deva, *Sustainable Business and Australian Corporate Law.*

[67] The Canadian case law suggests that management may take into account nonshareholder considerations such as the interests of the general community or the environment, if doing so would promote the success of the company, even if that would be to the detriment of the shareholders: *Peoples Department Stores Inc (Trustee of) v Wise*, 2004 SCC 28, [2004] 3 S.C.R. 461.

[68] See e.g. E. Elhauge, 'Sacrificing corporate profits in the public interest' (2005) 80(3) *New York University Law Review* 733; L. Stout, *The Shareholder Value Myth* (Berrett-Koehler Publishers, 2012); and D. Millon, 'Shareholder social responsibility' (2013) 36 *Seattle Law Review* 911.

[69] W.T. Allen, 'Our schizophrenic conception of the business corporation' (1992) 14 *Cardozo Law Review* 261, 274–6.

to the corporation and its shareholders, and not merely the interest of those who elected them,[70] the US courts do not recognise an enforceable duty towards other stakeholders in the corporation, except for creditors of insolvent corporations.[71] As we will see below, a strong business judgement rule means that the courts will almost always defer to the board's and management's decisions. While state law is moving in the direction of a more pluralist approach, management incentives and shareholder pressures, bolstered by the social norm of shareholder primacy, truncate in practice much of the discretion that the law creates.

In the UK, the Companies Act 2006 requires directors to act in the way they consider, 'in good faith, would be most likely to promote the success of the company for the benefit of its members as a whole', having regard to a non-exhaustive list of interests, including the 'likely consequences of any decision in the long term', employees, the environment, and the company's reputation.[72] The section was an important part of an attempt to enshrine 'enlightened shareholder value' at the heart of company law, in the belief that 'directors will be more likely to achieve long-term sustainable success for the benefit of their shareholders if their companies behave responsibly. Directors must therefore promote the success of the company in the collective best interest of shareholders, but must in doing so have regard to wider factors such as the interests of employees and the environment.'[73] The introduction of this section was more of a codification than a radical change to the law, and while the reformers went to great lengths to emphasise the business case for taking account of stakeholder interests, it is clear that pluralism was rejected in favour of shareholder value.[74] Johannes Heuschmid argues that the UK reform is a small step in the right direction.[75] However, we would suggest that the

---

[70] A.R. Pinto and F.A. Gevurtz, 'An overview of United States' corporate governance in publicly traded corporations', in Fleckner and Hopt, *Comparative Corporate Governance*, 1054 and 1059; *Katz v. Oak Indus., Inc.*, 508 A.2d 873 (Del. Ch. 1986).

[71] Pinto and Gevurtz, 'An overview of United States corporate governance in publicly traded corporations', 1059; e.g. *North American Catholic Educational Programming Foundation, Inc. v. Gheewalla*, 930 A.2d 92 (Del. 2007). A similar exception can be found in Australian law: see *Walker v. Wimborne* (1976) 137 CLR 1.

[72] Companies Act 2006 (UK), s. 172.

[73] See HC Deb., 11 July 2006, col 545, cited in Mukwiri, 'Myth of shareholder primacy', 230.

[74] See e.g. Department of Trade and Industry (DTI), *Modern Company Law for a Competitive Economy: Developing the Framework* (Department of Trade and Industry, 2000), Chapter 2.

[75] J. Heuschmid, 'The protection of workers under EU company law: the current position and future prospects', in S. Vitols and J. Heuschmid (eds.), *European Company Law and the*

reformers were overly influenced by arguments about agency cost and shareholder primacy, and, as Charlotte Villiers has also argued, the UK missed a rare opportunity to create a progressive and sustainable system of company law.[76] In other common law jurisdictions, such as Canada[77] and India,[78] a tendency towards a broader conception of the company interest is evident.[79]

Looking beyond common law jurisdictions, something akin to enlightened shareholder value can also be found in, for example, Portugal[80] and Spain.[81] Still, one of the strongest examples of shareholder influence can be found in China. In China, companies have an obligatory board of shareholders in addition to the management board and a supervisory board.[82] By virtue of this representation, it seems likely that the shareholder interest will be given preference over other stakeholder interests. This is confirmed by Jianbo Lou and Lei Tian, who classify China as a shareholder value jurisdiction.[83] Despite this shareholder value orientation, the concept of corporate social responsibility was introduced in 2005, leaving every

---

Sustainable Company: A Stakeholder Approach (European Trade Union Institute, 2012), 127.

[76] Villiers, *Mapping Paper: Sustainable Companies UK Report.*

[77] One Canadian case law decision states that 'the interests of the corporation' are broader than simply the financial interests of the shareholders, but the implications of this idea have not yet been worked out fully: *Peoples Department Stores Inc (Trustee of) v Wise*, 2004 SCC 28, [2004] 3 S.C.R. 461. For a helpful discussion, see C. Liao, *A Canadian Model of Corporate Governance: Insights from Canada's Leading Legal Practitioners* (Canadian Foundation for Governance Research, 2013), 10–13.

[78] See the new Companies Act which has several CSR-related provisions like a 2 per cent compulsory expenditure on CSR activities for large companies, referred to in S. Deva, 'Socially responsible business in India: has the elephant finally woken up to the tunes of international trends?' (2012) 41 *Common Law World Review* 299; See also *National Textile Workers' Union v. PR Ramakrishnan* (1983) S.C.R. (1) 922 at 943.

[79] For a nuanced comparative study of the common law jurisdictions, see C.M. Bruner, *Corporate Governance in the Common-Law World: The Political Foundations of Shareholder Power* (Cambridge University Press, 2013).

[80] Code of Commercial Companies, art. 64(1) (b), cited in J.M. Coutinho de Abreu, 'Portugal: synopsis on corporate governance', in Fleckner and Hopt, *Comparative Corporate Governance*, 795. Even though the wording of this article suggests a pluralist approach, Coutinho de Abreu argues that the shareholder interest still prevails over other interests (at 795–6).

[81] See E. Fernandez Rodriguez, S. Gomez-Anson, and A. Cuervo-Garcia, 'The stock market reaction to the introduction of best practices codes by Spanish firms' (2004) 12 *Corporate Governance: An International Review* 32, cited in J.A. Garcia-Cruces Gonzalez and I. Moralejo Menendez, 'Spain: listed companies' governance', in Fleckner and Hopt, *Comparative Corporate Governance*, 831 and 837.

[82] Liu and Pissler, 'China: corporate governance of business organizations', 161–2.

[83] Lou and Tian, *A Study on Sustainable Companies in the P. R. China*, sect. 2.1.1.

SHAREHOLDER PRIMACY

company engaging in business activity with a social responsibility.[84] This is reflected in the protection of stakeholders in both the Company Law of 2005 and other laws and regulations, where employees, creditors, governments, and society are included as matters that should be considered by the board.[85] Environmental protection is included as a public interest of society.[86] However, as Afra Afsharipour and Shruti Rana indicate, there is a long way to go before recent increases in CSR reporting translate into a reality of more environmentally and socially responsible business in China.[87]

Polish company law adopts a conventional shareholder focus, with the result that board and management may only lawfully consider stakeholder and environmental interests where they are relevant to producing returns for shareholders. While board and management have a broad legal discretion, these issues are rarely if ever litigated, and shareholder activism, while possible because of concentrated shareholdings, is rare.[88] However, remuneration of management board members follows US and Western European patterns,[89] encouraging the board to use their discretion to prioritise short-term shareholder value, and is justified by shareholder primacy ideology.

3.2.2   Pluralist approaches

At the opposite end of the spectrum from the common law shareholder value approach typified by the UK and, to a lesser extent, by the USA, we find those continental European jurisdictions, such as France, Germany, the Netherlands, as well as the Nordic countries, that favour a pluralist approach.

---

[84] Article 5 of the Company Law of 2005, see Liu and Pissler, 'China: corporate governance of business organizations', 202; Lou and Tian, *A Study on Sustainable Companies in the P. R. China*, 2.1.8.

[85] Lou and Tian, *A Study on Sustainable Companies in the P. R. China*, sect. 2.1.

[86] Lou and Tian, *A Study on Sustainable Companies in the P. R. China*, sect. 2.1.

[87] A. Afsharipour and S. Rana, 'The emergence of new corporate social responsibility regimes in China and India', (2014) 14, *UC Davis Business Law Journal*, 175–230, 205–—. See also L.-W. Lin, 'Corporate social responsibility in China: window dressing or structural change?' (2010) 28 (1), *Berkeley Journal of International Law*, 64–100.

[88] S. Soltysinski, 'Poland: corporate governance of joint-stock companies', in Fleckner and Hopt, *Comparative Corporate Governance*, 776. See also K. Oplustil and A. Radwan, 'Company law in Poland: between autonomous development and legal transplants', in C. Jessel-Holst, R. Kulms, and A. Trunk (eds.), *Private Law in Eastern Europe: Autonomous Developments or Legal Transplants?* (Mohr Siebeck, 2011), 430, 453–5.

[89] Soltysinski, 'Poland: Corporate governance of joint-stock companies', 772.

However, the pluralist approach is far from uniform. Some jurisdictions explicitly provide that the board must act in the interest of the company and its enterprise, understood as acting in the interest of all stakeholders and to a more or less clear extent including an interest of the enterprise in itself.[90] Others do not explicitly address the concept of 'company interest' at all, though by digging a little deeper we find support for a broader pluralist approach.[91] Finally, some pluralist jurisdictions emphasise one or more stakeholder groups, either in law or through social norms. Japan has a strong social norm that management should take account of employees, focusing on their benefits and rights. As that social norm operates within the scope of board and management discretion, it is under pressure from Anglo-American-style corporate governance codes that emphasise the primacy of shareholders and support the social norm of shareholder primacy.[92]

Under a pluralist approach, all stakeholder interests can or should be taken into account, and, in its purest form, this approach does not endorse any prioritisation of interests of stakeholders in relation to one another. Perhaps the most famous example of pluralism in its purest form is to be found in Germany, where the concept of the company interest has traditionally been, and still is, broader than the interests of the shareholders, also including the interest of the enterprise in itself, the employees, and public welfare. This broad conception of company interest was expressly stipulated in the so-called public welfare clause

[90] See e.g. the Netherlands, Art. 140, Book 2 of the Dutch Civil Code ('DCC'), supported by a recent Supreme Court case, ABN AMRO (JOR 2007, 178); J. Van Bekkum, et al., 'Netherlands: corporate governance in the Netherlands', in Fleckner and Hopt, Comparative Corporate Governance, 654, 655; Austria, Stock Corporation Act (Aktiengesetz, 'AktG') s. 70, which 'stipulates that the management board shall endeavor to promote the welfare of the company, taking into account the interests of the shareholders and the employees as well as the public interest', see S. Kalss, 'Austria: legal framework of corporate governance', in Fleckner and Hopt, Comparative Corporate Governance, 287.

[91] See e.g. B. Sjåfjell and C. Kjelland, 'Norway: corporate governance on the outskirts of the EU', in Fleckner and Hopt, Comparative Corporate Governance, 710, 722; Mähönen, 'Finland: corporate governance', 413.

[92] Japan's New Corporate Governance Principles of 2006 emphasise that corporate governance is intended to 'ensure company officers entrusted with responsibilities by shareholders fulfil the entrusted responsibilities', namely 'increasing long-term shareholder value': Japan Corporate Governance Forum (JCGF), 'New Corporate Governance Principles', General Rules, para 1.1, and see Nakamura, 'Japan: listed companies' corporate governance', in Fleckner and Hopt, Comparative Company Law, 233. However, recent research suggests that hedge funds have been unsuccessful in forcing shareholder primacy on Japanese management: J. Buchanan, D. Heesang Chai, and S. Deakin, Hedge Fund Activism in Japan: The Limits of Shareholder Primacy (Cambridge University Press, 2012).

SHAREHOLDER PRIMACY

of the Stock Corporation Act ('AktG') of 1937, but not included in the AktG 1965, apparently without this entailing any significant change in the law.[93]

While some voices in Germany argue in favour of 'shareholder value',[94] most German legal scholars offer a pluralist interpretation of *Unternehmensinteresse*.[95] That approach focuses on all interests that coincide in the German AktG.[96] Support for pluralism is found in the 2009 amendments to the German Corporate Governance Code,[97] though, unsurprisingly, as part of an international trend, the Code also encourages companies to adopt many of the instruments of shareholder primacy.[98] *Unternehmensinteresse* may also be said to be institutionalised in the German political economy through employee co-determination and works councils,[99] as it is in a number of other continental European countries[100] and to a lesser extent at the EU level. Of course, as David Millon points out in Chapter 2 in this volume, a focus on employee interests does not necessarily entail a broader consideration of environmental

---

[93] B. Grunewald, *Gesellschaftsrecht* (6th edn, Mohr Siebeck, 2005), p. 253. It has been suggested that an express formulation of the company interest was not necessary in the AktG 1965 because it was deemed to be obvious and therefore did not need to be specified. Also, there was concern that the order of interests might be perceived as a prioritisation, see A. Schall, L. Miles, and S. Goulding 'Promoting an inclusive approach on the part of the directors: the UK and German positions' (2006) 6 *Journal of Corporate Law Studies*, 308.

[94] P.O. Mülbert 'Marktwertmaximierung als Unternehmensziel der Aktiengesellschaft', in G. Crezelius, H. Hirte, and K. Vieweg (eds.), *Festschrift für Volker Röhrict* (OVS Verlag, 2005).

[95] H. Fleischer, *Handbuch des Vorstandsrechts* (Verlag C.H.Beck, 2006), s. 1, Rn 30; G Spindler, *Unternehmensinteresse als Leitlinie des Vorstandshandelns – Berücksichtigung von Arbeitnehmerinteressen und Shareholder Value* (Gutachten im Auftrag der Hans-Böckler-Stiftung, 2008).

[96] For further references and information, see Deipenbrock, *The Management Board of a German Aktiengesellschaft*, p. 11 f.

[97] See Article 4.1.1 of the Corporate Governance Code, which states: 'The board is responsible for independently managing the company in the interests of the company, that is, taking account of the interests of the shareholders, its employees and other stakeholders, with the objective of sustainable creation of value'. This amendment of the Corporate Governance Code was to strengthen stakeholder interests in order to meet 'public criticism of capitalism'; see www.corporate-governance-code.de.

[98] Heuschmid, 'The protection of workers under EU company law'.

[99] Albeit that co-determination is limited to the larger companies: Heuschmid, 'The protection of workers under EU company law'.

[100] Most countries that adopt a pluralist approach to the interests of the company mandate some level of employee participation in board decision-making, though there are vast differences in national approaches.

interests. Support for the inclusion of environmental interests therefore usually needs to be found elsewhere.[101]

In the Netherlands, exceptionally, the role of the works council also includes an environmental duty of care; it has 'to do everything in its power to promote environmental care on the part of the enterprise, including the taking or changing of policy-related, organisational or administrative measures relating to the natural environment'.[102] As argued by Tineke Lambooy, the works council can limit its environmental duty of care to the company's impact on the Dutch environment, or broaden this to 'the worldwide impact of the company's activities on nature and ecosystems services'.[103] The Netherlands is also a clearer example of the pluralist approach to the duties of the board. The board is required to act in the interest of the company and its enterprise,[104] understood to mean 'to act in the interest of all stakeholders', with the Supreme Court confirming that shareholder interests 'do not take priority over the interests of other stakeholders'.[105] This approach is also taken in the Dutch corporate governance code, the *Frijns* Code, of 2008, which provides that the management board is accountable to the supervisory board and to the general meeting, and should be 'guided by the interests of the company and its affiliated enterprise, taking into consideration the interests of the company's stakeholders'.[106]

Originally influenced by Dutch company law, Indonesian company law is an example of a shift towards a broader pluralistic approach as a matter of law on the books, with company law reforms undertaken with the aim of stimulating corporate social responsibility. The Indonesian Act regulating private companies sets out in its general provisions that social and

---

[101] For example, s. 87 I 2 AktG introducing sustainable development as a concept in German Aktienrecht, referred to by Deipenbrock, *The Management Board of a German Aktiengesellschaft*, p. 12 f.

[102] See the Dutch Works Council Act (DWCA), Art. 28 (4); see further T. Lambooy, 'A model code on co-determination and CSR. The Netherlands and CSR: A bottom-up approach', (2011) 8 (2–3), *European Company Law*, 74–82.

[103] Lambooy, 'A model code on co-determination and CSR'.

[104] While Dutch company law long has specified that 'the supervisory board members shall focus on the interest of the company and the connected enterprise', this was also codified for the management board in 2013, see further Lambooy, *The Possibilities for and Barriers to Sustainable Companies in Dutch Company Law*, mapping paper (Sustainable Companies Project, 2013), s. 2.1.

[105] van Bekkum, *et al.*, 'Netherlands: corporate governance in the Netherlands', 654–5.

[106] Principle II. For an in-depth discussion concerning Dutch corporate law and CSR issues, see T. Lambooy, *Corporate Social Responsibility: Legal and Semi-legal Frameworks Supporting CSR* (Kluwer, 2010), Chapter 3.

SHAREHOLDER PRIMACY 105

environmental responsibility 'shall be a commitment of the company to taking part in sustainable economic development in order to enhance the quality of life and environment'.[107] More specific requirements are made of companies in the field of natural resources.[108] However, due to a lack of clear definition of what this responsibility entails, among other things, these reforms are regarded as ineffective.[109] They do provide interesting examples of a legislative willingness to take new steps, however.

In the Nordic region, there is no uniform approach to the issue of the interests of the company. A thorough analysis of the legal sources of Norwegian company law indicates that Norway conceives of the company interest in a pluralist way in the purest sense, with no ex ante prioritisation of any of the interests, and the economic interest of the enterprise itself as the balancing point.[110] Environmental protection is arguably also making its way into the set of protected interests included in the interests of the company, and is certainly an interest that the board can legitimately consider. Indeed, boards are clearly being encouraged to do so.[111] In Denmark, Erik Werlauff advances a strongly pluralist view, but his is probably a minority view.[112] However, we can say that Denmark takes a pluralist approach to the interests of the company, albeit that its scope is not well defined.[113] Danish law gives the board scope to take account

---

[107] Limited Liability Company Law Article 1(3), A.F. Sukmono, 'The legal framework of CSR in Indonesia', in T.E. Lambooy, et al., (eds.), *CSR in Indonesia: Legislative Developments and Case Studies* (Konstitutisi Press, 2013), Chapter 2.

[108] Sukmono, 'The legal framework of CSR in Indonesia'.

[109] B. Sujayadi and F. Kurniawan, *Mapping on Indonesian Company Law*, mapping paper (Sustainable Companies Project, 2011).

[110] See Sjåfjell, *Sustainable Companies: Possibilities and Barriers in Norwegian Company Law*, s. 2.3.

[111] Through the environmental reporting requirement in Norway's Annual Accounts Act, which aims to internalise environmental externalities in the decision-making of the board, and reduce the negative environmental impact of the company year by year, see Sjåfjell, *Sustainable Companies: Possibilities and Barriers in Norwegian Company Law*.

[112] E. Werlauff, *Selskabsmasken: Loyalitetspligt og generalklausul i selskabsretten* (Gad, 1991), 70–2. He defines the interest of the company as 'the company's urge, on behalf of a number of involved interested parties, to preserve and augment those interests of capital and income belonging to the protected parties'; quote from the English summary, E. Werlauff, *Selskabsmasken* (Gad, 1991), 585.

[113] H. Lando, 'Shareholder eller stakeholder value? – En retsøkonomisk analyse af loyalitetspligten i aktieselskaber', (2001) 3(1) *Nordisk Tidsskrift for Selskabsret* 76; K. Dichow Blangsted, 'Interessesubjekter i selskabsretten – i et corporate governance perspektiv' (2001) 3 *Nordisk Tidsskrift for Selskabsret* 277, cited in K. Bühmann, et al., *Mapping of Danish Law Related to Companies' Impact on Environment and Climate Change*, Working

106   B. SJÅFJELL, A. JOHNSTON, L. ANKER-SØRENSEN, D. MILLON

of environmental concerns where there is a business case for doing so; the discretion may also extend beyond business case scenarios, an extension influenced by Denmark's CSR reporting requirements,[114] which are regarded by some commentators as quite progressive.[115] In contrast, Jukka Mähönen shows through an analysis of the legal sources that Finland has shifted from a pluralist to an enlightened shareholder value approach.[116] The same may be said of Sweden, where the in-depth discussion by Rolf Dotevall of the interests of the company may serve to illustrate the originally strong influence of the German *Unternehmensinteresse* in Nordic company law.[117]

As elsewhere in the world, all Nordic jurisdictions, under investor pressure, have introduced corporate governance codes that aim to encourage 'best practice'.[118] In doing so, they treat members of the board as 'agents' of the shareholders[119] as opposed to what is generally the case in Nordic company law.[120] This strong emphasis on accountability to shareholders, coupled with the language of shareholder primacy and the provision of high-powered incentives to the board and senior managers, is slowly moving the practice of pluralist systems towards compliance with the

---

Paper No. 10–36 (Nordic & European Company Law, 2013), 2. 2.1.1. By contrast, see S. Friis Hansen and J. Valdemar Krenchel, *Dansk Selskabsret – Kapitalselskaber* (Karnov Group, 2011), 50–2.

[114] Buhmann, et al., *Mapping of Danish Law Related to Companies' Impact on Environment and Climate Change*, s. 2.2.4. Danish corporate governance contains some CSR elements and also has recommendations on risk assessment that, according to Buhmann and others, include environmental risks (at s. 2.3).

[115] However, Sjåfjell is less enthusiastic about the game-changer effect of this type of regulation, which has also been introduced in Norway, see e.g. B. Sjåfjell, 'Why law matters: corporate social irresponsibility and the futility of voluntary climate change mitigation' (2001) 8(2–3) *European Company Law* 56.

[116] As noted by Mähönen, 'the similarity between the (Finnish) approach and the "enlightened shareholder value" ideology behind the 2006 Companies Act is remarkable': Mähönen, *Sustainable Companies Mapping Paper on Company Law Issues: Finland*, s. 2.1.

[117] R. Dotevall, *Bolagsledningens skadeståndsansvar* (2nd edn., Norstedts Juridik, 2008); Andersson and Segenmark, *Mapping Paper on the Company Law Barriers and Possibilities for Sustainable Companies*, s. 2.1.

[118] See S. Thomsen 'The hidden meaning of codes: corporate governance and investor rent seeking' (2006) 7 *European Business Organization Law Review* 845, 849–51. Thomsen even claims that the codes lack a 'theoretical or empirical rationale', to the extent that they are 'unlikely to do much good (and if so only by accident)' (at 846).

[119] Mähönen, 'Finland: corporate governance', 405.

[120] Exceptionally, in Finland, in the preparatory works of the Companies Acts, directors are denoted agents of shareholders, see Mähönen, *Sustainable Companies Mapping Paper on Company Law Issues: Finland*, s. 2.1.

SHAREHOLDER PRIMACY 107

social norm of shareholder primacy, even if the law on the books remains pluralist.[121] Under these codes and incentives, members of the board and senior managers simply do not use the discretion given to them by law to balance the various interests which are at stake. The trend towards inclusion of CSR in the corporate governance codes is not sufficient to counterbalance this.[122]

In France, in companies with a one-tier board, the managers (*les dirigeants*) are expected to manage the company in pursuit of *l'intérêt social* under the oversight of the powerful Président-Directeur-Général, with the remainder of the board (*le conseil d'administration*) determining strategy and overseeing its implementation. However, the meaning of *l'intérêt social* is highly contested, and the law is inconsistent.[123] Those taking a shareholder primacy approach have been bolstered by the arrival of Anglo-American corporate governance norms, including takeover regulation and incentive pay for executives, which are likely to limit the prospects of the *conseil d'administration* and the *dirigeants* taking a longer-term or pluralist approach to decision-making. However, the *Grenelle II* reforms demonstrate that concerns about sustainable development are also influencing policy, and corporate disclosures made in accordance with this law might allow stakeholders to put pressure on management.[124]

3.2.3 Group interest

In the context of corporate groups, a core question is whether a group interest can be recognised as an exemption from the general company law principle of separate legal entities and the duty of the board to promote the individual company's interest.[125] As we noted above, the shareholder interest is directly or indirectly included in the single company's interest. The board of a subsidiary is therefore normally obliged (also) to promote

---

[121] Mähönen, 'Finland: corporate governance', 440.

[122] See Sjåfjell and Anker-Sørensen, 'Directors' duties and corporate social responsibilities (CSR)', Chapter 7.

[123] For a helpful overview, see I. Tchotourian, 'Management renewal? Consequences of the new conception of the "best interests of the corporation' in North American and French Corporate Law' (unpublished, 2008); available at: https://papyrus.bib.umontreal .ca/jspui/bitstream/1866/2614/1/TextITchotourian.pdf.

[124] I. Tchotourian, 'Is corporate CSR reporting an expression of "law's being" or of lobbying? How much power does law really have? Debates and criticism around the latest French reform' (unpublished, 2012); available at: http://ssrn.com/abstract=2115845.

[125] Various jurisdictions apply various definitions and concepts in order to define a group. In our context, we only focus on the concept of 'group interest' without further discussion of legal or factual criteria.

the interest of the parent as a shareholder. Promoting the interest of the parent as shareholder will often lead to a promotion of a group interest. In other words, whether seen as a promotion of a shareholder interest included in the subsidiary's own interest, such as the situation is in Norway,[126] Sweden,[127] Denmark,[128] and Australia[129] or denoted as a concurrence of interests, as in the Netherlands,[130] many of the issues of promoting a group interest are resolved merely through the promotion of the subsidiary's interest. However, this would only apply in as far as the group interest is the same as the parent company's interest, and promoting this interest is not to the detriment of the subsidiary's own interest. The issue thereby comes to a head where the group interest is in conflict with the interest of the individual company, whether that of the parent or, more practically, the subsidiary. We will concentrate on the latter issue, namely whether there is recognition of a group interest that translates into a duty or discretion for the board of the subsidiary to promote the interest of the group even where that is not in the subsidiary's own interest. This can be found for subsidiaries without minority shareholders, as in, for example, Germany, where the law allows the subsidiary board to promote a group interest if related losses are 'equivalently compensated';[131] Turkey, which requires a 'pre-determined group policy' with a parallel parental liability scheme;[132] and China, where a group is required to have 'articles of association of the group as the common behavior criteria'.[133]

---

[126] In corporate practice, however, the tendency may be for boards of subsidiaries to see themselves as a part of a group without being aware of the legal responsibility they have as boards of an individual company. This cannot be an argument for changing the law to fit with practice unless one simultaneously addresses the issue of group liability, which is very unlikely to happen.

[127] Andersson and Segenmark, *Mapping Paper on the Company Law Barriers and Possibilities for Sustainable Companies*, s. 6.3.

[128] Buhmann, *et al.*, *Mapping: Denmark*, s. 6.2.

[129] *Equiticorp Finance Ltd v. Bank of New Zealand* (1993) 11 ACLC 952.

[130] S.M. Bartman, 'From autonomy of interests to concurrence of interests in Dutch group company law' (2007) 4(5) *European Company Law* 207.

[131] Sections 311 and §§ 317 f., AktG, see S. Grundmann, *European Company Law* (Intersentia, 2011), 722. However, the parent can only be held liable on a case-by-case basis where the claimant succeeds in providing proof of a detrimental parental interference, and a causal link between this interference and the damages or losses sustained by the subsidiary, see Reich-Graefe, 'Changing paradigms: the liability of corporate groups in Germany', pp. 791–2.

[132] Companies Act, Art. 203; Eroglu, *Obstacles and Possibilities for Sustainable Companies in Turkey*, p. 52.

[133] Measures for the Administration of Finance Companies of Enterprise Groups, Art. 3; see Lou and Tian, *A Study on Sustainable Companies in the P. R. China*, s. 6.1.

The German *Konzernrecht* has inspired other jurisdictions to regulate groups, and versions of the German understanding of group interest can be found, for example, in Slovenia[134] and Hungary.[135]

In contrast to the strict compensation regime in Germany, the French *Rozenblum* doctrine obliges the board of a subsidiary to further a group interest if four conditions are met: 'the group has to be structurally solid, the individual acts have to follow a coherent strategy of the group, it has to be expected that the single member of the group affected does not systematically have only disadvantages but that it also has advantages from this strategy and that at least its existence is not endangered'.[136] Consequently, if these conditions are met, the board of the subsidiary must direct the company in the direction laid out by the parent, even if that would harm the subsidiaries' creditors or employees in the short term.[137] The Italian model is arguably somewhere in between the above approaches: the law recognises a general group interest, but concurrently requests consideration of losses that have occurred and potential gains from synergies, and stipulates that the result should not be worse than without the group effects.[138] Similarly, in the Netherlands, the interest of the group could prevail if the synergies of being an affiliated company are profitable.[139]

In the EU, discussion of whether the concept of group policy or group interest should be recognised has flared up several times. The Commission-appointed High Level Group of Company Law Experts, chaired by Jaap Winter, suggested in 2002 that a parent company should be allowed to adopt and implement a co-ordinated group policy.[140] This advice was not followed. Based on the report from the Commission-appointed Reflection Group on the Future of European Company Law,[141]

---

[134] Companies Act, Art. 527; see J. Zrilič, *Mapping Paper on the Barriers and Possibilities for Integrating Environmental Sustainability into Slovenian Company Law* (Sustainable Companies Project, 2011), s. 5.1.

[135] Companies Act, Art. 56(3)(c), for the recognised group, and Art. 64(1)–(4), for the de facto group, referred to in P.J. Nikolicza, 'Hungary: corporate governance of listed companies', in Fleckner and Hopt, *Comparative Company Law*, 589.

[136] Grundmann, *European Company Law*, p. 722.

[137] Grundmann, *European Company Law*, p. 722.

[138] Grundmann, *European Company Law*, p. 773.

[139] Lambooy, *The Possibilities for and Barriers to Sustainable Companies in Dutch Company Law*, s. 6.1.

[140] J. Winter, *Report of the High Level Group of Company Law Experts on a Modern Regulatory Framework for Company Law in Europe* (European Commission, 2002), p. 96.

[141] Reflection Group, *Report of the Reflection Group on the Future of EC Company Law* (European Commission, April 2011).

B. SJÅFJELL, A. JOHNSTON, L. ANKER-SØRENSEN, D. MILLON

the most recent Action Plan from the Commission includes this topic as something that requires further investigation.[142]

3.2.4 Are we witnessing a convergence? If so, on what?

Not least in our context, a dynamic, forward-looking interpretation is arguably called for, rather than a retrospective, static view of the law.[143] As Benjamin Cardozo famously put it, 'Law never is, it is always about to be.'[144] In our context we may say that the concept of company interest is what society, notably through law, decides that the company interest should be. In that light, it is very interesting to note the two apparently opposing tendencies that we have identified in the above sections.

The first is the growing trend to prioritise shareholder interests in the conception of the company interest. In the Nordic countries, the formulation of the company interest may seem to be moving from a pluralist, continental European position towards a conception of the company interest that is much closer to the shareholder value approach taken by common law jurisdictions.[145] Certainly corporate practice and attitudes among commentators are influenced by and support the shareholder primacy drive. Case law distinguishing between the interests of the company and the interests of shareholders is regarded as surprising, and preparatory works referring to the interests of employees and local communities are perceived as old-fashioned and without significance.

The second trend is the growing societal awareness that companies have a significant impact on invaluable public goods, such as the global climate, as well as other 'social' interests. We are seeing an increasing inclination to include consideration of such interests in legislation,[146] as well as references to them in the corporate governance codes that are the hallmark of

---

[142] COM (2012) 740 final, sect. 4.6.

[143] The dynamic, teleological method of EU law may as such be an example to follow also outside the areas that are directly regulated by EU law, see Sjåfjell, 'Quo vadis, Europe?'

[144] The quote continues: 'It is realized only when embodied in a judgment, and in being realized expires': B. Cardozo, *The Nature of the Judicial Process* (Yale University Press, 1921), 126.

[145] This is perhaps especially clear in Finnish company law, see Mähönen, *Sustainable Companies Mapping Paper on Company Law Issues: Finland*, s. 2.1.

[146] Typically in new CSR and environmental reporting requirements, which on their own are insufficient.

the social norm of shareholder primacy.[147] While ethical norms may have been relevant to company law discussion in the past without clarity as to their content and impact,[148] the reference to them in soft-law instruments such as the OECD Guidelines for Multinational Enterprises[149] and the UN Guiding Principles on Business and Human Rights[150] is codifying and strengthening their position.[151] This growing awareness is also illustrated and supported by the shift in the EU's CSR definition away from the 'business-as-usual', marketing-friendly approach of treating it as a voluntary matter unconnected with companies' actual operations towards a broader, more inclusive, and more demanding definition. This defines sees CSR as companies' responsibility for their 'impacts on society', and requires an integration of 'social, environmental, ethical, human rights and consumer concerns into their business operations and core strategy'.[152] Although the EU Commission does not clarify how this responsibility is to be upheld and enforced, let alone its limits, and clearly stops short of setting out or proposing any enforceable legal duties,[153] growing societal awareness of these issues could inspire further reform.

In addition, in certain countries, there may be a growing tendency for shareholders to use their power not only through the dominant form of shareholder activism with its short-term, profit-maximising focus, but also for environmental and social reasons.[154] Environmental and broader CSR reporting requirements, especially those mandated by law, though insufficient on their own, do have the potential together with other initiatives to influence the ways in which the company interest is understood in some jurisdictions.[155]

---

[147] See D.G. Szabò and K. Engsig Sørensen, 'Integrating corporate social responsibility in corporate governance codes in the EU' (2013) 24(6) *European Business Law Review* 781.

[148] See Sjåfjell, *Sustainable Companies: Possibilities and Barriers in Norwegian Company Law*.

[149] *OECD Guidelines for Multinational Enterprises*, revised in 2011, available at: www.oecd .org/corporate/mne (see especially Chapter VI, Environment).

[150] *UN Guiding Principles for Business and Human Rights*, available at: www.business-humanrights.org/Documents/UNNorms.

[151] Over 40 countries and the EU have adhered to the OECD Guidelines.

[152] Sjåfjell and Anker-Sørensen, 'Directors' duties and corporate social responsibility'.

[153] Sjåfjell and Anker-Sørensen, 'Directors' duties and corporate social responsibility'.

[154] For example, Sjåfjell and Kjelland, 'Norway: corporate governance on the outskirts of the EU', 742; Hill, 'Australia: the architecture of corporate governance', s. III B 2; Liu and Pissler, 'China: corporate governance of business organizations', s. II B 4.

[155] See, for a further discussion of the relevance and impact of reporting requirements, Chapter 5 by Villiers and Mähönen in this book.

112   B. SJÅFJELL, A. JOHNSTON, L. ANKER-SØRENSEN, D. MILLON

In order to understand the extent to which a pluralist approach to the interests of the company can be translated into decision-making oriented to sustainability, two further issues must be explored. The first is the extent to which management or board decisions are scrutinised by the courts, in the event that litigation is brought. The second is the impact of the social norm of shareholder primacy in putting pressure on boards and managers to prioritise maximisation of short-term returns for shareholders, regardless of the company law duties of the board and management or the discretion the law gives them on how to act. These issues are discussed in the next two subsections of this chapter.

3.3   Directors' liability and the business judgement rule

In addition to their core duty to act in the interests of the company, members of the board of directors and senior managers normally owe duties of loyalty and care and skill to the companies that they direct.[156] The duty of loyalty (or fiduciary duty) prohibits members of the board and senior managers from self-dealing and profiting from their position, requiring them to prefer the interests of the company to their own. This duty is imposed to protect the interests of the company, and the shareholders who expect to share in its profits, against the possibility of directors abusing their power. As such, the duty is crucial for rendering members of the board liable for conferring benefits on themselves. The duty of loyalty operates to catch the worst examples of fraud, but does not say anything about the intensity with which the board pursues the generation of shareholder value. The duty of care and skill requires the board and senior managers to apply themselves to their roles with reasonable diligence and ability, taking account of their experience and the role they perform.

The power to litigate for a breach of duty is usually vested in the board of directors,[157] but most jurisdictions allow shareholders to enforce the

---

[156] See Oplustil and Radwan, 'Company law in Poland', where the issues of duty of loyalty are discussed (pp. 482–3) and the business judgement rule (pp. 483–4); Lou and Tian, *A Study on Sustainable Companies in the P. R. China*, s. 2.2.7.1; Lauraityte and Miliauskas, *Sustainable Companies under the Lithuanian Company Law*, s. 2.2.3; Parravicini, *Sustainability and CSR in Argentina: An Analysis Within Argentine Company Law*, s. 2.2.4.

[157] Exceptionally, Brazil appears to vest this decision in the general meeting, see Eizirik and Weber, 'Brazil: new developments in corporate governance', 1027.

company's rights on its behalf,[158] subject to certain safeguards,[159] or to sue members of the board or senior managers for harm caused to the company in breach of duty.[160] However, many jurisdictions have a business judgement rule (BJR) which marks out an area of decision-making free from interference by the courts. This rule has little or no impact on litigation in relation to the duty of loyalty, which often makes members of the board and senior managers strictly liable for profiting from their position or having a conflict of interest. However, the BJR makes litigation in relation to whether a particular decision was in the interests of the company very unlikely in most jurisdictions. A reason for this is that the law recognises that discretion for the decision-makers is at the heart of the firm. Hence, board and senior managers need to be able to take decisions safe in the knowledge that courts will not second-guess those decisions with the benefit of hindsight. Another effect of the BJR is that the duty of care and skill rarely if ever arises in private legal proceedings between companies and their board or senior managers concerning the quality of corporate decisions. Duty of care claims tend to arise in the context of liquidators or regulators bringing proceedings against board and senior management for failing to consider the interests of creditors when taking decisions,[161] or liquidators or regulators bringing proceedings against the board for failing to exercise adequate (or, indeed, any) oversight over the activities of senior management.[162] In restricting the scope of the duty of care, the BJR shows that the law recognises that it is a core function of the board and management to identify investment projects, which necessarily entails the risk that they will not succeed as expected. As such, it is inappropriate to use the duty of care to hold these groups liable if their decisions are not successful.

In what follows, we show that many legal systems expressly shield the board of directors from liability for good faith business decisions, giving

---

[158] This is the situation in France, see for example, 'France: the permanent reform of corporate governance', 491. Exceptionally, the Netherlands does not allow shareholders to bring either a direct or a derivative action against the directors: Bekkum, *et al.*, 'Netherlands: corporate governance in the Netherlands', 660.

[159] See e.g. Deva, *Sustainable Business and Australian Corporate Law*, s. IV; Clarke, *Irish Company Law Mapping Paper*, s. 4.1.

[160] See e.g. Lauraitytė and Miliauskas, *Sustainable Companies under the Lithuanian Company Law*, s. 4.1. In Turkey, shareholders can sue directors for indirect damage: Eroglu, *Obstacles and Possibilities for Sustainable Companies in Turkey*, s. A 9.

[161] See the UK Insolvency Act 1986, s. 214; Australia's Corporations Act 2001, s. 588G.

[162] For an example, see the case of *Australian Securities and Investments Commission v. Macdonald (No 11)* [2009] NSWSC 287.

the board a margin of discretion free from review by the courts.[163] The term 'business judgement rule' was first used in the USA to describe the courts' policy of non-intervention, though all common law jurisdictions share a strong and long-standing aversion to judicial intervention in management decision-making, stretching back to the courts' expectation that matters of internal management in partnerships would be dealt with by means of majority rule.[164] Delaware case law has driven the development of the BJR, with the courts applying: 'a presumption that in making a business decision the directors of a corporation acted on an informed basis, in good faith and in the honest belief that action taken was in the best interests of the company'.[165] Beyond the common law world, Gerner-Beuerle and Schuster argue that doctrines or rules similar to the Delaware BJR can be found in several European jurisdictions, albeit in varying forms.[166] The analysis that follows shows that jurisdictions differ with regard to the intensity with which courts scrutinise the board's decision-making.

Common law countries typically give the board of directors the broadest margin of discretion, though there are important differences between them. However, there is pressure to adopt a similar approach in some emerging economies.[167] Delaware's procedural approach has driven the development of the business judgement rule in the USA. Under Delaware company law, the courts will not interfere with a decision unless a shareholder plaintiff can show that the directors did not in good faith believe it to be in the long-term interests of the company; or that it was not based on relevant information; or that it was tainted by conflict of interest or bad faith.[168] The BJR thus functions both as a shield against liability and also as a presumption of appropriate conduct. A shareholder seeking to challenge a board decision must dispute the decision

---

[163] We still find examples of jurisdictions where the concept of the BJR is not developed clearly, such as Taiwan: see Wang and Tseng, 'Corporate governance of Taiwan', 13, and in China, where there is no formal BJR and the concept does not appear to have been developed judicially: Liu and Pissler, 'Corporate governance of business organizations', 174.

[164] K.W. Wedderburn, 'Shareholders' rights and the rule in Foss v Harbottle' (1957) 15 *Cambridge Law Journal* 194, 197–8.

[165] *Aronson v. Lewis*, 473 A 2.d 805, 812 (Del. 1984).

[166] For example, Croatian Companies Act, s. 252(1); German Stock Corporations Act, s. 93(1); Greek Codified Law 2190/1920, Art. 22a; Portuguese Commercial Company Act, Art. 72(2); see further Gerner-Beuerle and Schuster, 'Mapping directors' duties in Europe', 9–10.

[167] In H. Birkmose, M. Neville and K.Engsig Sørensen (eds), *Boards of Directors in European Companies*, (Kluwer Law International 2013), Liu and Pissler, 'Corporate governance of business organizations', 174.

[168] *Aronson v. Lewis*, 373 A2d 805 (Del. 1984); see Chapter 2 by Millon in this book.

process (focusing on matters such as adequacy of information or conflict of interest) rather than the substance of the decision in question.[169] Because of this emphasis on process and the presumption of proper conduct, Delaware's BJR provides disinterested directors with very broad protection. A similar procedural approach is also taken in, for example, Japan[170] and South Africa.[171]

In contrast, the UK has no formal BJR, either in statute or at common law, and the Company Law Review that preceded the 2006 legislation opposed a legislative BJR. However, the courts have traditionally 'shown a proper reluctance to enter into the merits of commercial decisions',[172] and subject decisions only to a test of subjective good faith. Section 172 of the Companies Act 2006 explicitly requires directors to take account of environmental impacts, along with other matters such as employee interests, in deciding how to promote the success of the company for the benefit of shareholders. The duty requires boards to at least try to anticipate the environmental consequences of their decisions within the limits of the information available to them.[173] However, the way in which a company trades off, say, employment and environmental considerations would not be justiciable; nor would a decision to ignore environmental considerations entirely, provided this is the 'director's subjective judgment, exercised in good faith' as to how best to promote the success of the company for the benefit of its shareholders.[174] In theory, a minority shareholder could litigate to challenge a board or management decision by alleging and proving that the directors in question did not honestly believe the decision would promote the interests of the company. In practice, this is virtually impossible, and there are few examples of cases where

---

[169] *Brehm v. Eisner*, 746 A.2d 244 (Del. 2000). In an extreme case, a court might apply the doctrine of waste or might conclude that a decision is substantively so harmful to the corporation as to suggest absence of good faith or sound process.

[170] The Japanese BJR excludes liability for directors who have done their best to perform their duties on a well-informed basis: Nakamura, 'Japan: listed companies' corporate governance', 222, 250.

[171] South Africa applies a version of the BJR very similar to that of Delaware, see Henning, et al., *Sustainable Companies, Climate Change and Corporate Social Responsibility in South African Law*, 37.

[172] Company Law Review Steering Group, *Modern Company Law for a Competitive Economy: Developing the Framework* (Department of Trade and Industry, 2000), 3.69–3.70.

[173] Villiers, *Mapping Paper: Sustainable Companies UK Report*, 26. Also in this direction, the Code of Corporate Governance (with which listed companies are expected to 'comply or explain') requires boards to 'focus on the sustainable success of an entity over the longer term', Villiers, *Mapping Paper: Sustainable Companies UK Report*, 28.

[174] Villiers, *Mapping Paper: Sustainable Companies UK Report*, 48.

litigants have succeeded. Many other jurisdictions grant the board a similarly large margin of discretion by applying only a subjective test; this is the approach taken in Ireland,[175] Switzerland,[176] Poland,[177] Australia,[178] and Slovenia,[179] for instance.

Other jurisdictions review the decision-making process more stringently. Some explicitly state that members of the board must prove that they have discharged their fiduciary duties towards the company (as in Finland[180] and France[181]), while other jurisdictions require that members of the board convince a judge that they acted in good faith (e.g. Brazil).[182] In Portugal, members of the board who cannot prove compliance with their duty to make reasonable decisions will still escape liability if they can discharge the lighter burden of proving that they did not act 'irrationally' (i.e. incomprehensibly or without any coherent explanation).[183] In

---

[175] Clarke, *Irish Company Law Mapping Paper*, 29.

[176] In all shareholder actions (e.g. liability lawsuits and challenges of general meetings' resolutions), the courts in Switzerland generally apply the BJR on behalf of boards and corporations, respectively. Courts follow a rather pragmatic approach, and no clear standard exists: see P.V. Kunz, 'Switzerland: the system of corporate governance', in Fleckner and Hopt (eds.), *Comparative Corporate Governance*, 887, 884.

[177] In Poland, directors have broad discretion under a de facto BJR to consider stakeholder interests, making challenge to decision-making unusual: Oplusti and Radwan, 'Company law in Poland', 482–4.

[178] The purely subjective common law BJR continues to apply in proceedings relating to duties other than the duty of care: Corporations Act 2001, s. 180(2).

[179] Under Slovenian law, management generally makes business decisions free from interference from the shareholders or the supervisory board, though failure to satisfy the will of the general meeting may result in removal (directly in a one-tier company, indirectly in a two-tier company): Zrilič, *Mapping Paper*, s. 2.2.

[180] According to the general Finnish procedural rules, the burden of proof is with the plaintiff. However, as far as the board and management are concerned, the reversed burden of proof is applied. One could also be held liable for negligence – insofar as the person liable cannot prove to have acted with due care: Mähönen, 'Corporate governance of Finland', 42.

[181] The Cour de Cassation has decided that a director is liable for a faulty decision taken by the board of directors (or by the managing board or supervisory board), unless the director can prove that they have fulfilled the duty of care, notably by opposing the decision. According to Conac, this decision clarifies the duties of care of directors and sets the bar quite high. In general, French courts do not tend to second-guess decisions from the board of directors or the management board as long as the company remains solvent: Conac, 'Corporate governance of France', 18–19, 27.

[182] Eizirik and Weber, 'Corporate governance of Brazil', 9.

[183] See Portugal CG, 18. Under Portuguese law, the director has to 'prove that he acted free from any personal interest, was fully informed, and according to the criteria of entrepreneurial rationality', Portuguese Commercial Company Code CSC Art. 72(2).

Australia, company directors who are sued for negligence must prove that they acted in good faith, without a personal interest, on information they reasonably believed to be appropriate and that they 'rationally believe[d]' the decision to be in the best interests of the corporation.[184] The latter criterion was interpreted as requiring the directors to show that they had engaged in a process of reasoning, but not to convince the court that the output of that process was '"reasonable" in an objective sense'.[185] The Australian approach is not wholly dissimilar to Delaware's approach, but it does reverse the burden of proof.[186] Less stringently, Argentina imposes a duty of vigilance, and a director who fails to prevent 'other directors from engaging in misconduct' will be liable unless they can show that they acted with due care.[187] However, this does not impinge on their discretion because 'Argentine courts tend to reject liability claims related to damages resulting from commercial decisions.'[188]

Other jurisdictions show greater willingness to engage with the substance of decisions. In the Netherlands, the Enterprise Chamber will order an inquiry into management where there are 'sound reasons to doubt the proper policies of the company and/or the conduct of its business'. If the court concludes that there has been mismanagement, that is, a breach of the 'elementary principles of responsible entrepreneurship', the members of the board will be liable.[189] In Luxembourg and Belgium, judges carry out a 'marginal' and 'a-priori' review, in which they place themselves at the moment when the decision was taken in order to decide whether it was wrongful, though a certain margin of error is permitted.[190] More specifically, in Belgium, the court will only hold members of the board or management liable if the decision 'clearly differs from all of the decisions that the company bodies could make at that time, particularly with regard to the corporate interest'.[191] In Indonesia, corporate managers

---

[184] Australia's statutory BJR, contained in s. 180(2) of the Corporations Act 2001, applies only in actions for breach of the duty of care.

[185] *ASIC v. Rich* [2009] NSWSC 1229, para [7289] per Austin J.

[186] Hill, 'The architecture of corporate governance', 127.

[187] *Forns, Eduardo A. v. Uantù S.A. y otros*, [2003-IV] JA, 897; Etcheverry and Manòvil, 'Corporate governance of Argentina', 982.

[188] Etcheverry and Manòvil, 'Corporate governance of Argentina', 983.

[189] van Bekkum, *et al.*, 'Corporate governance of the Netherlands', 659.

[190] Corbisier and Conac, 'Corporate governance of Luxembourg', 31. In 'Belgium – the legal system of corporate governance', Autenne comments (at 327) that this rule is similar to the American BJR.

[191] Autenne, 'Belgium – the legal system of corporate governance', 327.

have a duty to manage the business in accordance with the purposes of the company as stated in the articles, and face personal responsibility if they breach this duty.[192]

Some jurisdictions apply an objective test to the question of whether a decision could be considered to be in the interests of the company. Under German law, the members of the management board (*Vorstand*) will not be liable for damages for breach of duty[193] if they could 'reasonably believe, based on appropriate information, that they were acting in the best interest of the company'.[194] Hungarian law gives members of the management board a number of possibilities. They can be exempted from liability by showing: that they acted with due care and diligence and gave priority to the interests of the corporation, or that they did not take part in the decision-making process, or that they voted against the harmful board resolution; or by obtaining shareholder approval on the basis of true and sufficient information.[195] Finally, the recent reform of Albanian company law has arguably narrowed the scope of its BJR in cases concerning environmental protection by imposing a requirement that the board must take decisions in the best interest of the company as a whole, paying 'particular attention to the impact of its operation on the environment'.[196]

Whatever its precise formulation, the effect of the BJR in every jurisdiction considered here strengthens the discretion of the board and senior management that is the essence of the firm. All the

---

[192] B. Sujayadi and F. Kurniawan, *Mapping on Indonesian Company Law*, mapping paper (Sustainable Companies Project, 2011), s. 3 and s. 5.

[193] Section 93 II and III, Aktiengesetz. For more information on this and its enforcement, see Deipenbrock, *The Management Board of a German Aktiengesellschaft*, 20 f.

[194] Stock Corporation Act, s. 93(1). This applies analogously to entrepreneurial decisions of the managing directors, whose civil responsibility and liability are laid down in s. 43 GmbH-Gesetz. The supervisory board does not take part in management, and is obliged to bring claims for damages against management board members, though this is seldom done: Merkt, 'Germany: internal and external corporate governance', in Fleckner and Hopt, *Comparative Corporate Governance*, 543.

[195] Nikolicza, 'Hungary: corporate governance of listed companies'.

[196] The standard 'allows the court to consider all the aspects of a business decision, including the long-term advantages of a group decision even if measured against short-term disadvantages – factors likely to influence the decisions of the independent directors of subsidiary companies, who cannot but respect their company's embeddedness in the group', Albanian Companies Act, art. 98; see J. Dine, 'Jurisdictional arbitrage by multinational companies: a national solution?' (2012) 3(1) *Journal of Human Rights and the Environment* 68.

formulations of the BJR considered make it difficult for shareholders to challenge how members of the board and management define and formulate the 'interests of the company', and to challenge the quality of corporate decision-making in the courts. The rationale is that the exercise of business discretion is a matter that should be dealt with by means of the corporate governance process, using control rights over the company, rather than in the courts.

One important effect of the BJR is to give members of board and management greater scope to take account of environmental considerations in their decision-making than is apparent on the face of the law. In its strongest variant, board members need only be able to assert plausibly that a decision is in the interests of the company in question, and, even then, they are highly unlikely to be required to repeat this assertion in a court. Even in its weaker variant, the main burden on the members of the board is to show that they were properly informed. If they discharge this burden, the courts will not interfere with the substance of their decision. The logic here is that the courts' unwillingness to review the substance of decisions has the effect of insulating the board from shareholder litigation, giving the board scope to accord greater weight to environmental concerns, at least within the business case, and perhaps even beyond. However, the BJR also cuts the other way. Informal pressure from shareholders and short-term incentives might encourage the board to ignore the possibility of using its discretion to take account of environmental concerns.

On balance, the encroachment of the social norm of shareholder primacy into most jurisdictions arguably means that the BJR tends to have this latter effect. Indeed, one of the explicit goals of shareholder primacy is precisely to prevent members of the board and senior managers from imposing agency costs on shareholders in the form of satisfying the board's and senior managers' own preference for, for example, environmental protection by going beyond what the law requires. In order to achieve this, shareholder primacy has had to work around the strong protection given to corporate decisions by the BJR. We will see below that in those jurisdictions in which the shareholder primacy norm has taken root, shareholders have several ways of persuading management to pursue shareholder value, bypassing the BJR by removing any need to challenge specific decisions in court. Those who seek to safeguard the environment do not have similar tools at their disposal. Accordingly, when it operates in a shareholder primacy corporate governance context, the BJR has the effect of operating as a barrier to managerial decisions aimed at greater sustainability but which reduces short-term profitability.

In considering the relevance of the BJR for sustainable companies, it is also important to bear in mind that all jurisdictions have introduced specific legal regulations to deal with environmental issues.[197] Provided these regulations are enforced, either publicly or privately, as they at least in theory should be, the board must normally comply with them to avoid sanctions against them or the companies they direct. The BJR would not stand in the way of liability in such cases. The relevance of the BJR lies in giving the board a broader discretion as to how it discharges its core duty, that is, to promote the interests of the company. That discretion is particularly relevant where the law is silent on what the board is supposed to do in a particular situation – namely, in most ordinary, strategic and other business decisions.

3.4   The continued dominance of shareholder primacy

We have seen that, while legal systems can be divided into those that adopt a monistic (or 'shareholder value') approach to the interests of the company, equating it with the interests of the shareholders, and those that take a pluralist approach, directors in all jurisdictions benefit from considerable discretion in terms of defining the interests of the company. This is underpinned, and perhaps even broadened, by the BJR. That discretion opens up the prospect of the board using its authority to take account of sustainability considerations, even if this entails sacrificing profits and shareholder returns in the short term. The board can always argue that being seen as sustainable will create long-term shareholder value or be in the interests of the company (as the case may be), and the courts would be very unlikely to second-guess this business judgement. However, since the 1980s, this discretion has increasingly been pre-empted

---

[197] For example, US companies face potential civil and criminal liability for harm to the environment, based on state tort law and also on federal environmental statutes, though there are significant procedural and substantive hurdles. See further C.R. Taylor, *United States Company Law as it Impacts Corporate Environmental Behavior, with Emphasis on Climate Change*, Research Paper No. 2012–31 (University of Oslo Faculty of Law, 2012), available at: http://ssrn.com/abstract=2159659. In Poland, Art. 435 of the Civil Code and Art. 248 of the Environment Protection Act provide that companies that pose an extended risk by the nature of their activities may be strictly liable for environmental damages: see Radwan and Regucki, *The Possibilities for and Barriers to Sustainable Companies in Polish Company Law*, s. 4.2.

in both shareholder value and pluralist jurisdictions by the social norm of shareholder primacy,[198] which has been allowed to take root because of the lack of legislative definitions of the purpose and interests of the company, combined with the broad scope of discretion under the BJR.[199]

The social norm of shareholder primacy exploits the latitude given to the board and senior managers to decide how the company's resources should be allocated over time. As explained in Section 1 of this chapter, the rise of the shareholder primacy drive is informed by the postulates derived from the mainstream version of agency theory. Shareholder primacy justifies remuneration practices that reward executives for increasing the share price, and frames the matter in a way that excludes from consideration the enormous social and economic costs, and even the destruction of shareholder wealth, that have resulted. It trumpets as fact the efficient capital market hypothesis, which claims that the share price is the best available metric of corporate performance, and which, despite regular bouts of market inefficiency and dislocation, and persuasive academic criticism,[200] remains the dominant operating assumption of many economists and policy-makers. In corporations where shareholders are dispersed, these theories may merely provide theoretical cover for value extraction by short-term shareholders and corporate executives at the expense of long-term shareholders, stakeholders, and the company itself. This is certainly the case in the USA and the UK, where shareholders are widely dispersed.[201] In other jurisdictions, shareholdings are more concentrated than this. For example, large companies in Australia,[202] France, Sweden, and the Netherlands normally have large blockholding shareholders. Moreover, shareholders in many European countries use

---

[198] W. Lazonick and M. O'Sullivan, 'Maximizing shareholder value: a new ideology for corporate governance' (2000) 29 *Economy and Society* 13.

[199] 'Shareholder primacy originates not in company law, but rather in the norms and practices surrounding the rise of the hostile takeover movement in the Britain and America in the 1970s and 1980s. It is . . . essentially a cultural rather than a legal point of reference.' S. Deakin, 'The coming transformation of shareholder value' (2005) 13 *Corporate Governance: An International Review* 11, 13.

[200] Quiggin, *Zombie Economics*, Chapter 2; S. Keen, *Debunking Economics* (Zed Books, 2011).

[201] See e.g. the (somewhat dated) analysis in M. Goergen and L. Renneboog, 'Strong managers and passive institutional investors in the UK', and M. Becht, 'Beneficial ownership in the United States', in F. Barca and M. Becht (eds.), *The Control of Corporate Europe* (Oxford University Press, 2001), Chapters 10 and 11 respectively.

[202] A. Dignam and M. Galanis, 'Australia inside-out: the corporate governance system of the Australian listed market' (2004) 28 *Melbourne University Law Review* 623.

'control-enhancing mechanisms', such as multiple voting shares[203] and pyramid structures[204] to exercise control over corporate governance out of proportion to their shareholding. Large blockholding shareholders are arguably more likely to take a longer-term approach to the company's interests. However, these structures and shareholding patterns also create risks, inter alia, for minority shareholders, as controlling shareholders can use their position to enrich themselves at the expense of the minority and other interests through 'tunnelling' and other forms of value extraction.

While hopes are regularly expressed that shareholders, and institutional investors in particular, will become more active in promoting long-termism, including social and environmental goals,[205] major institutional shareholders themselves face pressures that encourage them to focus strongly on short-term share price maximisation.[206] Pension funds need cash to meet current obligations to retirees, and many mutual funds compete for investor dollars on the basis of quarterly or annual returns. Far from being a potential solution to the short-termism problem, institutional shareholders often exacerbate the problem. Their incentives combine with those of the board to resist decisions and strategies that require short-term costs that could produce economic or social (including environmental) benefits. The board may forego such benefits even when it is in their company's long-term financial interest to pursue them.

Through its influence on policy-makers, shareholder primacy has also found expression in takeover law, which in many jurisdictions[207] aims to establish a market for corporate control that removes boards and

---

[203] These are frequently used in Sweden, Finland (mainly in closed companies), France, and the Netherlands: see Shearman and Sterling LLP, *Report on the Proportionality Principle in the European Union* (Shearman and Sterling LLP, 2007), 18.

[204] These are commonly used in Sweden, Italy, and Belgium: Shearman and Sterling LLP, *Report on the Proportionality Principle in the European Union*, 19.

[205] This is the background for the EU Commission's reform package of April 2014, including a proposal to reform the Shareholder Rights' Directive with the explicit aim of using transparency requirements and soft law to encourage institutional shareholders to press for longer-term decision-making. See European Commission, *Proposal for a Directive Amending Directive 2007/36/EC as Regards the Encouragement of Long-Term Shareholder Engagement and Directive 2013/34/EU as Regards Certain Elements of the Corporate Governance Statement*, COM(2014) 213 final. For a critical commentary on the proposal, see A. Johnston and P. Morrow, *Commentary on the Shareholder Rights Directive*, Research Paper No. 2014-41 (University of Oslo Faculty of Law, 2014), available at: http://ssrn.com/abstract=2535274.

[206] J. Kay, *The Kay Review of UK Equity Markets and Long-Term Decision-Making* (House of Commons, Business, Innovation and Skills Committee, 25 July 2013); D. Millon, 'Shareholder social responsibility' (2013) 36 *Seattle University Law Review* 911.

[207] Delaware is an important exception here, giving directors considerable scope to defend unwanted takeovers.

senior managers under whose watch a company's share price has underperformed.[208] By incentivising a focus on the short-term share price, these practices and laws discourage members of the board and senior managers from using their discretion to consider issues such as sustainability, which will only be reflected in the share price in the very long term, if ever.[209] Although takeover law is meant to regulate an occurrence that is rare in the life of the individual company, the fear of takeovers has powerful effects on the decision-making of the board and senior management.

In the face of these myopic practices, and the development of the social norm of shareholder primacy, company law has remained largely silent. As we have seen, company law in some jurisdictions adopts a shareholder-centric approach, but even there does not require the short-term absolute prioritisation of shareholder interests. Such systems of company law are, at least in their current forms, simply incapable of counteracting short-termist decisions justified by reference to the social norm of shareholder primacy. Even in countries where the approach is less shareholder-centric, company law's permissiveness and the lack of concrete definitions of company purpose and interests have allowed the social norm of shareholder primacy to legitimate board and management decisions that focus on the short term. Social and environmental concerns are relegated to the 'business case' domain of corporate social responsibility. Germany is a good example of this dynamic. The growing financialisation of the German economy is resulting in increased pressure for enhanced short-term returns for shareholders. Management boards (*Vorstand*) are increasingly incentivised to interpret the corporate interest along shareholder primacy lines.[210] Although German company law has set some limits,[211] the lack of any hard norms relating

---

[208] See, for example, the chequered history of the European Takeover Directive, which sought to extend the UK's approach to takeover regulation across the whole EU.

[209] See the analysis of the EU Takeover Directive in light of the overarching EU goal of sustainable development in Sjåfjell, *Towards a Sustainable European Company Law*, Part V.

[210] For example, the average pay of directors in Volkswagen in 2011 was around 170 times the average pay of employees. This differential has increased considerably since 2005. See www.welt.de/wirtschaft/article121529657/Im-Schnitt-verdient-Ihr-Chef-50-Mal-mehr-als-Sie.html. While German companies 'do not rely as much on stock options as their US counterparts, they do as well rely heavily on short-term performance indicators.' See P. Duenhaupt, 'The impact of financialization on income distribution in the USA and Germany: a proposal for a new adjusted wage share' IMK Working Paper No 7/2011 (June 2011).

[211] In a landmark decision, the German Federal Court of Justice (*Bundesgerichtshof*), which is the country's highest court in civil matters, decided that stock options for members of

124   B. SJÅFJELL, A. JOHNSTON, L. ANKER-SØRENSEN, D. MILLON

to the *Unternehmensinteresse* has left considerable scope for the social norm of shareholder primacy to operate to legitimate these practices.[212]

It should be emphasised that this narrowing in practice of the discretion of members of the board and senior management is highly contentious and has not been the subject of an explicit policy choice.[213] The shareholder-centricity of common law is historically contingent, a reflection of the incomplete emergence of company law from partnership.[214] However, today, most mainstream corporate law scholars take shareholder-centricity for granted. Even in Nordic countries, the lack of clear rules as to the company interest has frequently been interpreted as an implicit instruction from the legislature that the shareholder interest should take priority. Under the influence of the law-and-economics-inspired, Anglo-American corporate governance debate, much of the Nordic legal scholarship has moved away from the broader, 'Germanic' position.[215]

The European Commission has, at least to date, played an important role in driving the shareholder primacy agenda in the EU and disseminating the social norm of shareholder primacy,[216] as has pressure from institutional investors. The social norm of shareholder primacy has become so entrenched that policy-makers respond to critiques that it has harmful effects with ever more elaborate attempts to steer boards and senior management towards a longer-term approach to shareholder value, rather than a more pluralist approach to corporate decision-making, which would encompass sustainability. So, for example, there is a move to give

---

the supervisory board are incompatible with the German Joint Stock Corporations Act (*Aktiengesetz*) because they inevitably lead to conflicts of interest, undermine the control function of the supervisory board, and are politically undesirable (see Bundesgerichtshof (Az.: II ZR 316/02) (16 February 2004)).

[212] Heuschmid, 'The protection of workers under EU company law'.

[213] This can be seen from the history of the EU Takeover Directive and the compromises which had to be reached for it to become law: see Sjåfjell, *Towards a Sustainable European Company Law*; Johnston, *EC Regulation of Corporate Governance*.

[214] For example, P. Ireland, 'Property and contract in contemporary corporate theory' (2003) 23 *Legal Studies* 453.

[215] Sjåfjell, *Sustainable Companies: Possibilities and Barriers in Norwegian Company Law*, s. 2.3.

[216] European Commission, *Recommendation 2004/913/EC of 14 December 2004 Fostering an Appropriate Regime for the Remuneration of Directors of Listed Companies*, OJ 2004 L 385/55, 2004; European Commission, *Modernising Company Law and Enhancing Corporate Governance in the European Union: A Plan to Move Forward*, COM (2003) 284 final, 21 May 2003.

shareholders greater say on pay,[217] and soft law is being used to encourage institutional investors to exercise greater stewardship over companies in order to promote a longer-term approach to corporate governance.[218] Even in the aftermath of the 2008 financial crisis, European Commission policy-makers rejected prescriptive regulation of executive pay in financial institutions, despite the enormous social costs to which this practice gave rise. It was the European Parliament that forced a cap on variable pay in the amended Capital Requirements Directive.[219]

Regardless of the tantalising prospects held out by the scope of action that national systems of company law – and the business judgement rule in particular – give to boards, corporate decision-making in an ever-growing number of jurisdictions is focused on short-term returns to shareholders, legitimated by the social norm of shareholder primacy. Social costs are thereby excluded from the analysis, left to external regulation or voluntary CSR. This is the fundamental barrier to the promotion of environmentally sustainable companies, as members of the board and senior managers who take account of sustainability typically will not maintain their control over companies for long. As long as the pre-eminence of the social norm of shareholder primacy prevails and institutional shareholders fail to see the importance of taking a long-term perspective, the business case approach that dominates the CSR agenda is unlikely to assist proponents of sustainability.[220]

While there are signs that the social norm is being increasingly widely questioned, in academia, in business, and in the media, there is a long way to go before the norm ceases to act as a potent barrier to sustainable companies. In our conclusion we will suggest that, as a starting point, there is a need for a clearer legislative statement of the purpose and the interests of the company, and for greater consideration to be paid to questions of enforcement.

---

[217] For example, Swiss voters approved the Minder Initiative giving shareholders a binding annual vote on compensation of directors and senior executives. At the time of writing, the EU was proposing to reform the Shareholder Rights Directive to give shareholders in listed companies a binding 'say on pay': see European Commission, COM(2014) 213 final, 9 April 2014, Art. 9a.

[218] See the UK Stewardship Code. The European Commission is proposing to require institutional investors, on a 'comply or explain' basis, to develop policies on engagement and disclose their implementation: see COM(2014) 213 final, Arts 3f–3h.

[219] See A. Johnston, 'Preventing the next financial crisis? Regulating bankers' pay in Europe' (2014) 41 *Journal of Law and Society* 6–27.

[220] See also Chapter 2 by Millon in this book.

4 Shareholder power within and beyond the scope of law

4.1 Introduction

The significance of shareholder primacy warrants an investigation into what shareholders themselves could do to promote or prevent the shift towards sustainable companies. Shareholders are of course not a homogeneous group and some distinctions need to be made. The obvious distinction is between minority and majority. Minority shareholders, even down to a holding of less than 1 per cent, have the potential to influence companies in a sustainable direction through socially responsible investment (SRI) and shareholder activism, as discussed by Benjamin Richardson in Chapter 6 in this book. All jurisdictions, albeit to a greatly varying degree, also allow minority shareholders (often subject to a minimum shareholding threshold) some influence on the company.[221] However, though there are some positive trends, SRI and the push by minority shareholders for sustainable companies are still too much of a fringe effort to be recognised as a significant driver towards sustainability.[222]

We will focus in this chapter on the majority shareholder as having the greatest potential to control or influence the company. Space does not allow us to cover all facets of this topic. With this caveat, the category of majority shareholders includes personal controlling shareholders (often the founding family), institutional or organisational shareholders (including foundations), and groups of shareholders who collectively control a majority of shares and who are bound to each other through shareholder agreements. In what follows, all of these shareholders will be referred to as majority shareholder(s) without distinction, and contrasted with a company as controlling majority shareholder, which we will refer to as the 'parent company'.

Corporate groups, consisting of a parent company and one or more subsidiaries, are traditionally divided into two different categories: equity groups and control groups. First, *equity groups* are established through share ownership that gives the parent the majority of votes in the subsidiary. In equity groups, the parent as a shareholder can dominate on issues of board appointments and thus the company's current business

---

[221] Directive 2007/36/EC of the European Parliament and of the Council of 11 July 2007 on the exercise of certain rights of shareholders in listed companies. For an analysis of the directive, see: P.E. Masouros, 'Is the EU taking shareholder rights seriously? An essay on the impotence of shareholdership in corporate Europe' (2010) 7 *European Company Law* 195.

[222] See further Chapter 6 by Richardson in this book.

operations by virtue of its shareholdings.[223] Second, so-called *control groups* (or factual groups) exist where the parent company can dominate on those same issues but with a lower level of share ownership. Whether this occurs as a factual matter will depend on both the structure of shareholdings and the company's statutes.[224] Both group concepts rely on a recognition of control, albeit control arising in different ways. As we will show, the parent company's control over a group amounts to a particularly extreme variant of shareholder primacy, in which all the implications of the relationship between companies and shareholders come to the fore. However, parent company control has the potential, as does shareholder control in general, to be wielded for a positive shift towards sustainability.

This section proceeds with a brief consideration of the potential influence of majority shareholders to adopt decisions at the general meeting of shareholders, including through their powers to change the articles of association; to appoint and dismiss the board; and, in some jurisdictions, even to give legally binding instructions to the board as to how the company should be run. As we did earlier with regard to the board, we ask whether majority shareholders use the rights given to them by law, and whether they are under any obligation to do so. We also discuss the actual influence of the shareholder beyond the scope of the law, a phenomenon that may be assumed to be especially prevalent in groups but also in companies with personal controlling shareholders.

We continue with a brief consideration of the possibility of sanctions where shareholders do not act in line with the purpose or interest of the company, and explore whether that can be used to ensure environmental sustainability. As there are few possibilities as regards sanctions where shareholder influence creates potential or hypothetical risk, we focus mainly on the question of shareholder liability for actual harm. Such liability is difficult to achieve both in relation to individual companies and in the corporate group context; few jurisdictions embrace the concept of group liability. There are some pioneering jurisdictions in this regard, but for the most part we are left with the uncertainties of the veil-piercing doctrine in company law; a few national examples of direct environmental liability for shareholders (as opposed to direct environmental liability of the company as a separate entity); and an evolving but uncertain

---

[223] Grundmann, *European Company Law*, 769.

[224] Grundmann, *European Company Law*, 769. In Albania, for instance, the concepts of control groups, factual groups, and effective control are defined by company law in Art. 207 (1): Dine, 'Jurisdictional arbitrage'.

international trend towards foreign direct liability claims within tort law. In each case we explore the extent to which these rights and obligations create scope for company decision-making that furthers sustainability.

4.2 Majority shareholder control

4.2.1 Power over the 'constitution' of the company

In all jurisdictions majority shareholders can change the articles of association, also denoted the constitution of the company, and thereby the company's specific purpose. This can affect the scope of the board's discretion or obligation to promote sustainability in its promotion of the interests of the company.[225] Changing the articles of association typically requires a supermajority vote at the general meeting and in some cases, such as when the company is no longer to have profit for its shareholders as part of its purpose, unanimity.[226] Company law, therefore, provides shareholders in a general meeting with full control over the constitution, and accordingly with broad scope for explicitly embedding sustainability in the constitution of an individual company. Conversely, these possibilities are barriers to boards or managers wishing to shift the business towards sustainability where majority shareholders disagree with this course of action. Indeed, as we will see below and have already indicated, even the possibility of shareholders using the control mechanisms granted to them by company law may deter boards from carrying out the necessary shift from business as usual towards an environmentally sustainable path.

4.2.2 Appointing and dismissing the board

The powers of the general meeting in most cases include appointing and dismissing the board. In many jurisdictions, the shareholders in a general meeting have the power to remove members of the board by simple majority.

This may be done directly, as in the UK where the general meeting can remove directors by an ordinary resolution.[227] Similarly, in Australia, the default rule is that the directors can be removed by a simple majority of the general meeting, a rule that is mandatory in

---

[225] For instance, the UK's Companies Act of 2006, s. 21. The company's directors will breach their duty to the company if they do not act in accordance with the company's constitution (s. 171(a)).

[226] See e.g. Sjåfjell, *Sustainable Companies: Possibilities and Barriers in Norwegian Company Law.*

[227] Companies Act of 2006, s. 168.

SHAREHOLDER PRIMACY

relation to public companies.[228] In the UK, appointments to the board are made in accordance with the articles, and by default this is either by ordinary resolution of the shareholders in a general meeting or by a decision of the directors.[229] However, where the board appoints directors, they must retire at the next annual general meeting, though they may offer themselves for reappointment by the shareholders.[230] In Australia, the default rule is that the general meeting has the power to appoint directors,[231] though companies typically include provision in their constitutions giving the board power to fill casual vacancies and to appoint additional directors up to the maximum.[232] The role of boards in practice in appointing directors in listed companies in these jurisdictions is reflected in the relevant corporate governance codes, which call for the establishment of a nomination committee consisting of a majority of independent non-executives to 'lead the process for board appointments' and 'make recommendations to the board'.[233]

The control of the general meeting over appointment and dismissal of the board may also be indirect, as in Norway, Germany, and Japan, where for certain categories of companies there may be a corporate assembly or supervisory board with shareholder- and employee-elected members, which appoints and dismisses the members of the board.[234] However, in these cases, the law may indirectly be seen to give the general meeting the

---

[228] Corporations Act 2001, ss. 203C and 203D.

[229] For the UK, see Model Articles for Public Companies, Art. 20. Where shareholders in public companies vote on appointments, there must be a separate vote on each director unless the shareholders vote without dissent not to follow this rule: Companies Act of 2006, s. 160.

[230] Model Articles for Public Companies, Art. 21.   [231] Corporations Act 2001, s. 201G.

[232] See R.P. Austin and I.M. Ramsay, *Ford's Principles of Corporations Law* (14th edn, Lexis-Nexis Butterworths, 2013) at 7.170.

[233] UK Corporate Governance Code, B.2.1; see also ASX, *Corporate Governance Principles and Recommendations* (3rd edn, 2014), Recommendation 2.1, noting the role of the nomination committee inter alia in making recommendations to the board in relation to 'board succession planning generally' and 'the appointment and re-election of directors'.

[234] In Norway, companies over a certain size may have the corporate assembly as an additional company law organ between the general meeting and the board, with the employees electing one-third of the members of the corporate assembly, which then appoints the board, see Sjåfjell and Kjelland, 'Norway: corporate governance on the outskirts of the EU', while in traditional two-tier jurisdictions such as Germany, the general meeting and the employees appoint the members of the supervisory board, which appoints the management board, see Merkt, 'Germany: internal and external corporate governance'. In Japan, the board of directors may appoint and dismiss the representative director and other executive officers: Nakamura, 'Japan – listed companies' corporate governance', 246–7.

final say in that the general meeting appoints the majority of the members of the corporate assembly and supervisory board. Moreover, corporate governance codes encourage the supervisory board to establish nomination committees. In Germany, that committee should consist exclusively of shareholder representatives who will propose candidates to the supervisory board for recommendation to the general meeting.[235] These powers and practices serve to enforce and exacerbate the misconception that members of the board are agents for shareholders as principals, with maximisation of shareholder returns as their main or only goal.

While these rights may in practice not be used in some companies, typically where the shareholders are dispersed and the cost of coordinating action to remove and replace the board serves as a deterrent, the very existence of these rights will tend to make the board more responsive to shareholders' wishes. Those wishes might be expressed directly but informally through engagement and activism, or indirectly through share sales creating downwards pressure on the share price. Such informal dialogue, in the shadow of a legal right to remove board members, allows shareholders to press their demands even in those jurisdictions, discussed below, where the shareholders in general meeting either are prohibited by law from giving direct instructions or rarely do so in practice.

This right to appoint and dismiss the board certainly brings shareholder interests to the forefront and may be used to promote the interests of the company in a narrow or broad sense. However, for this right to be deployed to influence board decision-making in the direction of environmental sustainability, the majority of shareholders – or at least a well-co-ordinated group of blockholders – would have to back the policy, and even then, there would sometimes be considerable costs of collective action. As we discussed earlier, in the absence of a clear statement of the purpose and interests of the company, these rights create a strong rhetorical suggestion that shareholders are the most important constituency, implicitly giving the social norm of shareholder primacy greater legitimacy.

4.2.3 Instructions

The general meeting may also influence the direction of the company by approving or rejecting proposals put before it concerning large investments and, of course, the payment of dividends to the shareholders. In many jurisdictions, notably in the EU, even minority shareholders have

---

[235] See German Corporate Governance Code (as amended on 26 May 2010), para. 5.3.3.

SHAREHOLDER PRIMACY 131

the right to submit a proposal before the general meeting.[236] In some states, majority shareholders in a general meeting can even issue legally binding instructions to the board, of a general or specific nature. However, the ability to instruct the board and thereby the company itself varies greatly between jurisdictions.

In the Nordic countries, with its strictly hierarchical system,[237] the general meeting is the highest authority. Notably in Norway, a simple majority at the general meeting has a broad competence to instruct the board which extends to specific situations (though this must not go so far as to override the division of labour between the company organs).[238] In Finland, only a unanimous general meeting may make decisions on matters falling within the general competence of the board or the general manager.[239]

In a German AG, the general meeting's competence is strictly and exhaustively delimited in law, consisting mainly of rights to approve issuance of new shares, discuss strategy in meetings and to hold management to account by reference to the company's financial accounts. Apart from these express rights, the shareholders in general meeting have no direct say over management, although management (*Vorstand*) may voluntarily put issues before the general meeting.[240] The effect of this is to entrench the management of an AG not only against the supervisory board but also against the shareholders in the general meeting. Poland adopts a similar approach, with the general meeting of public companies having no power to instruct the management board, although its power to remove the board means its wishes are likely to be listened to.[241] By contrast, the shareholders are the supreme decision-making body in the German GmbH.[242] And, in control groups, the management of controlled

---

[236] See Directive 2007/36, Art. 6.

[237] J. Lau Hansen, 'A Scandinavian approach to corporate governance', (2007) 50 *Scandinavian Studies in Law* 125–42, 133.

[238] Sjåfjell, *Sustainable Companies: Possibilities and Barriers in Norwegian Company Law.*

[239] Otherwise, the general competence is strictly in the hands of the board, as are matters of great importance (e.g. major structural matters). Additionally, Finnish law does not recognise the right to give instructions: Mähönen, *Sustainable Companies Mapping Paper on Company Law Issues: Finland*, s. 2.3.2.

[240] AktG, s. 119 II, see *Deipenbrock*, The Management Board of a German Aktiengesellschaft, 6.

[241] Radwan and Regucki, *The Possibilities for and Barriers to Sustainable Companies in Polish Company Law*, s. 2.2.2.

[242] Radwan and Regucki, *The Possibilities for and Barriers to Sustainable Companies in Polish Company Law*, 8 f.

AGs are under a legal obligation to act in accordance with instructions given by the controlling company, regardless of its corporate form.[243]

Most countries adopt an approach somewhere between these poles, but with marked variations. It is common to limit the ability of shareholders to interfere in board and management decisions. In France, the general meeting can probably lawfully give instructions to the board, but cannot deprive it of its management power entirely,[244] while in Spain, the general meeting has a default power to give instructions to the board or subject particular management issues to prior authorisation.[245] In Slovenia, the general meeting can only take over management if requested to do so by the management board.[246]

In most common law countries, shareholder intervention is a theoretical possibility in law but rarely if ever occurs in practice. In Ireland, the shareholders can exercise 'all the functions of the company' by voting in the general meeting but they normally adopt articles (internal regulations) in a standard form which vests all management powers in the board of directors, but grants the shareholders a (rarely used) power to give directions to the board of directors.[247] Certain matters are reserved to the general meeting by the legislation. The approach in the UK is broadly similar: the company's constitution defines the relationship between the general meeting and board. The default rule vests management in the board, but does allow the general meeting to instruct the directors by a 75 per cent majority.[248] In the absence of this provision in the articles, the shareholders have no power to instruct the directors.[249] Certain key decisions are reserved for the general meeting by legislation, but these do not touch upon the managerial prerogative. Exceptionally, individual shareholders might be able to litigate in the company's name by means of a derivative action, but any attempt by shareholders to bring a derivative action to challenge the directors' weighting of the various factors

---

[243] R. Reich-Graefe, 'Changing paradigms: the liability of corporate groups in Germany' (2005) 37 *Connecticut Law Review* 789.

[244] Conac, 'Corporate governance of France', 28–9.

[245] Escrig-Olmedo, *et al.*, *Sustainable Companies: Spanish Mapping Paper on Company Law Issues*, 17.

[246] Zrilič, *Mapping Paper*, 15.   [247] Clarke, *Irish Company Law Mapping Paper*, s. 2.2.

[248] See Article 4 of Model Articles for Public Companies. In contrast, Australian law does not give shareholders a default right to instruct the directors. In theory, such a power could be included in the company's constitution or articles, but, given that it is rarely if ever used in the UK and Ireland, shareholders would be unlikely to do this.

[249] *Automatic Self-Cleansing Filter Syndicate Co Ltd v. Cuninghame* [1906] 2 Ch 34.

contained in section 172 of the Companies Act 2006 would face virtually insurmountable 'practical and legal hurdles'.[250]

Among other examples, Canadian law allows shareholders by two-thirds majority to place restrictions on the board's authority at any time.[251] In practice, however, shareholders do not exercise meaningful control over management by virtue of their voting power. In Canada, shareholders (who comply with provincial-level requirements as to level of shareholding) may, in advance of a general meeting, present proposals for shareholder vote, including proposals related to the environment and to other CSR issues. Companies have the right to exclude proposals which are abusive, for example, because they are personally motivated or simply aim to 'secure publicity'. Oshionebo suggests that, while proposals on executive pay or environmental matters 'tend to attract publicity and public debate', publicity sought for the purposes of persuading other shareholders of the merits of the proposal 'may not amount to "abuse" of the shareholder's right to submit a proposal and would not justify its rejection'. Hence, in Canada, there is scope – albeit little explored – for shareholders to use proposals to push companies towards more environmentally friendly policies.[252] Similarly, in Ghana, the company's shareholders may pass resolutions relating to governance of the company, but the board is not required to follow them.[253] US federal law makes it possible for shareholders to recommend particular courses of action to the board, but they lack the power to mandate board action. In terms of voting, shareholders in the USA enjoy the right to vote only on major structural matters, which covers matters such as amendment of the corporate charter, merger, sale of all or substantially all assets, or liquidation, and on matters put before them by the board.[254]

4.2.4 Shareholder influence through informal channels

The concept of shareholder dialogue is not recognised by company law but is given some legitimacy by its inclusion in corporate governance codes. It typically consists of informal, private meetings between select

---

[250] Villiers, *Mapping Paper: Sustainable Companies UK Report*, 30–2.

[251] B.J. Richardson and G. Tanner, *Canadian Company Law: Barriers and Possibilities for Sustainable Companies*, mapping paper (Sustainable Companies Project, 2012), 16–17.

[252] Oshionebo, 'Shareholder proposals and the passivity of shareholders in canada: electronic forums to the rescue?' (2012) 37(2) *Queen's LJ* 619, 630–1.

[253] Schwartz, *Developing States and Climate Change: Solutions in Company Law?*, 18–19.

[254] Taylor, *United States Company Law as It Impacts Corporate Environmental Behavior*, s. 2.2.

shareholders and the chair of the board or the chief executive officer.[255] Such meetings are non-transparent and significant channels for shareholder influence. Although this also gives scope for influence by minority (institutional) investors, active majority shareholders will naturally have the most clout. Depending on the inclination of the most active shareholders, the board and management of the company may be guided by suggestions from shareholders, which is quite separate from the decision-making framework envisaged by company law. This may reduce company law to a formal structure with which companies must comply, but which has little or no impact on corporate decision-making.

Shareholder involvement in corporate governance – both formal and informal – tends to be viewed in the common law world as a solution to the short-term focus of board and senior management's decision-making under the shareholder primacy model. For example, in the UK, institutional shareholder 'involvement' is encouraged through the 'Stewardship Code', which aims 'to promote the long term success of companies in such a way that the ultimate providers of capital also prosper'.[256] Pension funds and other institutional investors may hold out the prospect of more socially responsible decision-making, given their longer-term time horizons. However, it should also be noted that those same funds have to earn sufficient returns to meet their obligations to existing beneficiaries at a time when central banks have locked down long-term interest rates.[257] Moreover, to the extent that the activism is being carried out by hedge funds, it may have the effect of reinforcing the short-term financial focus of shareholder primacy, curtailing board and management discretion.[258] Similar observations might be made about the trajectory of institutional

---

[255] For a helpful (if somewhat dated) overview, see M. Useem, *Investor Capitalism* (Basic Books, 1996). The legitimacy of such dialogue may be questioned when it is used as the only channel for shareholder influence beyond appointment of the board, as is the case, for example, in the controversies surrounding the Norwegian state's refusal to enter into any discussion of whether it should use its power as majority shareholder to instruct Statoil to withdraw from Canadian oil sand projects, see Sjåfjell, *Sustainable Companies: Possibilities and Barriers in Norwegian Company Law*, s. 1.3.

[256] Kay, *The Kay Review of UK Equity Markets and Long-Term Decision-Making*, which emphasises that 'engagement goes beyond merely voting' (at 53).

[257] See Millon, 'Shareholder social responsibility'.

[258] Gospel and Pendleton report that activist hedge funds sometimes purchase a stake in a company 'with the prior intention of securing changes' and typically aim 'to secure returns from activism within a year or so'; H. Gospel and A. Pendleton, 'Financialization, new investment funds, and labour', in H. Gospel, A. Pendleton, and S. Vitols (eds.), *Financialization, New Investment Funds, and Labour: An International Comparison* (Oxford University Press, 2014), 1, 13–18. See also 'US activist hedge funds form UK bridgehead for charge into Europe', *Financial Times*, 13 January 2014.

shareholder activism in the USA, though there is no analogue to the UK Stewardship Code. Although even the largest institutions typically hold small minority positions, they nevertheless can exert powerful influence, which more often than not pushes in the direction of current share price maximisation rather than long-term sustainability.

In the context of the corporate group, the parent company as shareholder of the subsidiaries may find communicating directly with the chair of the board or the manager of the subsidiaries more efficient. Members of the boards of subsidiaries may typically be employees of the parent company, rendering the idea of promoting an independent company interest as opposed to a group interest or parent company interest an academic exercise for which there is little space in everyday business life.

4.2.5 Fiduciary duties for shareholders?

The legal and factual powers of shareholders give rise to the question of whether the shareholders have any obligation to use their power in a particular way or in pursuit of specific goals. Generally speaking, shareholders are not under any obligation to focus on anything and are at liberty to pursue their own financial goals (though institutional investors typically have fiduciary responsibility to their beneficiaries to act in their best interests). As opposed to the board, which does not have a legitimate interest of its own and is given the duty of promoting the interests of the company, shareholders have a legitimate, company-law-protected right to act and vote so as to further their own self-interest. However, there are necessarily limits to this right and in a number of states majority shareholders may not secure undue advantages for themselves or others at the expense of the company or other shareholders. As such, the concept of the 'interests of the company' as a matter of law serves to limit how far the majority can go in promoting their own interest, as do a variety of minority-protection rules across jurisdictions.

Many states impose a duty of loyalty on the general meeting of shareholders, requiring it not to act in a way that is incompatible with the interests of the company. Shareholders may face liability where they take decisions that give undue or unjustifiable advantages to one or more shareholders, or favour third parties at the expense of shareholders.[259] This duty of loyalty usually applies to the shareholders when they act

---

[259] For example, Sjåfjell, *Sustainable Companies: Possibilities and Barriers in Norwegian Company Law.*

136 B. SJÅFJELL, A. JOHNSTON, L. ANKER-SØRENSEN, D. MILLON

in general meetings, but it may be more intense and wide-ranging for majority or controlling shareholders than for minority shareholders.[260]

Since the scope of this concept varies in different jurisdictions, the requirements of any duty of loyalty imposed on shareholders might be expected to vary depending on whether a particular country adopts a pluralist version or a narrower, shareholder value one. However, in most cases, this fiduciary duty operates primarily or exclusively as a means of protecting minority shareholders, reflecting the conventional concern of company law with conflicts between majority and minority shareholders. In Germany, the Federal Court of Justice has established a duty of loyalty of majority shareholders towards the company and its minority shareholders.[261] This effectively prohibits the majority shareholders from using their voting rights in a manner that could harm the interest of the company as a whole. This is also the case in the Nordic region, though the lack of court cases where the interests of the company as a separate entity are at stake has opened up scope for arguments that company law only protects the minority shareholders from majority abuse.[262] In France, the duty appears to be less far-reaching, with the courts finding an 'abuse of majority' where a majority shareholder votes against *l'intérêt social* in pursuit of the shareholder's own personal interest; however, this remedy, which is widely used in France, only operates to protect the interests of minority shareholders.[263]

Common law countries do not impose a general fiduciary duty on shareholders to act in the interests of the company. Company law in the USA requires that controlling shareholders deal fairly with the minority but does not go further.[264] Other common law jurisdictions impose a fiduciary duty on the general meeting in certain exceptional circumstances, such as when it is changing the constitution, or making other changes, which might adversely impact minority shareholders. However, it is certainly arguable that, if a company has a constitution which allows the general meeting to take management decisions, or if the general

---

[260] See e.g. the Portuguese Code of Commercial Companies (Còdigo das Sociedades Comerciais, 1986), Art. 83, where this point is illustrated by Coutinho de Abreu, 'Corporate governance of Portugal', 20.

[261] Merkt, 'Germany: internal and external corporate governance', 545.

[262] Andersson and Segenmark, *Mapping Paper on the Company Law Barriers and Possibilities for Sustainable Companies*, 9–10; Mähönen, *Sustainable Companies Mapping Paper on Company Law Issues: Finland*, 23; Buhmann, *et al.*, *Mapping: Denmark*, 12–13.

[263] Conac, 'Corporate governance of France', 30.

[264] For example, *Donahue v. Rodd Electrotype Co.*, 367 Mass. 578 (1975).

meeting exercises its power to instruct the board, it should act in the interests of the company (as defined in the law of the particular common law jurisdiction). Other jurisdictions, like Switzerland, do not impose fiduciary duties on shareholders at any level.[265] There is little more than the beginnings of an academic discussion about the imposition of a broader set of fiduciary duties for the shareholders, as in duties to ensure the achievement of the societal purpose of companies.[266]

Overall, then, to the extent that a fiduciary duty is imposed on shareholders, it offers little or nothing in terms of furthering sustainable decision-making in companies, because it is principally a means of protecting minority shareholders and may even act as a restraint on majority shareholders wishing to shift the company onto a sustainable path. Even when shareholders directly influence the company to violate environmental regulations or laws, the shield of limited liability tends to protect the shareholder. There are nevertheless some enforcement possibilities, as we will discuss in the next subsection.

4.3   Shareholder sanctions and liabilities

Any consideration of shareholder liability should distinguish between investor shareholders and controlling shareholders (parent company or personal controlling shareholder). Both types of shareholders benefit from the privilege of limited liability, which protects against any loss beyond the capital they contributed or the price they paid for their shares. This privilege is only removed in exceptional and extraordinary circumstances, referred to as 'veil piercing', a doctrine which is marred by confusion and inconsistency.[267] Kurt Strasser and Philip Blumberg refer to three sets of transactional costs as providing the 'modern justification' for the law's provision of limited investor liability (as it should be named to avoid confusion). First, shareholders do not have to concern themselves with, and monitor, the solvency of other shareholders. Second, shareholders do

---

[265] Kunz, 'Switzerland: the system of corporate governance', 887–8.

[266] I. Anabtawi and L. Stout, 'Fiduciary duties for activist shareholders' (2008) 60 *Stanford Law Review* 1255.

[267] Piercing the corporate veil refers to the shield of limited liability being disregarded by the court, resulting in an identification of shareholders (or parent company) and the company itself (subsidiary), leaving the shareholders (parent) liable for the company's (subsidiary's) affairs. Various jurisdictions apply different approaches to this doctrine, and some jurisdictions do not apply it at all. K. Vandekerckhove, *Piercing of the Corporate Veil* (Kluwer 2008).

138   B. SJÅFJELL, A. JOHNSTON, L. ANKER-SØRENSEN, D. MILLON

not have to monitor the board's activity out of fear of liability. Third, it facilitates investments because investors are assured that there will be no exposure of their 'personal assets to a greater risk of liability'.[268] The same authors argue that none of these rationales apply where the shareholder in question is a parent company.[269] We would certainly agree that they do not apply to the same extent to controlling shareholders (parent company or personal controlling shareholder) as they do to investor shareholders. In what follows, we will focus on parent companies.

In all the jurisdictions we survey, parent company shareholders, like investor shareholders, are protected by the corporate privilege of limited liability and the separate legal entity principle. Since legal systems recognised that companies can own shares, and therefore create subsidiary companies, corporate groups have evolved in a legal vacuum with little or no developed regulation. The German *Konzernrecht* is normally recognised as the most sophisticated regulatory scheme applicable to corporate groups, with explicit standards for parental liability.[270] Perhaps this is the reason for its influence on the legal regulation of groups in Portugal,[271] Brazil,[272] and Turkey,[273] among many examples.

The significance of the legal vacuum, in particular for jurisdictions without explicit regulation of corporate groups, comes to a head in cases regarding group liability and, of interest specifically in our context, parental liability for environmental externalities caused by subsidiaries.[274] Various approaches have been introduced to fill the legal vacuum, and

---

[268] K.A. Strasser and P.I. Blumberg, *Legal Models and Business Realities of Enterprise Groups: Mismatch and Change*, Research Paper No. 18/2009 (CLPE, 2009), 7.

[269] Strasser and Blumberg, *Legal Models and Business Realities of Enterprise Groups: Mismatch and Change*, 8.

[270] This liability scheme only addresses parent company shareholders and not individual investor-shareholders, and also applies differently to the two types of German group structure, see R. Reich-Graefe, 'Changing paradigms: the liability of corporate groups in Germany' (2005) 37 *Connecticut Law Review* 785, 788.

[271] Còdigo das Sociedades Comerciais, 1986, Art. 501, see Antunes, 'The law of corporate groups in Portugal', 29.

[272] V. Vizziotti, *et al.*, *Sustainable Companies under Brazilian Regulation: A Substantive and Procedural Overview*, Research Paper No. 2013–17 (University of Oslo Faculty of Law, 2013), available at: http://ssrn.com/abstract=2281095.

[273] Art. 195–209 of the New Turkish Commercial Code, cited in Eroglu, *Obstacles and Possibilities for Sustainable Companies in Turkey*, Part C.

[274] Corporate groups' environmental responsibility and possibly liability in a broader climate change context vary between jurisdictions, depending on factors such as *locus standi* rights, substantive environmental rules, and available remedies: P. Sands, *et al.*, *Principles of International Environmental Law* (Cambridge University Press, 2012), 15–16. See also L. Anker-Sørensen, *Parental Liability for Externalities of Subsidiaries: Domestic and*

SHAREHOLDER PRIMACY

they can be divided into liability schemes leaving corporate privileges intact, which are referred to as 'indirect liability' schemes and are based on parental wrongdoings, and liability schemes where corporate privileges are disregarded (or challenged), which may be referred to as 'direct liability' schemes.[275] In the latter type of scheme, parent companies can be held strictly liable without proving fault. The legal basis for both types of liability schemes can be either statutory or judicial. The statutory liability approach can be found within company and/or environmental legislation, and environmental law provides a strict (direct) liability in quite a few jurisdictions. Judicial liability takes many different forms, ranging from jurisdictions that do not broadly give judges specific discretion to pierce the corporate veil, such as Norway[276] and Denmark,[277] to those, such as India,[278] China,[279] and Ghana,[280] which give courts discretion to pierce 'when it is just and in the public interest to do so'.[281]

Within the range of national approaches, we find jurisdictions applying veil piercing in agency situations (and also in cases of fraud or concealing assets), where a controlling parent company is involved in all (or almost all) of the subsidiary's affairs, leaving the subsidiary as nothing more than the parent's puppet.[282] This, however, can be hard to prove, given

---

Extraterritorial Approaches, Research Paper No. 2014-36, (University of Oslo Faculty of Law, 2014), available at: http://ssrn.com/abstract=2506508.

[275] Germany applies both approaches; see the intragroup liability schemes in Germany described by Antunes as a 'dualist approach', see J.E. Antunes, *Liability of Corporate Groups: Autonomy and Control in Parent-Subsidiary Relationships in U. S., German and EEC Law* (Kluwer Law, 1994).

[276] Sjåfjell, *Sustainable Companies: Possibilities and Barriers in Norwegian Company Law*, s. 7.1.

[277] S. Friis Hansen and J. Valdemar Krenchel, *Dansk selskabsret 1* (3rd edn, Thomson Reuters, 2010), 139–44.

[278] S. Deva, *Sustainable Business and Indian Company Law: A Critical Review* (Sustainable Companies Project, 2011), s. VII.

[279] Lou and Tian, *A Study on Sustainable Companies in the P. R. China*, s. 7.1. The notion of enterprise liability can also be extended to foreign company's investing in Chinese companies, even though the situation with joint ventures is still unclear.

[280] Schwartz, *Developing States and Climate Change: Solutions in Company Law?*, 37.

[281] Schwartz, *Developing States and Climate Change: Solutions in Company Law?*

[282] A similar approach is taken by the Court of Justice of the EU in competition cases, where the doctrine of veil piercing, as in procedural matters, has been invoked from the early 1970s: see *International Chemical Industries*, C-48/69 [1972] ECR 619, where the court held that '[t]he fact that a subsidiary has separate legal personality is not sufficient to exclude the possibility of imputing its conduct to the parent company . . . in particular where the subsidiary, although having separate legal personality, does not decide independently upon its own conduct on the market, but carries out, in all material respects, the instructions given to it by the parent company'.

the fundamental notion that corporate privileges should not be dislodged without good reason, and. In jurisdictions such as the UK,[283] in the absence of an express agency agreement, the claimant must prove that the parent exercises such pervasive control over the subsidiary that the separation is a mere façade or that the subsidiary has 'no separate mind, will or existence of its own'.[284] Recent UK Supreme Court decisions have confirmed the courts' highly restrictive approach to veil piercing.[285]

Under indirect liability schemes, the parent company is held liable based on its own wrongdoings through the use of the concept of duty of care.[286] Such a duty of care was recognised by the UK Court of Appeal in *Chandler v. Cape plc.*[287] Here, the parent was held liable in negligence where its subsidiary's employees were exposed to asbestos.[288] Following the same line of reasoning within an environmental context, the Dutch court was in 2013 asked to consider three linked cases against Shell for environmental damages caused by a Nigerian subsidiary's oil spill.[289] The Dutch court followed the reasoning in *Chandler v. Cape plc*, where a parental duty of care is presumed to be established based on three criteria: foreseeable, proximity, and that it seems fair, just, and reasonable to establish a parental duty of care in the specific case. After applying the 'duty of care' test on Shell, the court concluded that the parent company in this specific case could not be held responsible for the environmental damages based on the lack of proximity, the potential number of beneficiaries, and that the parent company at most could be held responsible for preventing and mitigating the environmental harm, but not the damage itself. Similarly, claimants in Germany and Lithuania must prove detrimental parental influence, and a causal link between that interference and the loss or

---

[283] Villiers, *Mapping Paper: Sustainable Companies UK Report*, s. 6.1.

[284] *Adams v. Cape Industries* [1990] Ch. 433. See also a similar case from British Columbia, Canada: *International Trademarks Inc. v. Clearly Canadian Beverage Corporation* (1999), 47 B.C.L.R. (2d). 193.

[285] *Prest v. Petrodel Resources Ltd* [2013] UKSC 34; *VTB Capital plc v. Nutritek International Corp.* [2013] UKSC 5.

[286] Since it is based on a wrongful act made by the parent, no exception to the limited liability and separate legal personality is needed.

[287] *Chandler v. Cape plc* [2012] EWCA Civ. 525.

[288] Key to the decision was the fact that the parent had assumed responsibility to the employees in question to advise or ensure that there was a safe system of work, and therefore owed a duty of care to the employees of the subsidiary.

[289] See District Court of The Hague 30 January 2013. LJN BY9845; District Court of The Hague 30 January 2013, LJN BY9850; and District Court of The Hague 30 January 2013, LJN BY9854.

damage.[290] This approach is also used in the environmental legislation of some jurisdictions, such as Spain,[291] where a parent company can be liable for environmental damages caused by its subsidiary. In the EU, any natural or legal person that legally and factually exerts or has exerted a decisive influence resulting in the environmentally damaging activity can be held liable as an 'operator'.[292] This principle is derived from the EU Environmental Liability Directive.[293] The 'operator' approach aims to hold liable natural or legal persons where they have acted deliberately or negligently. The effect is a parental duty of care. By contrast, the US Supreme Court has explicitly rejected the notion that corporations can be considered as 'operators' in the context of environmental hazardous waste.[294]

In some direct liability schemes, the parent can be held liable solely on the formal basis of its relationship with its subsidiary.[295] This is evident, for example, in Portugal, where a parent company can be held liable for its subsidiary's debts where proceedings against the subsidiary have failed.[296] Similarly, direct parental liability can be found in environmental

---

[290] Reich-Graefe, 'Changing paradigms: the liability of corporate groups in Germany', 791–2; Procedurally, on the one hand, it is nearly impossible to prove such detrimental interference by the parent, but on the other hand, de facto single economic enterprises are often characterised by 'highly interconnected companies with a multitude of parental interference'. In Lithuania, this is regulated in Article 2.50(3) of the Civil Code; *UAB Göllnerspedition v. S. B. ir kt.* [2004] No. 3K-3–124/2004 (Supreme Court of Lithuania), cited in Lauraityte and Miliauskas, Sustainable Companies under the Lithuanian Company Law, s. 7.1.

[291] Environmental Responsibility Act 2007, Art. 10, with Arts 42 (1) and 18 of the Commercial Code.

[292] L. Bergkamp and B. Goldsmith, *The EU Environmental Liability Directive: A Commentary* (Oxford University Press, 2013).

[293] The Environmental Liability Directive (2004/35/CE), Art. 6 defines 'operator' as 'any natural or legal, private or public person who operates or controls the occupational activity or, where this is provided for in national legislation, to whom decisive economic power over the technical functioning of such an activity has been delegated, including the holder of a permit or authorization for such an activity or the person registering or notifying such an activity'.

[294] *United States v. Bestfoods*, 524 U.S. 51 (1998).

[295] See e.g. control groups in Germany, AktG § 291(1), translated in H. Schneider and M. Heidenhain, *The German Stock Corporation Act: Bilingual Edition with an Introduction to the Law* (Kluwer Law International, 2nd edn, 2000), 265; Reich-Graefe 2005, p. 789.

[296] Code of Commercial Codes 1986, Art. 501, referred to in J. Antunes, *The Law of Corporate Groups in Portugal*, Working Paper Series No. 84 (Institute for Law and Finance, 2008), 29.

142   B. SJÅFJELL, A. JOHNSTON, L. ANKER-SØRENSEN, D. MILLON

legislation, as in Finland[297] and Brazil,[298] which aims to hold a parent liable whenever damages are caused to the quality of the environment. However, the claimant still must prove a sufficient connection between the conduct of the parent company and the environmental damage, although there is no requirement that the parent should have behaved negligently.[299] In Finland, the competence autonomy of the subsidiary, the financial relationship between parent and subsidiary, and also possibly whether the parent has gained from the tortious activity, are taken into account in deciding whether the parent should be held liable.[300]

One key weakness of these liability schemes is the lack of an extraterritorial aspect. Environmental damage does not stop at national borders, and there is a need for legal mechanisms that mirror the structure of multinational enterprises and have traction over transnational environmental damage. An innovative statutory approach in this regard has been developed in the companies legislation of Albania[301] and Turkey,[302] including a conflict of laws provision that makes domestic and foreign parent companies equally responsible for environmental externalities wherever they occur.[303] Albania is also notable for its recognition of enterprise liability,

---

[297] A parent company's environmental liability is regulated in the Environmental Protection Act, Act on Compensation for Environmental Damage, and the Environmental Damage Insurance Act. Direct environmental liability is within ss. 7(1)–(2), and is imposed on anyone 'comparable' to the person carrying out the environmental damage: cited in Mähönen, *Sustainable Companies Mapping Paper on Company Law Issues: Finland*, ss. 4.1.1 and 4.1.3.

[298] Federal Bill No. 6938/81, Art. 14(1) and Federal Bill No. 9605/98, Art. 4; see also Art. 50 in Civil Code (general rule of piercing the veil): cited in Vizziotti, *et al.*, *Sustainable Companies under Brazilian Regulation*, s. C.1. The argument has also been made that the controlling shareholder generally has a duty to ensure that the company accomplishes its purpose and performs its social role: Eizirik and Weber, 'Corporate governance of Brazil', 1027.

[299] Eizirik and Weber, 'Corporate governance of Brazil', 1027; and Mähönen, *Sustainable Companies Mapping Paper on Company Law Issues: Finland*, s. 4.1.3.

[300] Act on Compensation for Environmental Damage, 1994, s. 7(1)(2), cited in Mähönen, *Sustainable Companies Mapping Paper on Company Law Issues: Finland*, s. 4.1.3.

[301] Law No. 9901, On Entrepreneurs and Companies, 2008, Art. 208(4). See further, Dine, 'Jurisdictional arbitrage', 44–69.

[302] Turkish Commercial Code, Arts 195(1) and 202(e): Eroglu, *Obstacles and Possibilities for Sustainable Companies in Turkey*, Part C.

[303] In the EU, Rome II Regulation on the Law Applicable to Non-contractual Obligations (EC/864/2007) Art. 7 provides plaintiffs of environmental damage claims a choice of law between (i) *lex loci damni* (place of the injury) and (ii) *lex loci delicti* (place of the tortious act). The understanding of the latter was further interpreted in the landmark *Bier* case (*Bier v. Mines de Potassse d'Alsace*, ECJ 21/76, 1976) by clarifying that victims

applicable to all affiliated companies, not just the parent.[304] However, the burden of proof on a claimant seeking to make a parent company liable for environmental damage caused by a subsidiary can be difficult to discharge in particular cases. In order to promote sustainable groups, we would support José Antunes' suggestion of a reversal of the burden of proof, so that once a claimant has proved that a subsidiary company has caused environmental damage, the parent company would be required to 'bring evidence as to whether the challenged decisions [or the environmental damage which occurred] have originated from its control or were taken autonomously by the subsidiaries'.[305]

4.4   Shareholder control is not the answer

The preceding analysis has shown that some jurisdictions give shareholders plenty of authority to influence the company's direction, while others restrict the ability of the shareholders in their general meeting to interfere with the board's decision-making, and some even prohibit it entirely.

Even where shareholder interference is a legal possibility, shareholders in large companies will often be dispersed with small stakes in the company, with the result that the costs of coordinating influence will normally be disproportionate to the benefit that may accrue to each from doing so. This is not to say that shareholders do not influence boards; the threat of dismissal makes the board responsive to (perceived) shareholder interests. In many jurisdictions it is theoretically possible for the requisite majority of shareholders to demand that the board pays greater attention to sustainability issues where there is a business case for doing so. Beyond the scope of the business case, minority protection rules may limit even the theoretical possibility of majority shareholders seeking environmental sustainability, making this a possibility only where there is a supermajority or unanimity in order to allow revision of the articles of association and any statement of that particular company's purpose. However, the BJR

---

of environmental degradation can sue the polluter in their home court, the place of pollution, or the place where the injury was caused.

[304] This is based on the identification that lies within the concept of a control group, where anyone (natural or legal person) who can invoke a tort claim, is to be regarded as a creditor to the entire corporate group, as a result of their claims: see Dine, 'Jurisdictional arbitrage', 66–7. A similar approach can be found in the USA: P.I. Blumberg, 'Accountability of multinational corporations: the barriers presented by concepts of the corporate juridical entity', (2001) 24 *Hastings Int'l & Comparative Law Review*, 297–320, 313.

[305] J.E. Antunes, *Liability of Corporate Groups* (Kluwer, 1994), 132, 384 and 493ff.; K. Vandekerckhove, *Piercing of the Corporate Veil* (Kluwer 2008), 544–5.

may allow the board to be influenced by a majority shareholder claiming to have a business case for environmental sustainability. Shareholders do not generally use the powers company law bestows on them across jurisdictions to move companies onto a sustainable path. Company law creates possibilities that could have been used to produce something akin to shareholder-driven pluralism, but in practice, these powers are used in line with the monistic approach, simultaneously driven by and enhancing the social norm of shareholder primacy. Also, when the largest corporate groups of the world embrace sustainability in their policies and marketing, the financial sustainability of their business is the focal point (however the group may present their sustainability efforts to the public), rather than ensuring that their business functions with the boundaries of a finite and vulnerable biosphere.[306]

Company law gives majority shareholders ample scope for action and influence where they want to use a particular company as a vehicle for contributing to environmental sustainability. In theory, company law also, albeit to a limited extent, erects certain barriers against majority shareholders who wish to promote the narrow, short-term shareholder interest only. The legal scope for such a shareholder strategy is, however, still too wide, and, in practice, company law does not impose meaningful limits on the destructive effects of the ethos of shareholder primacy.

5   The unexplored potential and way forward

5.1   The unexplored potential

Our analysis shows that there is much unfulfilled potential within company law regimes worldwide, as they currently exist, for companies to change from their generally short-termist, environmentally exploitative business models towards more responsible, long-term sustainability. In the mainstream corporate governance debate it is often said that the purpose of companies is the maximisation of shareholder value. As a matter of law, this is incorrect, particularly if we are referring to society's purpose with the company as an institution. Profit for shareholders is but one function of companies, and even where, exceptionally, a national system of company law turns this function into the primary goal by requiring

---

[306] See e.g. P. Dauvergne and J. Lister, *Eco-Business: A Big-Brand Takeover of Sustainability* (MIT Press, 2013).

the board to prioritise the shareholder interest, it is still understood that this is as a means to the end of increasing society's welfare.

Shareholders *could* use their power and influence to demand a departure from this misguided status quo. Many jurisdictions give broad powers to the general meeting, which would allow shareholders to steer the business of the company in a more sustainable direction. However, as Benjamin Richardson has shown, SRI so far seems destined to remain a modest, niche sector of the financial economy, unable greatly to influence the environmental practices of companies, in the absence of legal innovation. Conversely, the general influence of shareholders tends to amount to an uncritical push to maximise short-term returns to themselves.

Company law across many jurisdictions gives boards – and, by extension, management – perhaps surprising latitude to steer companies' business towards greater sustainability. No system of company law insists that boards should focus only on short-term returns to shareholders. In some countries, environmental sustainability has begun to make inroads into the duties of the board. All jurisdictions expect boards to ensure their companies comply with environmental law, and allow boards to go beyond the requirements of environmental law to internalise environmental externalities, at least in so far as they can articulate a business case argument for doing so. Some jurisdictions go further and allow companies to protect the environment beyond instrumental business case considerations. The BJR adopted in most nations broadens this discretion considerably.

5.2   The continued dominance of the social norm of shareholder primacy

While no system of company law requires the board to maximise returns to shareholders at all costs, the social norm of shareholder primacy provides incentives and pressures to do just this. Our analysis shows that, while company law does erect some barriers to the pursuit of sustainability, these are trivial compared with the social norm of shareholder primacy. This norm springs out of the historically contingent focus of company law on the position of shareholders (albeit one that varies a little across jurisdictions). Shareholder primacy has been allowed to develop because the law contains neither an explicit statement of what the societal purpose of companies is, nor of what the interests of the company are.

The influence of shareholder primacy means that there has been little exploration of how far boards – the strategy-setting, supervisory organ of companies – are legally permitted to go in shifting the management of business towards sustainable development. Boards frequently do not even choose the environmentally friendly, low-carbon option where there is an arguable business case, let alone challenge the outer boundaries of the rules by pursuing sustainability where the likely profitability of a particular decision may be questioned. The practice of companies in the aggregate is therefore detrimental both to those potentially affected by climate change and other environmental degradation (who, to date, have been primarily located in developing countries), and to vulnerable future generations. 'Business as usual' is detrimental to any shareholder with more than a very short-term perspective on their investment, including institutional investors such as pension funds and sovereign wealth funds. At the individual company level, shareholder primacy has negative implications for the long-term prospects of the firm itself as it discourages innovative long-term investments and tends to encourage increasing indebtedness to fund ever greater distributions to shareholders.

In the context of corporate groups, shareholder primacy is even more prominent, with the parent company's control of the group in practice virtually unrestricted by company law. The impact of this on sustainability is exacerbated by the sparse possibilities for holding the parent company liable for subsidiaries' environmental transgressions.

5.3   A way forward

While company law gives those who control companies ample scope to take account of sustainability, company law has also allowed the social imperative of shareholder primacy to develop to the point that it constitutes the most pernicious barrier to more sustainable companies. This trend has occurred because of what the law regulates and what it does not. It is here that we have tentatively identified a way forward. Since a major problem is a lack of regulatory clarity with regard to society's purpose in allowing companies to operate, and to the interests of the company, setting these key issues straight in a principles-based manner could be the foundation for a move towards a more environmentally sustainable direction for business.

The competence and duties of the board must be revised to reflect the redefined purpose of the company, with the concept of the interests of the company codified in a modern and inclusive manner. Building on the analysis in this chapter, a first tentative reform proposal intended for the Nordic countries by Beate Sjåfjell and Jukka Mähönen suggests that national companies acts should state that the societal purpose of companies is to create sustainable value within the planetary boundaries.[307] Such a redefined purpose of companies would need to be operationalised through integration of such a goal into the duties of the board. In a further development of this idea aimed at the EU level, Beate Sjåfjell suggests that the board be responsible for ensuring that the company formulates a long-term, life-cycle-based business plan, with key performance indicators against which the company could report annually.[308] Such a company law reform could potentially give more content to the non-financial reporting requirements that the European Parliament adopted in April 2014.[309] These and other tentative ideas for reform are discussed in the final chapter of this book, Chapter 8, where legal reform is also placed in the broader context of the sustainability discourse.

Shareholder primacy has become deeply entrenched through market pressure, necessitating legal reform to correct this market failure. Competitive advantage must be given to companies that contribute to sustainable development and taken away from those that do not. Reform of core company law, both at the level of broad principle, and at the level of its detailed structure, is a prerequisite to achieving sustainable companies. If done thoughtfully but ambitiously, it holds out the prospect of making more effective existing and future external regulation of companies, while allowing each company to realise its potential and contribute in its own creative and independent way to the mitigation of climate change and to broader environmental sustainability. Our position is not that reforming company law is the solution to all problems. Rather, it is a crucial piece of the jigsaw puzzle of sustainability that we urgently need to put into place.

---

[307] B. Sjåfjell and J. Mähönen, 'Upgrading the Nordic corporate governance model for sustainable companies' (2014) 11 *European Company Law* 58.

[308] B. Sjåfjell, 'Corporate governance for sustainability: the necessary reform of EU company law', in B. Sjåfjell and A. Wiesbrock (eds.), *The Greening of European Business under EU Law* (Routledge, 2015), Chapter 6.

[309] Discussed in depth in Chapter 5 by Villiers and Mähönen in this book.

4

The role of board directors in promoting environmental sustainability

BLANAID CLARKE

1 Introduction

In December 2012, the European Commission published an Action Plan on European Company Law and Corporate Governance ('Action Plan'), which was significantly sub-titled *A Modern Legal Framework for More Engaged Shareholders and Sustainable Companies*.[1] This initiative indicates the current focus of the Commission's attention on sustainability and its perception of the role that corporate governance plays in achieving this objective. This reference to 'sustainability', explained more fully in the Commission's Green Paper on EU Corporate Governance Framework[2] in 2011, refers more particularly to sustainable growth and long-term business performance. There is also, however, a growing awareness that companies have a crucial part to play in ensuring sustainability in the ecological sense of safeguarding the biosphere and minimising environmental damage. This is the sense in which the terms 'sustainability' and 'sustainable agenda' are used in the chapter. This is more consistent with the definition of corporate social responsibilit,y (CSR) introduced by the Commission in its communication *A Renewed EU Strategy 2011–14 for Corporate Social Responsibility*, which referred to 'the responsibility of enterprises for their impacts on society'.[3] While shareholders can play a role in engaging with their companies on this subject,[4] it is clear that it will fall largely to the board to champion environmental concerns over

[1] European Commission, Action Plan, *European Company Law and Corporate Governance: A Modern Legal Framework for More Engaged Shareholders and Sustainable Companies*, COM/2012/0740 final (2012).

[2] European Commission, *Green Paper: The EU Corporate Governance Framework*, COM (2011)164 final, (2011) 3.

[3] European Commission, *A Renewed EU Strategy 2011–14 for Corporate Social Responsibility*, COM(2011) 681, (2011), 6.

[4] B. Clarke, 'The EU's shareholder empowerment model in the context of the sustainable companies agenda' (2013) 2 *European Company Law* 103.

and above those required by the law and it will be their responsibility to embed them within the company's activities.

This chapter contributes to this book's understanding of the role of corporate law in facilitating or hindering environmentally responsible companies by analysing the role of boards of directors and, in particular, the role of corporate governance codes in disciplining boards to consider environmental concerns. The chapter builds on Chapter 3 by Sjåfjell and others in this book, and complements it by analysing how the role of the board of directors in the European Union (EU) and its Member States has been developed not through legislative reform but through revisions to corporate governance codes. These codes emphasise the importance of the board in monitoring and in strategic decision-making. It is submitted that in fulfilling both of these functions, directors must engage with the question of environmental sustainability. This is the case, not just for companies that adopt a broad, pluralistic interpretation of CSR but also for those whose focus is maximising shareholder returns over the long term. There is some evidence that this type of engagement improves financial performance. In addition, it is clearly an essential component of any effective risk management exercise to reduce the potential for regulatory sanctions and reputational damage to the company. Having set out what the board needs to do in this context, the chapter then examines the evolution of rules on board composition in order to determine whether directors are equipped to carry out this task. While this is also a matter left to soft law and corporate governance codes, the provisions in this respect have become more detailed and prescriptive. It is argued that this is a positive development in terms of the sustainable agenda. Based on existing empirical research, the new rules on independence, diversity, knowledge and character are likely to lead to the appointment of boards capable and more willing to engage with environmental issues proactively.

Section 2 of the chapter describes the manner in which corporate boards are regulated at both the EU and the national level in the Union. Section 3 examines the development of the role of non-executive directors and considers their role in embedding sustainability within the organisational framework. The chapter then turns to a consideration of the attributes and skills which directors and, in particular non-executive directors, are expected to possess. This involves an examination of: independence (Section 4); diversity (Section 5); knowledge and skills (Section 6); and character and integrity (Section 7).

2 Regulation of corporate boards

The structure of corporate boards varies across the EU. A before including mapping exercise of board structures in 2013 indicated that a one-tier-board system currently exists in seven Member States, including the UK, Ireland, and Spain.[5] Such a system also applies in the USA. A unitary board normally involves a single board comprising 'a combination of executive directors with their intimate knowledge of the business, and of outside, non-executive directors, who can bring a broader perspective to the company's activities'.[6] This board is the main decision-making organ within the company and its members are collectively responsible for the success of the company. This compares with a 'two-tier' system which generally involves a 'managing board' composed of the executive directors and a distinct 'supervisory board' responsible for overseeing the activity of the managing directors. A mandatory two-tier system exists in seven Member States, including Germany and Austria. In addition, 13 Member States, including France, Italy, and Portugal, permit companies to choose between one- and two-tier boards. The authors of the mapping exercise noted, however, that the board structures in a number of Member States 'cannot easily be classified according to the "monistic"/"dualistic" divide'.[7] They cited the example of the 'Nordic model' in Sweden, which is a hybrid form, incorporating elements of both the one-tier and the in two-tier systems.[8]

'One of the most significant events in modern corporate governance'[9] was the publication of a two-page Code of Best Practice by the UK Committee on the Financial Aspects of Corporate Governance in 1992. Referred to as the 'Cadbury Code' after the Committee's chairman, Sir Adrian Cadbury, it was designed 'to achieve the necessary standards of corporate behaviour'[10] by strengthening and increasing the effectiveness of corporate boards. Companies were required, as a condition of

---

[5] C. Gerner-Beuerle, P. Paech, and E. Schuster, *Study on Directors' Duties and Liability* (European Commission, DG Market, 2013) 4–12.

[6] Committee on the Financial Aspects of Corporate Governance, *Report of the Committee*, 1992, para. 4.1.

[7] Committee on the Financial Aspects of Corporate Governance, *Report of the Committee*, 1992, 7.

[8] Committee on the Financial Aspects of Corporate Governance, *Report of the Committee*, 1992.

[9] C. Jordan, *Cadbury Twenty Years On* (Center for Transnational Legal Studies Faculty Papers & Publications, 2012).

[10] Committee on the Financial Aspects of Corporate Governance, *Report of the Committee*, 1992, 11.

THE ROLE OF BOARD DIRECTORS IN SUSTAINABILITY   151

listing on the London Stock Exchange, to comply or to explain their non-compliance with the provisions of the Cadbury Code. This system of 'comply-or-explain' has been described as 'the trademark of corporate governance in the UK'.[11] Its introduction triggered a global debate on corporate governance and led to the development of similar codes across the globe.[12] It resulted in widespread acceptance that compliance with a voluntary code or disclosure of non-compliance is more effective than a statutory code in regulating corporate governance.

Although such a system lacks the clarity and precision that hard law would provide, it provides flexibility, allowing companies to adapt governance practices to their specific situations. It requires boards to publicly disclose the manner in which they have exercised their judgements in this respect and thus allows shareholders to factor this information into their assessment of the companies. Another advantage of a code over a traditional hard law instrument is its adaptability and speed. The UK's Financial Reporting Council, which is responsible for corporate governance in the UK, has emphasised that 'Its fitness for purpose in a permanently changing economic and social business environment requires its evaluation at appropriate intervals.'[13] The Cadbury Code has been amended a number of times since its introduction to take into account several reviews, including: a report by the Study Group on Directors' Remuneration under the chairmanship of Sir Richard Greenbury in 1995,[14] a report by the Committee on Corporate Governance under the chairmanship of Sir Ronald Hampel in 1998,[15] a review by Sir Derek Higgs of the role and effectiveness of non-executive directors in 2003,[16] a report by Sir David Walker on the governance of banks and other financial institutions in 2009,[17] and, most recently, a report by Lord Davies on board diversity in 2011.[18] Renamed 'the UK Corporate Governance Code' in 2010 and amended most recently in 2014, the code now extends to 20 pages and consists of principles and more detailed

[11] Financial Reporting Council (FRC), *UK Corporate Governance Code* (FRC, 2014), 4.
[12] The European Corporate Governance Institute's website (www.ecgi.org/codes/all_codes. php) provides a useful index of national and international codes.
[13] Financial Reporting Council (FRC), *UK Corporate Governance Code* (FRC, 2014), 1.
[14] *Directors' Remuneration: Report of a Study Group Chaired by Sir Richard Greenbury* (Gee Publishing, 1995).
[15] Committee on Corporate Governance, *Final Report* (Gee Publishing, 1998).
[16] D. Higgs, *Review of the Role and Effectiveness of Non-executive Directors* (Department of Trade and Industry, 2003).
[17] D. Walker, *A Review of Corporate Governance in UK Banks and Other Financial Industry Entities* (Walker Review Secretariat, 2009).
[18] Department of Business, Innovation and Skills (DBIS), *Women on Boards* (DBIS, 2011).

152   BLANAID CLARKE

provisions relating to leadership, effectiveness, accountability, remuneration, and relations with shareholders. The comply-or-explain regime is underpinned in the UK by a regulatory framework, including the Companies Act 2006.

At the EU level, soft law in the form of a Commission Recommendation has also been used to improve board governance. In 2005, the European Commission published a Recommendation on the role of non-executive or supervisory directors of listed companies and on the committees of the supervisory board.[19] Many of the proposals contained therein echo provisions in the UK Corporate Governance Code. The Recommendation is comprised of six main pillars: (1) an appropriate balance of executive and non-executive directors on boards, including a separation of the functions of chairman and chief executive officer; (2) a sufficient number of independent directors on the boards together with adequate disclosure on the determination of board members' independence; (3) board committees comprised largely of independent, non-executive directors; (4) regular evaluation of the board's functioning and competence; (5) greater transparency and communication with shareholders; and (6) a clarification of standards of qualification, competence, and availability for board members. Member States were invited to take the necessary measures to promote the application of this Recommendation either through legislation or through the application of a corporate governance code. A subsequent report by the Commission on the application of the Recommendation indicated that while progress had been made in improving governance standards in this field, a number of the recommended standards had not been followed in all Member States.[20]

The comply-or-explain principle was introduced into EU law by Directive 2006/46/EC which requires that listed companies refer in their corporate governance statement to a corporate governance code and that they report on their application of that code on a comply-or-explain basis.[21] A comparative study of corporate governance across EU Member

---

[19] Recommendation 2005/162/EC.

[20] European Commission, *Report on the Application by the Member States of the EU of the Commission Recommendation on the Role of Non-executive or Supervisory Directors of Listed Companies and on the Committees of the (Supervisory) Board*, SEC (2007) 1021 (2007).

[21] Directive 2006/46/EC of the European Parliament and of the Council of 14 June 2006 amending Council Directives 78/660/EEC on the annual accounts of certain types of companies, 83/349/EEC on consolidated accounts, 86/635/EEC on the annual accounts and consolidated accounts of banks and other financial institutions and 91/674/EEC on the annual accounts and consolidated accounts of insurance undertakings, O.J. EC No L 224, 2006.

THE ROLE OF BOARD DIRECTORS IN SUSTAINABILITY   153

States revealed that matters such as general board organisation, audit committees, statutory audit, and procedural shareholder rights tend to be regulated by law, often following European legislation.[22] Other topics such as board membership, independence, remuneration, internal control, and risk management are more often treated in corporate governance codes. The study indicated, however, that these categories are not clearly defined and vary between Member States. Surveys undertaken as part of the study indicate 'an overwhelming support' for the comply-or-explain regime from regulators, companies, and investors. However, while respondents considered it an appropriate and efficient regulatory tool, there was also near consensus that the mechanism does not function perfectly. Shortcomings were identified, for example, in the areas of enforcement and in the quality of disclosures in certain cases. In its Action Plan, the Commission announced its intention to take an initiative to improve the quality of corporate governance reports, and in particular the quality of explanations to be provided by companies that depart from the corporate governance codes.[23] In April 2014, the Commission published a draft Recommendation that seeks to provide guidance to listed companies, investors, and other interested parties in order to improve the overall quality of corporate governance statements published by companies.[24]

The success of the aforementioned codes in improving corporate governance standards clearly depends on the level of engagement by boards with key principles. In order to be effective, the Financial Reporting Council emphasised that '[t]he Boards must see good governance as a means to improve their performance, not just a compliance exercise'.[25]

3   The role of non-executive directors

The Corporate Governance Green Paper in 2011 identified the board of directors as being at the heart of good corporate governance, noting that

---

[22] RiskMetrics Group, *Study on Monitoring and Enforcement Practices in Corporate Governance in the Member States* (2009); available at: http://ec.europa.eu/internal_market/company/docs/ecgforum/studies/comply-or-explain-090923_en.pdf.

[23] European Commission, *Action Plan: European Company Law and Corporate Governance: A Modern Legal Framework For More Engaged Shareholders and Sustainable Companies*, COM/2012/0740 final. (2012), 2.2.

[24] A provisional version of the text for the draft recommendation is available at: http://ec.europa.eu/internal_market/company/modern/index_en.htm#corporategovernancepackage.

[25] Financial Reporting Council (FRC), *The UK Approach to Corporate Governance* (FRC, 2010), p. 6.

'high performing, effective boards are needed to challenge executive management'.[26] This echoes one of the opening statements in the Cadbury Committee's Report that 'every public company should be headed by an effective board which can both lead and control the company'.[27] The Committee's Report went on to emphasise the contribution of non-executive directors to the governance process in two ways: first, by reviewing the performance of the board; and management and, second, by 'taking the lead' in cases of conflict of interest. Such conflicts, it was stated, could arise where the interests of management and 'the wider interests of the company' diverged. While some academics argue that their role as auditors of management is the one that they are best qualified to play,[28] the Cadbury Report explained that the reason it was emphasising the non-executive directors' control function was because the rationale for the Committee's establishment was to review those aspects of corporate governance specifically related to financial reporting and accountability.[29] Accountability in this context was expressed only in relation to accountability to shareholders. It stated very clearly, however, that the primary contribution of non-executive directors as equal board members is to the leadership of the company. The Hampel Report commented that an 'unintended side-effect' of the Cadbury Code was to 'overemphasise the monitoring role'. It stated that it found 'general acceptance that non-executive directors should have both a strategic and a monitoring function'.[30] Nevertheless, the tension identified in these two reports between the non-executive directors' role as a monitor and their role as a contributor to strategic development remained and was referred to five years later in the Higgs Review.[31] Based on its own research, including 40 in-depth interviews with directors, the Higgs Review found that, while there might be a tension, there was no 'essential contradiction' between the two aspects of the non-executive directors' role. It suggested that:

---

[26] European Commission, *Green Paper: EU Corporate Governance*, 3.

[27] Committee on the Financial Aspects of Corporate Governance, para 4.1.

[28] R. Nolan, 'The legal control of directors' conflicts of interest in the United Kingdom: non-executive directors following the Higgs Report', in J. Armour and J.A. McCahery (eds.), *After Enron: Improving Corporate Law and Modernising Securities Regulation in Europe and the US* (Hart Publishing, 2006), 367.

[29] Committee on the Financial Aspects of Corporate Governance, *Report of the Committee*, 1992, para. 1.2.

[30] Hampel Committee, *Final Report* (European Corporate Governance Institute, 1998), paras 3.7 and 3.8.

[31] Higgs, *Review of the Role and Effectiveness of Non-executive Directors*, para. 6.1.

THE ROLE OF BOARD DIRECTORS IN SUSTAINABILITY 155

Polarized conceptions of the role, the research noted, bear little relation to the actual conditions for non-executive effectiveness. An overemphasis on monitoring and control risks non-executive directors seeing themselves, and being seen, as an alien policing influence detached from the rest of the board. An overemphasis on strategy risks non-executive directors becoming too close to executive management, undermining shareholder confidence in the effectiveness of board governance.[32]

While noting that companies differ in terms of what they require from their boards,[33] the Higgs Review suggested that the Code should state 'non-executive directors should constructively challenge and help develop proposals on strategy'. This text was accepted and remains as a Main Principle in the UK Corporate Governance Code.[34] The inclusion of this statement as a Main Principle is significant because listed companies incorporated in the UK must state in their annual financial reports how they have applied the Main Principles, whereas they may explain non-compliance with the other provisions.[35] Non-executive directors of listed companies are thus required to exercise both their control and strategic functions. This stipulation has important implications for the manner in which non-executive directors can promote sustainability in their companies.

In order to yield a real improvement in companies' environmental performance, directors should engage with environmental issues proactively and embed them into every aspect of their strategic thinking as well as considering them in the context of a risk management approach to prevent regulatory and reputational damage to the company.[36] A policy of integrating environmental concerns into companies' decision-making is a strategic matter that would thus clearly fall within the scope of the non-executive directors' role. They clearly have a part to play in putting environmental concerns on the board table and agreeing how these might be integrated with the broader activities of the company. This is also important in the sense of 'setting the tone from the top' as senior management is a principal source of the company's cultural beliefs and values. Non-executive directors in particular play a valuable role in the ethical aspects

---

[32] Higgs, *Review of the Role and Effectiveness of Non-executive Directors*, para. 6.2.

[33] Higgs, *Review of the Role and Effectiveness of Non-executive Directors*, para. 6.4.

[34] Financial Reporting Council, UK Corporate Governance Code (2014), para. A. 4.

[35] Financial Conduct Authority, Listing Rules, s. 9.8.6.5; available at: http://fshandbook.info/FS/html/FCA/LR/9/8.

[36] M. Rodrigue, M. Magna, and C. Cho, 'Is environmental governance substantive or symbolic? An empirical investigation' (2013) 114 *Journal of Business Ethics* 107.

of decision-making and in the process of creating and implementing ethical codes applicable to the activities of their companies.[37] By signalling the priority they attach to environmental matters, by promoting sustainable processes within the company, and embedding them within their systems, the board can influence the behaviour of management at all levels of the organisation.

In fulfilling their role as leaders of strategy, the question arises as to why directors should choose to support a programme of environmental sustainability. One possibility is that they may pursue environmentally friendly policies because they view them as being in the company's financial interest and they are seeking to maximise return for shareholders. Milton Friedman famously stated that a company has an obligation to act as a good citizen and that 'the social responsibility of business is to increase its profits'.[38] This attitude is not, of course, necessarily incompatible with a stakeholder welfare perspective. It involves viewing CSR not as an alternative to the traditional profit-maximisation objective but as an integral complementary part of the same process. In Jensen's 'enlightened value maximization objective', the corporate objective is still wealth maximisation, but the dependency of long-term wealth maximisation on stakeholder management is acknowledged.[39] This view is consistent with the 'triple bottom line concept' mooted by the Commission in its 2001 paper, *Promoting a European Framework for Corporate Social Responsibility*.[40] This concept involved companies voluntarily taking on board social and environmental concerns in addition to their economic ones on the basis that all three elements could dovetail to create more productive and profitable businesses. The challenge for companies in this context is 'how to make sustainability-centric approaches deliver not only on the financial bottom line but also on a broader platform of ecological and social accountabilities and goals that make up the sustainability blend'.[41] The evidence of a link between a company's corporate social performance

---

[37] L. Rodriguez-Dominguez, I. Gallego-Alvarez, and I. Garcia-Sanchez, 'Corporate governance and codes of ethics' (2009) 90 *Journal of Business Ethics* 187.

[38] M. Friedman, 'The social responsibility of business is to increase its profits' *New York Times Magazine*, 13 September 1970, 33.

[39] M.C. Jensen, 'Value maximization, stakeholder theory, and the corporate objective function', in J. Andriof, *et al.*, (eds.), *Unfolding Stakeholder Thinking* (Greenleaf Publishing, 2002).

[40] European Commission, *Green Paper: Promoting a European Framework for Corporate Social Responsibility*, COM(2001) 366 final, 2006.

[41] D. Vidal, *et al.*, *Sustainability Matters: Why and How Corporate Boards Should Become Involved*, Report No. R-1481–11-RR (Conference Board Research, 2012), 7.

record and its financial performance is mixed, as research tends to suggest only a mildly positive relationship between them.[42]

However, as might be expected, some evidence suggests that companies that are exposed as engaging in socially irresponsible or illegal behaviour experience decreases in their financial performance.[43] Environmental matters are thus relevant in the context of the non-executive directors' monitoring role. Together with the rest of the board, non-executive directors are responsible under the UK Corporate Governance Code for determining 'the nature and extent of the significant risks that the company is willing to take in achieving its strategic objectives and for maintaining sound risk management'.[44] Environmental risk and also consequential legal, regulatory, and reputational risk are elements that would be appropriately considered by the board in this context. The Corporate Governance Green Paper in 2011 acknowledges, for example, that 'some companies may face risks that significantly affect society as a whole: risks related to climate change, to the environment (e.g. the numerous dramatic oil spills) health, safety, human rights, etc.'.[45] In addition, in so far as research supports the view that improvements in environmental risk management are associated with lower costs of capital,[46] this becomes a matter of concern to boards in terms of liquidity or solvency risk.

In addition, while many companies disclose environmental information in their annual reports and on their websites in the form of sustainability and social reports, the boards of large companies and business groups will soon be required to explain their policies for dealing with environmental risks. In April 2014, the European Parliament adopted

---

[42] See e.g. J.D. Margolis, H.A. Elfenbein, and J.P. Walsh, 'Does it pay to be good . . . and does it matter? A meta-analysis of the relationship between corporate social and financial performance' (2009); available at: SSRN: http://ssrn.com/abstract=1866371; B. Lougee and J. Wallace, 'The corporate social responsibility (CSR) trend' (2008) 20 *Journal of Applied Corporate Finance* 96; R. Eccles, I. Ioannou, and G. Serafeim, *The Impact of a Corporate Culture of Sustainability on Corporate Behavior and Performance*, Working Paper No. 12–035 (HBS, 2011).

[43] See also J. Frooman, 'Socially irresponsible and illegal behavior and shareholder wealth: a meta-analysis of event studies' (1997) 36(3) *Business and Society* 221.

[44] UK Corporate Governance Code, para. C. 2.

[45] European Commission, *Green Paper: EU Corporate Governance*, para. 1.5. This is the only reference to the environment in the Green Paper and it might be viewed as relating more to damage to the company than damage by the company.

[46] R. Bauer and D. Hann, 'Corporate Environmental Management and Credit Risk' (2010); available at: SSRN: http://ssrn.com/abstract/1660470. See also M. Sharfman and C. Fernando, 'Environmental risk management and the cost of capital' (2008) 29 *Strategic Management Journal* 569.

a directive on disclosure of non-financial and diversity information by these companies.[47] Directive 2014/95/EU will enhance transparency on social and environmental matters. Applying on a comply-or-explain basis, the Directive requires these companies to disclose a statement in their annual report including material information relating to at least environmental, social, and employee-related matters; respect of human rights; anti-corruption, and bribery aspects. In these areas, the statement must include: a description of its policies; their results; and the risk-related aspects. This will oblige boards to consider these issues, though of course most boards would say that they do so anyway. By giving greater public prominence to these matters, the Directive will also expose companies to greater scrutiny from investors as well as from environmental agencies and NGOs. This has the potential to increase reputational damage for companies with poor environmental policies and to allow companies with policies that are viewed by investors and other stakeholders as effective and progressive to benefit from the positive reputational impact.[48] That is not to say, however, that there will necessarily be a direct follow-through in terms of environmental performance itself. There is a concern that corporate reporting may be used more as 'a tool for corporate legitimation'[49] than as a vehicle for increased transparency and accountability.[50] This concern would appear to be supported by research suggesting that companies with dubious environmental records use this disclosure as a tool for reducing the negative potential effects of actual performance information.[51]

---

[47] European Commission, Statement/14/124, 15 April 2014, available at: http://europa. eu/rapid/press-release˙STATEMENT-14-124˙en.htm. If properly implemented, Directive 2014/95/EU of the European Parliament and of the Council of 22 October 2014 amending Directive 2013/34/EU as regards disclosure of non-financial and diversity information by certain large undertakings and groups.

[48] D. Brown, R. Guidry, and D. Patten, 'Sustainability reporting and perceptions of corporate reputation: an analysis using Fortune most admired scores' (2010) 4 *Advances in Environmental Accounting and Management* 83; Group of 100, *Sustainability Reporting: A Guide* (KPMG Australia, 2004).

[49] D. Patten, 'Environmental disclosure as legitimation: is it in the public interest?' in S. Mintz (ed.) *Accounting for the Public Interest: Perspectives on Accountability, Professionalism and Role in Society* (Springer, 2014), 201. See also C. Cho, R. Guidry, A. Hageman, and D. Patten, 'Do actions speak louder than words? An empirical investigation of corporate environmental reputation' (2012) 37 *Accounting, Organizations and Society* 14; C. Deegan, 'The legitimizing effect of social and environmental disclosures: a theoretical foundation' (2002) 15 *Accounting, Auditing and Accountability Journal* 282.

[50] See the in-depth comparative analysis of corporate reporting requirements in Chapter 5 by Villiers and Mähönen in this book.

[51] Cho, *et al.*, 'Do actions speak louder than words? 14; C. Villiers and C. Van Staden, 'Where firms choose to disclose voluntary environmental information' (2011) 30 *Journal of Accounting and Public Policy* 504; C. Cho and D. Patten, 'The role of environmental

A second more liberal interpretation of a company's social responsibility, which might be more correctly described as a form of altruism, suggests that directors may act in the interests of stakeholders 'incurring uncompensatable costs for socially desirable but not legally mandated action'.[52] This involves a more pluralistic approach balancing the interests of constituent interests and not according priority to any group. Blair and Stout argued in their 'team production theory of corporate law' that 'a broad interpretation of [a company's interests] that permits directors to sacrifice shareholders' interests to those of other corporate constituencies... ultimately serves [shareholders'] interests as a class, as well as those of the other [constituencies] of the corporate coalition.'[53] A relentless focus on raising share price, Stout noted, can actually harm shareholders who:

> are real human beings with the capacity to think for the future and to make binding commitments, with a wide range of investments and interests beyond the shares they happen to hold in any single firm, and with consciences that make most of them concerned, at least a bit, about the fates of others, future generations, and the planet.[54]

In *A Renewed EU Strategy 2011–14 for Corporate Social Responsibility*, the Commission stated that 'corporate social responsibility concerns actions by companies over and above their legal obligations towards society and the environment'.[55] It stated further that:

> To fully meet their corporate social responsibility, enterprises should have in place a process to integrate social, environmental, ethical, human rights and consumer concerns into their business operations and core strategy in close collaboration with their stakeholders, with the aim of: maximising the creation of shared value for their owners/shareholders and for their other stakeholders and society at large; and identifying, preventing and mitigating their possible adverse impacts.

In addition, in the Corporate Governance Green Paper, the Commission acknowledged that boards have a 'vital part to play in the development

disclosures as tools of legitimacy: a research note' (2007) 32 *Accounting, Organizations and Society* 639.

[52] V. Brudney, 'The independent director – heavenly city or Potemkin village?' (1982) 95 *Harvard Law Review* 605.

[53] M. Blair and L. Stout, 'A team production theory of corporate law' (1999) 85 *Virginia Law Review* 248 at p. 305.

[54] L. Stout, *The Shareholder Value Myth: How Putting Shareholders First Harms Investors, Corporations, and the Public* (Berrett-Koehler Publishers, 2012), p. 6.

[55] COM(2011) 681 at 4.

160   BLANAID CLARKE

of responsible companies'.[56] These statements would seem to suggest a readiness to afford directors greater discretion in pursuing environmental strategies without having to prove a resulting benefit to shareholders.

In the UK, the Company Law Review Steering Committee, in considering the appropriate statutory response to the choice between approaches, favoured an 'enlightened shareholder value approach' over the alternative pluralistic interpretation.[57] It noted that 'an exclusive focus on the short-term financial bottom line, in the erroneous belief that this equates to shareholder value, will often be incompatible with the cultivation of co-operative relationships, which are likely to involve short-term costs but to bring greater benefits in the longer term'.[58] The resulting statutory duty, which is set out in Section 172(1) of the Companies Act 2006, provides that a director must 'act in the way he considers, in good faith, would be most likely to promote the success of the company for the benefit of its members as a whole'.[59] The reference to 'members' clearly gives primacy to the interests of shareholders.[60] Furthermore, though the term 'success' is not defined, the UK governmental guidance on the Act suggests that success in relation to a commercial company is considered to be its 'long-term increases in value'.[61] However, in keeping with the desire to adopt a more inclusive approach to other non-shareholder stakeholders, Section 172(1) continues by stating that in fulfilling this duty, a director must 'have regard (amongst other matters)' to a number of factors, including 'the likely consequences of any decision in the long term', 'the impact of the company's operations on the community and the environment', and 'the desirability of the company maintaining a reputation for high standards of business conduct'. Although this section highlights the salience of environmental concerns in corporate decision-making, the text is clear that the interests of employees and other non-shareholder stakeholders

---

[56] The Corporate Governance *Green Paper* (at 3) accords equivalent status to shareholder engagement and improvements to the application of the 'comply or explain' approach.

[57] The Company Law Review Steering Group, *Modern Company Law for a Competitive Economy: The Strategic Framework, a Consultation Document* (1999), Chapter 5.1.

[58] The Company Law Review Steering Group, *Modern Company Law*, para. 5.1.12.

[59] While this superseded the common law fiduciary duty to 'act in the interests of the company', it is important to note that the older case law still remains relevant to the interpretation of the new statutory provisions.

[60] It is also clear that a company in its constitutional document(s) may identify another stakeholder as taking priority over or taking joint priority with the interests of shareholders. This would allow a company to allow its directors discretion to adopt a more pluralist view.

[61] Ministerial statements, 'Companies Act 2006, Duties of company directors', (Department of Trade and Industry, 2007), 7–8; www.berr.gov.uk/files/file40139.pdf. See also Lord Goldsmith, Lords Grand Committee, 6 February 2006, col. 255.

THE ROLE OF BOARD DIRECTORS IN SUSTAINABILITY 161

are secondary to promoting the success of the company for the benefit of its members as a whole.[62] As Kershaw explains: 'This "regard list" in section 172 is less about what a "company's interests" are and more about regulating the process of acting: that is, in the process of making a decision, the director must consider the interests of the listed groups.'[63] It has been argued thus that while the enlightened shareholder value approach is seen as providing a radical reform, the approach is little different from the shareholder value approach.[64] It reflects the pragmatic view expressed by Jensen – that a company will not thrive if it ignores its important non-shareholder constituents.[65] It acknowledges the fact that paying attention to a company's environmental impact may thus be justified on the basis that this is in shareholders' best (financial) interests.

In the past 20 years, our expectations of the role to be played by non-executive directors and our ensuing demands in terms of their qualification, suitability, and representative base have grown exponentially. An article in *The Economist* in 1994, commenting on the legacy of the Cadbury Committee, claimed that an expectation had been raised that non-executive directors would 'behave as hard-nosed businessmen, referees, coaches, visionaries and saints, while giving only a few days a year to the job'.[66] Twenty years later, we could add to this list risk experts, internal auditors, stewards, and, on occasion, public servants. Bainbridge has gone so far as to describe board members as 'platonic guardians'.[67] The next four sections of the chapter will thus examine whether the boards are composed of the right people to fulfil the important and demanding role expected of them and in particular, to promote a sustainability agenda.

4 Independence

The Cadbury Code emphasised the importance of 'the calibre of the non-executive members of the board' but offered very little description

---

[62] *Palmers Company Law* (Thomson Sweet & Maxwell, 2014), para. 8.26021.

[63] D. Kershaw, *Company Law in Context: Text and Materials* (Oxford University Press, 2000), p. 382.

[64] A. Keay, 'Tackling the issue of the corporate objective: an analysis of the United Kingdom's "enlightened shareholder value approach"' (2007) 29 *Sydney Law Review* 577. See also A. Keay, 'Shareholder primacy in corporate law: can it survive? Should it survive?' (2010) 7 *European Company and Financial Law Review* 369.

[65] M. Jensen, 'Value maximisation, stakeholder theory and the corporate objective function' (2001) 7 *European Financial Management* 309.

[66] 'The invisible hand' *The Economist*, 8 October 1994, 81 at 81.

[67] S.M. Bainbridge, 'Director primacy: the means and ends of corporate governance' (2003) 97 *Northwestern University Law Review* 547.

or explanation of what was envisaged in this regard. It confined itself to stating that their calibre should be 'such that their views will carry sufficient weight in the board's decisions'.[68] In terms of qualification, the only concept referred to was 'independence of judgement'.

A distinction must be drawn at the outset between two different understandings of the term 'independence'. The first refers to an attitude and the second to a lack of ties to the company. As the Cadbury Committee noted: 'non-executive directors should bring an independent judgement to bear on issues of strategy, performance, resources, including key appointments, and standards of conduct'.[69] The Higgs Review described this as being 'willing and able to challenge, question and speak up',[70] but noted quite correctly that both executive and non-executive directors need to be independent in this sense. The UK Corporate Governance Code, while referring to directors being 'independent in character and judgement', does so only in the context of non-executive directors.[71]

The second way in which the term 'independence' is used is in relation to independence from the company or its stakeholders. The Cadbury Report recommended that the majority of non-executive directors on the board should be 'independent of the company', which it defined as directors viewed by the board as 'independent of management and free from any business or other relationship which could materially interfere with the exercise of their independent judgement'.[72] Fees and shareholdings were not considered in this context. The rationale for this is clearly linked to non-executive directors' role as monitors of management and acknowledges 'the natural potential for conflict between the interests of executive management and shareholders in the case of director remuneration, or audit . . . or indeed in a range of other instances'.[73] Thus, as the Higgs Review noted, although all directors are legally obliged to act in the best interests of the company, 'it has long been recognized that in itself this is insufficient to give full assurance that these potential conflicts will not impair objective board decision-making'.[74] It went further in recommending that at least half of the board,

---

[68] Financial Reporting Council (FRC), *UK Corporate Governance Code* (FRC, 2012), para. 4.11.
[69] Financial Reporting Council (FRC), *UK Corporate Governance Code*, para. 4.11.
[70] Higgs, *Review of the Role and Effectiveness of Non-executive Directors*, para. 9.1.
[71] *UK Corporate Governance Code*, para. B.1.1.
[72] Committee on the Financial Aspects of Corporate Governance, para. 4.12.
[73] Higgs, *Review of the Role and Effectiveness of Non-executive Directors*, para. 9.2.
[74] Higgs, *Review of the Role and Effectiveness of Non-executive Directors*, para. 9.3.

THE ROLE OF BOARD DIRECTORS IN SUSTAINABILITY 163

excluding the chairman, should be independent non-executive directors,[75] and this is the current position under the UK Corporate Governance Code.[76]

Requiring a high degree of independence has thus become a core theme of corporate governance. Based on the recommendations of the Higgs Review, the UK Corporate Governance Code defines this type of independence more broadly as free from 'relationships or circumstances which are likely to affect, or could appear to affect, the director's judgement'.[77] In a non-exhaustive list of factors, it considers whether the director has been an employee within the previous five years; has, or has had, within the previous three years, a material business relationship with the company; has received additional remuneration from the company; has close family ties with any of the company's advisers, directors, or senior employees; holds cross-directorships or has significant links with other directors through involvement in other companies or bodies; represents a significant shareholder; or has served on the board for more than nine years from the date of their first election.[78] These criteria may be viewed as quasi-presumptions for the boards to overcome in their classification of directors. The EU Recommendation on Non Executive Directors adopts a similar technique, listing nine circumstances 'frequently recognised as relevant' in the determination of independence.[79] It does so because it acknowledges correctly that it is not possible to list comprehensively all threats to directors' independence because 'the relationships or circumstances which may appear relevant . . . may vary . . . across Member States and companies, and best practices in this respect may evolve over time' and it suggests that the criteria should be tailored to the national context. Like the UK Corporate Governance Code, it refers to independence from more than the management. It thus includes in its list not only directors with a significant business relationship with the company, interlocking directors, and long-standing directors, but also directors representing controlling shareholders.

---

[75] Higgs, *Review of the Role and Effectiveness of Non-executive Directors*, para. 9.5.

[76] UK Corporate Governance Code, para. B.1.2. This does not apply, however, to smaller companies.

[77] UK Corporate Governance Code, para B.1.1.

[78] UK Corporate Governance Code. The Higgs Review referred to service on the board for a period of ten years rather than nine years.

[79] European Commission, *Recommendation on the Role of Non-executive or Supervisory Directors of Listed Companies and on the Committees of the (Supervisory) Board*, Annex II (2005/162/EC) (2005).

In the context of the sustainable agenda, one might ask the question whether non-executive directors and in particular independent non-executive directors might be more likely to consider the needs of the environment. An early body of empirical research was unable to find any strong association between board independence and firm value.[80] However, more recent research suggests that independent directors are associated with significantly better performance when their cost of acquiring information is low, and are associated with significantly worse performance when their cost of acquiring information is high.[81] Regarding environmental performance, however, the evidence is more positive, suggesting that the proportion of non-executive directors and, in particular, independent non-executive directors is positively associated with corporate social performance and environmental performance.[82] This finding supports earlier research that the presence of independent directors on a board leads to greater representation of the multiple points of view of the firm's role in the environment and among stakeholders.[83]

While the presence of independent directors on corporate boards may have a positive effect on their ability and willingness to prioritise sustainability within their companies, this outcome, of course, is not guaranteed. In the same way we have seen spectacular financial failure in credit institutions with strongly independent boards, we have seen environmental failures in firms like BP – a firm with a strong board comprising a majority of independent directors.[84] Despite BP's huge potential financial and environmental exposures, it did not appear to have a sound crisis response

---

[80] S. Bhagat and B.S. Black, 'The non-correlation between board independence and long-term firm performance' (2002) 27 *Journal of Corporation Law* 231; L. Ribstein, 'Market vs. regulatory responses to corporate fraud: a critique of the Sarbanes-Oxley Act of 2002' (2003) 28 *Journal of Corporate Law* 1; M.A. Fields and P.Y. Keys, 'The emergence of corporate governance from Wall St. to Main St.: outside directors, board diversity, earnings management, and managerial incentives to bear risk' (2003) 38 *The Financial Review* 1.

[81] R. Adams and D. Ferreira, 'A theory of friendly boards' (2007) 62 *The Journal of Finance* 217; M. Harris and A. Raviv, 'A theory of board control and size' (2008) 21 *Review of Financial Studies* 1797; R. Duchin, J.G. Matsusaka, and O. Ozbas, 'When are outside directors effective?' (2010) 96 *Journal of Financial Economics* 195.

[82] J. Zhang, H. Zhu, and H. Ding, 'Board composition and corporate social responsibility: an empirical investigation in the post Sarbanes-Oxley era' (2013) 114 *Journal of Business Ethics* 381; C. Mallin and G. Michelon, 'Board reputation attributes and corporate social performance: an empirical investigation of the US Best Corporate Citizens' (2011) 41 *Accounting and Business Research* 119; C. Post, N. Rahman, and E. Rubow, 'Green governance: boards of directors composition and environmental corporate social responsibility' (2011) 50 *Business and Society* 189.

[83] R.M. Haniffa and T.E. Cooke. 'The impact of culture and governance on corporate social reporting' (2005) 24 *Journal of Accounting and Public Policy* 391.

[84] All BP's non-executive directors were described as 'independent' in its 2009 annual report.

plan allowing it to react effectively to both prevent and manage an environmental disaster of such magnitude in the 2010 Deepwater Horizon offshore oil rig explosion. The board's fundamental risk management duties, which should have led it to anticipate and provide for such exposures, were ineffective in this regard.

5   Diversity

Diversity on corporate boards may be viewed in terms of factors such as nationality, ethnicity, religion, experience, expertise, age, and gender. Diversity is valued as a means of ensuring complementary perspectives are considered, mitigating groupthink, and generating diversity leads to more discussion, more monitoring, and more challenges in the boardroom.[85] Lord Davies' *Women on Boards* report in the UK noted: 'Inclusive and diverse boards are more likely to be effective boards, better able to understand their customers and stakeholders and to benefit from fresh perspectives, new ideas, vigorous challenge and broad experience. This in turn leads to better decision-making.'[86]

While increased gender diversity will ensure greater equality, an important objective in itself, the question as to whether it will make boards more effective remains moot and controversial. The European Commission has cited various studies that suggest that companies with a higher share of women at senior management levels deliver strong organisational and financial performance. It noted that: 'Studies have also shown that where governance is weak, female directors can exercise strong oversight and have a "positive, value-relevant impact" on the company. A gender-balanced board is more likely to pay attention to managing and controlling risk.'[87] However, the empirical evidence generally seems a little mixed[88] and, as acknowledged, even where correlations are found, this does not demonstrate causation.[89] From a sustainability perspective, the

---

[85] European Commission, *Green Paper: The EU Corporate Governance Framework*, COM (2011)164 final, at 5.

[86] Department of Business, Innovation and Skills, *Women on Board*, 7.

[87] See http://ec.europa.eu/justice/gender-equality/files/womenonboards/factsheet-general-1_en.pdf.

[88] See D. Carter, B. Simkins, and W.Simpson, 'Corporate governance, board diversity, and firm value' (2003) 38 *Financial Review* 33, suggesting a positive relationship; and R. Adams and D. Ferreira. 'Women in the boardroom and their impact on governance and performance' (2009) 94 *Journal of Financial Economics* 291, concluding the average effect of gender diversity on firm performance is negative.

[89] See e.g. S. Zahra and W. Stanton, 'The implications of board directors' composition for corporate strategy and performance' (1988) 4 *International Journal of Management* 229;

research findings are also equivocal,[90] though there appears to be a firmer link between boardroom diversity and improved CSR.[91] Women have been found to be particularly sensitive to, and influential in respect of, decisions pertaining to certain organisational practices such as CSR and environmental policies,[92] and also more likely to increase board consideration of the multiple interests of stakeholders.[93] What is irrefutable is that greater diversity will literally broaden the gene pool, providing a wider range of individuals reflecting different points of view and experiences. Christine Lagarde commented on this subject that: 'the point is certainly not to erase the differences between women and men but to enhance the talents of each individual'.[94] This, it is submitted, is a more productive line of argument.

In the UK, Lord Davies' report recommended inter alia that all chairpersons of FTSE 350 companies should set out the percentage of women they aim to have on their boards in 2013 and 2015 and that FTSE 100 boards should aim for a minimum of 25 per cent female representation by

---

R. Adler, 'Women and profits' (2001) 79 *Harvard Business Review* 30; R. Adams and D. Ferreira, 'Diversity and incentives in teams: evidence from corporate boards', Working Paper (Federal Reserve Bank of New York, 2002); L. Joy, *et al.*, *The Bottom Line: Corporate Performance and Women's Representation on Boards* (Catalyst, 2007); K. Campbell and A. Minguez-Vera, 'Gender diversity in the boardroom and firm financial performance' (2008) 83 *Journal of Business Ethics* 435; R. Adams and D. Ferreira, 'Women in the boardroom and their impact on governance and performance' (2009) 94 *Journal of Financial Economics* 291; D. Rhode and A. Packel, 'Diversity on corporate boards: how much difference does difference make?' Working Paper No. 89 (Rock Center for Corporate Governance at Stanford University, 2010).

[90] I. Boulouta, 'Hidden connections: the link between board gender diversity and corporate social performance' (2013) 113 *Journal of Business Ethics* 185.

[91] Zhang, *et al.*, 'Board composition and corporate social responsibility'; T. Hafsi and G. Turgut 'Boardroom diversity and its effect on social performance: conceptualization and empirical evidence' (2012) 112 *Journal of Business Ethics* 463; C. Post, N. Rahmanand, and E. Rubow, 'Green governance: boards of directors composition and environmental corporate social responsibility' (2011) 50 *Business and Society* 189; B. Coffey and J. Wang, 'Board diversity and managerial control as predictors of corporate social performance' (1998) 17 *Journal of Business Ethics* 1595. See, however, Rodriguez-Dominguez, *et al.*, 'Corporate governance and codes of ethics'.

[92] S. Nielsen and M. Huse, 'The contribution of women on boards of directors: going beyond the surface' (2010) 18 *Corporate Governance: An International Review* 136; N. Ibrahim and J. Angelidis, 'Effect of board members' gender on corporate social responsiveness orientation' (1994) 10 *Journal of Applied Business Research* 38.

[93] C. Mallin and G. Michelon, 'Board reputation attributes and corporate social performance: an empirical investigation of the US best corporate citizens' (2011) 41 *Accounting and Business Research* 119.

[94] C. Lagarde, 'Women, power and the challenge of the financial crisis' *New York Times* Opinion, 10 May 2010.

THE ROLE OF BOARD DIRECTORS IN SUSTAINABILITY 167

2015.[95] He also recommended that quoted companies should, as a legal requirement, disclose each year the proportion of women on the board, women in senior executive positions, and female employees in the whole organisation. The UK Corporate Governance Code states that 'the search for board candidates should be conducted, and appointments made, on merit, against objective criteria and with due regard for the benefits of diversity on the board, including gender'.[96] It also requires that a separate section of the annual report should describe the process the nomination committee uses in relation to board appointments. This should include a description of 'the board's policy on diversity, including gender, any measurable objectives that it has set for implementing the policy, and progress on achieving the objectives'.[97] Since Lord Davies published his report in 2011, the percentage of women on boards has increased from 12.5 per cent to 20.7 per cent in 2014 in the FTSE 100 companies.[98] Lord Davies has interpreted this as evidence that 'companies have got the message that better balanced boards bring real business benefits'.[99]

The average share of women on the boards of the largest publicly listed companies in the EU was 18.6 per cent in 2014.[100] In only five Member States – Finland, France, Latvia, Sweden, and the Netherlands – do women account for at least a quarter of board members.[101] This has given rise to concern that the divergence or absence of regulation at the national level was leading not only to the discrepancies in the number of women among executive and non-executive directors and different rates of improvement across Member States but also to the creation of potential barriers to the internal market through the imposition of different requirements on European listed companies operating across borders. The Commission confirmed that its objectives could not be sufficiently achieved by Member

[95] Department of Business, Innovation and Skills, *Women on Boards*.
[96] UK Corporate Governance Code, para. B.2.
[97] UK Corporate Governance Code, para. B.2.4.
[98] Department of Business, Innovation and Skills, *Women on Boards:. Davies Review Annual Report 2014* (DBIS, 2014).
[99] UK Government, 'Women on boards 2014: 3 years on', Press release, 26 March 2014, available at: www.gov.uk/government/news/women-on-boards-2014-3-years-on.
[100] See ec.europa.eu/justice/gender-equality/files/womenonboards/wob-factsheet_2014_en.pdf.
[101] Norway, the pioneering country in company law reform to ensure gender diversity on the board, has achieved the legislative goal of 40 per cent women on the boards of its public companies. For the innovative legislative approach and its history, see B. Sjåfjell and H.B. Reiersen, 'Report from Norway: gender equality in the board room' (2008) 5 *European Company Law* 191.

States on their own and would 'be better achieved through coordinated action at EU level rather than through national initiatives of varying scope, ambition and effectiveness'.[102]

There have been two recent legislative initiatives at the EU level seek to address this. First, in November 2012, the Commission announced a proposal for a directive in relation to gender representation on boards of listed companies other than SMEs.[103] This sets Member States a minimum objective of 40 per cent presence of the 'under-represented sex' among the non-executive directors of listed companies by January 2020. The rationale given for limiting this objective to non-executive directors was 'to strike the right balance between the necessity to increase the gender diversity of boards on the one hand and the need to minimize interference with day-to-day management of a company on the other hand'.[104] Companies are required to introduce 'a pre-established, clear, neutrally formulated and unambiguous criteria in selection procedures' in order to attain the percentage and, where candidates are equally qualified, priority must be given to women unless 'an objective assessment taking account of all criteria specific to the individual candidates tilts the balance in favour of the other sex'.[105] The second initiative is the afore-mentioned Directive on disclosure of non-financial and diversity information by large companies and groups.[106] It will require large listed companies to provide information on their diversity policy in their corporate governance statement or to explain non-compliance. Diversity is broadly defined in the Directive to include aspects concerning age, gender, geographical diversity, and educational and professional background. Companies should set out the objectives of its diversity policy, its implementation, and the results obtained.

Academic commentators have correctly expressed caution regarding the diversity point. It has been noted that diversity, like the notion of independence, 'does not bring absolute qualities to the board in the sense that more is always better' and that an excessive insistence on either

---

[102] European Commission, *Proposal for a Directive of the European Parliament and of the Council on Improving the Gender Balance among Non-Executive Directors of Companies Listed on Stock Exchanges and Related Measures*, 14.11.2012 COM (2012) 614 final, at 10.

[103] European Commission, *Proposal for a Directive of the European Parliament and of the Council on Improving the Gender Balance*. See Europa Press Release IP/12/1205, 'Women on boards: Commission proposes 40% objective' (14 November 2012).

[104] European Commission, *Proposal for a Directive on Improving the Gender Balance Among Non-Executive directors of Companies Listed on Stock Exchanges and related Measures*, Com(2012)614 final at 5.

[105] Article 4(3).

[106] Directive 2014/95/EU.

diversity or independence 'comes at the cost of expertise on the board'.[107] This is clearly sensible advice and a balanced approach to both is required.

6 Knowledge

In terms of knowledge, the UK Corporate Governance Code states clearly that 'to function effectively, all directors need appropriate knowledge of the company and access to its operations and staff.'[108] They also need to be supplied in a timely manner with 'information in a form and quality appropriate to enable it to discharge its duties'. Upon joining the board, directors must undertake induction and thereafter to 'continually update their skills and the knowledge and familiarity with the company required to fulfil their role'.[109] The Recommendation on non-executive directors is less prescriptive and its recitals acknowledge that 'most corporate governance codes recognise that . . . what constitutes proper qualifications should be left to the company itself because such qualifications will depend, *inter alia*, on its activities, size and environment and because they should be met by the board as a whole'.[110]

It has been suggested that boards might consider establishing a specialised committee "to support the board with regards to the sustainability agenda, strategy and performance of the company.[111] It might also be considered appropriate for the board to appoint a director with environmental skills and experience. This option may be considered particularly important for companies whose activities pose a threat to the environment, such as oil firms or chemical companies. Such persons will be able to fully appreciate the environmental risks involved and lead an appropriate risk management process. One concern often expressed is that having such a person on the board could give rise to a negative 'cacophony of conflicting morals' within the board. Yet, such a cacophony may not be a negative feature and may constitute instead a challenge to group think. A further argument against dedicated environmentalists on boards is that it

---

[107] P. Davies, *et al., European Company Law Experts' Response to the European Commission's Green Paper 'The EU Corporate Governance Framework* (2011), 7–8; available at: SSRN: http://ssrn.com/abstract=1912548.

[108] UK Corporate Governance Code, para B.4. Supporting Principles, para. 2.

[109] UK Corporate Governance Code, para. B.4.

[110] European Commission, *Recommendation on the Role of Non-executive or Supervisory Directors of Listed Companies and on the Committees of the (Supervisory) Board* (2005/162/EC), recital 16.

[111] R. Irwin World Business Council for Sustainable Development Response Paper "2014 Review of OECD Principles of Corporate Governance" available at http://www.oecd.org/daf/ca/WBCSD2015CGP.pdf.

allows other directors to abdicate responsibility on environmental matters, considering it to be no longer their concern and thus diluting its impact on the board. This argument is similar to that raised in the context of placing risk officers on the board and, arguably, is something that can be managed by proper training on the role and responsibilities of all directors for issues before the board.

A related idea that has been canvassed for a long time[112] is the question of public interest or 'special interest' directors who champion their particular causes. Stone proposed that a portion of each company's directors be designated to represent the public interest and in case of 'demonstrated delinquency' in a particular area, such as environmental protection, a 'special interest' director would be added for that area.[113] These directors would reflect the interests of those appointing them. This could involve directors receiving instructions from an environmental interest group, exercising their board role with this interest group in mind, reporting to the interest group, and being generally answerable to them. As Blumberg noted, 'the proposals for special interest representation' have objectives more profound than simply broadening the perspectives of the board. They seek to change the allocation of power within the corporation, to assure affected groups of participation in the decisions that involve them and to achieve accountability and legitimacy for the corporation.[114] A number of 'public interest directors' were appointed by the Minister for Finance in Ireland, for example, in order to promote 'the public interest' in 2008, at the time of the Irish Government's guarantee of the credit institutions.[115] Research has indicated that the proportion of directors with relevant experience and links to the firm's community is positively associated with corporate social performance, community performance, and environmental performance.[116] Such directors, it is argued, are 'less likely to tolerate environmental irresponsibility' because their

---

[112] P. Blumberg, 'Reflections on proposals for corporate reform through change in the composition of the board of directors: special interest or public directors' (1973) 53 *Boston University Law Review* 549; A.F. Conard, 'Reflections on public interest directors' (1976–1977) 75 *Michigan Law Review* 941.

[113] C.D. Stone, *Where the Law Ends: The Social Control of Corporate Behavior* (Harper & Row, 1975).

[114] Blumberg, 'Reflections on proposals for corporate reform through change in the composition of the board of directors' (1973) 53 *Boston University Law Review* 549.

[115] The appointments were made under the terms of the Credit Institutions (Financial Support) Scheme, 2008.

[116] M.C. Mallin and G. Michelon, 'Board reputation attributes and corporate social performance: an empirical investigation of the US Best Corporate Citizens' (2011) 41 *Accounting and Business Research* 119.

interests are more closely aligned with the interests of the community at large.[117]

In addition to the problems faced by directors who are environmental specialists and referred to in the previous paragraph, 'special interest' directors face particular challenges. Firstly, a potential conflict of interests may arise for the relevant director.[118] In Ireland, this was resolved by a statutory provision which applied to all directors of credit institutions covered by the State's 2008 blanket guarantee that the directors had a duty to have regard to the public interest-related issues contained therein and that this duty took priority over any other duty of the directors to the extent of any inconsistency.[119] Obviously this was an extreme situation and such a provision was considered justified in these circumstances. It is submitted that it would be less likely to find favour in a different context. It may be possible that the public interest director would be required to manage the conflict in the same way a director appointed by a major shareholder is required to do. In such a case, in cases of conflict, the interests of the company would be expected to take priority. It is difficult to imagine this happening in practice. A second problem is that the imposition of a special interest director on an unwilling board who has not fully accepted the particular interests might achieve little, and such a person would not be likely to influence the board. Conard has argued that such environmental interest directors are the least likely to be useful, even to environmentalists: '[s]ince defenders of the environment have few interests in common with representatives of investors, employees, customers, or consumers, they have little chance of making effective alliances with other constituencies'.[120] He thus described such individuals as 'gadflies' whose energies would be more productively spent in the political arena seeking to exert influence over voters.

There are further potential objections to the appointment of 'special directors'. Such an appointment would lead to the question of why this particular special interest deserves a seat on the board rather than another stakeholder interest such as consumer protection or employee interests. Finally, and most importantly perhaps, is the question of which organised constituency would have the authority to appoint such a special interest director to protect environmental interests. It would perhaps involve a

---

[117] G. Kassinis and N. Vafeas, 'Corporate boards and outside stakeholders as determinants of environmental litigation' (2002) 23 *Strategic Management Journal* 399.
[118] Kassinis and Vafeas, 'Corporate boards and outside stakeholders', 564.
[119] Credit Institutions (Stabilisation) Act 2010, s. 48.
[120] Conard, 'Reflections on public interest directors', 959.

172 BLANAID CLARKE

government minister charged with responsibility for business or for the environment. The difficulty is that this would amount to a substantial interference in the business affairs of the company, and the political appetite for such a measure is likely to be limited. In light of the many difficulties faced by such directors, it might be considered that their influence on companies might be better exercised as external stakeholders, either using the external pressures of regulation and law suits, as Sax has argued,[121] or using lobbying and public pressure to make these issues a reputational matter for the companies involved.

7 Character

As noted above, one vital attribute of a director referred to in the Cadbury Code is 'independence of judgement'.[122] This has been described as 'the ability to exercise objective, independent judgement after fair consideration of all relevant information and views without undue influence from executives or from inappropriate external parties or interests'.[123] The Recommendation on non-executive directors requires the independent director to undertake inter alia 'to maintain in all circumstances his independence of analysis, decision and action' and 'to clearly express his opposition in the event that he finds that a decision of the (supervisory) board may harm the company'.[124] Arguably, this standard should apply to every director, not just non-executive ones.

Plato's *Republic* referred to the classic virtues of wisdom, courage, temperance, and justice. These are all attributes that would be desirable on a company board at an executive and non-executive level. Looking to the field of 'virtue ethics', Colombo suggested that one might add to this list the Aristotelian virtues of truthfulness, good temper, honesty, and pride. Again, these attributes could be described as the character traits one would seek in a director. Unlike regulations which simply require better behaviour, the application of virtue ethics seeks 'to lead [directors] to better behaviour via an improvement of character'.[125] This is crucial when one considers that the law cannot anticipate every possible misfeasance,

---

[121] J. Sax, *Defending the Environment* (Alfred A. Knopf, 1971), 175–230.

[122] Committee on the Financial Aspects of Corporate Governance, para. 4.12.

[123] Basel Committee on Banking Supervision, *Principles for Enhancing Corporate Governance* (October 2010), 10.

[124] Basel Committee on Banking Supervision, *Principles for Enhancing Corporate Governance*, Annex II, section 2.

[125] R.J. Colombo, 'Toward a nexus of virtue', Research Paper No. 11–17, (Hofstra University Legal Studies, 2011), 4.

THE ROLE OF BOARD DIRECTORS IN SUSTAINABILITY   173

and it is not possible, therefore, to prescribe a response to meet every situation. Where individuals have integrity and act in an ethical manner, this becomes less of a problem. Virtue, Colombo argued, 'is capable of restraining the individual from exploiting a loophole that he or she discovers in the law – a loophole that would cause the individual's misconduct to evade detection and/or punishment'.[126] This is an attractive argument and one that appears consistent with research suggesting investors have a strong interest in business ethics because it has a positive association with firm value.[127] By ensuring that the directors are individuals of strong moral fibre and character, one might be more assured of their ability to make the right decisions for the company and all its stakeholders. This quality is attractive, particularly in the context of a sustainable company's agenda.

Arguments have been put forward as to the need to have an 'ethical code for directors' incorporating some of these virtues.[128] The difficulty with this request, of course, is that it is hard to define and to measure such qualities. It involves qualitative judgements. It would not be possible to prescribe criteria to be used by a nominations committee, for example, in identifying an appropriate candidate. However, it is submitted that the law does have a role in this regard – it can make it easier for individuals to develop the habit of acting virtuously. It does this not just by establishing social norms and best business practices through soft law. Hard law can also serve to create an environment that facilitates rather than undermines individuals' ability to do good.[129] The introduction of directors' duties in Section 172 of the UK Companies Act 2006 is arguably a worthy example in that it may be seen as promoting such virtuous conduct. It does so by allowing directors to take into account the broader range of interests, which include environmental considerations, and not punishing them or finding them in breach of their duties for doing so. A report for the European Parliament's Legal Affairs Committee, identifying initiatives and instruments at the EU level that could enhance legal certainty in the field of CSR, suggested inter alia that a duty like Section 172 be enshrined at the EU level to bring together the various elements of directors' obligation of diligence.[130]

---

[126] Colombo, 'Toward a nexus of virtue', 14.

[127] Rodriguez-Dominguez, *et al.*, 'Corporate governance and codes of ethics'.

[128] See e.g. M. Schwartz, T. Dunfee, and M. Kline, 'Tone at the top: an ethics code for directors?' (2005) 58 *Journal of Business Ethics* 79; H. Siebens, 'Concepts and working instruments for corporate governance' (2002) 39 *Journal of Business Ethics* 109.

[129] Colombo, 'Toward a nexus of virtue,' 20.

[130] D. Jean-Philippe, 'Corporate social responsibility: identifying what initiatives and instruments at EU level could enhance legal certainty in the field of corporate social

8 Conclusion

Non-executive directors can play a valuable role in ensuring that companies adopt high environmental standards. Corporate governance codes allow them to play a role both in strategic decision-making, which includes agenda setting, and in monitoring management. The former role should allow directors to ensure that sustainability is embedded within the firm and is an integral part of all decisions taken, rather than a superficial add-on in homage to political correctness. The responsibility of non-executive directors to control management also involves them in tasks such as monitoring compliance with environmental regulations and managing environmental risks. Even where CSR is viewed more in terms of an enlightened shareholder value approach rather than a purer form of altruistic stakeholderism, directors will have a responsibility to pursue environmental sustainability.

The question of who will be entrusted with this important role is key. It has been argued in this chapter that a diverse board comprised of independent, skilled, and knowledgeable directors will be most likely to achieve this to the benefit of all stakeholders. An effective board appointment and board assessment process will play a crucial role in this context. Care must be taken, however, to strike a correct balance and not to sacrifice expertise or experience in our quest for independence or indeed diversity. Finally, independence of judgement and virtue should be promoted as a means of strengthening boards. In order, then, to derive the full benefit from these highly qualified persons, our legal systems must give them sufficient support in the sense of allowing them to pursue a sustainable agenda.[131]

responsibility' (European Parliament, 2012); available at: www.europarl.europa.eu/meetdocs/2009_2014/documents/juri/dv/pe462464_/pe462464_en.pdf.

[131] How this can be achieved is discussed further in Chapter 8 of this book.

5

Accounting, auditing, and reporting: supporting or obstructing the sustainable companies objective?

CHARLOTTE VILLIERS AND JUKKA MÄHÖNEN

1 Introduction

We are facing a deep ecological crisis. Climate change and its potentially catastrophic effects on biodiversity are widely accepted as an impending threat. Abundant scientific research evidence warns of the increasingly likely effects of global warming and other environmental impacts wrought by human activities. The possible solutions to this approaching calamity are a source of controversy. Among the different strategies for tackling climate change, company law and accounting law have a potentially important role in disciplining companies and directing them towards more sustainable behaviour. Company disclosure requirements are relevant to this objective. As was stated recently by the European Commission: '[b]etter disclosure of non-financial information may be a tool to further increase the number of European enterprises fully integrating sustainability and responsibility into their core strategies and operations in a more transparent way'.[1] With clearer reporting rules, companies and investors may be able to focus more clearly on sustainability issues and companies' environmental performance might more easily be evaluated.[2]

In this chapter we explore the role of accounting, reporting, and auditing in responding to the unsustainability crisis. The chapter focuses on the reporting and auditing requirements regarding the impact of corporate activity on the environment. Across the jurisdictions represented in the

---

[1] European Commission, *Disclosure of Non-Financial Information by Companies: Public Consultation Questionnaire* (European Commission, DG for Internal Market and Services, 2011), 3.

[2] European Commission, *Green Paper: Audit Policy: Lessons from the Crisis*, COM 561 final (2010), 8.

175

Sustainable Companies Project, from which this book is derived, there is a strong and well-established corporate financial accounting culture. The progress made by jurisdictions in environmental or sustainability accounting, however, is quite variable. While recognition of the potential relevance of accounting to improvement of environmental performance might indicate that accounting and reporting can improve sustainable corporate behaviour, these mechanisms may also hinder such improvements. This chapter explores the obstacles to and possibilities of improved sustainability through accounting and reporting as well as related audit and other assurance processes. Through the cross-jurisdictional analysis, the chapter will help identify a more progressive role for sustainability-related reporting and auditing.

The chapter begins with a discussion of the conceptual considerations of accounting and sustainability, including the role of accountants and accounting as a methodology of capitalism. The chapter next provides an overview of the accounting requirements across some of the jurisdictions represented in the Sustainable Companies Project. Much of the information in this section has been obtained from the 'mapping papers' that were completed for the Project.[3] The chapter closes with analysis of the overarching themes that emerge from that multi-jurisdictional overview before offering some suggestions for reforms.

2 Some general conceptual considerations of accounting and sustainability

2.1 The role of accountants

2.1.1 The positive role

Company activities can readily cause trauma to the biosphere, principally through rapacious use of natural resources and the emission of pollutants such as greenhouse gases (GHGs). How companies report on their activities may influence such impacts. The Institute of Chartered Accountants in England and Wales (ICAEW) suggests that disclosure of 'information can promote better markets, in the broader sense of markets that have outcomes that meet public policy objectives',[4] and the ICAEW

---

[3] Most of these mapping papers are included in the University of Oslo Faculty of Law Legal Studies Research Paper Series on SSRN, and several have been published or are forthcoming in the *International and Comparative Corporate Law Journal.*

[4] Institute of Chartered Accountants in England and Wales, *Information for Better Markets, Sustainability: The Role of Accountants* (ICAEW, 2004).

identifies eight different mechanisms through which accountants might support information flows to address expectations and attitudes towards sustainability: (1) corporate policies; (2) supply chain pressure; (3) stakeholder engagement; (4) voluntary codes; (5) rating and benchmarking; (6) taxes and subsidies; (7) tradable permits; and (8) requirements and prohibitions.[5]

The ICAEW suggests that accountants are well equipped to play an influential role in formulating company policies, developing business cases for action and managing the impacts of sustainability issues in an integrated way. Thus, they might help to identify, measure, and manage business risks and help companies 'navigate the new world of increased transparency'.[6] Accountants might also 'provid[e] some form of assurance that company policies are being operated throughout the organisation and its related businesses' through the 'design and use of performance indicators to test the effectiveness of company policies and the reliability of related information'.[7] Accountants might also have a role in the management of supply chains by designing and operating those management systems and also through their assurance work on supplier performance and the application of codes of conduct in the supply chain.[8] Accountants might be able to advise on and support engagement with stakeholders, which increasingly requires provision and assurance of social, environmental, and economic data.[9] Effective socially responsible investments require rating and benchmarking based on sustainability criteria, and this also requires the timely publication of relevant, comparable, and reliable information. Accountants appear well placed to collect and present such data and to have a role in interpreting the results of benchmarking as well as assisting in raising the quality and credibility of the benchmarking processes.[10] Accountants also assist in the development of management accounting for use in internal as well as external reporting of social and environmental impacts, performance measurement[11] as well as the assurance processes related to such reporting and enhancing trust in information.[12] These benefits suggested by the ICAEW are illustrative

[5] ICAEW, *Information for Better Markets, Sustainability.*
[6] ICAEW, *Information for Better Markets, Sustainability*, 21.
[7] ICAEW, *Information for Better Markets, Sustainability.*
[8] ICAEW, *Information for Better Markets, Sustainability*, 27.
[9] ICAEW, *Information for Better Markets, Sustainability*, 35.
[10] ICAEW, *Information for Better Markets, Sustainability*, 48.
[11] ICAEW, *Information for Better Markets, Sustainability*, 81.
[12] ICAEW, *Information for Better Markets, Sustainability*, 88–9.

178 CHARLOTTE VILLIERS AND JUKKA MÄHÖNEN

of the kinds of arguments that other national accounting bodies make about the positive role of accountants.

2.1.2 The negative role

While it seems clear from the foregoing observations from an influential national accounting body that accountants have a potentially supportive role in sustainable business activity, there are also risks in relying on them for this purpose. As traditional accounting focuses on the relationship between investors and the firm with the goal of calculating the net profits distributable to the investors, there will be challenges for sustainability advocates since this function arguably narrows the perspective of the accountants. In addition, the neutral stance that the ICAEW has presented might not accurately reflect the nature of accountants' interest in the sustainability agenda.

There are some potential concerns. Lovell and MacKenzie note, for example, that authority is gained through promoting the uptake of certain seemingly neutral practices and techniques (e.g. the application of financial accounting principles and techniques to climate change – double-entry book-keeping; quantitative and narrative formats), and through discourse (e.g. the discursive positioning of accountancy as the 'natural home' for the professional management of carbon).[13] Other examples of such neutralising and narrowing of the agenda from the accountants' perspective might include the emphasis on measurement from a narrow, business-oriented view so that the natural world is redefined in accounting terms that fit the corporate agenda of commercial exploitation or generation of profits; current accounting techniques are based on neoclassical economics, which privileges market mechanisms, economic instruments and property rights, and these largely ignore the social, organisational and political aspects of accounting; numerical quantification is not necessarily compatible with the natural world, and there is an emphasis on monetary value that can exclude non-monetary externalities; and technical accounting practices such as the short-term annual time horizons tend to overlook enduring environmental impacts.[14]

Lovell and MacKenzie thus remind us that accountants are more powerful than is suggested by the picture of them as passively reacting to a situation. Indeed, while accountancy can make things appear 'anti-political'

---

[13] H. Lovell and D. MacKenzie, 'Accounting for carbon: the role of accounting professional organisations in governing climate change' (2011) 43 *Antipode* 706.

[14] Lovell and MacKenzie, 'Accounting for carbon', 725–27.

ACCOUNTING, AUDITING, AND REPORTING 179

and seemingly uncontroversial, the technical debates about accountancy rules and standards in reality sometimes involve intense power struggles. The potential for carbon accountancy rules having a huge influence on company profits and liabilities has made it a site of conflict.[15] Thus, accountants help to shape the social processes involved, and accountancy plays a constitutive role in those social processes.[16] As critiqued by Miller:

> [A]ccounting is, above all, an attempt to intervene, to act upon individuals, entities and processes to transform them and to achieve specific ends. From such a perspective, *accounting is no longer to be regarded as a neutral device* that merely documents and reports 'the facts' of economic activity. Accounting can now be seen as a set of practices that affects the type of world we live in, the type of social reality we inhabit, the way in which we understand choices...[17]

Lovell and MacKenzie observe that the accountancy professions have responded to climate change by seeking to mould the global warming problem to fit into existing accounting discourse and practices. As they say, the new carbon economy represents 'business as usual' for accountants. Climate change presents accountants with a new policy space[18] in which they are able to make further financial gains. Indeed, the ICAEW talks of 'responding to new market opportunities'[19] and the Association of Chartered Certified Accountants (ACCA) states that 'ACCA members will need to understand how the carbon crisis will affect businesses, and whether there are investment opportunities.'[20] These responses indicate a focus on profits, both for their own profession and for their corporate clients, a motivation that limits the potential for business to change towards sustainability.

2.2 Accounting and capitalism as a challenge to sustainability

This profit-oriented response is hardly surprising given that financial accounting and double-entry book-keeping are closely connected to

---

[15] Lovell and MacKenzie, 'Accounting for carbon', 709.
[16] Lovell and MacKenzie, 'Accounting for carbon', 707–8.
[17] P. Miller, 'Accounting as social and institutional practice', in A.G. Hopwood and P. Miller (eds.), *Accounting as Social and Institutional Practice* (Cambridge University Press, 1994), 1 (emphasis added). Cited by Lovell and MacKenzie, 'Accounting for carbon', 708–9.
[18] Miller, 'Accounting as social and institutional practice', 725–6.
[19] ICAEW, *Information for Better Markets: Sustainability*, 11.
[20] Association of Chartered Certified Accountants, *The Carbon Jigsaw* (ACCA, 2009), cited by Lovell and MacKenzie, 'Accounting for carbon', 721.

180 CHARLOTTE VILLIERS AND JUKKA MÄHÖNEN

capitalism.[21] Capitalism is based on private profit-maximising firms that gain their financing from private, profit-maximising investors. With its emphasis on economic growth, the market mechanism, and private wealth creation, capitalism itself could be perceived as innately in conflict with sustainability.[22] Accounting itself, argue some critics, contributes to the economic self-interest by constructing accountability in such a way that an entity has no choice but to pursue only its own good.[23] According to Li, 'Under capitalism, there has been a systematic tendency for population, production and consumption to expand on increasingly larger scales.'[24] Although this environmentally unsustainable tendency is not unique to capitalist systems, Li explains further that:

> First, the capitalist world system is based on inter-state competition...
> [which makes it difficult]... for global environmental regulation to func-
> tion effectively. Second, the existing physical and technical infrastructure
> of the global capitalist economy is based on non-renewable resources and
> ecologically unsustainable technologies. Even if economic growth can be
> made compatible with sustainability under idealized technological con-
> ditions, it would nevertheless take several decades to replace the existing
> infrastructure with a new, ecologically sustainable infrastructure.[25]

The foregoing dynamic of capitalism suggests that, at best, it can only accommodate a weak form of sustainable development.[26] Accounting is complicit in this capitalist structure. As Jones describes:

[21] W. Sombart, *Der moderne Kapitalismus* (Duncker and Humbolt, 1916); K.S. Most, *Sombart on Accounting History* (Academy of Accounting Historians, 1979). See also M. Weber, *The Protestant Ethic and the Spirit of Capitalism*, translated by T. Parsons (Allen & Unwin 1930); M. Weber, *General Economic History*, translated by F.H. Knight (Allen & Unwin, 1927). See further R.A. Bryer, 'The history of accounting and the transition to capitalism in England – Part One: theory' (2000) 25 *Accounting Organizations and Society* 131; R.A. Bryer, 'The history of accounting and the transition to capitalism England – Part Two: the evidence' (2000) 25 *Accounting Organizations and Society* 327; J.S. Toms, 'Calculating profit: a historical perspective on the development of capitalism' (2010) 35(2) *Accounting, Organizations and Society* 205.

[22] J.G. Speth, *The Bridge at the Edge of the World: Capitalism, the Environment, and Crossing from Crisis to Sustainability* (Yale University Press, 2008); M. Li, 'Capitalism, climate change and the transition to sustainability: Alternative scenarios for the US, China and the world' (2009) 40(6) *Development and Change* 1039.

[23] See C.C. Ngwakwe, 'Rethinking the accounting stance on sustainable development' (2012) 20(1) *Sustainable Development* 30, citing T. Shearer, 'Ethics and accountability: From the for-itself to the for-the-other' (2002) 27(6) *Accounting, Organizations and Society* 541.

[24] Li, 'Capitalism, climate change and the transition to sustainability', 1040–1.

[25] Li, 'Capitalism, climate change and the transition to sustainability', 1041.

[26] H.E. Daly, 'Economics and sustainability: in defence of a steady-state economy', in M. Tobias (ed.), *Deep Ecology* (Avant Books, 1985), 90.

ACCOUNTING, AUDITING, AND REPORTING 181

> [C]urrent accounting with its focus on profit measurement as a precursor to dividend payments primarily serves the interests of the big companies and their shareholders. Other stakeholder groups and interests, including environmental interests, remain unsatisfied . . . conventional accounting elevates the measurement, calculation, valuation and disclosure of financial assets and profits. Other activities which remain unmeasured are disregarded.[27]

Some critics go so far as to malign accounting as 'the originator of managerial capitalism', with adverse consequences such as concentrating power in the hands of few individuals, and increasing the gap between rich and poor.[28]

Even where sustainability reporting has been developed, questions remain over the viability of current models and practices in the context of managerial capitalism. Gray highlights the rhetoric surrounding the term 'sustainability' and notes that it has come to be synonymous with other notions such as social responsibility or environmental management and 'most especially, becomes a term that offers no threat to corporate attitudes and activity'.[29] He notes also that there is in the business claims an additional signifier for sustainability, that of the sustainability of the business itself, which ultimately 'adapts more comfortably with the preconceptions of "business as usual"'.[30] Such narratives are 'powerful fictions; fairy tales to help the children sleep at night'.[31] Ultimately, accountants stand accused as complicit in environmental mismanagement through their collaboration with corporations and their unsustainable business operations.[32]

2.3 Accounting and capitalism as a potential contribution to a sustainable future

These criticisms of modern capitalism are clearly quite devastating. However, in capitalism there may also be some solutions. Speth, for example,

---

[27] M.J. Jones, 'Accounting for the environment: towards a theoretical perspective for environmental accounting and reporting' (2010) 34 *Accounting Forum* 129.

[28] Ngwakwe, 'Rethinking', 30.

[29] R. Gray, 'Is accounting for sustainability actually accounting for sustainability . . . and how would we know? An exploration of narratives of organisations and the planet' (2010) 35 *Accounting Organizations and Society* 49.

[30] Gray, 'Is accounting for sustainability actually accounting for sustainability?'

[31] Gray, 'Is accounting for sustainability actually accounting for sustainability?', 50.

[32] Ngwakwe, 'Rethinking', 30, citing K.T. Maunders and R.L. Burritt, 'Accounting and ecological crisis' (1991) 4(3) *Accounting, Auditing and Accountability Journal* 9.

182   CHARLOTTE VILLIERS AND JUKKA MÄHÖNEN

highlights the creativity, innovation, and entrepreneurship of businesses operating in a vibrant sector, as essential to designing and building a prosperous and sustainable economy.[33] Advocates of natural capitalism[34] argue that companies can gain a competitive advantage and profit by practising four key principles: (1) profiting from advanced resource productivity; (2) closing materials loops; (3) eliminating waste; and (4) reinvesting in natural capital.[35] Porrit argues that as capitalism is 'the only game in town', we have no choice but to rely on capitalism to reorient itself towards sustainability. He suggests that we extend the concept of capital to include natural capital and to change sustainability into a positive agenda by showing that it is as much about new opportunities for responsible wealth creation as about outlawing irresponsible wealth creation, and to speak to people's desire for long-term prosperity, enlightened self-interest, and higher quality of life. This agenda is more likely to yield positive results than the pursuit of utopian dreams.[36] A change in investment, production, and consumption patterns is thus required. It is unlikely that a viable economic system to rival capitalism will emerge in the near term to deal with the challenges of climate change and other ecological damage, and thus these changes will have to be made partly through market governance mechanisms.[37] Accounting law and company law will therefore be key features in this process of change.

There is clearly much to be done. Accounting, reporting, and auditing provide a platform for such progress, and this might be made achievable by using the tool of reflexive law.[38] Consumers, companies, the accounting

---

[33] J.G. Speth, 'The bridge at the end of the world: capitalism, the environment and crossing from crisis to sustainability', available at: www.aclimateforchange.org/profiles/blogs/the-bridge-at-the-edge-of-the-world.

[34] See e.g. *The Natural Capital Declaration*, available at: www.naturalcapitaldeclaration.org.

[35] See e.g. L. Hunter Lovins and A.B. Lovins, *Natural Capitalism: Path to Sustainability?* (Natural Capital Solutions, 2001).

[36] See J. Porrit, *Capitalism as If the World Matters* (Earthscan, 2007). See also P. Hawken, B. Lovins, and L. Hunter Lovins, *Natural Capitalism: The Next Industrial Revolution* (Earthscan, 1999).

[37] See M. Paterson, 'Global governance for sustainable capitalism? The political economy of global environmental governance', in N. Adger and A. Jordan (eds.), *Governing Sustainability* (Cambridge University Press, 2009), 99 at 116–17.

[38] D. Hess, 'Social reporting: a reflexive law approach to corporate social responsiveness' (1999) 25 *Journal of Corporation Law* 41 at 43. R.D. Hines, 'The FASB's conceptual framework, financial accounting and the maintenance of the social world' (1991) 16 *Accounting, Organizations and Society* 313 at 314. On the origins of reflexive law, see G. Teubner, 'Substantive and reflexive elements in modern law' (1983) 17 *Law & Society*

ACCOUNTING, AUDITING, AND REPORTING 183

professions, and regulators are still at the learning stage with regard to accountability for environment impacts such as climate change. For this reason, accounting law and practice are often framed as a 'reflexive law forum'.[39]

In reflexive law theory and strategic practice, authorities are given the role of creating a procedural framework 'which allows societal actors to interact and formulate norms based on learning about needs and expectations held by other actors'.[40] Reflexive law is 'employed to promote the internalisation of externalities within organisations'.[41] It is 'the establishment of procedural frameworks and the self-regulatory processes that take place' for exchange and learning.[42] This learning is essential to this relatively new area of accounting, and in reflexive law theory, such learning is achieved through a continuous self-observation and self critique. In reality, however, we are faced with a challenge of social engineering that reveals epistemological and teleological tensions that underlie the reflexive regulation project. The accounting, reporting, and auditing context highlights these tensions. Section 3 of this chapter describes the regulatory structure for accounting relevant to sustainability.

3 Accounting requirements and practices: comparative perspectives

3.1 Regulatory structure

Across the jurisdictions represented in the Sustainable Companies Project, there is much sustainability and CSR reporting activity but it is of variable quality, coming from a variety of hard and soft regulatory bases, with some jurisdictions appearing to be more progressive than others. Accounting law, as well as company law and environmental protection legislation, are all relevant, as are accounting standards promulgated by professional accounting organisations, including the International Financial Reporting Standards (IFRS) and the US Generally Accepted Accounting Principles (US GAAP), as well as locally applicable national standards

---

Review 239; G. Teubner, 'Autopoiesis in law and society: a rejoinder to Blankenburg' (1984) 18 *Law and Society Review* 291; E.W. Orts, 'Reflexive environmental law' (1995) 89 *Northwestern University Law Review* 1227.

[39] See K. Buhmann, *The Danish CSR Reporting Requirement as Reflexive Law: Employing CSR as a Modality to Promote Public Policy* (University of Oslo Faculty of Law Research Paper No. 2011–36), available at: http://ssrn.com/abstract=1964220, 14.

[40] Buhmann, *The Danish CSR.*   [41] Buhmann, *The Danish CSR.*

[42] Buhmann, *The Danish CSR.*

and principles (local GAAP), such as those created by the Accounting Standards Board in the UK. Listed companies are often subject to further requirements imposed by securities law regulation and securities exchanges. Corporate governance codes and joint- and self-regulatory or voluntary corporate practices are also widespread, but these vary in how they treat issues such as environmental protection and sustainable business. Many companies subscribe to guidance provided by bodies such as the Global Reporting Initiative (GRI) or as members of CSR-oriented organisations.

There is less developed practice in auditing and assurance. According to the survey carried out for the Sustainable Companies Project, there is no jurisdiction with compulsory auditing or assurance of sustainability reports.[43] Even in the most progressive jurisdictions, only a fraction of the reports are audited. The problem lies in the structure of reporting. Financial accounts follow a reporting structure different from the management or annual report. The management report and the annual report, within its operating review section, provide narrative explanations of the company's performance. Sustainability reports are either included in management reports or are published as separate reports.

3.2 IFRS/GAAP

The jurisdictions represented in the research are divided into those applying IFRS, created by the International Accounting Standards Board (IASB), the international standard-setting body of the IFRS Foundation,[44] and others applying local GAAP. In our project, most countries follow the IFRS, possibly because those which are members of the European Union (EU) or of the European Economic Area (EEA)[45] are bound to do so. According to the IFRS, the principal objectives of its Foundation are:

to develop a single set of high-quality, understandable, enforceable, and globally accepted International Financial Reporting Standards (IFRSs)

---

[43] For information about the Sustainable Companies Project, see jus.uio.no/companies, under Projects.

[44] The IFRS Foundation is an independent, not-for-profit, private sector organisation working in the public interest: see www.ifrs.org/About-us/Pages/IFRS-foundation-and-iasb.aspx.

[45] The EEA was established in 1994 and today comprises countries within the EU together with Iceland, Lichtenstein, and Norway, who participate in the EU's internal market without being members of the European Union.

through its standard-setting body, the International Accounting Standards Board (IASB);

to promote the use and rigorous application of those standards;

to take account of the financial reporting needs of emerging economies and small and medium-sized entities (SMEs); and

to promote and facilitate adoption of IFRSs, being the standards and interpretations issued by the IASB, through the convergence of national accounting standards and IFRSs.[46]

To meet these goals, major economies have established time lines to converge with or adopt IFRSs. European legislation requires Member States to adopt IAS/IFRS for the consolidated accounts of listed or publicly traded companies.[47]

The popularity of the IFRS makes convergence possible with the potential for greater comparability and consistency, and enabling more standardised reporting. However, the IASB has largely concentrated on financial accounting. There are no IFRS on directors' reports or CSR reporting. Indeed, the IFRS Practice Statement on the Management Commentary remains non-binding, its role being to assist company management in presenting its commentary on the company's financial statements. According to van Mourik, 'All the IASB board members share the same positivist ontology focusing on accounting as a technical tool aimed at faithfully representing an entity's financial reality, rather than as a social construct which generates intended and unintended economic, social and environmental consequences.'[48] The experience to date appears to confirm the views of Lovell and Mackenzie noted above that accountants present their role as neutral when in reality they wield significant social and political influence. The IASB has given support to the development of sustainability reporting by its involvement in the recently formed International Integrated Reporting Council (IIRC),[49] whose role has been to create a globally accepted framework for sustainability

---

[46] IFRS, available at: www.ifrs.org/About-us/Pages/IFRS-Foundation-and-IASB.aspx.

[47] Regulation (EC) No 1606/2002 of the European Parliament and of the Council of 19 July 2002 on the application of international accounting standards, OJ 2002 No. L243, 11 September 2002, p. 1.

[48] C. van Mourik, *Response to the IFRS Foundation's Report of the Trustees' Strategy Review* (IFRS, July 2011).

[49] The IIRC is a global coalition of regulators, investors, companies, standard setters, the accounting profession, and NGOs leading the development of a global framework for integrated reporting, see www.theiirc.org.

186 CHARLOTTE VILLIERS AND JUKKA MÄHÖNEN

accounting.[50] The first such IIRC framework was published in December 2013.[51]

Some other jurisdictions follow the alternative local GAAP, the standard framework of guidelines for financial accounting used in any given jurisdiction. Local GAAP include the standards, conventions, and rules accountants follow in recording and summarising transactions, and in the preparation of financial statements.

3.3 The European Union: the Accounts Modernisation Directive

In the EU, the Accounts Modernisation Directive[52] is very important to the foregoing issues.[53] Paragraph 9 of the Preamble explains:

> The annual report and the consolidated annual report are important elements of financial reporting. [F]or these to present a fair review of the development of the business and of its position . . . the information should not be restricted to the financial aspects of the company's business. [The fair review] should lead to an analysis of environmental and social aspects necessary for an understanding of the company's development, performance or position.

Article 46 of the Fourth Directive on annual accounts,[54] as amended by the Accounts Modernisation Directive, requires a company's annual report to 'include at least a fair review of the development and performance of the company's business and of its position, together with a description of the principal risks and uncertainties that it faces'. The review, analysing the company's development, performance, and position, must include both

---

[50] For further information on progress of this project, see IIRC: www.theiirc.org/about/.

[51] Available at: www.theiirc.org/wp-content/uploads/2013/12/13–12–08-THE-INTER NATIONAL-IR-FRAMEWORK-2-1.pdf.

[52] Directive 2003/51/EC of the European Parliament and of the Council of 18 June 2003 amending Directives 78/660/EEC, 83/349/EEC, 86/635/EEC and 91/674/EEC on the annual and consolidated accounts of certain types of companies, banks and other financial institutions and insurance undertakings, OJ 2003 No. L178, 17 July 2003, p. 16.

[53] For an interesting analysis of how this Directive has been applied in EU countries, see T. E. Lambooy and N. van Vliet, 'Transparency on corporate social responsibility in annual reports' (2008) 5(3) *European Company Law* 127, and also T.E. Lambooy, *Corporate Social Responsibility: The Legal and Semi-legal Frameworks Supporting CSR* (Kluwer, 2010).

[54] Fourth Council Directive 78/660/EEC of 25 July 1978 based on Article 54 (3) (g) of the Treaty on the annual accounts of certain types of companies, OJ 1978 No. L222, 14 August 1978, p. 11.

ACCOUNTING, AUDITING, AND REPORTING 187

financial and, where appropriate, non-financial key performance indicators relevant to the particular business, including information relating to environmental and employee matters. The Fourth Directive, as well as the Seventh Directive on consolidated accounts, have been replaced by the New Accounting Directive of 2013.[55] Paragraph 26 of the Preamble and Article 19 of the New Accounting Directive codifies the above-mentioned parts of the Accounts Modernisation Directive.

National implementation of the Accounts Modernisation Directive has varied, though for EU Member States and the three EFTA states of the EEA, the Directive is at the heart of the national requirements for environmental reporting. The European Commission reports:

> Some Member States have privileged 'report or explain' models, where companies can choose between actual reporting, or, alternatively, disclosing the reasons for not doing so. Others establish an outright legal requirement, which may be quite prescriptive. Some Member States target large companies, while others focus on certain listed companies or government-owned companies only. Some Member States refer to international guidelines (although often different ones), while others are developing their own national reporting guidelines.[56]

An impact assessment study on non-financial information disclosure by EU companies, published by the Commission in 2013, reveals that the current EU legislation is not effective. Although an increasing number of companies do disclose non-financial information in their annual reports, or in stand-alone sustainability reports, both from a quantitative as well as a qualitative viewpoint, the disclosures do not satisfy stakeholders.[57]

---

[55] Directive 2013/34/EU of the European Parliament and of the Council of 26 June 2013 on the annual financial statements, consolidated financial statements and related reports of certain types of undertakings, amending Directive 2006/43/EC of the European Parliament and of the Council and repealing Council Directives 78/660/EEC and 83/349/EEC, OJ L 182, 29.6.2013, p. 19.

[56] European Commission, *Proposal for a Directive of the European Parliament and of the Council amending Council Directives 78/660/EEC and 83/349/EEC as regards disclosure of non-financial and diversity information by certain large companies and groups,* Strasbourg, 16.4.2013 COM (2013) 207 final (hereafter 'EC 2013').

[57] European Commission, *Impact Assessment Accompanying the Document Proposal for a Directive of the European Parliament and of the Council Amending Council Directives 78/660/EEC and 83/349/EEC as Regards Disclosure of Non-financial and Diversity Information by Certain Large Companies and Groups,* SWD(2013) 127 final, p. 11. Of the 443 EU companies featuring in the FTSE All World Index between 2005 and 2009,

In terms of quantity, it is estimated that 94 per cent of the total of approximately 42,000 large companies in the EU do not disclose non-financial information at all. As a remarkable outcome, more than 50 per cent of the reports that have been published in the EU come from companies established in the UK, Denmark, Spain, and France, that is, countries with additional national disclosure requirements.[58] As regards the quality of the information disclosed, the impact assessment study revealed that 'a majority of users considered that information is often not sufficiently material, balanced, accurate, timely, and comparable'.[59]

The mapping papers undertaken for this Sustainable Companies Project confirm this level of variation among different jurisdictions. Thus, some states have adopted a minimalist approach, such as Slovenia, which has copied the text into its legislation without publishing guidance,[60] and others have introduced more extensive reporting requirements, such as Hungary.[61] As a reaction, the European Commission published in April 2013 a proposal to amend Article 46 of the Fourth Directive (and Article 36 of the Seventh Directive).[62] The proposed amendment requires companies to provide a non-financial statement with information relating to 'at least environmental, social and employee matters, respect for human rights, anti-corruption and bribery matters'.

On 15 April 2014, the plenary of the European Parliament adopted a directive based on the Commission proposal. The new directive, now amending the New Accounting Directive, will enter into force once it is adopted by the Council and published in the EU *Official Journal*. The directive requires companies to disclose information on policies, risks and outcomes as regards environmental matters, social and employee-related

---

fewer than one in six reported GHG emissions that covered all corporate activities, while others did not say which activities their data referred to. See also the survey conducted by Leeds University/Euromed on a sample of 4,000 CSR reports, available at: www.leeds.ac. uk/news/article/2696/doing_good_or_just_talking_about_it.

[58] European Commission, *Impact Assessment*, p. 10, referring to Global Winners & Reporting Trends: see www.corporateregister.com/crra/help/CRRA-2012-Exec-Summary.pdf.

[59] European Commission, *Impact Assessment*, p. 11.

[60] J. Zrilič, *Mapping Paper on the Barriers and Possibilities for Integrating Environmental Sustainability into Slovenian Company Law* (Sustainable Companies Project, 2011).

[61] D.G. Szabó, *The Possibility of Sustainable Companies under the Hungarian Company Law Regime* (Sustainable Companies Project, 2011).

[62] European Commission, Proposal for a Directive of the European Parliament and the Council amending Council Directives 78/660/EEC and 83/349/EEC as regards disclosure of non-financial and diversity information by certain large companies and groups, COM/2013/0207 final.

ACCOUNTING, AUDITING, AND REPORTING 189

aspects, respect for human rights, anti-corruption and bribery issues, and diversity in their board of directors.[63]

In Section 4, we outline the key reporting requirements in some of the countries represented in the Sustainable Companies Project.

4 Comparative reporting requirements for the environment and sustainability

Environmental reporting requirements vary greatly among jurisdictions. Alongside the provisions that implement the EU Accounts Modernisation Directive, most countries have additional disclosure obligations relating to environmental protection, as set out in further legislation or by the listing authorities or accounting bodies who set accounting standards. Most jurisdictions have developed rules on corporate governance, many mirroring the UK, with quasi-regulatory Corporate Governance Codes[64] that are to be applied on a comply-or-explain basis. Some corporate governance regimes are more specific than others in their disclosure requirements.

In this summary of our findings, we first present the EU and the EFTA states of the EEA, followed by other jurisdictions that are not required to implement EU law.

4.1 EU and EEA Member States

4.1.1 Primary legislation

Nearly all countries have primary legislation with provisions relating to company reporting. Either commercial codes or company or accounting legislation contain such provisions. For example, Section 289 of the German Commercial Code (*Handelsgesetzbuch*, HGB) requires major companies to provide economic reports containing information on non-financial performance indicators on the environment and employee matters.[65] Similarly, the Swedish law of annual accounts (ÅRL)[66] states

---

[63] See http://ec.europa.eu/finance/accounting/non-financial_reporting/index_en.htm.

[64] C. Villiers, Mapping Paper: Sustainable Companies UK Report, Research Paper No. 2013–16 (University of Oslo Faculty of Law, 2013), available at: http://ssrn.com/abstract=2280350.

[65] G. Deipenbrock, *The Management Board of a German Aktiengesellschaft, the Managing Directors of a German GmbH, the Unternehmensinteresse and the Goal of Sustainable Development of Companies – Some Fundamentals* (Sustainable Companies Project, 2011).

[66] *Årsredovisningslag* [Annual Reports Act] (1995: 1554).

190   CHARLOTTE VILLIERS AND JUKKA MÄHÖNEN

that all companies are required to report non-financial information relevant to the business in the directors' report, including information relating to the environment and to employees. Companies engaged in activities that require permits or notification under the Environmental Code[67] should always provide information about the impacts on the environment.[68] Recent amendments were made in France to the Commercial Code, under the new Grenelle 2 Law,[69] which extends corporations' obligations to report annually on the non-financial consequences of their activities.[70] Similarly, the Spanish Company Capital Act, Article 262, requires management reports with contents mirroring the specifications laid down in the Accounts Modernization Directive.[71] Some countries provide these requirements in their environmental laws, such as Macedonia,[72] while others set them out in their accounting legislation, such as Finland.[73]

4.1.2 Implementation of the Accounts Modernisation Directive

The level of detail with which states have implemented the EU Directive varies considerably. Most countries have requirements that largely match those set out in the Directive, such as the UK, in Section 417 of the Companies Act 2006, which closely resembled Article 46 of the Directive.[74] Section 417 has since been repealed and replaced by new Sections 414 A to 414 C of the Companies Act 2006 (Strategic Report and Directors'

---

[67] *Miljöbalk* [Environmental Code] (1998: 808).

[68] J.B. Andersson and F. Segenmark, *Mapping Paper on the Company Law Barriers and Possibilities for Sustainable Companies: Sweden*, Research Paper No. 2013–09 (University of Oslo Faculty of Law, 2013), available at: http://ssrn.com/abstract=2248584.

[69] *Loi n° 2010–788 du 12 juillet 2010 portant engagement national pour l'environnement* [Act on the National Commitment to the Environment].

[70] I. Tchotourian, 'When CSR drives new corporate governance: does the latest French law reform (the 'Grenelle 2 Law') confirm the end of "business as usual"?', in S. Boubaker and D.K. Nguyen (eds.), *Board Directors and Corporate Social Responsibility* (Palgrave Macmillan, 2012), p. 255.

[71] E.E. Olmedo, *et al.*, *Sustainable Companies: Spanish Mapping Paper on Company Law Issues*, Research Paper No. 2012–36 (University of Oslo Faculty of Law, 2012), available at: http://ssrn.com/abstract=2181337.

[72] J.S. van Rumpt, *Macedonia Company Law Barriers and Possibilities for Sustainable Companies*, mapping paper (Sustainable Companies Project, 2011).

[73] J. Mähönen, *Sustainable Companies Mapping Paper on Company Law Issues: Finland* (Sustainable Companies Project, 2011).

[74] Villiers, *Sustainable Companies UK Report*.

ACCOUNTING, AUDITING, AND REPORTING 191

Report) Regulations 2013[75] and requires large and medium-sized companies to provide a 'strategic report' within the directors' report (instead of a 'business review'). While some countries, such as Macedonia, have adopted a minimalist approach and have done no more than copy the text,[76] others have gone beyond the Directive and been more comprehensive in their approach, such as Hungary in its Accounting Act, which demands information on measures and actions that facilitate or plan to facilitate environmental protection in general.[77]

Thus, companies are required to disclose their environmental policy and the steps undertaken for environmental protection regardless of whether they have any significant effect on the company's own development or financial performance.[78] In Hungary, the environmental impact of the company is seen as relevant independently of other impacts. The Hungarian model might therefore be seen as more supportive of sustainability in and of itself rather than as related merely to the company's economic or market position. Norway's Accounting Act is also more detailed than the standard set by the EU Directive. The Norwegian Accounting Act requires the inclusion in the directors' report of several social, environmental, and health and safety issues. Notably the Norwegian law also requires that the report include information about measures that can prevent or mitigate negative environmental impacts. Further, the Norwegian Accounting Act, in implementing the EU Directive, requires that 'if relevant for the development, performance or position' of the company, environmental matters are to be included in the report. The board's annual report must also include information on 'not insignificant impact on the external environment'.[79] In contrast to Norway, Turkey, which is working towards accession to the EU, provides only basic sustainable and environmental reporting requirements in its legislation.[80]

---

[75] Statutory Instrument No. 2013/1970.
[76] van Rumpt, *Macedonia Company Law Barriers and Possibilities for Sustainable Companies.*
[77] Szabó, *The Possibility of Sustainable Companies under the Hungarian Company Law Regime.*
[78] See especially Sections 94–95 of the Act C 2000 on Accounting [2000. évi C. törvény a számvitelről, Kihirdetve: 2000. IX. 21], available in English at: www.ecovis.hu/angol/accounting.pdf.
[79] B. Sjåfjell, *Sustainable Companies: Possibilities and Barriers in Norwegian Company Law,* Research Paper No. 2013–20 (University of Oslo Faculty of Law, 2013), available at: http://ssrn.com/abstract=2311433.
[80] M. Eroglu, *Obstacles and Possibilities for Sustainable Companies in Turkey,* Research Paper No. 2013–04 (University of Oslo Faculty of Law, 2013), available at: http://ssrn.com/abstract=2218220.

4.1.3 Additional reporting requirements

Disclosure obligations on companies are commonly also found in collateral codes and supplementary regulations. The information provided for the different countries in the Sustainable Companies Project indicates a trend in which stock exchanges have posited demands for information but these do not always require environmental disclosures.[81] Thus, in Ireland, the Irish Stock Exchange Listing Rules, Chapter 6, also set out continuing obligations for disclosure but there is no provision for environmental reporting. However, the EU Market Abuse (Directive 2003/6/EC) Regulations 2005 set out the requirements for and the timing of disclosure of information to the market, and this includes price-sensitive information under which, suggests Clarke, 'it is conceivable that the information required to be disclosed here may relate to environmental matters'.[82] In Spain, the Sustainable Economy Act 2011 requires listed companies to describe the main characteristics of their internal control systems and risk management about the process of issuing financial information. It also specifies management principles to be incorporated in the strategic plans of state-owned commercial companies. The latter must submit annual reports on corporate governance and sustainability reports in accordance with commonly accepted standards.[83] Germany has supplemented its Commercial Code with provisions in the German Stock Corporation Act (AktG) which state that the management board must provide the supervisory board with the information it needs to supervise the work of the management board and that such reports must cover intended business policy and business plans.

In some countries the professional accounting boards have provided guidance on non-financial disclosures. In 2003, the Finnish Accounting Board issued guidance on the recognition, measurement, and disclosure of environmental issues as a part of a company's financial statement. The guidance was amended in 2006 when the disclosure requirements were expanded to cover the board's mandatory Review of Operations. The Finnish Accounting Board's general guidance defines a set of environmental and social performance indicators and related qualitative

---

[81] For further discussion on links between corporate governance codes and CSR in the EU, see: D.G. Szabó and K.E. Sorensen, *Integrating Corporate Social Responsibility in Corporate Governance Codes in the EU*, LSN Research Paper Series, No 10–28 (LSN, 2013).

[82] B.J. Clarke, *Irish Company Law Mapping Paper*, Research Paper No. 2012–35 (University of Oslo Faculty of Law, 2012), available at: http://ssrn.com/abstract=2178420.

[83] Olmedo, *et al.*, *Sustainable Companies: Spanish Mapping Paper*.

ACCOUNTING, AUDITING, AND REPORTING 193

information to be disclosed in the review of operations, when this information is material for financial reporting purposes. This is tied to the financial situation of the company.[84]

Similarly, in the UK, the Accounting Standards Board published a Reporting Statement of Best Practice for the Operating and Financial Review to supplement the requirements in Section 417 of the Companies Act 2006. This was not mandatory but it provided comprehensive guidance for discussing in the business review the main factors underlying the company's performance and financial position. Adherence to the Accounting Standards Board's Statement of Best Practice was not commonly found among companies.[85] The Financial Reporting Council has the remit of providing guidance for companies in the preparation and publication of their strategic reviews. The Department for Environment, Food and Rural Affairs also issued Reporting Guidelines on Key Performance Indicators and Guidance for Measuring Greenhouse Gas Emissions. In June 2012, the Department announced at the Rio+ 20 Summit that reporting GHG emissions would become compulsory for large companies from April 2013,[86] and these requirements now appear in the Companies Act 2006 (Strategic Report and Directors' Report) Regulations 2013. The Department believes that mandatory reporting by companies is a first step towards the reduction of such emissions.[87]

While the main provisions are now found in Sections 414 A–D of the Companies Act 2006, in addition, the UK Pensions Act 1995, Section 35, as amended by the Pensions Act 2004, obliges the trustees of pension schemes to prepare, maintain, and periodically review a statement of investment principles that discloses the extent (if at all) to which social, environmental, and ethical factors have been taken into account in the selection, realisation, and retention of investments.[88] In order to attract investment, this provision might incentivise companies to make such information

---

[84] Mähönen, *Sustainable Companies Mapping Paper: Finland.*

[85] Villiers, *Sustainable Companies UK Report.* For further information on the background and the impact of the ASB's Statement of Best Practice, see O. Aiyegbayo and C. Villiers, 'The enhanced business review: has it made corporate governance more effective?' (2011) 7 *Journal of Business Law* 699.

[86] Villiers, *Sustainable Companies UK Report.*

[87] See DEFRA, 'Leading businesses to disclose greenhouse gas emissions', press release (20 June 2012), available at: www.defra.gov.uk/news/2012/06/20/greenhouse-gas-reporting/.

[88] The Occupational Pension Schemes Amendment Regulations 1999, cl. 2 4 (UK). See also Occupational Pension Schemes (Investment) Regulations 2005. See further, D. Hess,

available for pension trustees and asset managers to consider.[89] However, Richardson's review of implementation of this reform and similar efforts in several other EU Member States and non-EU states reveals that though many pension funds have published policies disclosing their commitment to socially responsible investing (SRI), the quality of their disclosures is often poor or perfunctory with little insight provided into their application and impact.[90]

In Macedonia, implementation of the Modernisation Directive's requirements for non-financial information is left to its environmental legislation and the 'CSR Agenda', which are explained in the Corporate Governance Manual of 2007 for public companies. The latter lists information on the members of the governing bodies, directors, and employees, information on shareholders, related party transactions, risk factors, stakeholders, information on corporate governance structure, and policy. The CSR Agenda states that 'the government should require companies of a certain size and active in certain specified industries to report on their environmental and social impact and to develop a guideline on how to apply the GRI and select the most important indicators for the Macedonian business community'.[91] Similarly, the Turkish Corporate Governance Principles, published by the Capital Market Board in 2005, require annual reports to be prepared in a manner to ensure public access to information regarding the company's activities and employees' social rights. Professional training and environment protection rights may also be incorporated in this annual report.[92]

Denmark also has relatively sophisticated reporting requirements. The Environmental Protection Act has led to Statutory Order 210/2010 which establishes mandatory environmental reporting requirements for certain industrial activities (those which are more polluting: in the construction sector and those emitting toxic waste into the environment).[93] Since January 2009, certain large companies (by number of employees or asset thresholds) have also been required, under a new Section 99a,

---

'Public pensions and the promise of shareholder activism for the next frontier of corporate governance: sustainable economic development' (2007) 2 *Virginia Law and Business Review*, 222.

[89] Villiers, *Sustainable Companies UK Report*.

[90] B.J. Richardson, *Fiduciary Law and Responsible Investing: In Nature's Trust* (Routledge, 2013), 170–3.

[91] van Rumpt, *Company Law Barriers and Possibilities for Sustainable Companies*.

[92] Eroglu, *Obstacles and Possibilities for Sustainable Companies in Turkey*.

[93] Buhmann, et al., *Mapping: Denmark*.

inserted into the Financial Statements Act, to submit CSR reports which may include consideration of human rights, societal, environmental, and climate change conditions as well as combating corruption in their business strategy and activities.[94] Similar requirements issued by the Danish Financial Supervisory Authority also cover institutional investors, mutual funds, and other listed financial enterprises. The legislation exempts those companies that have prepared a progress report pursuant to their accession to the UN Global Compact or the UN Principles for Responsible Investment.[95] Alongside the requirements posited by the Environmental Protection Act 210/2010 and the amended Danish Financial Statements Act, similar reporting requirements apply to institutional investors, mutual funds, and other listed financial enterprises not covered by the Financial Statements Act, introduced in statutory orders issued by the Danish Financial Supervisory Authority. Such information required includes the company's social responsibility policies; how the company implements its social responsibility policies in practice; the company's evaluation of what has been achieved through social responsibility initiatives during the financial year and any expectations regarding future initiatives. The Agency for Companies and Commerce requires companies to publish the main contents of their CSR policy or at least to state that they have no such policy, if that is the case.[96] Norway, in 2013, inspired by the Danish rule, has added another layer of a broader CSR reporting requirement to its existing provisions, requiring that large companies report on the work they do to integrate human and labour rights concerns and environmental concerns and anti-corruption measures.[97]

4.2 Reporting requirements outside the EU

4.2.1 Corporate law or environmental law

In jurisdictions outside of the EU and the three EFTA members of the EEA, where the Accounts Modernisation Directive is not applicable, a

---

[94] See Act 1403 of 27 December 2008, amending *Årsregnskabsloven* (Danish Financial Statements Act).

[95] Sections 6 and 7 of Act 1403 of 27 December 2008. See further, Danish Government Guidance: *Reporting on CSR*, available at: www.CSRgov.dk.

[96] Buhmann, *et al.*, *Mapping: Denmark*.

[97] See Sjåfjell, *Sustainable Companies: Possibilities and Barriers in Norwegian Company Law*. She casts into doubt the use of the new rule, as companies can choose to merely report that they have no CSR guidelines, and there is little indication that this new provision will be enforced any more than the original CSR provisions have been.

variety of provisions relevant to environmental reporting exist. In some such jurisdictions these requirements are found in the company laws, such as in Australia, where the Corporations Act 2001 requires the reporting of information relevant to a company's future prospects.[98] This obligation is understood to include reporting on past, present, and future environmental performance to the extent that it is likely to affect the business strategy and future financial prospects. India's new Companies Act 2013 also contains extensive information requirements for CSR disclosure.[99]

In China, the annual report must contain environmental information. Under Article 65 of the Chinese Securities Law, an annual account must be published each accounting year and an interim report must be sent to the securities regulatory authority and stock exchange with details of major litigation and environmental events that may considerably affect the trading price of the company's shares. Mandatory disclosures are to be made by companies that discharge excessive pollutants, including the name, address, and legal representative of the enterprise, the name of the main pollutants, and how they are discharged and in what quantities, environmental protection facilities, and prepared emergency plans for pollution accidents.[100]

In other jurisdictions, environmental reporting requirements are found in environmental law, for example, in Japan[101] and in Argentina.[102] This chapter, however, does not provide the space to delve into the details of such reporting standards in these or other jurisdictions.

4.2.2   The role of securities regulators

Notably, in these non-EU and non-EEA jurisdictions, the securities regulators also play an important role in mandating non-financial disclosures, particularly where such information is deemed as 'material' or as 'price-sensitive'. In the USA, the Securities and Exchange Commission (SEC)

---

[98] Sections 299 and 299A.   [99] Act No. 18 of 2013.

[100] J. Lou and L. Tian, *A Study on Sustainable Companies in the P. R. of China*, Research Paper No. 2013–05 (University of Oslo Faculty of Law, 2013), available at: http://ssrn.com/abstract=2218284.

[101] J. Ueda, *Sustainable Companies: Mapping Paper for Japan* (Sustainable Companies Project, 2011).

[102] D. Parravicini, *Sustainability and CSR in Argentina: An Analysis Within Argentine Company Law*, Research Paper No. 2013–01 (University of Oslo Faculty of Law, 2013), available at: http://ssrn.com/abstract=2197774.

ACCOUNTING, AUDITING, AND REPORTING 197

specifically addresses climate change disclosure obligations, in addition to requiring disclosure of financially 'material' environmental issues. The SEC Guidance advises that Item 101 of Regulation S-K Description of Business must include disclosure regarding certain costs of compliance with environmental laws, and Item 303 of Regulation S-K on Management's Discussion and Analysis requires registrants to identify and disclose known trends, events, demands, commitments, and uncertainties that are reasonably likely to have a material effect on financial condition or operating performance, that is, such information for which there is 'a substantial likelihood that a reasonable shareholder would consider it important in deciding how to vote or make an investment decision or if the information would alter the total mix of available information'.[103] Guidance on corporate disclosure of financially-material climate change matters was issued by the SEC in 2010.[104] The Dodd Frank Wall Street Reform and Consumer Protection Act 2010[105] also directs the SEC to regulate on specific disclosures such as conflict minerals and mining and oil and gas extraction companies, which the SEC addressed in August 2012.[106]

In the EU, the corresponding requirements are found in Chapter 10 of the New Accounting Directive, to be implemented shortly by the Member States.[107] The new provisions apply to all public-interest entities, including all listed companies, and also to large unlisted undertakings.[108]

In Canada, where there is no national equivalent of the SEC but rather a confederation of provincially-based Canadian Securities Administrators, there is an absence of reporting guidance on climate change, despite

---

[103] See further-SEC, *Interpretation: Commission Guidance Regarding Management's Discussion and Analysis of Financial Condition and Results of Operations*, Release Nos 33–8350; 34–48960; FR-72; and *TSC Industries, Inc.* v. *Northway, Inc.*, 426 US 438 – Supreme Court 1976.

[104] SEC, *Commission Guidance Regarding Disclosure Relating to Climate Change Matters*, Release Nos 33–9106; 34–61469; FR-82 (2 February 2010).

[105] Dodd-Frank Wall Street Reform and Consumer Protection Act (Pub. L. 111–203, HR 4173). And see SEC, *Conflict Minerals*, Release No. 34–67716 (22 August 2012).

[106] C.R. Taylor, *United States Company Law as it Impacts Corporate Environmental Behavior, with Emphasis on Climate Change*, Research Paper No. 2012–31 (University of Oslo Faculty of Law, 2012), available at http://ssrn.com/abstract=2159659.

[107] According to Article 53(1) of the Directive, the Member States shall bring into force the laws, regulations, and administrative provisions necessary to comply with the Directive by 20 July 2015 (but there is provision to delay implementation until 2016).

[108] Article 42(1).

lobbying for such guidance from socially responsible investors. However, some direction on environmental reporting does exist, including guidance issued in 2010.[109] To illustrate the provincial legal standards, there are mandatory requirements under the Ontario Securities Act 1990 (as amended) requiring companies to file a prospectus that provides 'full, true and plain disclosure of all material facts relating to the securities issued or proposed or to be distributed' and also, in the prospectus, discussion of factors 'that have affected the value of projects such as environmental issues'.[110] Continuous disclosure is required by National Instrument 51–102 and its accompanying forms, which include requirements to disclose environmental issues.[111] A reporting public company must also disclose in its annual information form any social or environmental policies fundamental to its operations. The form must include information relating to any risk factors, including environmental issues and risks posed by the application of any environmental laws, also legal proceedings, but not if the claim is for damages valued at less than 10 per cent of the company's assets. The MD&A (management, discussion, and analysis) section of a company's report is also required to contain information on important trends and risks that have affected the financial statements, and as well as trends and risks that are reasonably likely to affect them in the future. This information could include environmental matters incidentally.[112]

The Australian Securities and Investment Commission (ASIC) is also empowered to develop guidelines and has done so since 2000 in relation to the product disclosure statements (PDS) that issuers of public securities must release. The ASIC's measures aim to improve the integrity of the market for SRI. Securities rules in the companies legislation oblige applicable entities (primarily investment companies and superannuation funds) in their 'product disclosure statements' (PDS) to explain 'the extent to which labour standards or environmental, social or ethical considerations are taken into account in the selection, retention or realization of the investment'.[113] This obligation is buttressed by the ASIC's

---

[109] Canadian Securities Administrators (CSA), *Environmental Reporting Guidelines*, CSA Staff Notice 51–333 (CSA, 2010).

[110] R.S.O. 1990, s. 56(1).

[111] Canadian Securities Administrators, *National Instrument 51–102 Continuous Disclosure Obligations*, 31 October 2011.

[112] B.J. Richardson and G. Tanner, *Canadian Company Law: Barriers and Possibilities for Sustainable Companies* (Sustainable Companies Project, 2010).

[113] *Corporations Act*, 2001 (Cth), s. 1013D(1)(l).

regulatory guidelines, which expect an explanation of the criteria for measuring investment standards or considerations, a general description of whether adherence to the methodology is monitored, and an explanation of actions taken when a specific investment no longer adheres to the stated investment policy.[114]

Among examples from developing countries, the Argentine Securities Exchange Commission (Comisión Nacional de Valores, 'CNV') also issued Resolution No. 559/09 applying to listed companies. It imposes disclosure obligations to report material facts, environmental surveys/audits, adaptation programmes, and compliance with insurance obligations/environmental management plans of the company. However, this Resolution is not applicable until the CNV issues supplementary regulations. It is a controversial provision and is opposed by companies on the basis of confidentiality issues.[115]

In South Africa, the King Code III, in force since 2010,[116] requests reporting that integrates social and environmental performance with all other dimensions of the company's activities. Chapter 9 of the Code defines integrated reporting as companies putting into their report information sufficient to show how the company has positively and negatively impacted the economic life of the community and its social and environmental and governance issues, and also to report on its likely impact during the coming year. This form of integrated reporting is mandatory for all companies listed on the Johannesburg Stock Exchange, on a 'comply-or-explain' basis.[117]

4.2.3 Specific legislation

Some jurisdictions have specific legislation for dealing with certain nonfinancial and environmental disclosures. In Australia, the National Greenhouse and Energy Reporting Act 2007 requires companies that exceed specified GHG emissions or energy thresholds to register and report

---

[114] ASIC, *Section 1013 Disclosure Guidelines* (ASIC, 2003); and ASIC, *Policy Statement 168: Product Disclosure Statements* (ASIC, 2005).

[115] Parravicini, *Sustainability and CSR in Argentina.*

[116] Chapter 6, King Report on Corporate Governance for South Africa and King Code of Governance Principles (King III), available at: IOD in Southern Africa: http://african.ipapercms.dk/IOD/KINGIII/kingiiicode/.

[117] J.J. Henning, *et al.*, *Sustainable Companies, Climate Change and Corporate Social Responsibility in South African Law* (Sustainable Companies Project, 2012).

annually to the Greenhouse and Energy Data Officer about their emissions and energy consumption. In addition, the National Pollutant Inventory requires reporting of emissions of specified chemicals to air, land, and water. A key objective of the Australian legislation is for community involvement and participation in environmental protection through enhanced access to information regarding corporate pollution. In Japan, Section 9(1) of the Act Concerning the Promotion of Business Activities with Environmental Considerations by Specified Corporations 2004 requires specified businesses to provide an annual report on their environmental considerations. The Ministry of the Environment has also, since 2003, published Environmental Reporting Guidelines.[118] The Argentine Corporation Law No. 19550 requires companies with more than 300 employees to prepare and submit a social report with employee-related information to the relevant trade union.[119]

4.2.4 Professional standards and principles, and professional guidance

As with the EU and EEA jurisdictions, other countries also rely quite extensively on the promulgation of principles and guidance by the professional accounting organisations. Notably, the US Financial Accounting Standards Board (FASB) Financial Accounting Standard 5 of 1975 deals with loss contingencies appearing in company disclosure. This might include climate-related loss contingencies covering liabilities or asset impairments arising from violation of or required compliance with climate change law; damage to property and obligations triggered by climate change events, though in practice so far, the financial impacts of climate change have largely gone unreported and unmeasured. There are also industry-specific regulations such as insurance firms' obligations to disclose financial risks due to climate change and any action taken to mitigate such risks.[120]

5 Emerging themes

From the above survey of the regulatory structure for environmental-related accounting and reporting across the jurisdictions inside and outside the EU and the EEA, a number of themes can be distilled. For example,

---

[118] Ueda, *Sustainable Companies: Mapping Paper for Japan.*
[119] Parravicini, *Sustainability and CSR in Argentina.*
[120] Taylor, *United States Company Law as It Impacts Corporate Environmental Behavior.*

what is reported and to whom are relevant to an analysis of the contribution of accounting and corporate law to sustainability. In addition, the self-regulatory and voluntary aspects of this activity are of relevance, particularly given the claims in reflexive law theory of their potential importance for learning and behavioural change.

5.1   What is reported?

Sustainability reporting covers a diverse menu of issues, which varies across jurisdictions, markets, and industries, Typically, the subjects reported on include costs of environmental management processes, litigation risks, and pollution costs as well as GHG emissions, water supply, health and safety, employee relations, and customer and supplier interests. Many nations focus on financially-material factors affecting the company. The definition of materiality is not uniform, but by and large it covers factors that are likely to affect investment decisions or the share price.

Numerous jurisdictions refer in their legislation or supplementary guidelines to 'material factors affecting the company and risk factors' but normally these are not clearly or exhaustively defined. Some guidance is offered in the Market Abuse Directive in the EU.[121] But outside the EU other jurisdictions have also provided guidance on this issue. Thus, for example, in Ghana, the Securities Exchange Commission and the Ghanaian Stock Exchange Listing Regulations require that listed companies provide investors with information of a price-sensitive nature, including information on issues that materially affect inter alia the financial and operating results of the company and material foreseeable risk factors. Companies 'are also encouraged to include information on their non-financial affairs', in annual reports. Such information can include 'information on employment; environmental matters; social responsibility; and matters of customer and supplier interest'. In short, in Ghana, 'while the financial aspects tend to underpin the legislation, it does not preclude consideration of environmental aspects by company directors and boards', and 'requirements to comply with other laws and governance or codes could make those provisions viable supplements to the Ghanaian Companies Code and vice versa'.[122] A variety of other nations canvassed

---

[121]   Directive 2003/6/EC of the European Parliament and of the Council of 28 January 2003, on insider dealing and market manipulation. OJ L, 12 April 2003, at 16.

[122]   P. Schwartz, *Developing States and Climate Change: Solutions in Company Law?*, Research Paper No. 2013–15 (University of Oslo Faculty of Law, 2013), available at: http://ssrn.com/abstract=2275177.

in this chapter contain regulations and associated rules that span a similar smorgasbord of social and environmental issues.

5.2 Who are the recipients of the information?

In most jurisdictions the key recipients of the environmental information found in corporate annual reports and other disclosures are shareholders, other investors, and bank financiers. However, some jurisdictions recognise other stakeholders and encourage wider public participation in environmental protection. Consider South Africa, Australia, and France, for example. In Australia, 'the audience for this information may be environmental groups and community members but it is equally likely to attract the attention of shareholders, investors, financiers and insurers'.[123] Furthermore, 'these reporting obligations open the possibility of stakeholders impeaching the behaviour of companies both for not disclosing enough information and for providing misleading information'.[124] In South Africa, Chapter 6 of the King Code promotes 'transparent communication with stakeholders'.[125] The French Grenelle II Law refers to stakeholders external to companies, such as consumer associations and NGOs.[126] In practice, only a small group of such stakeholders will have the status of interested persons for the purposes of legally challenging corporations for failure to comply with the disclosure obligation.[127] Another determinant of who should receive the company's reports is the company's boardroom structure. Thus, in Germany, companies with supervisory boards must operate a process whereby the management board presents the company's reports to the supervisory board for its approval.[128]

5.3 Where and how is the information to be published?

One further determinant of who should receive the company's information will be the place in which it is published. If the shareholders in an annual general meeting (AGM) are the only recipients, this alone may well

---

[123] S. Deva, *Sustainable Business and Indian Company Law: A Critical Review* (Sustainable Companies Project, 2011), 8.

[124] Deva, *Sustainable Business and Indian Company Law*.

[125] Henning, *et al.*, *Sustainable Companies, Climate Change and Corporate Social Responsibility in South African Law*.

[126] Commercial Code, Art. 225–102, para. 6.

[127] See Tchotourian, 'When CSR drives new corporate governance'.

[128] Deipenbrock, *The Management Board of a German Aktiengesellschaft*.

limit the effectiveness of a company's environmental protection agenda. However, in most jurisdictions discussed in this chapter, the information is not only provided to the AGM but is accessible by the general public, such as when securities regulators place information with a national registrar. Of course, making information public is one of the prices that the company's shareholders have to pay for the privilege of limited liability. This public nature of company information is crucial to the development of an environmental protection policy.

Some jurisdictions also require publication on websites. Turkey, for example, obliges companies to have a website with a special section dedicated to statutory shareholder communication.[129] In China, listed companies also must publish their environmental reports on both the website of the Ministry of Environmental Protection and on their own websites.[130] Denmark has quite stringent rules governing website reporting to make it accessible, such as the requirement that the mandatory CSR report be accessible for at least five years and that mandatory information must be segregated from non-mandatory information.[131]

5.4   'Soft' measures adopted

Around the world there is widespread implementation of voluntary measures for environmental and social reporting. The GRI is particularly extensively applied. There are 20,000 stakeholders from over 80 countries, representing corporations, governments, and numerous types of non-governmental stakeholders, within the GRI network. According to the GRI website, thousands of organisations in diverse economic and industry sectors, in addition to public authorities and non-profits, have published reports that adopt part or all of the GRI Guidelines.[132] Another CSR disclosure and best practice standard developed through a multi-stakeholder process is the ISO 26000 Guidance on Social Responsibility, which was completed in November 2010.[133] The GRI's participation in that process and the links being made with the GRI suggest that the ISO 26000 will also be used widely.[134]

---

[129] Eroglu, *Obstacles and Possibilities for Sustainable Companies in Turkey.*
[130] Lou and Tian, '*Sustainable Companies in the P. R. of China.*
[131] Buhmann, *et al., Mapping: Denmark.*   [132] See www.globalreporting.org.
[133] A. Johnston, 'ISO 26000: guiding companies to sustainability through social responsibility?' (2012) 9(2) *European Company Law* 110.
[134] GRI, *GRI and ISO 26000: How to Use the GRI Guidelines in Conjunction with ISO 26000* (GRI, 2011).

In addition to these broad, widely adopted international guidance initiatives, there are other voluntary measures applied globally. Environmental management schemes, for example, are popular inside and outside the EU, such as in Denmark and in Argentina. Up to the end of December 2009, at least 223,149 ISO 14001 certificates had been issued in 159 countries and economies.[135] In reality, however, environmental management schemes tend to have no real pattern and thus, globally, the schemes appear to be haphazard and unstructured in practice. There can be lack of consistency in their application. For example, in Hungary, there is evidence that 80 per cent of companies providing separate sustainability and CSR reports use the GRI principles, but many of those reports do not receive the A+ or A grades. Instead, they tend to be minimalistic and perfunctory.[136]

Corporate governance recommendations and guidance documents are also common. For example, in Macedonia, the CSR Agenda suggests that 'governments should require companies of a certain size and active in certain specified industries to report on their environmental and social impact... and to develop guidelines on how to apply the GRI and select the most important indicators for the Macedonian business community'.[137] In practice, however, companies in Macedonia tend to restrict themselves to the minimum legal requirements. Most firms lack a history of disclosing CSR information.[138] Many corporate governance codes operate on a 'comply-or-explain' basis. In India, there was virtually no compulsory environmental reporting before the Companies Act 2013, with its new CSR reporting rules, but companies have been increasingly using voluntary initiatives to disclose, as noted in the Carbon Disclosure Project's national reports on India.[139] In Japan, the government issued Environmental Reporting Guidelines 2003 and the 2004 Act Concerning the Promotion of Business Activities with Environmental Consideration by Specified Corporations as well as supplements to the 2004 Act in 2007.[140] A notable group that promotes voluntary reporting exists in

---

[135] ISO, 'ISO 9001 certifications top one million mark, food safety and information security continue meteoric increase', press release (25 October 2010).

[136] Szabó, *The Possibility of Sustainable Companies under the Hungarian Company Law Regime*, p. 6.

[137] van Rumpt, *Company Law Barriers and Possibilities for Sustainable Companies.*

[138] See United Nations Development Programme (UNEP), *Baseline Study on CSR Practices in the New EU Member States and Candidate Countries* (UNEP, 2007), p. 47.

[139] Carbon Disclosure Project, available at: www.cdp.net/EN-US/WHATWEDO/Pages/India.aspx.

[140] Ueda, *Sustainable Companies: Mapping Paper for Japan.*

ACCOUNTING, AUDITING, AND REPORTING 205

Germany. ECONSENSE[141] is a forum for promoting sustainable development of German businesses whose members are leading, globally active German companies and businesses.[142]

Among other notable voluntary measures, in Australia, soft disclosure guidelines are included in the Principles issued by the Corporate Governance Council of the Australian Securities Exchange.[143] Principle 7.1 states that companies should establish policies for the oversight and management of material business risks and disclose a summary of those policies. Companies should also identify all material risks including operational, environmental, sustainability, compliance, strategic, ethical conduct, reputation or brand, technological, product or service quality, human capital, financial reporting, and market-related risks.[144] In China, Article 19 of the Measures for the Disclosure of Environmental Information of 2007 'encourages' enterprises to disclose voluntarily information on a host of performance metrics and outcomes, including annual environmental protection targets and achievements, annual gross resources assumption volume of the enterprise, agreements on voluntary environmental improvements, social responsibilities fulfilment, and other environmental information regarding companies that discharge excessive pollutants.[145] In Canada, in 2010, the Canadian Securities Administrators for public companies issued a new environmental reporting guidance that recommends that companies explain the purpose of their environmental policies, the environmental risks such policies are meant to address, and how such policies are being monitored and updated. So far, however, no guidance exists on the climate change-related disclosures.[146]

5.5 Auditing and assurance of reports

According to the definition set out in the International Standards on Auditing (ISAs) promulgated by the International Auditing and Assurance Standards Board (IAASB) of the International Federation of Accountants

---

[141] Forum for Sustainable Development of German Business, see www.econsense.de.
[142] Deipenbrock, *The Management Board of a German Aktiengesellschaft*.
[143] See ASX Corporate Governance Council, *Corporate Governance Principles and Recommendations with 2010 Amendments*, 2nd edn, available at: www.asx.com.au/documents/asx-compliance/cg_principles_recommendations_with_2010_amendments.pdf.
[144] S. Deva, *Sustainable Business and Australian Corporate Law*, Research Paper No. 2013–11 (University of Oslo Faculty of Law, 2013), available at: http://ssrn.com/abstract=2248621.
[145] Lou and Tian, *Sustainable Companies in the P. R. of China*.
[146] Richardson and Tanner, *Canadian Company Law: Barriers and Possibilities for Sustainable Companies*.

(IFAC), the purpose of an audit is to enhance the degree of confidence of intended users in the financial statements.[147] Assurance is defined as engagements other than audits or other reviews of historical financial information covered by ISAs or International Standards on Review Engagements (ISREs).[148] At an international level, the IAASB promulgates both auditing standards (ISAs) and assurance standards (International Standard on Assurance Engagements (ISAE) 3000).[149]

The problem with auditing is that it deals with historical financial reporting only, and not with non-financial reporting such as annual or management reports. Sustainability reports may be included in the management reports section of the annual report or they may be published as separate documents. In both cases, they are not audited. In the EU, however, the auditor makes a 'consistency check' between the accounts and the annual report. According to Article 51(1)(2) of the Fourth Directive[150] on annual accounts, the statutory auditors are required to express an opinion concerning the consistency or otherwise of the annual report with the accounts for the same financial year. Under this rule, though only if it is included in the annual report, sustainability reports are checked at least cursorily by the auditor.[151]

If the sustainability report is published separately, no such consistency check is done. A positive exception is, again, Denmark, where the audit check is extended to all publication forms.[152] In some jurisdictions, such as Finland and Japan, the management report falls under the purview of statutory auditing, which is a step forward since sustainability information in management reports is then ostensibly fully audited.[153] According to the FEE, auditing of such information may raise questions in relation to the auditability of information that is judgemental and subjective in nature.

---

[147] International Standard on Auditing 200, *Overall Objectives of the Independent Auditor and the Conduct of an Audit in Accordance with International Standards on Auditing*, para. 3.

[148] International Standard on Assurance Engagements 3000, *Assurance Engagements Other than Audits or Reviews of Historical Financial Information* (International Federation of Accountants, 2005), para. 1.

[149] International Standard on Assurance Engagements (ISAE) 3000, *Assurance Engagements.*

[150] Fourth Council Directive 78/660/EEC of 25 July 1978 based on Article 54(3)(g) of the Treaty on the annual accounts of certain types of companies OJ L 222, 14 August 1978, 11–31.

[151] For a discussion, see FEE, 'Discussion paper: sustainability information in annual reports: building on implementation of the modernisation Directive' (December 2008).

[152] Buhmann, *et al.*, *Mapping: Denmark.*

[153] Mähönen, *Sustainable Companies Mapping Paper: Finland*; Ueda, *Mapping Paper for Japan.*

ACCOUNTING, AUDITING, AND REPORTING 207

Thus, the FEE calls for recommendations concerning good practice and worthy examples to 'take the auditability and verifiability aspect into account in suggesting disclosures'.[154]

Assurance of separate, voluntary CSR reports is totally discretionary. If these reports are scrutinised by auditors, reviews usually follow the general ISAE 3000 applicable to assurance engagements. Another important assurance standard is published by the Accountability Organisation as AA 1000 AS 2008.[155] It is generally followed by special CSR assurors, separate from the auditing firms. AA 1000 AS requires that the assurance provider complies with the ethical requirements and follows the guidelines for planning and performing the assurance engagement set in the Standard. The aim of the Standard is to assure the credibility and quality of the reporting organisation's sustainable performance and reporting by providing a means for assurance providers to go beyond mere verification of data, to evaluate the way reporting organisations manage sustainability, and to reflect that management and resulting performance in its assurance statements. Available evidence suggests significant variability in the adoption of assurance standards, indicating that more work is required in this area.[156]

In most countries external statutory auditing is based on national or international legal and self-regulatory standards. Statutory auditors are in some cases regarded as company organs, alongside the board or directors, for example, in Finland and Japan.[157] The most widely adopted international auditing regulation scheme is the ISA, issued by IFAC through the IAASB. The ISAs are usually recognised as part of national standards on auditing, for example, in Finland, Ghana, Macedonia, Slovenia, and Turkey. In the EU, statutory auditing is based on the Auditing Directive of 2006,[158] as amended by Directive 2014/56/EU.[159] According to Article 26

---

[154] See FEE, 'Discussion paper: sustainability information in annual reports', at 41.

[155] See www.accountability.org/images/content/0/5/056/AA1000AS%202008.pdf.

[156] P. Perego and A. Kolk, 'Multinationals' accountability on sustainability: the evolution of third-party assurance of sustainability reports' (2012) 110 *Journal of Business Ethics*, 173.

[157] Mähönen, *Sustainable Companies Mapping Paper: Finland*; Ueda, *Mapping Paper for Japan*.

[158] Directive 2006/43/EC of the European Parliament and of the Council of 17 May 2006 on statutory audits of annual accounts and consolidated accounts, amending Council Directives 78/660/EEC and 83/349/EEC and repealing Council Directive 84/253/EEC, OJ 2006 No. L157, 9 June 2006, p. 87.

[159] Directive 2014/56/EU of the European Parliament and of the Council of 16 April 2014 amending Directive 2006/43/EC on statutory audits of annual accounts and consolidated accounts, OJ 2014 No. L158, 27 May 2014, p. 196.

of the Directive, Member States shall require statutory audits to be undertaken by official auditors and audit firms in compliance with international auditing standards adopted by the Commission. According to Article 9 of the new Public-Interest Entities Auditing Regulation,[160] the same applies to statutory audit of public-interest entities. As no ISAs have been adopted by the Commission as of July 2014, implementation still depends on the individual Member State. In many non-EU jurisdictions, compulsory statutory auditing depends on either the type or size of a company. For instance, in Australia, only public companies fall under statutory audit.[161] In Canada, small, private companies are excluded from the process.[162] In the EU, the Auditing Directive entitles the Member States to exclude small, unlisted companies from a statutory audit. In most jurisdictions, these audits are undertaken by accredited external auditors and auditing firms, and occasionally by a supervisory body (e.g. in Australia, by the ASIC).

In some jurisdictions, such as Finland, Japan, and Turkey, the auditors review both the management and financial reports. In the EU, according to the Fourth Directive, the statutory auditors need only express an opinion concerning the consistency of the annual report governed by Article 46 with the annual accounts for the same financial year.[163] The same applies to corporate governance statements governed by Article 46, as far as a description of the main features of the company's internal control and risk management systems in relation to the financial reporting process and the information required by the Takeovers Directive is concerned.[164] Otherwise, the statutory auditor is required to check that the corporate governance statement has been produced.[165] These provisions mean that the annual report requirements of Article 46(1)(b) on non-financial key performance indicators relevant to the particular business, including information relating to environmental and employee matters, do not fall under a statutory audit.[166] In Germany, the report on the economic

---

[160] Regulation (EU) No 537/2014 of the European Parliament and of the Council of 16 April 2014 on specific requirements regarding statutory audit of public-interest entities and repealing Commission Decision 2005/909/EC, OJ 2013 No. L158, 27 May 2014, p. 77.

[161] Deva, *Sustainable Business and Australian Corporate Law*.

[162] Richardson and Tanner, *Canadian Company Law: Barriers and Possibilities for Sustainable Companies*.

[163] Article 51(1), second subparagraph.

[164] Directive 2004/25/EC of the European Parliament and of the Council of 21 April 2004 on takeover bids, OJ 2004 No. L142, 30 April 2004, p. 12.

[165] Article 46(2).

[166] See e.g. Zrilič, *Barriers and Possibilities for Integrating Environmental Sustainability into Slovenian Company Law*.

ACCOUNTING, AUDITING, AND REPORTING   209

position of a public company (AG) must be audited together with the annual financial statements and the bookkeeping.[167] The auditors must examine whether the report on the economic position reflects the annual financial statements and whether it gives an accurate view on the position of the company, including its business risks.[168]

As noted above, in Denmark, the compulsory CSR reports are subject only to a consistency check. However, the auditing process must ensure consistency between the reporting on policies, on practices for implementing the policies, and on results and expectations. Additionally, when the CSR reports are published on the company website or through a Global Compact or UNPRI report, the auditor must verify that information in the general report on where the CSR report may be found is correct, and that the report is listed under the required title reference and contains the information legally required. Monitoring of consistency between CSR information and actual performance is left to others – generally civil society, investors, buyers, and other interested stakeholders.[169]

In Denmark, when a management's report declares that a company provides CSR reporting pursuant to its accession to the Global Compact or UNPRI, the auditing must assess whether the company fulfils those surrogate reporting mechanisms. For companies declaring they have made a Global Compact Communication on Progress, the auditor must check that this Communication is available to the public on the Global Compact website. For organisations declaring they have made a UNPRI Communication on Progress, auditing must perform a similar due-diligence check. For CSR reporting through the Global Compact or UNPRI processes, the auditor has no further obligations. The auditor, therefore, is not required to assess the Communication on Progress. A Global Compact or UNPRI Communication on Progress uploaded on the Global Compact website is not subject to formal auditing. As Buhmann states, monitoring of the latter, due partly to resource and staffing constraints, is effectively left to civil society groups.[170]

In regard to voluntary sustainability reports, there are no specific auditing or assurance rules governing them, unless the report is included in annual or management reports regulated by auditing or conformity checks. In many jurisdictions, including Finland, Hungary, Japan, South

---

[167] Section 316 et seq. of the German Commercial Code, see Deipenbrock, *The Management Board of a German Aktiengesellschaft.*

[168] Section 316 et seq. of the German Commercial Code.

[169] Buhmann, *et al., Mapping: Denmark.*   [170] Buhmann, *et al., Mapping: Denmark.*

Africa, and Spain, voluntary assurance practices are reported. If auditors' or auditing firms' activities are governed by international standards, this will usually include the ISAE 3000 applicable to assurance engagements (other than audits or reviews of historical financial information).

6 Evaluation

From the above multi-jurisdictional survey of regulatory mechanisms and approaches governing accounting, reporting, and auditing requirements, several observations can be made about their potential contribution to sustainability. There are positive and negative features that can be identified. First, there is a wide variety of different regulations, from direct, substantive law to self-regulation and voluntary measures. In the EU, the Accounts Modernisation Directive provides a framing provision that the EU and EEA Member States have implemented, though with a range of proficiency and diligence. In other jurisdictions, the securities and exchange regulators feature strongly in providing the governance framework for auditing and reporting, though again with variable quality and stringency. Further relevant provisions appear in diverse legal portfolios, including accounting law, company and securities law, and environmental law.

Corporate governance codes also shadow these governance regimes, and operate usually on a 'comply-or-explain' basis while allowing for a variety of approaches that may stimulate innovation by firms, some of which could result in greenwashing through reporting that is neither reliable nor relevant.[171] Corporate governance codes are essentially about stewardship and accountability. However, the anecdotal evidence suggests that many companies do not recognise the link to CSR and rely only on the narrower aspect of the corporate governance codes. Such codes, based largely on the Anglo-Saxon model, emphasise the relationship between management and shareholders while other stakeholders are not well acknowledged.[172] Companies also make wide use of voluntary measures, whether by establishing their own policies and reporting and

---

[171] For a recent discussion of greenwashing by multinational companies, see C. Marquis, and M.W. Toffel, *When Do Firms Greenwash? Corporate Visibility, Civil Society Scrutiny, and Environmental Disclosure*, Working Paper No. 11–115 (Harvard Business School, Organizational Behavior Unit, 2012).

[172] G. Aras and D. Crowther, 'Governance and sustainability: an investigation into the relationship between corporate governance and corporate sustainability' (2008) 46 *Management Decision* 433. See also D.G. Szabó and K. Engsig Sørensen, 'Integrating corporate

ACCOUNTING, AUDITING, AND REPORTING

other procedural requirements or by signing up to third-party initiatives such as the GRI.[173] What is reported also varies, though a few subjects are dealt with quite universally. The information recipients are primarily shareholders but increasingly other stakeholders are recognised as relevant recipients. In Germany, supervisory boards have an important role. Auditing and assurance come across as somewhat 'hit and miss' initiatives, and in this arena financial reporting still receives most attention. Perhaps the most innovative steps are the environmental management initiatives and the provisions for integrated reporting, as encouraged by the King Code in South Africa.[174]

6.1   Barriers to and opportunities for sustainability reporting and sustainable business

The foregoing discussion reveals that environmental and sustainable reporting is widely practised globally and regarded as important and relevant corporate activities. The survey allows us to identify barriers and opportunities for development of sustainable business practices. At this point it might be observed that, sometimes, what might be identified as a barrier can also lead observers in the direction of a potential solution. A barrier might therefore also be turned into an opportunity.

6.1.1   The definition of sustainability

A major potential problem is the lack of clarity in the concept of sustainability. Indeed, as discussed in Chapter 1 of this volume, the definition of sustainability can be ambiguous and contentious. Consequently, disclosures and evaluations of corporate performance may be 'flawed and simplistic'.[175] Gray notes that the focus on sustainability *of the business* is more compatible with a 'business as usual approach' but this is unlikely to be the principal aim of those concerned with sustaining the planet and

---

social responsibility in corporate governance codes in the EU' (2013) 24(6) *European Business Law Review* 781.

[173] European Commission, *A Renewed EU Strategy 2011–14 for Corporate Social Responsibility,* 25 October 2011, COM(2011) 681 final.

[174] See Henning, *et al., Sustainable Companies, Climate Change and Corporate Social Responsibility in South African Law.*

[175] G. Aras and D. Crowther, 'Corporate sustainability reporting: a study in disingenuity?' (2009) 87 *Journal of Business Ethics Supplement* 279.

212 CHARLOTTE VILLIERS AND JUKKA MÄHÖNEN

the health of the biosphere.[176] Others note that terms such as 'sustainable', 'social', and 'environmental' have been replaced by 'corporate responsibility' or 'responsible investing', thereby resulting in an increased risk of managerial capture and constricted, technical interpretations of CSR or SRI.[177] A clearer and more robust definition of sustainability with clearly identified key performance indicators (KPIs) is required. Current corporate governance approaches are arguably too narrow to provide direction to this goal. An obvious starting point will be the widely cited definition offered by the 1987 Brundtland Report:

> Sustainable development is development that meets the needs of the present without compromising the ability of future generations to meet their own needs. It contains within it two key concepts: the concept of 'needs', in particular the essential needs of the world's poor, to which over-riding priority should be given; and the idea of limitations imposed by the state of technology and social organization on the environment's ability to meet present and future needs.[178]

It can be seen from this definition, however, that sustainable development necessarily appears to include economic, ecological, and social dimensions but how these competing elements are prioritised or reconciled is not made clear.[179] Critics doubt that indefinite economic growth is compatible with ecological sustainability.[180] The Agenda 21 Action Plan endorsed by the Earth Summit 1992[181] sought to divide sustainable development into a two-part endeavour encompassing the socio-economic and the biophysical spheres. The CSR movement has emphasised a three-part

---

[176] R. Gray, 'Is accounting for sustainability actually accounting for sustainability... and how would we know? An exploration of narratives of organisations and the planet' (2010) 35 *Accounting, Organizations and Society* 47 at 49.

[177] D.L. Owen and B. O'Dwyer, 'Corporate social responsibility: the reporting and assurance dimension', in A. Crane, *et al.* (eds.), *The Oxford Handbook of Corporate Social Responsibility* (Oxford University Press: 2008), 384.

[178] World Commission on Environment and Development, *Our Common Future* (Oxford University Press, 1987), Chapter 2.

[179] G. Lamberton, 'Sustainability accounting: a brief history and conceptual framework' (2005) 29 *Accounting Forum* 7 at 13.

[180] R. Costanza and H. Daly, 'Natural capital and sustainable development' (1992) 1 *Conservation Biology* 37.

[181] The first UN Conference on Environment and Development (UNCED Earth Summit) was held in Rio de Janeiro in 1992. Here, world leaders adopted Agenda 21, a blueprint to attain sustainable development in the twenty-first century. For information, see UNESCO, *The Rio Declaration on Environment and Development* (1992), available at: www.unesco.org/education/nfsunesco/pdf/RIO_E.PDF.

division, captured in Elkington's notion of the 'triple bottom line'.[182] These approaches have left considerable room for deceptive claims and practices by companies masquerading as 'sustainable' businesses.[183]

An alternative approach to differentiate performance has been to identify a continuum from weak to strong sustainability.[184] Weak sustainability is one that does not question the present mode of economic development, whereas strong sustainability does question it and seeks to redefine our societal objectives.[185] The latter approach has been substantiated through the elaboration of a number of prescriptive policy principles, including polluter pays, the precautionary approach, and environmental justice. In any event, because of the value judgements and uncertainty involved, determining the definition of sustainability demands debate on many key questions, including sustainability for what, sustainability for whom, sustainability in what way, sustainability for how long, clarification of what we wish to sustain, the extent of change required, and the nature of the process for sustainability.[186]

Although these issues cannot be resolved simply within the framework of corporate CSR reporting and auditing, these procedures provide an expression of diverse understandings of sustainability. Owen and O'Dwyer have traced the development of social and environmental reporting and the move towards sustainability reporting. Increasingly, companies are providing sustainability reports in which social and economic issues have been incorporated into what were previously purely environmental reports.[187] They note that the terms 'sustainability' and 'social and environmental' are being replaced by 'corporate responsibility' as the preferred title.[188] Such reports have two dimensions: the integration of triple bottom line considerations, in which social, environmental, and usually economic issues are covered within one report, and the facilitation of dialogue and stakeholder engagement.

---

[182] J. Elkington, *Cannibals with Forks: The Triple Bottom Line of 21st Century Business* (Capstone, 1987).

[183] J.M. Moneva, P. Archel, and C. Correa, 'GRI and the camouflaging of corporate unsustainability' (2006) 30 *Accounting Forum* 121.

[184] Moneva, *et al.*, citing J. Bebbington, 'Sustainable development: a review of the international development, business and accounting literature' (2001) 25 *Accounting Forum* 128.

[185] Moneva, *et al.*, 'GRI and the camouflaging', 123.

[186] Moneva, *et al.*, 'GRI and the camouflaging', 122 and 124.

[187] Owen and O'Dwyer, 'Corporate social responsibility', 394.

[188] Owen and O'Dwyer, 'Corporate social responsibility'.

6.1.2 The emphasis on financial reporting

Accountants and accounting organisations are powerful political institutions, so if their world-view is narrow or deficient, this will limit what can be achieved through reporting and disclosure. Their pre-eminent focus on financial issues can be detrimental to the sustainability objective. Such institutions need to be encouraged to be more proactive in non-financial matters. There are signs of such activity. The new International Integrated Reporting Committee, for example, has the remit to create a globally accepted framework for sustainability accounting. It was set up by the GRI and Accountants for Sustainability,[189] and has the backing of the IASB.[190] Its work is still at an early stage so there is an opportunity for sustainability experts and other stakeholders to influence the shape of any requirements promulgated.

The accountancy profession expresses confidence in its ability to move towards a more nuanced approach that accommodates non-financial issues. The ICAEW highlights the accounting profession's 'ability to bring together the necessary qualities: knowledge of relevant law, numeracy, objectivity and integrity'.[191] In a report published by the ACCA, the following observation was made:

> Accountants have much to offer in terms of core skills which are essential to developing more robust, consistent, effective and useful sustainability reports for national governments and the public sector more widely. Accountants are well placed to understand the regulatory environment, manage risk and develop efficient frameworks to measure information that can be monetised.
>
> However, sustainability reporting also provides a number of challenges and opportunities for accountants, in particular, professional development, including establishing a deeper understanding of the interdependence of social, environmental and economic issues; long-term and future-focused accounting practices; and working alongside other professions.[192]

6.1.3 Lack of consistency

An additional problem is the multiplicity and lack of consistency between guidance documents and reporting processes and presentations. This

---

[189] See www.theiirc.org.

[190] A. Leck, 'Integrating reporting could complete the vast jigsaw of business reviews', *City*, 14 September 2011.

[191] Leck, 'Integrating reporting', 11.

[192] H. Jones, *Sustainability Reporting Matters: What Are National Governments Doing About It?* (ACCA, 2010), 7.

ACCOUNTING, AUDITING, AND REPORTING

situation can be confusing or unclear for reporting organisations and stakeholders alike, as is acknowledged in a survey by the Fédération des Experts Comptables Européens (FEE) of guidelines for sustainability reporting.[193] The heterogeneity of approaches arises partly because the EU legislation itself lacks a common framework for ensuring an adequate level of comparability and leads to a lack of cohesion of reporting by companies. This hinders comparative assessment of companies' CSR activities, as observed by the European Commission in its consultation on non-financial reporting.[194] To remedy the EU barriers, the FEE recommends integration of sustainability into the business model; raising awareness of good practices across countries and promoting best practice; identification of KPIs, and that entities should indicate how they have selected and determined the relevance of their KPIs; providing assurance highlighting the relevance of verifiability; and auditability.

The variety of accounting and reporting methods and requirements among different jurisdictions makes comparability and verifiability difficult to attain. While the take-up of IFRS has been widespread, this trend is largely because IFRS is mandatory in most regions. However, IFRS tends to focus on financial reporting. International measures for CSR reporting are generally not mandatory or sufficiently detailed to generate comparable reports. The IFRS Practice Statement on the Management Commentary is not binding and is a principles-based document that is designed to give companies flexibility to tailor reports according to their specific circumstances. This approach is unlikely to result in consistency or uniformity of reporting. The GRI is also considered to be insufficient because, while it provides specific indicators, it allows a company to choose which indicators to report on.[195]

A further difficulty is the multiplicity of units of measurement to assess performance. First, the many indicators to measure performance towards sustainability can be confusing and obfuscatory, and the quality of data required to calculate environmental performance indicators and perform life-cycle analysis is questionable.[196] Measurements used by screening firms may cover issues as diverse as environmental impact,

---

[193] Federation of European Accountants, *Environmental, Social and Governance (ESG) Indicators in Annual Reports: An Introduction to Current Frameworks* (FEE, 2011), p. 4.

[194] European Commission, *Summary Report of the Responses Received to the Public Consultation on Disclosure of Non-Financial Information by Companies* (April 2011), p. 2.

[195] D.L. Levy, H. Szejnwald Brown, and M. de Jong, 'The contested politics of corporate governance: the case of the Global Reporting Initiative' (2010) 49 *Business and Society* 88.

[196] Lamberton, 'Sustainability accounting', 21.

regulatory compliance, and organisational processes.[197] Measurements might include, for example, natural capital inventory accounting that involves the recording of stocks of natural capital over time and using changes in stock levels as an indicator of the shifting quality of the natural environment.[198] Another type of measurement might include input-output analysis of the physical flow of materials and energy inputs, and product and waste outputs in physical units.[199] Measurements used for screening by sustainable investors might necessitate trade-offs, for example where the management of some environmental problems has more direct impact on the firm's bottom line than others.[200] Ultimately there is little transparency regarding the metrics used to evaluate CSR performance and the trade-offs that such evaluations will involve.[201]

In addition, what might look impressive in the law books does not necessarily lead to successful practices. Hungary, for example, appears to regulate over and above the EU Directives' requirements – as do Norway and Denmark – but in practice, companies there appear to report the minimum necessary to comply, offering little meaningful information.[202] One potential result, if there is significant differentiation in regulation, is a state regulatory competition and a 'race to the bottom' in terms of quality of standards. If it is possible for a company to get away with the minimum, there may be little incentive to do more. To avoid this dilemma requires, inter alia, improved awareness and promotion of best practices.

6.1.4 The Global Reporting Initiative (GRI)

The GRI is widely used by many companies worldwide and is therefore normatively authoritative. It arguably makes sense to push for making this standard mandatory. However, the GRI has limitations. First, according to Levy and others, the GRI does not sufficiently identify specific information to report.[203] The GRI has an overriding aim to enhance

---

[197] M. Delmas and V. Doctori Blass, 'Measuring corporate environmental performance: the trade-offs of sustainability ratings' (2010) 19 *Business Strategy and The Environment* 245 at 246.

[198] Lamberton, 'Sustainability accounting', 9.

[199] Lamberton, 'Sustainability accounting', 10.

[200] Delmas and Doctori Blass, 'Measuring', 247.

[201] Delmas and Doctori Blass, 'Measuring', 245.

[202] Szabó, *The Possibility of Sustainable Companies under the Hungarian Company Law Regime.*

[203] Levy, *et al.*, 'The contested politics', 104.

ACCOUNTING, AUDITING, AND REPORTING   217

'the quality, rigour and utility of sustainability reporting' with such reporting entailing 'measuring, disclosing and being accountable for organisational performance towards the goal of sustainable development'.[204] The Guidelines contain extensive guidance on economic indicators and also on social indicators that, in the 2006 version of the guidance, call for more quantitative disclosure than previous versions, which had been more limited to qualitative issues such as policy and description of associated programs.

The implementation of the GRI has been evaluated by some scholars. Notably, Owen and O'Dwyer observed an increase in the social information disclosed, though it still appears to be somewhat unbalanced with more information on employees than the space devoted to communities, customers, and suppliers combined. They also note that many of these social reports are concerned with a desire to reap reputational gains and manage stakeholder expectations, and these objectives are not necessarily the same as conveying accountability to affected parties. A process of managerial capture has taken place with 'managers exhibiting a clear tendency to interpret CSR concepts in a highly constricted fashion consistent with corporate goals of shareholder wealth maximization'.[205] Owen and O'Dwyer highlight the lack of completeness of much corporate reporting practice in which managers operate a one-way communication process and do not enable all relevant stakeholders to participate. The powerful stakeholders are engaged, but to the exclusion of the economically weak.[206] Mandatory, standardised, and externally verifiable corporate sustainability reporting is probably required, but is unlikely in the climate of voluntarism that dominates matters of CSR policy in general.[207]

Overall, the GRI may not really challenge the existing order. Arguably it is 'nested in the existing neoliberal framework and little different from conventional profit first business approaches... Many companies apply it as a brand enhancing tool rather than as a genuine disciplinary mechanism.'[208] The GRI still competes with other standards, which has led to the generation of data that is not easily comparable across

---

[204] Global Reporting Initiative, *Guidelines* (2006), 4.
[205] Owen and O'Dwyer, 'Corporate social responsibility', 397.
[206] Owen and O'Dwyer, 'Corporate social responsibility', 399.
[207] Owen and O'Dwyer, 'Corporate social responsibility', 400.
[208] Levy, *et al.*, 'The contested politics', 101.34. See also T. Hahn, *et al.*, 'Trade-offs in corporate sustainability: you can't have your cake and eat it' (2010) 19 *Business Strategy and the Environment* 217.

companies.[209] It appears that the GRI has often been used as a tool for managing corporate sustainability efforts, assessing and protecting corporate reputation, and enhancing brand values.[210] Consequently NGOs and other stakeholders have not benefited from the GRI as had been hoped. The existing situation suggests a degree of stagnation, with many Western countries not witnessing much growth in recent years in the take-up of the Guidelines. Additionally, this might be because they are set in a win-win approach to sustainability while the reality is perhaps that of trade-offs and compromises.[211] Accountants, auditors, consultants, and certifiers of CSR performance reports have benefited as 'GRI entrepreneurs'. Moreover, while accountants are crucial to the success of the Guidelines, they have not yet fully worked out the technologies and accounting processes appropriate for the Guidelines.[212]

The latest version of the GRI[213] tries to tackle some of these problems. G3.1 is an update and completion of the third generation of the GRI's Sustainability Reporting Guidelines, launched on 23 March 2011. G3.1 includes expanded guidance for reporting on human rights, local community impacts, and gender. Although organisations can still report using G3, the GRI recommends that new reporters begin their reporting journey using G3.1, as it enables greater transparency on a wider range of issues. Organisations can decide if the expanded Guidance in G3.1 is relevant to them by following the Technical Protocol – Applying the Report Content Principles. This resource helps organisations to produce relevant reports more easily, and can be used with the G3.1 and G3 Guidelines. Organisations can decide if the expanded Guidance in G3.1 is relevant to them by following the Technical Protocol – Applying the Report Content Principles.

The principal problem with the GRI and other sustainability reporting tools such as the AccountAbility Principles Standard (AA1000APS) on sustainability principles[214] or the Social Accountability International's SA8000 standard focusing on the workers' and human rights is that they are typically *voluntary* reporting channels. This risks limiting the extent and robustness of auditing.

---

[209] Levy, *et al.*, 'The contested politics', 89.
[210] See Moneva, *et al.*, 'GRI and the camouflaging'.
[211] Hahn, *et al.*, 'Trade-offs'.
[212] It might therefore be premature to make them mandatory at this stage.
[213] G3.1, launched in 2011.
[214] AA1000 AccountAbility Principles Standard, *AA1000APS* (AccountAbility, 2008).

6.1.5   Audit and assurance

If the voluntary reports are assured by auditing firms or auditors, they usually follow the general ISAE 3000 standard applicable to assurance engagements other than audits or reviews of historical financial information, or its national counterpart. Another important assurance standard is AA 1000 AS, which is generally followed by special CSR assurors. It requires that the assuror or the auditing firm comply with ethical requirements, and plan and perform the assurance engagement to obtain limited assurance whether any matters come to its attention that causes it to believe that the report does not provide a balanced and reasonable representation of the company's sustainability performance based on the company's applicable reporting guidelines, usually the GRI.

Doubts over assurance practice applied to environmental reports reveal concerns over their rigour and usefulness. AA1000 AS provides assurance guidelines as recommended by the FEE and the GRI. For example, the GRI Guidelines state that the GRI 'encourages the independent assurance of sustainability reports and the development of standards and guidelines for the assurance process to be followed by assurance providers'.[215] How beneficial the AA1000 AS guidelines are is open to question. Adams and Evans argue that they do not, at present, adequately cover all aspects of the environmental and social assurance process.[216] Another problem is that of management control of the assurance process. Unlike the auditors, whose activities are regulated by law and who follow regulated working practices like the International Standards on Auditing (ISA) and who are selected by the shareholders, the managers appoint the assurance providers and they can impose limits upon the exercise. Attempts to combine the procedural and presentational rigour of ISAE 3000 and AA1000AS on stakeholder responsiveness may resolve this problem.[217]

Essentially, a crucial problem is that no institutional forum is provided by which any meaningful form of stakeholder power may be utilised. Owen and O'Dwyer conclude that 'administrative reform, in the shape of new reporting systems, in isolation can do little to achieve real social change . . . Rather, reform must be designed to empower shareholders and

---

[215] See especially GRI, 2002, paras 17–18.

[216] C. Adams and R. Evans, 'Accountability, completeness, credibility and the audit expectations gap' (2004) 14 *Journal of Corporate Citizenship* 97, at 114.

[217] See e.g. PwC Comments on Proposed ISAE 3000 (Revised), Assurance Engagements Other Than Audits or Reviews of Historical Financial Information: PwC comment letter (IFAC), by Global Accounting Consulting Services, 15 September 2011.

220 CHARLOTTE VILLIERS AND JUKKA MÄHÖNEN

other stakeholders by instituting more participatory forms of corporate governance.'[218]

6.1.6 Enforcement and engagement

Reporting alone is arguably not a sufficient form of discipline to promote CSR. It also requires enforcement mechanisms and sanctions, as well as opportunities for engagement for the recipients of such reports. In a number of jurisdictions, such as China and Denmark, fines for non-compliant reports may be imposed.[219] Whether or not this occurs in practice is another matter. In Norway, for example, though fines may be imposed, companies that do not comply with the environmental reporting requirements set out in the Annual Accounts Act generally go unpunished. Empirical evidence suggests scepticism about the effectiveness of some of the legal requirements, referring to reports of low compliance rates by Norwegian companies, probably because of lack of enforcement and lack of political and social drivers.[220]

In the UK, the Conduct Committee, a subsidiary body of the Financial Reporting Council (FRC), together with the Financial Reporting Review Panel, has the power to pursue non-compliant companies through the courts.[221] This power has not so far been used (as of mid 2014), but the FRC has required at least one company to provide further information to make its report compliant with Section 417 of the Companies Act 2006.[222]

---

[218] Owen and O'Dwyer, 'Corporate social responsibility', 405. The authors might substitute the shareholders referred to with stakeholders. For further discussion, see B. O'Dwyer, D. Owen, and J. Unerman, 'Seeking legitimacy for new assurance forms: the case of assurance on sustainability reporting' (2011) 36 *Accounting, Organizations and Society* 31.

[219] Lou and Tian, *Sustainable Companies in the P. R. of China*; Buhmann, *et al.*, *Mapping: Denmark*.

[220] See Sjåfjell, *Sustainable Companies: Possibilities and Barriers in Norwegian Company Law*. The problem may be not the rule but the lack of follow-up of the rule, which does not bode well for the additional CSR layer that has been added in Norway, inspired by the Danish rule. There is no proper auditing requirement with the new rule either, merely a consistency check, which is waived where the companies report according to international standards like Global Compact. See also I. Vormedal and A. Ruud, 'Sustainability reporting in Norway: an assessment of performance in the context of legal demands and socio-political drivers' (2006) 18(4) *Business Strategy and the Environment* 207.

[221] Villiers, *Sustainable Companies UK Report*.

[222] See Statement by the Financial Reporting Review Panel in respect of the report and accounts of Rio Tinto Plc (15 March 2011). For further discussion, see C. Villiers, 'Narrative reporting and enlightened shareholder value under the Companies Act 2006' in J. Loughrey (ed.), *Directors Duties and Shareholder Litigation in the Wake of the Financial Crisis* (Edward Elgar, 2013), 97.

ACCOUNTING, AUDITING, AND REPORTING 221

Connected to this issue is the problem of liability for directors. Their lawyers are likely to advise them against giving too much information. Moreover, safe harbour provisions are generally not trusted by directors and they are not encouraged to be forthcoming in their reports.[223] In addition, NGOs and other outside stakeholders do not have opportunities to directly challenge directors in breach of the reporting rules or for harms revealed. Indeed, shareholders also have limited *locus standi* for such actions.

In conclusion, Schaltegger and Burritt observe that 'in the drive to ensure or encourage acceptable corporate behaviour, it has not been enough to confront the corporation with the threat of negative profit outcomes for unacceptable behaviour (e.g. fines and removal of licences), or to take legal action against the corporation or key business officials for non-compliance with the myriad of legal rules laid down.'[224]

6.1.7 Emergence of alternate models of social accounting

The development of sustainability reporting is crucial in supporting business actors to improve CSR. This goal requires going beyond the conventional accounting and reporting methods of financial and cost accounting to find new informational tools for transparency procedures that appropriately address matters such as ecological health and their carrying capacities, thresholds, and cumulative effects.[225] Conceivably, many corporations are ill-placed to provide or analyse such information, and perhaps such roles should be assumed by other stakeholders such as government environmental agencies or independent NGO watchdogs. But, at a minimum, the business sector should cooperate in the multi-party development of more nuanced and accurate sustainability reporting paradigms.

The development of such non-financial information should also be tailored to the needs of as many stakeholders as possible rather than only investors. In order to avoid deceptive practices such as 'greenwashing', consideration must be given to the practical usefulness of disclosures and to move from the procedural tasks that emphasise report preparation, information verification, and disclosure, towards behavioural change within corporations that leads to better sustainability performance.[226]

---

[223] Aiyegbayo and Villiers, 'The enhanced business review'.

[224] S. Schaltegger and R.L. Burritt, 'Sustainability accounting for companies: catchphrase or decision support for business leaders?' (2010) 45 *Journal of World Business* 375 at 378.

[225] Schaltegger and Burritt, 'Sustainability accounting for companies', 377.

[226] Schaltegger and Burritt, 'Sustainability accounting for companies', 383.

Schaltegger and Burritt suggest that on this basis sustainability reporting remains at a nascent stage of development and 'is still more of a buzz word than a well defined approach'.[227] A major step in this direction can be identified in the attempts made towards integrated reporting in which the company's reporting discloses and explains the relationship between the financial, social, environmental, and governance issues faced by a company. Rather than having a separate sustainability report, the company integrates sustainability issues into its main report, but also adopts integrated strategic thinking and decision-making. Steps have been taken towards this ambitious form of reporting in South Africa but also more generally through the work of the IIRC.[228] New metrics are also relevant to these developments, along with new ways of disseminating company information with increasingly more sophisticated usage of the Internet to communicate with dispersed stakeholders and investors. One innovative theoretical example is the Sustainable Stakeholder Accounting Statement, which combines an environmental income profit-and-loss statement with an environmental equity balance sheet account.[229]

7 Conclusion

Much remains to be done to improve corporate reporting for sustainability. Clear definitions of core concepts such as 'sustainable development', both generally and within the business context, and 'materiality' need further refinement. That task should underpin the clarification of key non-financial performance indicators. Accounting techniques for non-financial issues are still at a nascent developmental stage, and the role of accountants and auditors and their professional bodies, nationally and internationally, will be extremely important to the goals identified in this chapter. Much CSR reporting remains left to voluntary and discretionary measures, leading to risks of corporate capture, lack of comparability, inconsistency, and uncertainty in benchmarking.

The Accounts Modernisation Directive has at least nudged the EU and EEA Member States to introduce legislation that puts CSR and

---

[227] Schaltegger and Burritt, 'Sustainability accounting for companies', 383.

[228] See Henning, et al., *Sustainable Companies, Climate Change and Corporate Social Responsibility in South African Law*. For a discussion, see e.g. M.P. Krzus, 'Integrated reporting: if not now, when?' (2011) *IRZ Heft* 271.

[229] See R. Sherman, 'Corporate social responsibility, corporate social performance and sustainable stakeholder accounting' (2002) 1 *International Business and Economics Research Journal* 43.

ACCOUNTING, AUDITING, AND REPORTING 223

sustainability issues in each company's line of vision. Importantly, attempts have begun to foster integrated reporting,[230] recognising that the problem is not only a lack of information but also a lack of clarity of purpose regarding what information is presented and how. On 15 April 2014, the plenary of the European Parliament adopted a new Directive amending these rules.[231] Companies concerned will need to disclose information on policies, risks, and outcomes as regards environmental matters, social and employee-related aspects, respect for human rights, anti-corruption and bribery issues, and diversity in their board of directors. However, the new rules will only apply to some large companies with more than 500 employees. According to the Commission, the scope includes some 6,000 large companies and business groups across the EU.[232]

The Directive leaves significant flexibility for companies to disclose relevant information in the way that they themselves consider most useful, or in a separate report. Companies may use international, European, or national guidelines that they consider appropriate (for instance, according to the Commission, the UN Global Compact, ISO 26000 standards, or the German Sustainability Code). The regulatory principle chosen in the Directive is that of 'comply-or-explain'. Comply-or-explain in this context means that if a company does not pursue any policies in relation to environmental, social, and employee matters, respect for human rights, anti-corruption, and bribery matters, it is not obliged to so, but must provide an explanation for not doing so. The Directive does not yet have any enforcement provisions.

Progress in corporate reporting for sustainability is essential in order to provide a basis for response and engagement by stakeholders. More emphasis must also be given to the audit and verification of information published. As the European Commission states on the topic of CSR information: 'In order to ensure the sufficient quality and credibility of the reported information, the question should be raised whether there might be a need for an independent check on the reported information and whether auditors should play a role in this regard.'[233] This requires more standardisation and legislative actions, even mandatory rules on compulsory assurance.

---

[230] With the IIRC Framework. The European Commission's proposal offers a step in the direction of integrated reporting but more would be required to make this a reality.
[231] See http://ec.europa.eu/finance/accounting/non-financial_reporting/index_en.htm.
[232] See http://ec.europa.eu/finance/accounting/non-financial_reporting/index_en.htm.
[233] European Commission, *Green Paper*, p. 8.

224 CHARLOTTE VILLIERS AND JUKKA MÄHÖNEN

The possibility of using separate reports is of great importance as far as the assurance of the reports is concerned. According to Article 34 of the New Accounting Directive, the statutory auditor(s) or audit firm(s) shall express an opinion on whether the management report and consolidated management report is consistent with the financial statements for the same financial year, and whether the management report has been prepared in accordance with the applicable legal requirements, and must state whether, in the light of the knowledge obtained in the course of the audit, the auditor has identified material misstatements in the management report. These requirements do not apply to separate non-financial reports at all.

The new Directive heralds a step forward, but the flexibility given to companies on which framework they will apply might undermine comparability. The Directive applies to large companies and it might be hoped that in future SMEs would also be covered. Enforcement possibilities and opportunities for challenges to be made by stakeholders in relation to company information might also be a further step forward in the future. Further promising precedents identified in this chapter include South Africa's integrated reporting system and Australia's internalising of the objectives of more comprehensive reporting into company law itself rather than relying on external legislation. It must be emphasised, however, that the new EU Directive will not require integrated reporting. As the Commission stresses, the Directive:

> focuses on environmental and social disclosures. Integrated reporting is a step ahead, and is about the integration by companies of financial, environmental, social and other information in a comprehensive and coherent manner. To be clear, this Directive does not require companies to comply with integrated reporting.[234]

However, the Commission is monitoring with great interest the development of the integrated reporting concept, and, in particular, the work of the IIRC.[235]

It is still in its early days, but the approach of integrated reporting offers a positive step. Without understanding and demonstrating the links between corporate strategies and financial performance with the environmental, social, and economic contexts, a formidable barrier to

---

[234] Disclosure of non-financial and diversity information by large companies and groups – 'Frequently asked questions', 15.4.2014, para. 8, available at: http://europa.eu/rapid/press-release_MEMO-14-301_en.htm.

[235] See http://europa.eu/rapid/press-release_MEMO-14-301_en.htm.

ACCOUNTING, AUDITING, AND REPORTING 225

sustainability will remain. By recognising and working with the links between corporate activity and the environmental, social, and corporate governance contexts, these two dimensions may be better reconciled. The institutional and policy framework has not yet been completed. Reform is a matter of urgency since currently many of those companies deemed to provide the best reports are in fact among the worst offenders.[236] To make genuine progress towards sustainable companies, correct and reliable environmental reporting is essential. Some companies, of course, offer excellent reports that will surpass the legal requirements and standards issued by any jurisdictions. However, without clear and enforceable standards, it is likely that investors' preferences will often determine the effectiveness of environmental reporting, and this could have a limiting effect.[237] Ultimately, it may be necessary to introduce enforceable mandatory disclosure and assurance of integrated or sustainability reports. Steps must be taken to improve corporate disclosure for sustainability. Better reporting will clear a path towards better business behaviour and a healthier planet. Time is of the essence.[238]

---

[236] See e.g. S. Berthelot, M. Magnan, and D. Cormier, 'Environmental disclosure research: review and synthesis' (2003) 22 *Journal of Accounting Literature* 1, especially at 20.

[237] See e.g. Aiyegbayo and Villiers, 'The enhanced business review'.

[238] I. Ioannou and G. Serafeim, *The Consequences of Mandatory Sustainability Reporting*, Research Working Paper No. 11–100, 2011 (Harvard Business School, 2011).

6

Financial markets and socially responsible investing

BENJAMIN J. RICHARDSON

1 Finance capitalism and the 'unseen' polluters

The goal of promoting environmentally sustainable business is not just for regular corporations in the productive economy, as other chapters in this book discuss, but extends also to those companies' investors and financiers. This chapter investigates how the financial sector shapes the environmental performance of the economy, and assesses whether the burgeoning global movement for socially responsible investing (SRI) can foster sustainable companies, especially in the absence of credible governmental regulation. The chapter concentrates on five areas of potential SRI influence. The principal argument is that the financial sector continues to have negative environmental characteristics and impacts, both in its own right and on the companies the sector funds, and presently SRI has only a modest remedial influence. SRI will likely only acquire greater significance through a more enabling regulatory and public policy framework rather than continued reliance on voluntary goodwill.

This first part of the chapter outlines the often hidden environmental impacts of the financial economy and why it should assume greater accountability for promoting sustainable development. Section 2 briefly maps the history, aspirations, and methods of SRI while Section 3 conceptualises SRI as a means of market governance that, at least for some proponents, seeks to discipline companies and improve their social and environmental behaviour. Thereafter, Section 4 (SRI's financial rationale), Section 5 (altering the cost of capital to business), Section 6 (corporate engagement), Section 7 (voluntary codes of conduct), and Section 8 (public policy reforms) examine the efficacy of the principal means of influence available to social investors. Section 9 concludes this chapter with a warning of the need for more concerted action if SRI is to leverage positive change for sustainable business.

No discussion of corporate environmental behaviour today is complete without recognition of the role of financial institutions, both as often

FINANCIAL MARKETS AND SOCIALLY RESPONSIBLE INVESTING   227

significant corporate actors in their own right, as is the case with banks and insurance companies, and as financiers and investors in conventional firms. The late twentieth-century transformation of the global economy into a system of 'finance capitalism' has propelled financial markets into a position of pre-eminence in shaping economic development. In recent years the financial economy has been worth at least US$212 trillion,[1] and approximately 40 of the world's 100 largest companies are financial entities, such as banks.[2] Yet its hegemony and institutional sustainability are in doubt. The Global Financial Crisis (GFC) that erupted in 2008 revealed profound weaknesses in the financial economy and the need to reset it on socially responsible foundations. The recent 'Occupy Movement' is testament to the clusters of public unease about the role and governance of financial markets.

While finance capitalism has been widely excoriated as a vector of economic crisis and irrational exuberance,[3] its complicity in environmental *unsustainability* is less openly acknowledged.[4] Institutional investors such as pension funds and insurance companies, as well as retail investors who buy into mutual funds, and the banking sector, have not traditionally regarded themselves as agents of or relevant to environmental decision-making. Although some commentators believe '[t]here is nothing inherent in the structure of the financial system which necessarily leads to environmental destruction',[5] such a belief is credible only at a theoretical level.

The evidence is mixed. Positively the financial economy can play a constructive role in mobilising investors to support carbon markets, which in 2010 totalled approximately US$141 billion in trades.[6] Financiers may also help mobilise resources for poor communities and households, such as through microfinance. On the other hand, the separation between

---

[1] C. Boxburgh, S. Lund, and J. Piotrowski, *Mapping Global Capital Markets 2011* (McKinsey Global Institute, 2011), 2 (economic statistic for the end of 2010).

[2] M. Stichele, *Critical Issues in the Financial Industry: Somo Financial Sector Report* (Stichting Onderzoek Multinationale Ondernemingen, 2005), 58.

[3] See R.J. Shiller, *Irrational Exuberance* (Princeton University Press, 2000); J. Bogle, *The Battle for the Soul of Capitalism* (Yale University Press, 2005); F. Jameson, 'Culture and finance capitalism' (1997) 24(1) *Critical Inquiry* 246.

[4] But see W. Sun, C. Louche, and R. Pérez (eds.), *Finance and Sustainability: Towards a New Paradigm? A Post-Crisis Agenda* (Emerald Books, 2011).

[5] M.A. White, 'Environmental finance: value and risk in an age of ecology' (1996) 5 *Business Strategy and the Environment* 198, at 200.

[6] CityUK, 'Carbon markets: July 2011', available at: www.thecityuk.com/research/our-work/reports-list/carbon-markets-2011.

those who provide capital and control a business, the hallmark of corporate capitalism, has leveraged the separation between investment and social responsibility. Easy access to capital through financial markets removes corporate financing constraints that might otherwise curb economic growth and thus its environmental consequences. Passive investors also tend to be physically remote from the activities that directly impact the environment, thus weakening the sense of responsibility they might have for taking corrective action. Further fraying any sense of ethical responsibility is that investors' portfolios tend to comprise only tiny fractional stakes in a multitude of companies, and the ease of selling securities helps diminish the perceived importance of their relationship with the company. The overall result is diminution of any sense of moral agency of investors for the economic activities and companies they fund.

Structural features of the finance system suggest it has become a major factor behind corporate unsustainability and environmental degradation.[7] The system lacks an innate mechanism to scale the economy within biosphere limits or to take into account very long-term environmental considerations such as climate change. Its tendencies towards myopic and speculative investment, often of little productive value and without factoring in environmental risks and costs, make the financial market an impediment to sustainability. In a sense, therefore, investors can be viewed as the economy's *unseen* polluters, contributing to environmental problems that they fund and profit from, yet rarely held directly accountable; instead, such problems are habitually attributed to the 'frontline' companies that produce goods and services.

If industries and businesses in the productive, 'real' economy were perfectly regulated, we presumably would ignore financiers' behaviour because all environmental costs and benefits would be accounted for. The cost of capital would fully reflect sustainability performance, with polluters incurring higher operational costs, and thereby competitive disadvantages in raising finance. But such hopes are naïve. A half-century of environmental law reform in the modern era has only mitigated, not ended, humanity's unsustainable path.[8] Even nations with relatively sophisticated environmental laws are usurped by soaring cross-border investments in jurisdictions without robust legal controls. In a global

---

[7] G. Clark and D. Wójcik, *The Geography of Finance: Corporate Governance in the Global Marketplace* (Oxford University Press, 2007).

[8] See B.J. Richardson and S. Wood (eds.), *Environmental Law for Sustainability* (Hart Publishing, 2006).

FINANCIAL MARKETS AND SOCIALLY RESPONSIBLE INVESTING 229

financial system, allowing investors in one country to profit from development in another, it is imperative to inculcate environmental responsibility into the very inception of economic decision-making when financing is considered.

A further reason to discipline the financial sector, and even hold it accountable to higher standards than those applicable to the companies it funds, is the economic and environmental significance of financial institutions. The banking and debt crises in North America and Europe in the aftermath of the GFC show how failings in the financial sector can cause enormous collateral damage.[9] Apart from any environmental effects attributable to the financial economy, many commentators have long argued that on traditional economic policy grounds, financiers should be controlled and monitored more closely than regular firms.[10] The sector contains propagation mechanisms that can amplify initial, small shocks throughout the real economy; insolvency of a bank usually has far greater ramifications for the economy than the collapse of a non-financial company.[11] Regulators need to impose measures that reduce systemic risks posed by the financial economy, such as requiring fuller disclosures, higher capital reserves, greater environmental risk analysis, and longer term investment planning.

Ultimately, perhaps the most basic reason for targeting financiers is simply that in deriving profits from companies engaged in environmentally degrading and socially harmful activities, financiers are complicit in such harm. These 'unseen' polluters should be exposed for their contribution to unsustainability. Capital financing influences development choices; those who enable, and benefit from, those choices through financial investment should also share in the responsibility. Financial institutions have developed to mobilise capital and to facilitate financial returns for investors. Money has to be actively managed and be reinvested to generate profit for financiers. This pervasive drive to put capital to use, to make more capital, creates a process that fosters social and

---

[9] R.C. Whalen, 'The subprime crisis: cause, effect and consequences' (Networks Financial Institute, 2008); G. Soros, *The New Paradigm for Financial Markets: The Credit Crisis of 2008 and What It Means* (PublicAffairs, 2008).

[10] D. Heremans, *Corporate Governance Issues for Banks: A Financial Stability Perspective* (Katholieke Universiteit, 2006); J. Macey and M. O'Hara, 'The corporate governance of banks' (2003) 9(1) *Economic Policy Review* 91.

[11] Some non-financial corporations of course are extremely significant economically, and their collapse would produce wide-ranging economic effects. The motor vehicle industry is an example.

230 BENJAMIN J. RICHARDSON

environmental changes. So though the financial sector may lack operational control of polluting developments, it cannot be construed as an unknowing or helpless bystander to such impacts. While the financial sector rarely acknowledges such connections, they are increasingly made by nongovernmental organisations, such as Oxfam, whose 2014 report, *Banking on Shaky Grounds*, reveals how some major Australian banks have allegedly financed dubious land acquisitions in developing countries that are contributing to environmentally destructive land use practices.[12]

Regrettably, however, few states have favoured regulating the financial economy to resolve these problems. Legal measures to promote more socially and environmentally sensitive investing have emerged in some countries over the past decade or more, but they eschew structural problems of the financial economy that impede long-term investment or accounting for environmental externalities.[13] Under the sway of free market ideology, lightly regulated financial markets are still viewed by most policy-makers as efficient and conducive to economic growth.[14] There have been some countervailing pressures to expand state control to correct market abuses and financial crises,[15] though few tangible legal reforms have been adopted.

The current reforms promote incentive and informational policy instruments that leave investors with considerable discretion. One example is the requirement for funds to disclose their policies for SRI, and policies for exercising their shareholder proxy votes. These transparency reforms were introduced in several EU states, as well as in Australia and New Zealand, and particularly target pension funds.[16] Australian pension legislation also gives beneficiaries the right to choose where their monies are invested, thereby enabling social investors to switch to one of the

[12] Oxfam Australia, *Banking on Shaky Grounds: Australia's Big Four Banks and Land Grabs* (Oxfam Australia, 2014).

[13] B.J. Richardson, *Socially Responsible Investment Law: Regulating the Unseen Polluters* (Oxford University Press, 2008).

[14] E. Shaw, *Financial Deepening in Economic Development* (Oxford University Press, 1975); A. Singh, 'Financial liberalisation, stock markets and economic development' (1997) 107(442) *The Economic Journal* 771; R. Berkowitz and T.N. Toay (eds.), *The Intellectual Origins of the Global Financial Crisis* (Fordham University Press, 2012).

[15] J. Cioffi, *Corporate Governance Reform, Regulatory Politics, and the Foundations of Finance Capitalism in the United States and Germany*, Comparative Research in Law and Political Economy Research Paper 1/2005, (York University, 2005), 1–2.

[16] For example, the UK's Occupational Pension Schemes (Investment) Regulations, 2005: cl. 2(3)(b)(vi)–(3)(c); Australia's Corporations Act, 2001 (Cth), s. 1013D(1)(l); France's Projet de loi sur l'épargne salariale, 7 February, 2001, No 2001–152, Arts 21, 23; and New Zealand's KiwiSaver Act, 2006, s. 205A.

FINANCIAL MARKETS AND SOCIALLY RESPONSIBLE INVESTING 231

burgeoning ethical or green funds.[17] Another reform, adopted in Canada and the USA, requires mutual funds to disclose their shareholding proxy voting policies and voting records.[18] Its aim is to discourage fund managers from colluding with corporate management, and to improve the quality of corporate governance through a more active proxy voting process. Research on implementation of some of these standards, however, reveals shortcomings. Mandated disclosures sometimes entail vague, perfunctory statements that do not illuminate how investment decisions are implemented and their impacts.[19] Process standards have rarely extended to democratising investment policy-making, which remains dominated by fund managers, investment consultants, and other professed experts. Economic incentives to alter the cost-benefit calculations of financiers in favour of sustainable development have also been introduced. A notable example is the Netherlands' Green Project Directive,[20] which several studies credit as having significantly boosted funding for local environmental-friendly projects,[21] though unfortunately the scheme was phased out in 2014. Conversely, economic incentives can discourage financing of environmentally unsound projects. Imposing liability on lenders for pollution connected to their borrowers was upheld by courts in the USA under the 'Superfund' legislation,[22] and its drastic effects in dampening bank lending to the chemical industry contributed to modification of the scheme in 1996 to limit lenders' potential liability.[23]

---

[17] Superannuation Legislation Amendment (Choice of Superannuation Funds) Act, 2005 (Cth).

[18] SEC, 'Disclosure of proxy voting policies and proxy voting records by registered management investment companies' (SEC, 31 January 2003); Canadian Securities Administrators (CSA), *National Instrument 81–106 Investment Fund Continuous Disclosure and Companion Policy 81–106CP* (CSA, 2005).

[19] UK Sustainable Investment and Finance Association (UKSIF), *Focused on the Future: 2000–2010 Celebrating Ten Years of Responsible Investment Disclosure by UK Occupational Pension Funds* (UKSIF, 2010).

[20] The scheme was revamped and extended in 2002 and 2005: Regeling groenprojecten buitenland, Staatscourant 1 (2 January 2002), 31; Regeling groenprojecten, Staatscourant 131 (11 July 2005), 13.

[21] Vereniging van Beleggers voor Duurzame Ontwikkeling (VBDO), *Socially Responsible Savings and Investments in the Netherlands: Developments in Volume and Growth of Socially-responsible Savings and Investments in Retail Funds* (VBDO 2005), 11; KPMG, *Sustainable Profit: An Overview of the Environmental Benefits Generated by the Green Funds Scheme* (KPMG, 2002), 6.

[22] Comprehensive Environmental Response, Compensation and Liability Act, 1980, Pub. L. No. 96–510.

[23] M. Greenberg and D. Shaw, 'To lend or not to lend – that should not be the question: the uncertainties of lender liability under CERCLA' (1992) 41(4) *Duke Law Journal* 1211; and,

232 BENJAMIN J. RICHARDSON

Many areas of legal governance of financial markets remain unreformed. Fiduciary law is a significant omission.[24] Fiduciary law provides the broad legal standards governing how trustees, fund managers, and other custodians of investment assets act on behalf of their beneficiaries. Fiduciary finance law problematically tends to view financial institutions as just ordinary private trusts, despite their often public-like characteristics and social impacts. Under prevailing legal understandings, fund managers usually cannot accommodate sustainability considerations without investment benefits, unless the affected investors consent or the legal instrument establishing the fund provides a mandate. Financial trustees' duties to invest 'prudently' and act in beneficiaries' 'best interests' are typically interpreted by courts to exclude consideration of social and environmental 'returns' unless they can offer at least comparable financial benefits.[25] Furthermore, it is difficult in law to defend costly decisions that defer benefits (such as climate-friendly investments) to beneficiaries until many decades. Fiduciary law expects beneficiaries to benefit in a direct, quantifiable way, rather than amorphously, for instance, as members of the greater public may benefit from cleaner air or purer water. The impact of fiduciary law on the scope for SRI has seldom attracted serious attention from governments; a rare example is the July 2014 report of the English Law Commission on to the fiduciary responsibility of investment intermediaries in the UK, but without recommendations on how to harness fiduciary law as a tool to promote SRI or sustainable companies.[26]

2 Socially responsible investing (SRI)

The foregoing structural barriers in the financial economy to supporting sustainable companies should not imply that all financiers and investors are disinterested in the concerns raised by this book. In fact, a global movement for SRI has emerged that purports to prioritise different goals.[27]

---

on the 1996 statutory amendments: O. de S. Domis, 'New law finally limits environmental liability' (1996) 161(189) *American Banker* 3.

[24] See B.J. Richardson, *Fiduciary Law and Responsible Investing: In Nature's Trust* (Routledge, 2013).

[25] B.J. Richardson, 'Fiduciary and other legal duties', in K. Baker and J.R. Nofsinger (eds.), *Socially Responsible Finance and Investing* (John Wiley & Sons, Ltd, 2012), 69.

[26] Law Commission, *Fiduciary Duties of Investment Intermediaries*, LAW COM No. 350 (UK Government, 2014).

[27] Examples of the pioneering literature include A. Domini and P. Kinder, *Ethical Investing* (Addison-Wesley, 1984); P. Kinder, S. Lydenberg, and A. Domini, *The Social Investment Almanac: A Comprehensive Guide to Socially Responsible Investing* (Henry Holt, 1992); R.

FINANCIAL MARKETS AND SOCIALLY RESPONSIBLE INVESTING   233

The long-standing SRI crusade has embraced a variety of concerns, of which environmental performance has become a pre-eminent theme. SRI can be viewed as a reaction to the impacts of the economic system and the failure of states to regulate them. The fair trade movement, green consumerism, and social investment share the quality of citizens seeking alternate means to express their impeded ethical values.

SRI uses a variety of methods that can be distilled into two principal tactics: to avoid or favour investing in certain industries or companies because of characteristics of their products or operations, or to engage with specific businesses so as to induce behavioural changes. These methods are respectively known as portfolio screening and corporate engagement. SRI is also a diverse movement,[28] known by labels such as 'ethical investment', 'mission investment', 'social investment', and 'sustainable finance'. The terminological differences are not in themselves necessarily significant, as they partly reflect cultural, historical, and political differences in international markets. More important are the underlying conceptual differences and lack of 'definitional clarity' in SRI.[29] Some proponents believe SRI involves merely 'taking into account' social and environmental issues that might have a bearing on financial performance,[30] while others see it as about prioritising unadulterated ethical considerations.[31]

Faith-based investors were pioneers of SRI, beginning in the eighteenth century when the Quakers proscribed financial ties to the transatlantic slave trade. During the early twentieth century the churches screened their portfolios to avoid alcohol, tobacco, gambling, and other 'sin stocks'.[32] In the 1970s, South Africa's apartheid regime was targeted by SRI activists, with religious investors again featuring highly. These early SRI gestures that were seen as a moral crusade tended to rely on strict negative portfolio screens and occasionally confrontational shareholder activism.

Sparkes, *Socially Responsible Investment: A Global Revolution* (John Wiley & Sons, Ltd, 2002); M. Jeucken, *Sustainable Finance and Banking: The Financial Sector and the Future of the Planet* (Earthscan, 2001).

[28] J. Sandberg, *et al.*, 'The heterogeneity of socially responsible investment' (2009) 87(4) *Journal of Business Ethics* 519.

[29] W. Ransome and C. Sampford, *Ethics and Socially Responsible Investment: A Philosophical Approach* (Ashgate Publishing, 2011) at 9.

[30] UNEP-FI, *The Materiality of Social, Environmental and Corporate Governance Issues in Equity Pricing* (UNEP-FI, 2004).

[31] B.J. Richardson and W. Cragg, 'Being virtuous and prosperous: SRI's conflicting goals' (2010) 92(1) *Journal of Business Ethics* 21.

[32] J. Brill and A. Reder, *Investing from the Heart* (Crown Publishers, 1992).

In this vein, therefore, SRI reflects a style of market governance. It provides rationales and means by which ethical investors may challenge corporate irresponsibility when states do not act. Since most firms rely on debt or equity funding to sustain their activities, in theory, investors can influence corporations by tying finance to environmental and social considerations.[33] SRI suggests that economic agents need not only a legal licence to operate, but also a 'market' or 'social licence'.[34] Companies and financial institutions should not only operate within juridical boundaries, but also respect extra-legal social standards of reasonableness, fairness, and environmental responsibility.

The recent market spread of SRI has distanced itself from this stance, partly because it is perceived to be financially imprudent,[35] and most financiers today would reject any pretensions to 'policing' the market. As mainstream investors such as pension funds have embraced SRI – for a variety of reasons, including to placate NGO pressure, to stave off state regulation, and for their financial self-interest – they have refashioned it, purging its more radical ethical agenda and reframing SRI as values-neutral financial risk management. Rather than view SRI as an agent of positive change, 'environmental, social, and governance' (ESG) issues – to use financial industry parlance – are presented as 'extra-financial' issues that may have financial consequences for investors requiring due diligence.

3   SRI as a means of market governance

A crucial dimension of this book's focus on the barriers to, and opportunities, for sustainable companies is the role of social investors in leveraging positive change. Although SRI manifests in various guises, a seminal idea is that it 'considers both the investor's financial needs and an investment's impact on society. SRI investors encourage corporations to improve their practices on environmental, social, and governance issues.'[36] However,

---

[33] P. Rivoli, 'Making a difference or making a statement? Finance research and socially responsible investment' (2003) 13(3) *Business Ethics Quarterly* 271.

[34] On 'social licence', see N. Guningham, R.A. Kagan, and D. Thornton, 'Social license and environmental protection: why businesses go beyond compliance' (2004) 29(2) *Law and Social Inquiry* 307.

[35] J.M. Leger, 'Socially responsible funds pique interest, but results often have been unimpressive' *Wall Street Journal*, 18 November 1982, 33; D. Shapiro, 'Social responsibility mutual funds: down the down staircase' (1974–75) *Business and Society Review* 90.

[36] US-SIF, 'Sustainable and responsible investment facts', available at: http://ussif.org/resources/SRIguide/SRIfacts.cfm. See also D. Ross and D. Wood, 'Do environmental and social controls matter in Australian capital investment decision-making?' (2008) 17(5)

FINANCIAL MARKETS AND SOCIALLY RESPONSIBLE INVESTING   235

SRI's societal impact has received relatively little attention from scholars, who have generally focused their investigations on its financial impacts and returns.[37]

One example of the hope that some might have that SRI can improve corporate behaviour concerns how investors scuttled an environmentally controversial pulp mill on the island of Tasmania, in Australia. In May 2008, the Australian and New Zealand (ANZ) Bank declined to fund a pulp mill proposed by Gunns, a major local forestry operator.[38] Although the ANZ publicly declined to elaborate its reasons for shunning the project,[39] worth about A\$2 billion, the bank was undoubtedly concerned about the pulp mill's potential environmental impacts, or at least negative publicity about such impacts.[40] ANZ incurred a lot of bad press and pressure from some of its shareholders.[41] As a signatory to the Equator Principles,[42] a global voluntary SRI code, the ANZ was surely conscious of the environmental due diligence standards it had pledged to follow. The lender's stance is particularly curious given that the pulp mill satisfied government regulations.[43] Other lenders and investors subsequently also increasingly became wary of Gunns and its pulp mill, and the company is now in grave financial distress.[44]

This story raises interesting questions about the capacity and role of investors and financiers to act, in effect, as surrogate environmental 'regulators' of the market. As mechanisms of corporate financing, in theory,

---

Business Strategy and the Environment 294; Worldwide Fund for Nature (WWF) and BankTrack, *Shaping the Future of Sustainable Finance: Moving from Paper Promises to Sustainable Performance* (WWF, 2008).

[37] M. Barnett and R. Salomon, 'Beyond dichotomy: the curvilinear relationship between social responsibility and financial performance' (2006) 27 *Strategic Management Journal* 1101; N. Kreander, *et al.*, 'Evaluating the performance of ethical and non-ethical funds: a matched pair analysis' (2005) 32(7/8) *Journal of Business Finance and Accounting* 1465; R. Bauer, J. Derwall, and R. Otten, 'The ethical mutual fund performance debate: new evidence from Canada' (2007) 70 *Journal of Business Ethics* 111–24.

[38] M. Wilkinson and B. Cubby, 'ANZ exit from pulp mill project confirmed' (28 May 2008) *Melbourne Age* 3.

[39] 'ANZ quiet on Gunns funding', *Sydney Morning Herald*, 22 May 2008, available at: www.smh.com.au/business/anz-quiet-on-gunns-funding-20080522-2h52.html.

[40] 'Lobby group ups pressure on ANZ', *ABC News*, 7 April 2008, available at: www.abc.net .au/news/2008–04–07/lobby-group-ups-pressure-on-anz/2395140.

[41] M. Bowman, 'The role of the banking industry in facilitating climate change mitigation and the transition to a low-carbon global economy' (2010) 27 *Environmental and Planning Law Journal* 448, at 456.

[42] See www.equator-principles.com.

[43] A. Darby and D. Welsh, 'Contentious pulp mill wins federal approval', *The Sydney Morning Herald* 11 March 2011, 7.

[44] A. Krien, *Into the Woods: The Battle for Tasmania's Forests* (Black Inc., 2012), 268–70.

the financial industry can influence firms' development choices and, cumulatively, wider economic trends.[45] Also, as shareholders, investors acquire a voice in companies to potentially leverage change. Thereby, SRI might complement official regulation to help improve the social responsibility of the market. In addition to this empirical enquiry into the behavioural influence of SRI, there is the theoretical question of what should be the relationship between SRI and official regulation. If a company complies with environmental legislation, such as obtaining permits for its polluting activities, should the legal system bother with investors wishing to foster behaviour that goes *beyond compliance*? These issues thus invite a wider debate about the role of financial markets as a means of governance for sustainable business.

While social investors have strong financial objectives, which the SRI industry increasingly prioritises, the legitimacy of SRI remains strongly framed by its difference from conventional investment through offering 'social returns' in addition to financial gains.[46] Providing 'social returns' implies that SRI can influence corporate environmental and social behaviour. In this guise, SRI is not just a matter of – as it was with faith-based ethical investing – about eschewing profit from 'sin stocks', but about reducing the amount of 'sin' (i.e. ethically problematic activities, from the perspective of religious dogma).

There are five ways in which SRI has sought to exert influence, which this chapter examines:

1. Promoting SRI as a profitable alternative to conventional investment.
2. Altering the cost of capital of targeted companies, such as by divestment, and thereby creating pressure for improved corporate behaviour. Positive investment, such as impact investing, can also reward and stimulate good behaviour.
3. Advocating change in companies as shareholders or lenders, such as by filing shareholder resolutions and informal engagement with corporate management.
4. Designing codes of conduct for investors to engender more systemic changes across the market.
5. Encouraging reforms to public policy and official regulations pertaining to the financial economy.

---

[45] J. Froud, A. Leaver, and K. Williams, 'New actors in a financialised economy and the remaking of capitalism' (2007) 12(3) *New Political Economy* 339.

[46] H.G. Fung, S.A. Law, and J. Ya, *Socially Responsible Investment in a Global Environment* (Edward Elgar, 2010), 46.

The notion of having 'influence', as discussed in this chapter, is about possessing some power to affect a thing or a course of events. It denotes some degree of leverage that financial institutions may exert over borrowers, clients, and their portfolio companies regarding their sustainability performance. Such influence might range from dissuading a company from initiating or operating a project that is environmentally harmful, to making modest adjustments to its operations, or even encouraging a business to take positive measures to improve its environmental performance. Importantly, investors' influence might transcend individual companies to acquire broader strategic significance in shaping the public policy and regulatory agenda, such as contributing to changes in securities regulation or environmental standards. Measuring or quantifying such an influence can be difficult, however, because of the complexity of attributing changes in the environmental behaviour of targeted firms to the actions of investors. Thus, an assessment of SRI's influence is inevitably somewhat conjectural and qualitative in nature in the absence of detailed empirical studies (which have not yet been undertaken).

In each of the aforementioned five areas of influence, we should account for investors' diverse aims. SRI might merely serve to avoid sponsoring companies that perpetrate environmental and social wrongs. In other words, in this minimalist approach, SRI merely aims to avoid encouraging harm. Alternatively, some social investors seek positive change, such as through community impact investment and financing the 'green and clean tech' sector, in order to promote sustainable development. Thus, when evaluating the influence of SRI, the success of its strategies must be seen in light of the level of ambition.

A further important variable is institutional differences among financial actors. The financial industry is populated by a diverse crowd, including pension funds, insurance companies, banks, mutual funds, and investment foundations, and their ability and means to exert influence likely vary somewhat. Some commentators contend that the largest players share the characteristic of being 'universal investors', a trait that may sensitise them to the imperative of sustainable development.[47] The notion of 'universal investor' (sometimes also known as 'universal owner') was coined in

---

[47] J. Hawley and A. Williams, *The Rise of Fiduciary Capitalism* (University of Pennsylvania Press, 2000); J. Hawley and A. Williams, 'The universal owner's role in sustainable economic development' (2002) 9(3) *Corporate Environmental Strategy* 284; F. Amalric, 'Pension funds, corporate responsibility and sustainability' (2006) 59(4) *Ecological Economics* 440; UNEP-FI, *Universal Ownership: Why Environmental Externalities Matter to Institutional investors* (UNEP-FI, 2011).

238 BENJAMIN J. RICHARDSON

recent years to denote large institutional investors, such as pension funds, which hold huge and diverse (i.e. 'universal') portfolios that give them major stakes in the productive economy. This quality implies that an institutional investor benefiting from a company that externalises its social and environmental costs might ultimately suffer financially when these externalities adversely affect other assets in its portfolio. Therefore, universal investors should have an incentive to practise SRI, such as by reducing negative externalities (e.g. pollution and corruption) and increasing positive externalities (e.g. robust corporate governance and respect for human rights) across their portfolios. So far, there has been limited empirical evidence to validate these effects, and indeed there are reasons to doubt the theory. Investors have difficulty in coordinating their activities towards common altruistic purposes, such as fighting climate change, when operating in a competitive market.[48] Furthermore, the theory struggles to explain how environmental externalities collectively become internalised in the economy. Many environmental problems have a tendency to manifest slowly, over many decades, and often imperceptibly.[49] The gradualism of environmental decay and degradation can lull us into complacency, and blind investors to the unfolding quicksand of climate change.

The overall size of the SRI sector is also pertinent to an analysis of its influence. The media and practitioner literature sometimes paints a misleading picture.[50] While recent research from 2012 in North America and Western Europe by leading SRI associations heralds the sector as having captured between 10 and 20 per cent of these investment markets,[51] the survey methodologies are not robust and may tend to exaggerate the numbers. We lack similar data for responsible lending in the banking sector, though some qualitative research does raise concerns.[52] The fundamental problem is that surveys often include as SRI the entire portfolio of a fund

---

[48] Richardson, *Fiduciary Law and Responsible Investing*, 80–1.

[49] R. Nixon, *Slow Violence and the Environmentalism of the Poor* (MIT Press, 2011).

[50] For example, P. Aburdene, *Megatrends 2010: The Rise of Conscious Capitalism* (Hampton Roads Publishing, 2005), 140; T. Grant, 'Social investment assets soar', *Globe and Mail*, 22 March 2007, B17.

[51] European Social Investment Forum (Eurosif), *European SRI Study 2012* (Eurosif, 2012); US-SIF (Forum for Sustainable and Responsible Investment), *Report on Sustainable and Responsible Investment Trends in the United States 2012* (US-SIF, 2012).

[52] One 2006 study concluded that 'with few exceptions bank policies are lagging significantly behind relevant international standards and best practices': WWF and BankTrack, *Shaping the Future*, 4; see also International Finance Corporation (IFC), *Banking on Sustainability: Financing Environmental and Social Opportunities in Emerging Markets* (IFC, 2007).

that ethically screens only for a single or limited number of issues, or engages with only a few firms from its portfolio. In the USA, for example, the Forum for Sustainable and Responsible Investment (US-SIF) reports that 11.3 per cent of assets under professional management are linked to SRI.[53] Yet, this and earlier surveys include funds that screen merely against tobacco, alcohol, or gambling; indeed, 25 per cent of nominal SRI funds in one of the US-SIF's surveys screened only on the basis of *one* of these activities.[54] Further deceptive claims are found in the 2012 benchmark study made by Canada's Social Investment Organization, which trumpets that SRI is worth C\$600 billion and holds 20 per cent of all assets under management in Canada.[55] About 90 per cent of this figure seems to be based on the estimated value of investment portfolios of funds that engage with firms representing only a small fraction of their portfolio companies.[56] The Canadian survey egregiously counts the *entire* value of these investment portfolios rather than the tiny portion relating to SRI-driven corporate engagement. A likely more realistic figure for the SRI in Canada is about 2–3 per cent of the market, as recognised by this Canadian study in its earlier separate measurement of investment tied to 'core' ethical screens.[57]

4   SRI's financial rationale

A cursory review of recent literature on social investing reveals its preoccupation with SRI's financial justification. Rather than assess how SRI contributes to sustainability, as an ethical goal of value in its own right, many focus on how SRI can be financially advantageous.[58] SRI's philosophy has thus morphed dramatically, paralleling the same trend in

---

[53] US-SIF, *Report on Sustainable and Responsible Investment Trends in the United States 2012*, 11.

[54] US-SIF, *2005 Report on Socially Responsible Investing Trends in the United States: A 10-Year Review* (SIF, 2005), 9.

[55] Social Investment Organization (SIO), *Canadian Socially Responsible Investment Review 2012* (SIO, 2013), 4. This organisation is now known as the Responsible Investment Association.

[56] Social Investment Organization (SIO), *Canadian Socially Responsible Investment Review 2012*, 27.

[57] Social Investment Organization, *Canadian Socially Responsible Investment Review 2012*, 9.

[58] The literature is vast: e.g. P. Camejo, *The SRI Advantage: Why Socially Responsible Investing Has Outperformed Financially* (New Society Publishers, 2002); M. Barnett and R. Salmon, 'Beyond dichotomy: the curvilinear relationship between social responsibility and financial performance' (2006) 27(11) *Strategic Management Journal* 1101.

240   BENJAMIN J. RICHARDSON

the CSR discourse as documented by David Millon in Chapter 2 of this book.

While the ethical rationale still enlightens the 'protest' wing of the SRI sector, through their campaigns on a miscellany of causes spanning land mines to animal welfare, and some retail banks profess to give precedence to ethical principles over maximising profits, such as the Banca Etica (Italy) and Ekobanken (Sweden),[59] the dominant style of SRI has gravitated elsewhere. In trying to woo more adherents, many SRI proponents have rebranded it as a savvy business strategy. Investors are cajoled to scrutinise firms' ESG performance not primarily for ethical reasons, but because such issues might affect financial returns. Such attitudes permeate the industry-sponsored research and practice guides. The UNEP-FI has advised, 'The first – and arguably for investors the most important – reason to integrate environmental, social and governance issues is, simply, to make more money.'[60] Thereby, SRI is redefined as a sophisticated model of financial analysis in which ESG factors are assessed for materiality and effect on risk and returns.

A busy research industry has mushroomed to substantiate and promote claims about the financial advantage of SRI. The research generally concludes that SRI offers comparable or superior risk-adjusted financial returns relative to conventional investments.[61] Proponents of SRI contend that unethical businesses will harm their value in the long term due to extra costs, such as the increased chance of litigation or reputational damage.[62] Nonetheless, one might dispute the survey methodologies that rely on inconsistent definitions of 'socially responsible' when comparing SRI to conventional finance,[63] and some research findings are contrary.[64] Even if SRI out-performs the market, there may be a simple explanation.

---

[59] O. Weber and S. Remer, 'Social banking: introduction', in O. Weber and S. Remer (eds.), *Social Banks and the Future of Sustainable Finance* (Routledge, 2011), 1.

[60] UNEP-FI, *Show Me the Money: Linking Environmental, Social and Governance Issues to Company Value* (UNEP-FI, 2006), 4.

[61] UNEP-FI and Mercer Consulting, *Demystifying Responsible Investment Performance: A Review of Key Academic and Broker Research on ESG Factors* (UNEP-FI, 2007); M. Schroeder, 'The performance of socially responsible investments: investment funds and indices' (2004) 18(2) *Financial Markets and Portfolio Management* 122.

[62] L. Renneboog, J.T. Horst, and C. Zhang, 'Socially responsible investments: institutional aspects, performance, and investor behavior' (2008) 32(9) *Journal of Banking and Finance* 1723, at 1734.

[63] For a synthesis of many such studies, see M. Orlitzky, F. Schmidt, and S. Rynes, 'Corporate social and financial performance: a meta-analysis' (2003) 24(3) *Organization Studies* 403.

[64] Ransome and Sampford, *Ethics and Socially Responsible Investment*, 92; R. Copp, M.L. Kremmer, and E. Roca. 'Should funds invest in socially responsible investments during

As Haigh and Hazelton explain, 'The reason for correlations between the performance of conventional and SRI funds may be that the portfolios of SRI funds are not markedly different to those of conventional mutual funds.'[65] In other words, SRI can be too inclusive, merely screening out a few tobacco producers, for instance, but otherwise mimicking the market (as appears in the SRI industry survey methodologies discussed).[66]

Modern corporate finance theory suggests that if SRI screens out significant portions of the market on ethical grounds, it cannot financially outperform the market as a whole.[67] One of its principal concepts, modern portfolio theory, holds that a diversified investment universe is more likely to produce optimal, risk-adjusted returns than a narrowly constructed portfolio.[68] Exclusionary ethical screens that reduce the investment pool therefore should increase risks without compensatory higher returns.[69] Even if markets in the 'real world' do not necessarily reflect theoretical models, as some commentators plausibly contend,[70] SRI does not necessarily enjoy an advantage because an inefficient market may under- or over-rate both ethical and unethical businesses equally.[71] SRI that relies on corporate engagement rather than exclusionary screens should retain a reasonably diversified portfolio, though both methods may carry higher expenses and administrative overheads than regular funds due to the additional ESG research and active shareholding.

The appeal to SRI's financial credentials nonetheless appears to be a savvy strategy to overcome the sector's traditional marginalisation. For moral arguments to prevail on investors, there likely needs to be a substantial preponderance of opinion among the general public behind

---

downturns? Financial and legal implications of the fund manager's dilemma' (2011) 23(3) *Accounting Research* 254.

[65] M. Haigh and J. Hazelton, 'Financial markets: a tool for social responsibility?' (2004) 52(1) *Journal of Business Ethics* 59, at 65.

[66] Other research suggests there are material differences between SRI and non-SRI portfolios: see, e.g. K.L. Benson, T.J. Brailsford, and J.E. Humphrey, 'Do socially responsible fund managers really invest differently?' (2006) 65(4) *Journal of Business Ethics* 337.

[67] J. Langbein and R. Posner, 'Social investing and the law of trusts' (1980) 79 *Michigan Law Review* 72; M. Knoll, 'Ethical screening in modern financial markets: the conflicting claims underlying socially responsible investment' (2002) 57 *Business Lawyer* 681.

[68] H. Markowitz, 'Portfolio selection' (1952) 7(1) *Journal of Finance* 77. Returns, for instance, include dividends paid by firms as well as appreciation of the firms' stock prices.

[69] A. Rudd, 'Social responsibility and portfolio performance' (1981) 23(4) *California Management Review* 55.

[70] See, e.g. R. Ball, 'The theory of stock market efficiency: accomplishments and limitations' (1995) 30(2–3) *Journal of Applied Corporate Finance* 4.

[71] Knoll, 'Ethical screening in modern financial markets', 706.

242   BENJAMIN J. RICHARDSON

such arguments, such as the immorality of profiting from apartheid. Financial self-interest can be a very powerful stimulant to act: depicting environmental threats such as climate change as financial risks or opportunities seemingly provides a sturdier basis to galvanise investors' interest than amorphous pious talk.[72] And over the very long term – decades or longer periods – the business case for addressing environmental externalities should materialise because the costs of climate change and other ecological degradation can usually only be deferred but not avoided entirely.

Several countervailing considerations weigh against such optimism for the financial case for SRI. First, environmental due diligence is still far from integrated into conventional financial practices among mainstream investors.[73] A flourishing ESG research industry has emerged,[74] which is helping to inform new sustainability performance standards. An excellent example is the Climate Bonds Standard and Certification Scheme, offering investors an assurance regarding the low carbon quality of screened assets such as corporate bonds.[75] But such initiatives are not widespread in the financial industry and many impediments to robust ESG analysis have been identified, including scepticism about the link between environmental factors and investment performance; behavioural impediments rooted in the organisational culture of institutional funds and their agents, where short-term outlooks dominant decision-making; and the difficulty of monetising intangible ESG information.[76] By contrast, investment professionals prefer to focus on financial information such as return on equity, sales growth, price/earnings ratios, and other 'hard' indices of financial performance.[77]

Thus, though we may know that a company's sustainability performance is in some way relevant to its financial performance, especially

---

[72] Mercer, *Climate Change Scenarios: Implications for Strategic Asset Management* (Mercer, 2011).

[73] McKinsey, 'Valuing corporate social responsibility: McKinsey Global Survey results', *McKinsey Quarterly*, February 2009; European Centre for Corporate Engagement (ECCE), 'Use of extra financial information by research analysts and investment managers' (ECCE, 2007).

[74] For example, Trucost (UK) and Jantzi Sustainalytics (Canada).

[75] See http://standards.climatebonds.net.

[76] H. Jemel-Fornetty, C. Louche, and D. Bourghelle, 'Changing the dominant convention: the role of emerging initiatives in mainstreaming ESG', in W. Sun, C. Louche, and R. Pérez (eds.), *Finance and Sustainability: Towards a New Paradigm? A Post-Crisis Agenda* (Emerald Group, 2011) 85, at 89–91.

[77] Jemel-Fornetty, *et al.*, 'Changing the dominant convention', 90.

FINANCIAL MARKETS AND SOCIALLY RESPONSIBLE INVESTING 243

over the long term, cognitively it seems too difficult for investors to make the connections and then act on that knowledge. Climate integrity is often seen by fund managers and trustees as too nebulous for workable financial quantification, and thus warranting serious consideration.[78] Environmental issues usually cannot be accurately reflected in conventional financial accounting systems unless they are associated with specific expenses or income attributable to an entity, as Chapter 5 in this book by Charlotte Villiers and Jukka Mähönen explains.[79] The SRI industry is trying to develop new valuation methods,[80] and the value of environmental performance to a company's brand name is one area where firms might be responsive.

Another dilemma for SRI arises when a countervailing business case for financing environmentally damaging companies exists. The extensive market and regulatory failures to control environmental externalities provide temptations for financiers. The international commodities market boom before 2008 is one such example of intensified exploitation of natural resources.[81] Growing investment in the fossil fuel economy, such as Canada's oil sands, persists, despite talk about the menace of climate change.[82] In other words, if SRI is contingent on profitability, that logic will also sometimes give reasons to act unethically. While social investors increasingly argue a business case for investing responsibly over the long term,[83] many factors blunt acting as though the future mattered: fund managers hired on two-year performance contracts have incentives to act strongly for the near term; corporations themselves are structured strongly around short-term financial measurements, such as quarterly financial reporting; and uncertainty about the financial cost of distant

---

[78] J. Solomon, *Pension Fund Trustees and Climate Change* (Association of Certified Chartered Accountants, 2009), 21–3.

[79] See also S. Goodman and T. Little, *The Gap in GAAP: An Examination of Environmental Accounting Loopholes* (Rose Foundation for Communities and the Environment, 2003).

[80] S. McGeachie, M. Kiernan, and E. Kirzner, *Finance and the Environment in North America: The State of Play of the Integration of Environmental Issues into Financial Research* (Innovest, 2005), 57.

[81] 'The commodities boom on 2011: coal will be the new gold' (23 February 2011) MoneyMorning.Com, available at: http://moneymorning.com/2011/02/23/commodities-boom-2011-coal-will-be-the-new-gold.

[82] E. Crooks, 'Oil sands: ice thaws on Canadian projects', *Financial Times,* 11 March 2011, available at: www.ft.com/cms/s/0/2bf6bb96–50f9–11e0–8931–00144feab49a.html#axzz1aLC3tPKE.

[83] S. Lyndenberg, 'Universal investors and socially responsible investors: a tale of emerging affinities' (2007) 15(3) *Corporate Governance: An International Review* 467, at 471 (stating that pension funds have 'inherently long investment horizons').

244 BENJAMIN J. RICHARDSON

environmental harms, which depends partly on the extent of government regulation to penalise polluters, persists.[84]

5 Altering the cost of capital

Another way SRI might nudge companies towards sustainability is by altering firms' cost of capital. Social investors might believe they can financially reward ethical companies by channelling additional investment to them, while punishing or disciplining unethical ones by divesting from them, and thereby imposing higher costs of raising money.[85] If sufficient social investors dominate the market, they might be able to have this effect, thereby creating something analogous to a Pigouvian tax.[86] If responsible financiers could differentiate the cost of capital on the basis of environmental or social performance, they could motivate companies to improve their behaviour in order to entice social investors wishing to invest.

Corporate finance theory, however, suggests otherwise. In an efficient stock market, suggests the literature, there are limitations to investors' ability to affect the price of a firm's shares or bonds.[87] The standard textbook theory is that the current price of a firm reflects a combined assessment of the current value of the firm relative to reported earnings and expectations of any changes in value in the near-to-medium term. The notion of 'elasticity' is used by economists to describe the fractional change in the quantity demanded for each fractional change in price, and there tend to be salient differences in the demand curve (elasticity) for corporate securities compared to typical goods and services in the productive economy. Whereas investors may buy and sell blocks of shares without significantly affecting the share price, for many commodities, changes in demand can significantly affect price. Thus, an Israeli boycott against cottage cheese in 2011, aimed at protesting against recent food price rises in Israel, led to a reduced demand, and less cheese sold led major supermarkets to reduce significantly the retail price of this food

---

[84] Richardson, *Socially Responsible Investment Law*, 120–58.

[85] T. Hebb, *No Small Change: Pension Funds and Corporate Engagement* (Cornell University Press, 2008), 22; R. Sparkes and C. Cowton, 'The maturing of socially responsible investment: a review of the developing link with corporate social responsibility' (2004) 52 *Journal of Business Ethics* 45, at 45.

[86] A. Pigou, *The Economics of Welfare* (Macmillan, 1932).

[87] C. Loderer, *et al.*, 'The price elasticity of demand for common stock' (1991) 46 *Journal of Finance* 621.

staple.[88] On the other hand, because the stock of a particular company often has many similar substitutes for investors (e.g. a variety of companies operating in a particular economic sector, such as IT or energy), the demand for its securities is more elastic. Consequently, a small change in share price will trigger a large change in the quantity demanded or, conversely, a large increase in the quantity demanded will result in only a small price change.

The foregoing essentially implies that social investors are price-takers rather than price-makers. Changes in the price for stock should only reflect underlying changes in the perceived financial prospects of the company (i.e. anticipated future cash flows to the company). As any divesting by social investors on ethical criteria does not per se alter the expected cash flow of the firm's activities, its stock prices should not change.[89] Social investors who shun a business on ethical grounds therefore would not prevail as other (conventional) investors stand by to buy the stock. Of course, business case SRI that educates the market on the financial consequences of firms' sustainability performance might have some influence (but, as already explained, the business case presently offers an imperfect lens of corporate behaviour).

Other research highlights variables that might enable social investors to exert a market influence in specific or unusual circumstances. Pietra Rivoli, who extrapolates from the reality that markets do not always behave according to textbook dogma, predicts that social investors may alter the cost of capital when the stock is particularly unique (i.e. has few substitutes) or trades in small, restrictive markets.[90] Such conditions might exist for a firm that operates a niche, boutique business or is a market leader and innovator. Some research also tracks fluctuations in stock prices from the addition or deletion of stocks from major stock indexes, such as the S&P 500. Index tracking funds typically adjust their own portfolios to reflect changes in the underlying index, and a group of such indexes have been created for social investors such as the Dow Jones Sustainability Indexes. Standard finance theory would predict that

---

[88] R. Rozenberg and A.D. Meseritz, 'Cottage cheese sales plummet as Israeli consumers revolt over price', *Haaretz*, 19 June 2011, available at: www.haaretz.com/themarker/cottage-cheese-sales-plummet-as-israeli-consumers-revolt-over-price-1.368458.

[89] W. Davidson, D. Worell, and A. El-Jelly, 'Influencing managers to change unpopular corporate behavior through boycotts and divestitures' (1995) 34(2) *Business and Society* 171.

[90] P. Rivoli, 'Making a difference or making a statement? Finance research and socially responsible investment' (2003) 13(3) *Business Ethics Quarterly* 271.

changes in demand for a stock added or removed from an index should not affect the stock price, because they do not per se reflect changes in the company's financial prospects. But several studies of the S&P 500 found such an effect, mainly owing to the accompanying benefits of increased liquidity and inclusion in a larger investor base.[91]

Another situation where SRI might be influential is of course where all or the overwhelming majority of investors were socially oriented; by their sheer force of numbers, they might sway companies. We lack research that predicts informatively the tipping point for such an effect,[92] but as already noted, SRI markets are relatively small and nowhere near this threshold. Presently, no individual financier or coalition of investors could ever come near to monopolising all sources of development and corporate finance to make SRI obligatory (but they might at least make it more expensive for targeted companies that resist social investors to seek finance from other sources).

Turning to the empirical evidence, the impact of SRI campaigns is ambiguous. The South African boycott is the most comprehensively studied example, and many researchers conclude it had only modest effect on the economic performance of targeted companies.[93] The more recent crusade against the tobacco industry also appears to have had limited effect on targeted firms' stock prices.[94] The recent fossil fuels divestment campaign, spearheaded by networks such as Fossil Free,[95] is attracting good support from a number of public sector funds, philanthropic foundations, and religious investors, but has yet to make serious inroads into the mainstream financial industry. Other research into changes in the cost of capital in light of information released to the market about firms' environmental behaviour, such as news of a pollution scandal or, conversely, commendations for exemplary achievements, suggests such factors can

---

[91] A. Lynch and R. Mendenhall, 'New evidence on stock price effects associated with changes in the S&P 500 Index' (1997) 70(3) *Journal of Business* 351.

[92] However, see the limited stab at modelling an answer: R. Heinkel, A. Kraus, and J. Zechner, 'The effect of green investment on corporate behavior' (2001) 36(4) *Journal of Financial and Quantitative Analysis* 431.

[93] S. Teoh, I. Welch, and C.P. Wazzan, 'The effect of socially activist investment policies on the financial markets: evidence from the South African boycott' (1999) 72 *Journal of Business* 35; but compare to R. Kumar, W. Lamb, and R. Wokutch, 'The end of South African sanctions, institutional ownership, and the stock price of boycotted firms' (2002) 41(2) *Business and Society* 133.

[94] T. Burroughes, 'Ethical investors losing out as tobacco stocks burn up Britain's equity markets' *The Business*, 24 February 2007.

[95] See http://gofossilfree.org.

affect stock prices or the cost of borrowing.[96] However, the market impact tends to be short-lived.[97]

In gauging SRI's influence, we must also distinguish between the role of equity and debt financing, the former being the focus of the preceding discussion. Debt financing is primarily through bank loans and corporate bonds. Banks also have an influence through their financial advice and selling investment products. As lender, a bank should be able to exert reasonable influence over borrowers, especially small, private enterprises with few financing options, as well as established firms seeking large loans.[98] A thriving social banking sector, comprising lenders focusing on poverty alleviation (mainly in developing countries) and ethical banking (mainly in Western countries), is providing targeted financial support for businesses, communities, and households that contribute to sustainable development.[99] Lenders may also have self-interested reasons to heed environmental factors. 'Climate risk' has become a boutique area of environmental risk assessment that banks are increasingly incorporating into their due diligence procedures.[100] Westpac, an Australian bank reputed to be an SRI leader in its sector, believes '[t]he role of the leader is not just to look at themselves but to also look outwardly at who they can influence. As a bank we are in a good position to do that because nearly all businesses have a banking relationship.'[101] Gunns (discussed earlier in this chapter), for example, sought a huge loan from the ANZ Bank for its controversial Tasmanian pulp mill, which was denied. Lenders most commonly scrutinise borrowers' environmental practices when they might engender

---

[96] N. Lorraine, D. Collison, and D. Power, 'An analysis of the stock market impact of environmental performance information' (2004) 28 *Accounting Forum* 7; S. Dasgupta, B. Laplante, and N. Mamingi, *Capital Market Responses to Environmental Performance in Developing Countries* (World Bank, 1998).

[97] D. Cormier, M. Magnan, and B. Morard, 'The impact of corporate pollution on market valuation: some empirical evidence' (1993) 8 *Ecological Economics* 135.

[98] M. Jeucken, *Sustainable Finance and Banking: The Financial Sector and the Future of the Planet* (Routledge, 2001); P. Thompson, 'Bank lending and the environment: policies and opportunities' (1998) 16(6) *International Journal of Bank Marketing* 243.

[99] Weber and Remer, 'Social banking', at 2.

[100] Among reports that have evaluated banks' climate-related policies and practices: D.G. Cogan, *Corporate Governance and Climate Change: The Banking Sector* (Ceres, 2008); B. Furrer, M. Swoboda, and V. Hoffman, *Banking and Climate Change: Stumbling into Momentum? An Analysis of Climate Strategies in More Than 100 Banks Worldwide* (WWF and SAM, 2009).

[101] G. Paterson, 'CSR official, Westpac', quoted in A. De Lore 'How the companies compare: a network of high achievers is showing the way' (Special Report on Corporate Responsibility Index), *Sydney Morning Herald* 20 May 2008, 2.

costly environmental liabilities. They may consequently adjust the cost of a loan to reflect unresolved environmental risks, require the borrower to adopt specific environmental safeguards, or demand more valuable security against the loan.[102]

But there are market constraints to how high an ethical lender can raise the bar. In a competitive credit market, lenders have incentives not to be too demanding for risk of losing clients to less scrupulous financiers. While banks' influence in the financial sector has increased as market deregulation allows them to extend their range of services and activities to include insurance and retail investing, as direct lenders, banks' influence has waned as alternative sources of financing have become available to firms through institutional investors. In the USA, the banks' share and the other depository institutions' share of financial assets declined from 54.9 per cent in 1967 to 23.7 per cent in 2007, while the share of pension funds and mutual funds surged from 15.4 per cent to 37.8 per cent.[103] The trend has benefited both public and private companies, as the growth of private equity funds since the 1970s has provided another source of cash for private companies.[104]

In conclusion, the ability of SRI to influence the availability and cost of money to companies is presently limited. In certain contexts, social investors and lenders might be able to nudge some firms to improve their behaviour by tightening the purse strings, but this is still far from common.

6 Corporate engagement

6.1 The shift from 'exit' to 'voice'

The growth of the SRI market in recent decades has paralleled an evolution in its methods, with more reliance on 'voice', such as by engaging with corporate managers, and less use of 'exit' (e.g. selling shares or denying loans). As Sjåfjell and her co-authors discussed in Chapter 3 of this book, reliance on shareholder voice to discipline companies has generally not offered a decisive challenge to the myopic and environmentally problematic practices of business. Without wishing to repeat their analysis of the

---

[102] Paterson, 'CSR official, Westpac'.

[103] J. D'Arista and S. Griffith-Jones, 'Agenda and criteria for financial regulatory reform', in S. Griffith-Jones, et al. (eds.), *Time for a Visible Hand: Lessons from the 2008 World Financial Crisis* (Oxford University Press, 2010), 126 at 133–4.

[104] E. Talmor and F. Vasvar, *International Private Equity* (John Wiley & Sons, Ltd, 2011).

FINANCIAL MARKETS AND SOCIALLY RESPONSIBLE INVESTING   249

legal and social obstacles to transforming the limitations of shareholder primacy in corporate governance, this section examines in more specific detail how social investors have sought to engage with companies. Such investors, sometimes acting in concert with NGOs and activists, may seek to influence companies through dialogue and pressure from within, rather than by divesting or exclusionary screening. These strategies have also occasionally been used, explains Cook, 'by well organised shareholder coalitions to achieve public policy changes, thereby extending their reach beyond targeted firms'.[105] Faith-based investors and public sector pension funds have tended to be the most active and most likely to raise SRI issues, and occasionally NGOs such as Amnesty International and the Sierra Club have bought corporate stock in order to acquire an additional platform to voice their concerns.

The rise of institutional, 'universal' investors in global financial markets over recent decades has raised hopes for greater shareholder oversight of corporate management. Berle and Means's pioneering work in the 1930s suggested that the twentieth-century development of business corporations entailed a dispersal of shareholding to much of the general public, with a consequential loss of shareholder control over corporate managers.[106] Today, some commentators see the rise of institutional funds as challenging those assumptions, by reconcentrating share ownership and providing greater economies of scale and incentives to monitor and discipline managers.[107] Importantly, the reconcentration is not simply at the level of individual funds but through their ability to work in concert. While each institutional fund commonly holds only a small fraction of the stock of any single firm, together they might hold a sufficient stake to exert influence.

Traditionally, institutional investors tended to be rather passive shareholders. The GFC, explained a European Commission (EC) policy paper in 2010, 'has shown that confidence in the model of the shareholder-owner who contributes to the company's long-term viability has been severely shaken'.[108] Institutional shareholders can be unwilling or unable

---

[105] J. Cook, 'Political action through environmental shareholder resolution filing: applicability to Canadian oil sands?' (2012) 2 (1) *Journal of Sustainable Finance and Investment*, 26–43.

[106] A. Berle and G. Means, *The Modern Corporation and Private Property* (Transaction Publishers, 1932).

[107] See Hebb, *No Small Change*, 28.

[108] European Commission, *Green Paper: Corporate Governance in Financial Institutions and Remuneration Policies*, COM (2010) 285 final, 8.

250   BENJAMIN J. RICHARDSON

to exert influence through engagement, owing to myriad factors, including lacking knowledge and incentives to monitor companies because of the costs involved, the difficulties of coordinating action, and conflicts-of-interest.[109] The opportunities for free riders, who benefit from the share price increases resulting from successful corporate engagement without shouldering any of its costs, can undermine collaborative engagement. The traditional lack of investor-related activism is also partly attributable to legal barriers to shareholder voice and networking, as discussed in other chapters in this book, though increasingly these have been mitigated by legislative reform.

Extensive engagement and activism are not necessarily desirable. Shareholders cannot and should not micromanage a company. Engagement best focuses on issues that could increase the long-term and sustainability performance of the firm.[110]

6.2   Current engagement practices

Institutional funds' engagement with companies over ESG concerns, while increasing,[111] can be rather episodic and fleeting. Further, the effectiveness of shareholder campaigns appears to be more pronounced in the largest firms and businesses operating close to their ultimate consumers, as presumably these corporations' brand image and reputational value are more significant and sensitive to challenge.[112]

The quality and extent of institutional investors' engagement have been mixed in recent years. Some institutions such as the California Public Employees Retirement System (CalPERS) and Hermes have good

---

[109] J. Parkinson, *Corporate Power and Responsibility: Issues in the Theory of Company Law* (Clarendon Press, 1995), 168–9; B.S. Black, 'Shareholder activism and corporate governance in the United States', in P. Newman (ed.), *The New Palgrave Dictionary of Economics and the Law* (Palgrave, 1998) 459; A. Schleifer and R.W. Vishny, 'Value maximization and the acquisition process', (1988) 2(1) *Journal of Economic Perspectives* 7.

[110] R. Barker, 'Ownership structure and shareholder engagement: reflections on the role of institutional shareholders in the financial crisis', in W. Sunn, *et al.* (eds.), *Corporate Governance and the Global Financial Crisis: International Perspectives* (Cambridge University Press, 2011) 144, at 149.

[111] S. Davis, J. Lukomnik, and D. Pitt-Watson, *The New Capitalists: How Citizen Investors Are Reshaping the Corporate Agenda* (Harvard Business School Press, 2006) at 15–16.

[112] G.L. Clark, J. Salo, and T. Hebb, 'Social and environmental shareholder activism in the public spotlight: US corporate annual meetings, campaign strategies, and environmental performance, 2001–04' (2008) 40(6) *Environment and Planning A* 1370; M.P. Lee and M. Lounsbury, 'Domesticating radical rant and rage: an exploration of the consequences of environmental shareholder resolutions on corporate environmental performance' (2011) 50(1) *Business Society* 155.

FINANCIAL MARKETS AND SOCIALLY RESPONSIBLE INVESTING   251

records of active ownership. Research by Proffitt and Spicer[113] and Lee and Lounsbury[114] on the ascendance of institutional investors highlights both their cumulative victories as active shareholders that challenge corporate management on SRI issues and some corresponding, wider political influence over policy-makers. But measuring the extent and impact of corporate engagement is methodologically challenging, given that much of it is informal and 'behind-the-scenes', and showing cause and effect of engagement and changes in corporate behaviour is difficult.

One recent Canadian example is the planned Enbridge Northern Gateway Project involving twin pipelines through British Columbia, a monstrous project that has inspired some shareholders to file resolutions calling on Enbridge to adopt mitigating measures or abandon it altogether. A group of SRI funds led by NEI Investments filed a shareholder proposal on risks associated with aboriginal people's opposition to the pipeline at Enbridge's annual shareholder meeting in May 2012, with 28.5 per cent voting for and 10.7 per cent abstaining – a relatively strong rebuke, indicative of growing investor unease.[115]

Investors can use an array of engagement strategies. Most commonly, they prefer polite, informal dialogue with company executives. Other options include active proxy voting and occasionally filing or supporting dissent shareholder proposals. The Universities Superannuation Scheme (USS), one of the UK's most active funds, has singled out climate change as a priority issue for engagement.[116] It is difficult, however, to gauge the extent and quality of USS's corporate engagement (as with other funds) because it relies on a low-key, private approach to raising its concerns.[117] By contrast, the Californian financial behemoth, CalPERS, pushes a more public and confrontational style of engagement that sometimes includes the media to 'name-and-shame' recalcitrant companies.[118]

There is worrying research suggesting that most institutional investors have little engagement with investee companies.[119] A study conducted by Riskmetrics Group and others found that 'the institutional investor community consists of two distinct parts: a small active minority and

[113] W.T. Proffitt, Jr. and A. Spicer, 'Shaping the shareholder activism agenda: institutional investors and global social issues' (2006) 4(2) *Strategic Organization* 165.
[114] Lee and Lounsbury, 'Domesticating radical rant and rage'.
[115] A. Hasham, 'Pipeline protest rolls into T.O.: First Nations group taking fight to Enbridge', *Toronto Star* 9 May 2012, A6.
[116] Universities Superannuation Scheme (USS), *Climate Change: A Risk Management Challenge for Institutional Investors* (USS, 2001).
[117] Hebb, *No Small Change*, 63.   [118] Hebb, *No Small Change*, at 65.
[119] Barker, 'Ownership structure', 149.

a majority of more passive investors'.[120] A study by Goergen and others suggests that UK institutional investors do not routinely monitor investee firms.[121] Choi and Fisch found that many US pension funds typically kept a low and non-confrontational profile.[122] A more wide-ranging survey by the International Corporate Governance Network (ICGN) in 2009 found that 'insufficient trust' between companies and investors hindered constructive engagement.[123]

Jurisdictional differences in the extent of investor activism are apparent. It remains predominantly a North American tradition, and not as widely practised among European social investors or in other markets such as Australia.[124] Investor-related activism, suggests Schaefer, writing in 2004, 'neither has tradition nor meaning in the system of German corporate governance'.[125] The number of shareholder resolutions on SRI issues that went to a vote in the USA has fluctuated little between 194 and 176 per year between 2004 and 2013, and over this time the average supporting vote increased from 12 per cent to 21 per cent, according to data compiled by FundVotes.[126] Among environmental issues raised by shareholders, climate change has been the dominant concern; from 2004 to 2013 the number of resolutions about it that went to a vote annually rose from 9 to 18.[127] Many resolutions are filed but never voted on, sometimes because shareholders withdraw their resolution if management agrees to discuss or address their concerns. Shareholder proposals rarely garner a majority of votes, and ordinarily are not legally binding and may thus be ignored by corporate management.[128]

---

[120] Riskmetrics Group, *et al.*, *Study on Monitoring and Enforcement Practices in Corporate Governance in the Member States* (Riskmetrics Group, September 2009), 15.

[121] M. Goergen, *et al.*, 'Do UK institutional shareholders monitor their investee firms?' working paper (European Corporate Governance Institute, 2007) at 12.

[122] S. Choi and J.E. Fisch, 'On beyond CalPERS: survey evidence on the developing role of public pension funds in corporate governance' (2008) 61 *Vanderbilt Law Review* 315, at 329.

[123] S.C.Y. Wong, 'Shareholder-company engagement: a comparative overview' (2009) *International Corporate Governance Network Yearbook* 61.

[124] Corporate Monitor, *Responsible Investment: A Benchmark Report on Australia and New Zealand by the Responsible Investment Association Australasia* (Corporate Monitor, 2008), 23.

[125] H. Schaefer, 'Ethical investment of German non-profit organizations – conceptual outline and empirical results' (2004) 13(4) *Business Ethics: A European Review* 269, at 271.

[126] FundVotes, 'Shareholder resolutions: average shareholder support by category', available at: www.fundvotes.com/resolutionsbycategory_countavg.php.

[127] FundVotes, 'Shareholder resolutions: average shareholder support by category'.

[128] Davis, *et al.*, *The New Capitalists*, 16–18.

FINANCIAL MARKETS AND SOCIALLY RESPONSIBLE INVESTING   253

In the retail fund sector, including SRI mutual funds, fierce market competition leads fund managers to 'focus on straightforward [trading] strategies and quarterly performance metrics in an effort to attract and retain investors. With some exceptions, mutual funds tend not to invest significant monies in their analysis of corporate governance issues.'[129] The US mutual fund industry is dominated by Fidelity, Vanguard, and American Funds, and they tend to vote routinely with corporate management. These fund groups compete on returns and low fees without any incentive to invest in ESG analysis and active shareholding. By contrast, the proxy voting record of dedicated SRI mutual funds in North America suggests they 'are far less supportive of management' and commonly offer 'strong support for shareholder initiatives'.[130]

Outsourcing corporate governance to proxy advisors, as if often done by institutional investors, may generate additional problems. The quality of voting recommendations of proxy advisors can vary dramatically by company and market. The market for proxy voting in North America and Western Europe has become highly concentrated, and conflicts of interest may arise from proxy advisors who serve both companies and their institutional investors.[131] Dominant proxy advisory providers such as ISS and Glass Lewis may have business ties to companies whose shares are being voted on their advice, such as consultancy services for improving corporate governance and selling data about companies' comparative ESG performance and rating.

Collaboration between investors can enable engagement to flourish and be more effective. Although each investor may hold a small stake in individual companies, investors could increase their control over companies through collaboration. Hebb traces a trend since the late 1990s towards increasing collaboration among institutional funds, especially among public sector pension plans in North America and the UK, directed towards improving corporate governance, including greater accountability to shareholders, more transparency, and managerial oversight. More well-qualified and independent directors are among the corporate

---

[129] American Bar Association (ABA), *Report of the Task Force of the ABA Section of Business Law Corporate Governance Committee on Delineation of Governance Roles & Responsibilities* (ABA, 2009), 19.

[130] L. O'Neill and J. Cook, *Proxy Voting by Canadian Mutual Funds 2006–2009* (SHARE and FundVotes, 2010), 3.

[131] OECD, *Corporate Governance and the Financial Crisis: Key Findings and Main Messages* (OECD, 2009), 54.

governance best practices sought.[132] Much of this institutional collaboration is clustering around specific SRI codes of conduct, such as the Carbon Disclosure Project, whose effect is analysed later in this chapter, as well as networks such as the Council of Institutional Investors (in the USA) and the National Association of Pension Funds (in the UK).

Public sector funds, perhaps because of their more politicised roots, tend to be more active shareholders than their private counterparts. In particular, some sovereign wealth funds such as the New Zealand Superannuation Fund and the Norwegian Government Pension Fund-Global (NGPF-G) are becoming active shareholders and supporting shareholder resolutions on sustainability issues.[133] Their work suggests that divestment and engagement are not necessarily mutually exclusive strategies. The NGPF-G uses both techniques to fulfil its legal mandate to invest ethically, and its policy is to engage with targeted companies before potentially excluding them from its investment portfolio. The Fund's ethical investment regulations require that companies proposed for exclusion be given a chance to respond and be told the reasons for the proposed exclusion.[134] This process may trigger some dialogue, and persuade the firm to make amends (such as by cancelling a controversial project).[135]

Because corporate engagement can be very time-consuming and labour-intensive, it is usually done very selectively. Even the ability to monitor companies – a precondition to engagement – is beyond the capacity of many pension funds and many other financial institutions.[136] Active, one-to-one engagement with targeted firms is typically done in few cases at one time. With over 3,000 firms in its portfolio, the Canada Pension Plan is only able to engage closely with about 15 firms annually, though it communicates on SRI issues with many more portfolio companies through questionnaires and proxy voting.[137] Likewise, the NGPF-G, in 2012, held shares in approximately 8,300 companies, with an average

---

[132] Hebb, *No Small Change*, 1–2.

[133] B.J. Richardson, "Sovereign wealth funds and socially responsible investing: an emerging public fiduciary' (2013) 2 *Global Journal of Comparative Law* 125.

[134] Guidelines for Observation and Exclusion from the Government Pension Fund Global's Investment Universe (2010), s. 5(3).

[135] This option tends not to be available to companies liable to be excluded because of the very *nature* of their business (e.g. producing tobacco).

[136] Hebb, *No Small Change*, 76.

[137] Canada Pension Plan Investment Board (CPPIB), *2011 Report on Responsible Investing* (CPPIB, 2011), 8–20.

FINANCIAL MARKETS AND SOCIALLY RESPONSIBLE INVESTING 255

ownership stake in each of about 1.3 per cent,[138] and only engages with about 100 firms annually.[139]

Engagement by banks involves a different legal and economic context. Through lending, banks may have a close, on-going relationship with companies. The contractual terms of a loan can give banks leverage to scrutinise a company's activities and even impose covenants regarding its handling of environmental activities and risks. This leverage may be strongest in the traditionally bank-based economies of continental Europe and East Asia, where lenders have been more important than the capital markets for corporate financing. In Germany, such intimate relationships between banks and companies gave rise to the '*Hausbank*' phenomenon, involving loans to corporate clients being secured by the bank holding shares in the firm.[140] In the USA and the UK, by contrast, such relationships have traditionally been more at arm's length, with banks generally distancing themselves from corporate governance and operational affairs.

Some recent research suggests these inter-jurisdictional differences in regard to creditors' engagement practices are decreasing. German company law and capital markets regulation are increasingly gravitating towards the Anglo-American model.[141] Conversely, Tung contends that Anglo-American banks habitually influence corporate managerial decision-making, even regarding routine operational matters rather than simply when borrowers are in distress.[142] Banks may also exert influence through research and advisory work; Bowman discusses how some banks have partnered with NGOs and companies 'to commission and disseminate research that influences policy-makers as well as corporate actors', and she cites Westpac's partnering with other parties through the Australian Business Roundtable on Climate Change to commission research on the business case to address climate change.[143]

---

[138] Norwegian Ministry of Finance, *The Management of the Government Pension Fund in 2013 (2013–2014) to the Storting* (Government of Norway, 2014), 67.

[139] Interview, Ola Mestad, Chair, Council on Ethics, NGPF-G, October 2012.

[140] A. Hackethal, 'German banks and banking structure', in J.P. Krahnen and R.H Schmidt (eds.), *The German Financial System* (Oxford University Press, 2004), at 71.

[141] F.J. Preu and B.J. Richardson, 'German socially responsible investment: barriers and opportunities' (2011) 12(3) *German Law Journal* 865.

[142] F. Tung, 'Leverage in the board room: the unsung influence of private lenders in corporate governance' (2009) 57 *UCLA Law Review* 115, at 118–19.

[143] Bowman, 'Role of the banking industry', 463.

6.3   Legal milieu of corporate engagement

Although it is an indelible part of the fiduciary responsibility of fund managers and trustees to exercise shareholder rights in companies in a manner that best maximises beneficiaries' interests (though the law does not generally stipulate what those interests are), the legal milieu governing shareholder rights can hinder corporate engagement, as can be gleaned from a few cursory examples. In Australia, institutional investors have expressed concern that collaboration on corporate governance outside shareholders meetings would violate certain provisions of the *Corporations Act*.[144] In Britain, the provisions of the Takeover Code and the Financial Service Authority's (FSA) controller's regime may deter collective engagement.[145] In the USA, low levels of engagement have been fuelled by concerns over potential infringement of securities regulation, particularly the *Regulation Fair Disclosure* (Regulation FD).[146] This states that when a company discloses material non-public information to certain individuals or entities, it must also make public disclosure of that information. To comply with Regulation FD, the companies may insist on procedures that restrict interaction with shareholders.[147]

Legal reform or a reinterpretation of old rules has in recent years also helped increase investor activism, including changes to securities law to facilitate communication between shareholders and to lower their transactions costs in both monitoring and coordinating responses. In order to address the concerns that have been raised over the extent to which engagement would be inconsistent with other regulatory requirements, the UK's FSA has issued guidance which advises the existing regulatory regime: 'do not prevent collective engagement by institutional shareholders designed to raise legitimate concerns on particular corporate issues, events or matters of governance with the management of investee companies'.[148]

---

[144] R. McKay, *Collective Action by Institutional Investors is More Than a Passing Fad* (Australian Council of Superannuation Investors, 2007), 2.

[145] Rule 9.1(a) of the City Code on Takeovers and Mergers provides that a mandatory offer should be made to all shareholders when any person acquires . . . an interest in shares which (taken together with shares in which persons acting in concert with him are interested) carry 30% or more of the voting rights of a company: Panel on Takeovers and Mergers, 'City Code on Takeovers and Mergers', 129, available at: www.thetakeoverpanel .org.uk/wp-content/uploads/2008/11/code.pdf.

[146] SEC, Fair Disclosure, Regulation FD, available at: ww.sec.gov/answers/regfd.htm.

[147] Barker, 'Ownership structure', 149.

[148] S. Dewar, 'Shareholder engagement and the current regulatory regime', FRC, 19 August 2009, available at: www.frc.org.uk/documents/pagemanager/Corporate_Governance/ Related_documents/shareholder_engagement_FSA_letter.pdf.

FINANCIAL MARKETS AND SOCIALLY RESPONSIBLE INVESTING   257

In Germany, the *Risk Limitation Act* of 2008 has reaffirmed that coordinated conduct in single cases (i.e. coordination between investors regarding issues raised in general meetings or arrangements to affect the composition of the supervisory board) will not be deemed to be 'acting in concert' and thus will be spared the onerous regulatory consequences that would follow.[149] In Canada and the USA, securities regulators decided in 2003 and 2005 respectively to encourage more vigilant shareholding by requiring mutual fund companies to disclose their shareholder voting policies and practices.[150]

Another area of legal reform has improved shareholder rights to file proposals and challenge corporate management. Amendments to the Canadian Business Corporations Act (CBCA) in 2001 curbed company management's discretion to disallow a shareowner proposal that promoted political, social, or similar objectives. The revised rule only requires a shareowner to 'demonstrate that the proposal relates in a significant way to the business or affairs of the corporation'.[151] Shareholder activism has since increased; the volume of shareholder proposals in Canada increased from fewer than three in each year before the mid-1990s to 63 in 2000 and 148 in 2005.[152]

National corporate governance codes rather than hard regulation are the main mechanisms used to encourage shareholder engagement in some jurisdictions. The 2008 Dutch Corporate Governance Code explicitly calls for shareholders to be willing to 'engage in a dialogue with the company and their fellow shareholders'.[153] Similarly, the UK Corporate Governance Code stipulates: 'There should be a dialogue with shareholders based on the mutual understanding of objectives. The board as a whole has responsibility for ensuring that a satisfactory dialogue with shareholders takes place.'[154] These codes are usually based on a soft-law approach that

---

[149] Risikobegrenzungsgesetz, Bundesgesetzblatt (2008) at 1666.

[150] SEC, 'Disclosure of proxy voting policies and proxy voting records by registered management investment companies' (31 January 2003); Canadian Securities Administrators, *National Instrument 81–106 Investment Fund Continuous Disclosure and Companion Policy 81–106CP* (2005).

[151] Section 137(5)(b)(i).

[152] Statistics on shareholder proposals filed in Canada are available at Shareholder Association of Education and Research, available at: www.share.ca/shareholderdb/.

[153] Corporate Governance Code Monitoring Committee (CGCMC), *Dutch Corporate Governance Code Principles of Good Corporate Governance and Best Practice Provisions* (CGCMC, 2008), 34.

[154] Financial Reporting Council (FRC), *The UK Corporate Governance Code* (FRC, 2010), 25.

seeks to foster dialogue between shareholders and corporations through the application of the 'comply-or-explain' principle. Consequently, companies can deviate from code requirements as long as they explain their reasoning to shareholders.[155]

Other contributors in this volume, especially Chapter 3 by Sjåfjell and others on 'shareholder primacy', provide further analysis of shareholder rights in corporate governance. The main point to note here is that corporate law can hinder engagement by social investors, but it is not a determinating factor is far less influential than other variables considered in this chapter.

7 Voluntary codes of conduct

7.1 Governing for systemic change

Following the growth in CSR codes and standards, the financial industry has drafted its own suite of codes to promote SRI.[156] These codes may help coordinate, standardise, and facilitate responsible financing. This function may be especially valuable in moving SRI beyond its traditional emphasis on targeting discrete issues – such as tobacco, weapons, or apartheid – towards systemic, economy-wide concerns. In practice, however, SRI codes have yet to fulfil this aim. Major collective action problems in financial markets prevent social investors from cooperating to address these systemic concerns, such as the difficulty of controlling 'free-riders' in a competitive market, and the 'public good' characteristics of many environmental amenities, such as the global climate.

Mostly drafted by financial institutions, though sometimes involving governments or NGOs, the numbers of SRI codes have increased significantly. The codes are voluntary and not legally binding per se, and have attracted considerable interest from mainstream financial institutions.[157] Miles explains that 'voluntary codes for the financing sector are making a positive impact', including 'through the rejection or modification of environmentally damaging projects, the raising of environmental

---

[155] Barker, 'Ownership structure', 150.

[156] M.D. Berry, 'Frameworks for socially responsible investing', *Thomson Reuters*, 9 August 2013, available at: http://sustainability.thomsonreuters.com/2013/08/09/frameworks-for-socially-responsible-investing.

[157] B.J. Richardson, 'Financing sustainability: the new transnational governance of socially responsible investment' (2007) *Yearbook of International Environmental Law* 73.

FINANCIAL MARKETS AND SOCIALLY RESPONSIBLE INVESTING   259

awareness amongst the financing sector...and the harmonization of lending standards'.[158] On the other hand, drawbacks of the codes include lack of robust compliance controls and while they may target specific environmental concerns (e.g. climate change), specific actors (e.g. institutional investors) or methods of accountability (e.g. greater disclosure), the structural and systemic constraints that the financial economy imposes on sustainability are generally not strongly addressed.

The SRI codes span a range of methods, structures, and objectives that can be broadly categorised into two types, though a single instrument may combine both. First, there are normative frameworks that set out the substantive principles and guidance on desirable performance. They include the Collevecchio Declaration on Financial Institutions[159] and the UNPRI.[160] Process standards, enabling the assessment, verification, and communication of performance, constitute a second approach to governing the market. A key example is the Equator Principles.[161] Process standards do not dictate social and environmental outcomes, but rather establish a procedure such as environmental reporting that may spur improvements in signatories' performance.

Table 6.1 lists the principal SRI-related codes. Most entries were selected because they explicitly address the financial sector, while two examples – the Ceres Principles and the Sullivan Principles – have wider application to the business community. Apart from their voluntary nature, the most distinctive characteristic of these SRI codes is their *global* reach; most are intended as universal standards for an international market. Their broad scope contrasts with the patchwork intergovernmental regulation of financial markets.

These SRI codes are complemented by a plethora of voluntary standards for CSR and corporate governance that indirectly or implicitly affect the financial sector.[162] While financial institutions are not usually signatories to CSR codes, they may assist social investors by providing information about best practice standards in a particular industry sector, as well as insights into the behaviour of individual companies.

---

[158] K. Miles, 'Targeting financiers: can voluntary codes of conduct for the investment and financing sectors achieve environmental and sustainability objectives?' in K. Deketelaere, *et al.* (eds.), *Critical Issues in Environmental Taxation*, vol. 5 (Oxford University Press, 2008) 947, at 948.

[159] See www.foe.org/camps/intl/declaration.html.   [160] See www.unpri.org.

[161] See www.equator-principles.com/index.shtml.

[162] W. Cragg (ed.), *Ethics Codes, Corporations and the Challenge of Globalization* (Edward Elgar, 2005).

260 BENJAMIN J. RICHARDSON

Table 6.1 *Major SRI-related codes and standards*

Code	Principal sponsor
Carbon Disclosure Project, 2002	Rockefeller Philanthropy Advisors
Carbon Principles, 2008	Consortium of US banks
Climate Principles, 2008	Climate Group
Ceres Principles, 1989	Coalition for Environmentally Responsible Economies (Ceres)
Collevecchio Declaration on Financial Institutions, 2003	Coalition of nongovernmental organisations
Equator Principles, 2003	Consortium of multinational banks and the World Bank's International Finance Corporation
Eurosif Transparency Guidelines, 2004	European Social Investment Forum (Eurosif)
Global Sullivan Principles: 1977	Reverend Leon Sullivan
Green Bond Principles: Voluntary Process Guidelines for Issuing Green Bonds, 2014	Coalition for Environmentally Responsible Economies (Ceres)
Investor Network on Climate Risk Action Plan, 2003	Coalition for Environmentally Responsible Economies (Ceres)
London Principles of Sustainable Finance, 2002	UK Department of Environment and Corporation of London
Natural Capital Declaration, 2011	UNEP-FI, Global Canopy Programme, & Getulio Vargas Foundation
Principles for Responsible Agricultural Investment, 2014	United Nations Conference on Trade and Development and other UN bodies
Principles for Sustainable Insurance, 2012	UNEP-FI
UK Stewardship Code, 2010	UK Financial Reporting Council
UN Principles for Responsible Investment (UNPRI), 2005	United Nations
UNEP Statement by Financial Institutions on the Environment and Sustainable Development, 1997	UNEP-FI

FINANCIAL MARKETS AND SOCIALLY RESPONSIBLE INVESTING 261

The main potential advantages of SRI codes are their ability to coordinate action on common concerns, to facilitate the exchange of information and best practices, and build a network for peer pressure to minimise unscrupulous and unethical financing. Some codes have been heavily subscribed to; most notably, the UNPRI as of July 2014 boasted 1,270 signatories, including many large, mainstream financial institutions.[163] Yet, when it comes to influencing corporate behaviour – ultimately the most relevant indicator of success – evidence is less verifiable. The most successful demonstrated effect has been greater disclosure of corporate social and environmental performance, such as pursuant to the Carbon Disclosure Project (it enables social investors to better discriminate between corporate leaders and laggards on dealing with GHG emissions and to apply pressure accordingly). Transparency standards may also foster greater reflection and learning among participants about their practices and impacts, which in turn may stimulate positive behavioural changes.[164]

The most obvious barrier to the influence of these codes is their *voluntary* character.[165] Considerable literature has scrutinised the motivations and impact of corporate self-regulation, which does not need to be rehearsed in detail.[166] British Petroleum is a prime example of a company that, despite projecting a reputation as being 'green' – it was listed on the Dow Jones' Sustainability Index and a signatory to the UN Global Compact – was responsible for the Deepwater Horizon explosion in 2010 that spawned massive environmental and economic costs in the Gulf of Mexico, including damage to the company itself.[167]

Further, variations in the goals and tools of codes, and how they are drafted and more subsequently monitored, can lead to differences in their efficacy. Some SRI codes give signatories considerable discretion, while

---

[163] Listed at: www.unpri.org/signatories.

[164] A. Kolk, D. Levy, and J. Pinkse, 'Corporate responses in an emerging climate institutionalization and commensuration of carbon disclosure' (2008) 17(4) *European Accounting Review* 719.

[165] See I. Maitland, 'The limits of business self-regulation' (1995) 27(3) *California Management Review* 132.

[166] For example, J. Moon, 'The firm as citizen? Social responsibility of business in Australia' (1995) 30(1) *Australian Journal of Political Science* 1; R. Gibson (ed.), *Voluntary Initiatives: The New Politics of Corporate Greening* (Broadview Press, 1999); S. Wood, 'Voluntary environmental codes and sustainability', in B.J. Richardson and S. Wood (eds.), *Environmental Law for Sustainability* (Hart Publishing, 2006), 229.

[167] J. Balmer, 'The BP Deepwater Horizon débâcle and corporate brand exuberance' (2010) 18 *Journal of Brand Management* 97.

others are rather prescriptive. Some codes contain generic performance targets (e.g. to prevent or minimise adverse environmental impacts) while others are specific (e.g. to reduce GHG emissions by a specific quantity and in a specific time-frame). A good example of the more prescriptive approach is the Collevecchio Declaration, while the UNPRI reflects the more discretionary, open-ended approach. Yet, raising the performance has drawbacks; investors have shunned the Collevecchio Declaration, drafted by NGOs. Investors usually favour discretionary and procedural-based standards, such as self-reporting. While transparency measures can have beneficial effects, they probably will not induce major changes in investors' underlying goals, especially if there is no independent auditing and verification. Information on pollution or human rights violations must compete for attention in a crowded field with often seemingly more pressing and tangible concerns. Voluntary mechanisms also typically lack credible enforcement mechanisms, so compliance depends more on peer pressure, market discipline, or NGO scrutiny.

The ostensible voluntariness of SRI codes does not mean they are necessarily without legal implications. A code may be legally binding by virtue of contracts between participating institutions; a bank, for example, may include in its contract with a borrower a term that the parties adhere to the Equator Principles' provisions regarding environmental assessment. A code may also have consequences for regulatory compliance; Denmark's *Financial Statements Act* provides that an investment institution's requirement to report annually on its sustainability performance may choose to refrain from doing so if it has submitted a progress report in connection with its accession to the UNPRI.[168] The legal consequences may depend somewhat on the degree of specificity of a code's provisions; some contain brief aspirational declarations, as in the London Principles of Sustainable Finance, while others posit highly specific operational rules and performance indicators, such as the Collevecchio Declaration. The significance of such differences is that the less-specific codes may not be self-executing without additional effort to define their working requirements. Another variable is the governance function performed by codes. A variety of such functions may be fulfilled by SRI codes, such as agenda-setting, rule making, including setting targets, administration (such as facilitating exchange of information and verification of

---

[168] Act amending the Danish Financial Statements Act ('Årsregnskabsloven'), 8 October 2008. s. 99a(7).

FINANCIAL MARKETS AND SOCIALLY RESPONSIBLE INVESTING 263

compliance), and dispute settlement.[169] Typically, most codes straddle several of these regulatory functions rather than performing merely one.

The most successful codes – though it is empirically hard to quantify their effect – appear to possess two attributes: (1) they were drafted through a multi-stakeholder process; and (2) they are embedded in a wider institutional regime for on-going dialogue, education, and monitoring. These forms of 'civic regulation', as some commentators describe them, provide frameworks for business and non-profit NGOs to work collaboratively together.[170] The UNEP-FI regime perhaps best exemplifies these traits, and it has garnered considerable support from many investors.[171] Research by John Conley and Cynthia Williams on the Equator Principles, which apply to project financing, suggests they have generally had a positive influence in changing the culture of lenders, and they identify the presence of NGO watchdogs as instrumental in making the Principles function well.[172]

The following sections examine in more detail two examples – the Equator Principles and the UNPRI – that provide contrasting examples of the different approaches found in SRI codes. The Equator Principles apply to bank lending, whereas the UNPRI apply to institutional investors. Also, these examples are highlighted because of their widespread support in the financial community, and thus one might presume therefore that they are relatively more influential.

7.2   The Equator Principles

The leading SRI code for banks is the Equator Principles (EPs), which provide lenders with a framework to manage the social and environmental impacts associated with projects seeking finance, such as dams, factories, and mines.[173] Formulated by the banking industry under the auspices of the World Bank's International Finance Corporation (IFC), the EPs target

---

[169] See M. Priest, 'Five models of self-regulation' (1997–98) 29 *Ottawa Law Review* 233, at 239.

[170] D.J. Vogel, 'Private global business regulation' (2008) 11 *Annual Review of Political Science* 261.

[171] UNEP-FI: available at: www.unepfi.org.

[172] J. Conley and C. Williams, 'Global banks as global sustainability regulators? The Equator Principles' (2011) 33(4) *Law and Policy* 542.

[173] T. O'Riordan, 'Converting the Equator Principles to equator stewardship' (2005) 47(4) *Environment* 1.

264 BENJAMIN J. RICHARDSON

commercial lending, especially in emerging economies where competent environmental regulation may be absent. Motivated to avoid both public criticisms that they supported controversial projects and the loss of business to unscrupulous lenders, a cohort of banks sought to level the playing field for project financing by drafting the Principles.[174] Involving the IFC, the World Bank's private-sector lending arm, boosted the credibility of the EPs.

The EPs are not entirely self-contained standards, but incorporate references to the IFC's Safeguard Policies for social and environmental impact assessment (SEIA), forestry, dam safety, indigenous peoples, and other topics. The EPs were released in June 2003,[175] and revised in July 2006,[176] and again in June 2013.[177] In July 2010, a set of governance rules were formally adopted, introducing integrity measures to improve implementation of the EPs, and establishing the Equator Principles Association, comprised of representatives of member signatories.[178] All signatories pledge to provide loans only to borrowers who conform to the Principles. The EPs apply to projects with a total capital cost of at least US$10 million (US$50 million before the 2006 revisions). They require lenders to rate projects they plan to finance, based on the magnitude of potential impacts and risks in accordance with the screening criteria of the IFC.[179] These criteria categorise projects as A, B, or C (high, medium, and low), depending on their potential environmental and social impacts. A or B project borrowers must undertake a SEIA based on IFC standards to address the issues identified in the screening process. Project financing banks must also prepare an Environmental and Social Action Plan and an accompanying Environmental and Social Management System based on the conclusions of the SEIA.[180] For category C projects, no further assessment is required beyond the initial screening.

Financiers of category A and B projects must also ensure that the borrower has consulted with affected local communities 'in a structured

---

[174] N. Affolder, 'Cachet not cash: another sort of World Bank Group borrowing' (2006) 14 *Michigan State Journal of International Law* 156.

[175] See www.equator-principles.com.

[176] See E. Morgera, 'Significant trends in corporate environmental accountability: the new performance standards of the international finance corporation' (2007) 18 *Colorado Journal of International Environmental Law and Policy* 151.

[177] See www.equator-principles.com/index.php/ep3. The latest consolidated version of the EPs is available at: The Equator Principles (June 2013), available at: www.equator-principles.com/resources/equator‘principles‘III.pdf.

[178] Equator Principles Association, *Governance Rules* (July 2010).

[179] Principle 1.   [180] Principle 4.

and culturally appropriate manner'.[181] This requirement was extended by the 2013 revisions to the EPs to provide additional protection for indigenous peoples with the requirement that 'projects with adverse impacts on indigenous peoples will require their Free, Prior and Informed Consent'.[182] Furthermore, proponents must make the SEIA report and Action Plan available in a local language for public comment and for independent expert review.[183] Financiers must include a 'grievance mechanism' to hear complaints 'by individuals or groups from among project-affected communities'.[184] And prior to drawing on the loan, the borrower must covenant with the lender to implement an environmental management plan and to monitor any impacts.[185]

Given that the banking sector drafted the EPs, the high number of signatories among global banks is unsurprising. As of August 2014, 80 banks and related financial institutions in 34 countries, accounting for about over 95 per cent of the global project financing market, had endorsed the EPs.[186] Most signatories are North American or Western European lenders, especially large banks with international operations.[187] As early as 2005, two years after the EPs were adopted, a study by the British law firm Freshfields Bruckhaus Deringer rejoiced that the Principles' 'impact on the financial market generally and their success in redefining banking considerations has been far greater than anyone could have predicted'.[188] Through common standards and procedures for timely and more granular risk assessment, the EPs have helped signatory banks to minimise the reputational risks associated with development projects, and offered public relations benefits to deflect NGOs' scrutiny.[189]

The 2006 and 2013 revisions to the EPs have ostensibly improved their accountability, transparency, and enforceability, though potentially some weaknesses remain.[190] A lender's categorisation of a project or the scope of an SEIA or management plan cannot readily be challenged. The categorisation of a project crucially influences the types of environmental

---

[181] Principle 5.   [182] Principle 5.   [183] Principle 7.
[184] Principle 6.   [185] Principle 8.
[186] Equator Principles, *Members and Reporting*, available at: www.equator-principles.com/index.php/members-reporting/members-and-reporting.
[187] P. Kulkarni, 'Pushing lenders to over-comply with environmental regulations: a developing country perspective' (2010) 22(4) *Journal of International Development* 470.
[188] Freshfields Bruckhaus Deringer (FBD), *Banking on Responsibility* (FBD, 2005), 1.
[189] See D. Schepers, 'The impact of NGO network conflict on the corporate social responsibility strategies of multinational corporations' (2006) 45(3) *Business and Society* 282.
[190] B. Baue, 'Revised Equator Principles fall short of international best practice for project finance', *SocialFunds.com*, 2 July 2006.

standards and procedures that subsequently apply. Further, while affected groups may publicly comment on a SEIA or a proposed management plan, they cannot legally challenge their adequacy, except perhaps in the case of indigenous peoples where the EPs contain more emphatic language on the requirement to observe national and global legal standards. The 2013 revisions brought further improvements to the EPs, including: to widen the application of the code to other forms of banking finance, including bridging loans and project-related corporate loans; to improve public reporting incorporating implementation of the EPs and making available online the social and environmental assessment summary and specific reporting on GHG emissions for major polluting projects; and the assessment process to give more attention to climate change and human rights due diligence, and in some cases to apply the principle of 'free prior informed consent' to allow local communities to reject a proposed project.

Implementation of the EPs had received mixed reviews prior to the 2013 revisions. BankTrack, an umbrella organisation of NGOs pooling their advocacy on financial issues, has found various lapses.[191] Conversely, a report by Freshfields suggested, more optimistically, that the Principles have led some Equator banks 'into more structured dialogue with stakeholders and NGOs about social and environmental aspects of their lending'.[192] Several international project financing deals have tested the credibility of the EPs. These include the Baku–Tbilisi–Ceyhan pipeline project, to bring Caspian Sea oil to Western Europe,[193] the Sakhalin-II oil and gas project in Eastern Russia,[194] and the Uruguayan pulp mills, bordering Uruguay and Argentina.[195] The latter project, financed by Calyon and other lenders, has been particularly controversial, leading to litigation between these states in the International Court of Justice.[196] On the other hand, the ANZ Bank, another EPs signatory, rejected an environmentally

[191] M. Chan-Fishel, *Unproven Principles: The Equator Principles at Year Two* (BankTrack, 2005).
[192] Freshfields, *Banking on Responsibility*, 10.
[193] BankTrack, *Principles, Profit or Just PR?* (BankTrack, 2004).
[194] M. Bradshaw, 'The "greening" of global project financing: the case of the Sakhalin-II offshore oil and gas project' (2009) 51(3) *Canadian Geographer* 255.
[195] V. Lee, 'Enforcing the Equator Principles: an NGO's principled efforts to stop the financing of a paper pulp mill in Uruguay' (2008) 6(2) *Northwestern Journal of International Human Rights Law*, available at: http://scholarlycommons.law.northwestern.edu/cgi/viewcontent .cgi?article=1077&context=njihr.
[196] Pulp Mills on the River Uruguay (Argentina v. Uruguay), ICJ, 13 July 2006; (2006) 45 ILM, 1025.

controversial pulp mill in Tasmania, as discussed earlier in this chapter. Even financiers (or their clients) with good intentions may encounter difficulties implementing the EPs, given the cited deficiencies in their environmental and social expertise, which may lead to their not being able to identify risks to biodiversity or local communities in a timely or comprehensive manner.[197]

7.3   The UN Principles for Responsible Investment (UNPRI)

The UN Principles for Responsible Investment (UNPRI) have become the most prestigious and widely endorsed voluntary code for SRI, though its architects and signatories tend to see the Principles as a statement of good investing practice rather than a tool for 'social' change. Designed primarily for institutional ('universal') investors, the Principles were developed by the investment community under the auspices of the UN through its UNEP-FI and UN Global Compact initiatives. While a multi-stakeholder working group with representatives from environmental NGOs, academia, and other non-commercial stakeholders was consulted when preparing the Principles, the financial sector was the most influential voice. The present governance of the UNPRI includes the Advisory Council of 11 elected representatives from investor signatory organisations and two representatives from the UN. Day-to-day operations are managed by the UNPRI Secretariat, which is financed by fees paid by signatories, of which there were 1,270 in July 2014.

The UNPRI combine process and performance standards in their six brief clauses and supplementary guidance on 'possible actions'. The expectations are broadly defined and do not provide yardsticks to which investors could easily be held measurably accountable. To illustrate, Principle 1 vaguely declares: 'We will incorporate environmental, social and corporate governance (ESG) issues into investment analysis and decision-making processes.' More helpful as an educative tool is the supplementary guidance; for example, for the second principle on active shareholding, the suggested actions include to 'exercise voting rights', 'develop an engagement capability', and 'file shareholder resolutions consistent with long-term ESG considerations'. Through such actions, the UNPRI secretariat sees several benefits:

---

[197] E. Hamman, 'The finance sector's role in environmental transgressions', paper presented at Environmental Finance Symposium, Macquarie University, 25 July 2014.

> While these Principles are designed to enhance the delivery of long-term returns to clients and beneficiaries, their implementation will also focus greater attention on ESG issues throughout the investment and corporate sectors... The PRI will also stimulate increased active ownership on ESG issues by investors... In this way, the Principles for Responsible Investment will contribute to improved corporate performance on environmental, social and governance issues.[198]

The UNPRI have been highly successful in improving awareness of SRI and creating peer pressure on investors to at least outwardly profess support for change. But the UNPRI is very much reformist rather than revolutionary. Among the list of possible actions for the first principle, there is no stated expectation that investors will actually incorporate ESG factors into their ultimate portfolio choices; the principle focuses on 'investment analysis' and 'decision-making processes', but does not ensure that final decisions achieve specific targets, such as avoiding financing carbon-intensive developments. The Principles do not require a signatory to demonstrate any particular performance standards with regard to human rights or environmental protection. The UNPRI do not refer to divestment; rather, active engagement, shareholder resolutions, ESG analysis, and reporting are proposed as methods of SRI. However, nothing is said about the eventual outcome of these actions and what should be done if they are ineffectual. Another lacuna is that the second principle on active ownership focuses on participation in investee companies, but ignores the need to democratise decision-making within financial institutions. Nor do the UNPRI insist on any independent audit or verification mechanism to assess the quality of signatories' implementation, though since 2013 they must publicly report on aspects (but not all) of their implementation of the Principles.[199] The UNPRI Secretariat reassures investors that: 'There are no legal or regulatory sanctions associated with the Principles. They are designed to be voluntary and aspirational... a direction to head in rather than a prescriptive checklist with which to comply.'[200] Finally, in addition to voluntary compliance, the UNPRI caution that 'investors publicly commit to adopt and implement them, *where consistent with our fiduciary responsibilities*.[201] Thus, any regard to ESG factors is potentially severely constrained by the fiduciary legal duties of institutional investors.

---

[198] UNPRI, available at: www.unpri.org/about-pri/faqs.
[199] UNPRI, 'Reporting framework', available at: www.unpri.org/areas-of-work/reporting-and-assessment/reporting-framework.
[200] UNPRI, 'Frequently asked questions': available at: www.unpri.org/faqs.
[201] UNRPI, available at: www.unpri.org/principles (emphasis added).

8 Public policy and legal reforms

This book emphasises the importance of the legal architecture of companies to enable sustainable business practices. So, too, some social investors have recognised this message in strategising how to exert influence. Regulation can help overcome the limitations of voluntary approaches. Once self-regarded as an alternative to such regulation, the SRI movement is starting to concede the need for government help, such as reforms to corporate governance to facilitate shareholder activism, and corporate environmental reporting standards to enable investors to track firms' sustainability performance.[202] In regard to climate finance, carbon taxes or cap-and-trade schemes can help price emissions for the benefit of investors.[203] Recognition of the importance of this means of SRI echoes David Vogel's advice that the definition of CSR must be expanded to include not only what companies do voluntarily but also the position the company takes with respect to public policy.[204] If business opposes expansions of public authority that would strengthen industry-based responsibility, can they really be considered 'socially responsible'?

Efforts to target regulators have focused on the legal infrastructure governing companies rather than those for investors. In Australia, several banks made submissions to the federal government's Garnaut Review in 2010 about the proposed carbon emission trading scheme, and some such as Westpac have advocated the scheme to ensure an efficient carbon-pricing mechanism.[205] In Canada, the Responsible Investment Association (formerly called the Social Investment Organisation), which represents the country's SRI industry, and the Shareholder Association of Research and Education (SHARE) have lobbied the provincial and federal governments for reform, campaigning particularly for greater disclosure of SRI policies by pension funds.[206] Earlier, in 2001, these bodies and other Canadian SRI groups successfully lobbied for revisions to the *Canadian*

---

[202] Richardson, *Socially Responsible Investment Law*, 303–75; T. Hebb and D. Wójcik, 'Global standards and emerging markets: the institutional investment value chain and CalPERS' investment strategy' (2005) 37(11) *Environment and Planning* 1955, at 1971.

[203] See S. Labatt and R. White, *Carbon Finance: The Financial Implications of Climate Change* (John Wiley & Sons, Ltd, 2007).

[204] D. Vogel, *The Market for Virtue: The Potential and Limits of Corporate Social Responsibility* (Brookings Institution Press, 2005).

[205] Bowman, 'Role of the banking industry', 463.

[206] See L. O'Neil, *Pension Fund Investment and Disclosure: Acknowledging Environmental, Social and Governance Considerations. Submission to the Federal Department of Finance, Financial Sector Division* (SHARE, 2009).

Business Corporations Act to reduce barriers to the filing of shareholder proposals on SRI issues.[207] In the USA, major public sector pension funds such as CalPERS in early 2010 successfully petitioned the SEC to oblige listed companies to disclose the way climate change investment risks affected their business.[208] Not only are social investors targeting national regulators, they also occasionally lobby international standard-setters. Canada's NEI Investments (also known as Ethical Funds), in March 2012, wrote to the Office of the High Commissioner for Human Rights in response to the call for input for the UN Secretary-General's report on implementation of the Ruggie Guiding Principles on business and human rights throughout the UN system.[209] NEI asked that the concept of fiduciary duty be added to the list of influential areas of policy and business law that require review with a human rights lens. Not all such efforts, however, are successful; one example was the UK Social Investment Forum's (UKSIF) proposal to amend the *Financial Services and Markets Act* 2000 to include the provision of environmental financing within the Financial Services Authority's mandate.[210]

Shareholder campaigns are one means by which social investors sometimes undertake strategies to achieve changes, not only at the company level, but also at the policy or regulatory level. Macleod and Park describe collaboration among institutional shareholders on issues such as climate change as 'investor-driven governance networks'.[211] One quite successful example from the USA, focusing on environmental issues, was organised by Ceres (Coalition for Environmentally Responsible Economies) to address climate change. The Ceres' climate campaign highlighted the significant risks to shareholders from global warming in four areas: litigation, regulation, physical damage, and reputation impacts. Among its

---

[207] M.R MacLeod, *Forging Private Governance of Climate Change: The Power and Politics of Socially Responsible Investment*, PhD dissertation (Columbian College of Arts and Sciences, George Washington University, 2008), 148.

[208] SEC, 'SEC issues interpretive guidance on disclosure related to business or legal developments regarding climate change' (27 January 2010), available at: http://sec.gov/news/press/2010/2010-15.htm.

[209] Submission from NEI, 26 March 2012, available at: www.neiinvestments.com/neifiles/PDFs/5.5%20Public%20Policy%20and%20Standards/Business%20and%20Human%20Rights%20Framework%20Implementation%20UN%20System.pdf.

[210] UKSIF, 'UK Social Investment Forum tells MPs of need to include environment in framework for financial services regulator', Press release, 19 April 1999.

[211] M. Macleod and J. Park, 'Financial activism and global climate change: the rise of investor-driven governance network' (2011) 11(2) *Global Environmental Politics* 54.

FINANCIAL MARKETS AND SOCIALLY RESPONSIBLE INVESTING 271

strategies, Ceres coordinates the filing of shareholder resolutions, and net-works and engages with targeted companies, institutional investors, and government policy-makers.[212] In her analysis of the Ceres' climate cam-paign, and other examples, Cook reveals 'that resolution filing with broad investor appeal and linked to a policy agenda can achieve change beyond targeted companies'.[213] The impact on the policy agenda arose because 'management is forced to publicly defend its position when activists use the SEC-mediated proxy process'.[214] Shareholder resolutions published in proxy materials become part of the public record and the issues con-tained therein are brought to the attention of securities regulators. Con-comitantly, their impact on the policy agenda can be amplified when shareholder activists use other channels of influence including 'participa-tion on policy committees, meetings with politicians and regulators and the production of research with policy implications'.[215]

The Ceres' campaign concentrated on reform of SEC's disclosure regu-lations. With support from major public pension funds such as CalPERS, the campaign petitioned over 2007–2009 the SEC to oblige public com-panies to disclose the way climate change might affect their shareholders' investments.[216] In January 2010, the SEC responded favourably by releas-ing new interpretative guidance on existing SEC disclosure regulations relating to climate change.[217] This guidance was a major step towards reg-ulators recognising the materiality of climate disclosures, and strengthens the prospects for litigation to request climate risk information from public companies that do not adequately disclose.[218]

While the SRI industry is sometimes willing to advocate such reform, the financial industry more generally is not. In 1996, the American bank-ing industry successfully lobbied Congress to amend the Superfund leg-islation to immunise itself from lender liability suits for the costs of remediating contaminated lands.[219] Also, the mutual fund industry in

---

[212] Cook, 'Political action', 34–5.   [213] Cook, 'Political action', 26.
[214] Cook, 'Political action', 29.   [215] Cook, 'Political action', 30.
[216] L. Riddell, 'Pension funds throw green weight around', *Carbon Insider*, 16 July 2008, available at: http://carboninsider.com/?p=25.
[217] SEC, 'SEC issues interpretive guidance on disclosure related to business or legal develop-ments regarding climate change', SEC, 27 January 2010.
[218] G. Erion, The stock market to the rescue? Carbon disclosure and the future of securities-related climate change litigation' (2009) 18(2) *Review of European Community and Inter-national Environmental Law* 164.
[219] Asset Conservation, Lender Liability and Deposit Insurance Protection Act 1996, ss. 2501–04.

North America fiercely resisted new securities regulations in the mid-2000s to make it disclose how fund managers vote shares belonging to their beneficiaries.[220] This helps explain why legal reforms to promote SRI that have emerged in some countries since 2000 have generally just tinkered with the underlying problems of the financial economy that hinder sustainability. The reforms have concentrated on market-based and informational tools that alter the procedures of SRI decision-making, without seriously facilitating or obliging SRI. Any more ambitious reforms have been reserved for public financial institutions, such as mandating sovereign wealth funds to avoid unethical investments.

9 Conclusion

SRI both impeaches and challenges financial markets. It indicts long-standing investment practices for impairing ecological health, while also presenting an opportunity to reform those practices to respect environmental and social values essential to the long-term health of the economy. But, at present, any claims that an SRI revolution is under way are exaggerated. The institutional and economic barriers to the SRI market remain entrenched, and core legal standards to which financiers are held to account remain largely unaltered. Most financial institutions' behaviour remains unchanged, and any evaluation of environmental impact, even by avowed social investors, tends to be made narrowly in terms of financial advantage. The enormity of the challenge requires, fundamentally, 'a financial paradigm shift towards a broad sense of sustainability'.[221]

The final chapter of this book, Chapter 8, will touch on some possible legal reforms to promote sustainable companies, and some of these proposals relate to the financial economy and measures to facilitate SRI. It is therefore not necessary to conclude this chapter by duplicating those comments about how to improve conditions for SRI. An extensive literature has also emerged in the wake of the GFC, offering ideas to address the systemic weaknesses of the financial economy.[222] While many of these proposals are persuasive, such as improved transparency of financial transactions, enhanced capital reserves to buffer against market

---

[220] Davis, et al., The New Capitalists, 73.

[221] Sun, et al., 'Finance and sustainability', 3, 14.

[222] For example, R.W. Kolb (ed.), Lessons from the Financial Crisis: Causes, Consequences, and Our Economic Future (John Wiley & Sons, Ltd, 2010); K. Davis, Regulatory Reform Post the Global Financial Crisis: An Overview (Australian Centre for Financial Studies, 2011).

instabilities, and more intensive supervision of financial markets, they do not directly address the environmental impacts of the financial sector and its hindrance to creating sustainable companies.

More ambitious reforms that we might contemplate, such as mandatory SRI duties and the democratisation of fund governance, may seem far-fetched, but with the biosphere slipping into a crisis, even more seemingly draconian alternatives may one day be contemplated, if the financial sector is not disciplined now to be more environmentally responsible. These are not challenges unique to any country, and are of global importance requiring solutions at both the national and international levels. Until then, SRI will likely remain a modest, niche sector of the financial economy, only occasionally influencing the environmental practices of companies.

7

Limits to corporate reform and alternative legal structures

CAROL LIAO

1 Introduction

An ongoing environmental crisis, an imperative to strengthen the social economy, and an escalating demand for greater worldwide sustainability have pushed financially beleaguered states to their limits. Now more than ever, there is a pressing need to reap the benefits of sustainable governance from the private sector. The growth of corporate social responsibility (CSR) over the past several decades has been effective in tempering some of the negative externalities that arise under the shareholder primacy model of governance. The period when CSR only referred to corporate philanthropic donations has long passed. Contemporary CSR is intimately intertwined with the 'Green' movement, and sustainability is an 'emerging megatrend' that may soon 'force fundamental and persistent shifts in how companies compete'.[1] The cross-sector expansion of CSR is growing increasingly apparent on the global stage.

Nevertheless, while developments in the CSR movement are worthwhile and efforts to reform the shareholder primacy model must continue, there are certain ideological and practical limitations that make true reformation of this model difficult. Empirical studies have shown that CSR trends have been consistent with theories of strategic CSR and rational, profit-seeking management decision-making.[2] 'Greenwashing' – where companies spend significantly more time and money on green advertising rather than on environmentally sound practices – is a real

---

[1] D.A. Lubin and D.C. Esty, 'The sustainability imperative' (May 2010) *Harvard Business Review* 2 at 2.

[2] See e.g. D. Siegel and D. Vitaliano, 'An empirical analysis of the strategic use of corporate social responsibility' (2007) 16 *Journal of Economic and Management Strategy* 773; R. Fisman, G. Heal, and V. Nair, *A Model of Corporate Philanthropy*, Working Paper (Columbia Business School, 2007).

concern. The pure economic incentives driving much CSR mean sustainable practices automatically lose out when those practices do not dovetail with the financial bottom line. There are legitimate fears that CSR may just become another commodity that businesses sell in the service of short-term shareholder wealth maximisation, rather than serving as a catalyst for achieving substantive change.

It is important, therefore, that in the midst of ongoing reform efforts, one does not lose sight of available alternatives. The cooperative model, for example, is the oldest corporate structure in history, but on the topic of corporate reform, it seems to operate in separate circles of discussion. This is despite the fact that the cooperative has been recognised by the United Nations (UN) as playing a critical role in economic development and social innovation throughout the world.[3] In addition, a new breed of alternative legal structures is emerging. These corporate structures – commonly called 'hybrids'[4] – blend traditional for-profit and non-profit legal characteristics in their design to support sustainable and community-oriented practices beyond the traditional parameters of the for-profit company. Governance features within these hybrids not only enable, but require, CSR concepts to be embodied within corporate practices. The development of corporate hybridity is signalling a new wave of reform in the CSR movement. While the topic of CSR has become prevalent in academic scholarship, the role of corporate law in necessitating CSR practices has been limited. The growth of the 'social enterprise', a term with no legal import and a variety of meanings across for-profit and non-profit sectors, is beginning to generate a legislative response. Hybrids may be a key contributor in establishing the critical infrastructure to help solve some of the most pressing social and environmental issues of our time.

This chapter continues in Section 2 by addressing some of the formidable barriers facing reformation of the shareholder primacy model. The section will not delve into long-standing arguments for and against shareholder primacy, which are canvassed adequately in other chapters of this book. Instead, the section will highlight factors that, regardless of the validity of one's theoretical arguments for or against shareholder

[3] United Nations, 'International year of cooperatives', available at: http://social.un.org/coopsyear.
[4] Also known as 'blended enterprises', see e.g. D. Brakman Reiser, 'Governing and financing blended enterprise' (2010) 85 *Chicago-Kent Law Review* 619.

276   CAROL LIAO

primacy, perpetuate the continued domination of this mainstream model. These factors include entrenched ideological beliefs that have permeated the psyche of corporate governance practices in global capital markets and path dependence. The reasoning leads one to conclude that those seeking transformative change should consider innovative new avenues to supplement the pathway to true corporate reform. Section 3 provides a closer look at the cooperative as an existing alternative to the mainstream model, and how this structure has played an integral role in the growth and development of some local communities throughout the world. The remainder of the chapter is dedicated to exploring a new generation of corporate hybrid alternatives that have appeared in the last decade in the UK, Canada, and the USA. Section 4 explores some of the main types of hybrids, examining the governance features that are attempting to support the space between the for-profit and non-profit arenas, the reasons behind these features, the main challenges these models face, and the potential advantage. The chapter concludes by suggesting that more effort is needed to foster the growth and development of alternative legal models. Increased research and analysis, particularly economic analysis, are necessary and may spell the difference between the success and failure of hybrids in the pursuit of long-term sustainable development.

2   Limitations to reforming the for-profit corporation

For as long as the concept of shareholder primacy has existed in legal scholarship, a great deal of research has been dedicated to critiquing many features inherent in the model.[5] With such an earnest desire to reform the existing model, why does it continue to thrive? The following discussion suggests that the resilience of the model depends not so much on the truth behind its advocates' arguments, but whether beliefs supporting the model are widely held and ideologically entrenched. Moreover, path dependence almost assures the continued dominance of shareholder primacy for the foreseeable future.

---

[5] See e.g. J. Bakan, *The Corporation: The Pathological Pursuit of Profit and Power* (Free Press, 2004) (and the subsequent film documentary of the same name); K. Greenfield, *The Failure of Corporate Law: Fundamental Flaws and Progressive Possibilities* (University of Chicago Press, 2006); L. Stout, *The Shareholder Value Myth: How Putting Shareholders First Hurts Investors Corporations and the Public* (Berrett Koehler Press, 2012).

LIMITS TO CORPORATE REFORM AND ALTERNATIVE STRUCTURES 277

2.1 Entrenched ideological beliefs

2.1.1 Shareholder wealth maximisation benefits society

One reason for shareholder primacy's dominance is the common belief that the fundamental purpose of the corporation should be to maximise the wealth of its shareholders, which in turn will increase the wealth of society. This dogma has been at the core of modern economics since Adam Smith's *An Inquiry into the Nature and Causes of the Wealth of Nations*, where he famously opined: 'It is not from the benevolence of the butcher, the brewer, or the baker, that we expect our dinner, but from their regard to their own interest.'[6] Smith's concept of the 'invisible hand' has resonated within the theoretical underpinnings of corporate law for some time now. It postulates that shareholders have powerful incentives to maximise the value of the firm and monitor corporate directors' and officers' conduct. Managers, as shareholders' agents, seek to maximise shareholders' wealth through the increase of share value and dividend payments, which presumably includes ensuring that stakeholders are appeased[7] and ultimately this translates into benefits to consumers and society as a whole. Advocates of shareholder primacy may point to improved consumer products and innovative research and development as some examples of societal benefits that are realised through the competitive drive for increased profit.[8] On the other hand, counterarguments have been made that expenditures such as research and development are vulnerable to cuts due to short-termism under the model.[9]

---

[6] A. Smith, 'An inquiry into the nature and causes of the wealth of nations' (1776) 1 *Eighteenth Century Collections Online* 1.1.2.

[7] See e.g. R. Kraakman, *et al.*, *The Anatomy of Corporate Law: A Comparative and Functional Approach*, 2nd edn (Oxford University Press, 2009), 61–6.

[8] See e.g. C. Elson, 'Five reasons to support shareholder primacy', NACD Directorship Blog, 15 April 2010, available at: www.nacdonline.org/Magazine/Article.cfm?ItemNumber=9187; see also A. Loten, 'Can firms aim to do good if it hurts profit?' *The Wall Street Journal*, 11 April 2013, B6, quoting Elson: 'It's politically correct to suggest that a company benefit the public rather than its investors. But investors are the public.'

[9] See e.g. B. Sjåfjell, *Towards a Sustainable European Company Law* (Kluwer Law International, 2009), 339–40, where she discusses the argument whether takeover concerns lead boards to 'focus excessively on the short term and share price, leading . . . to insufficient resources being allocated to research and development', and cites inconclusive results found in W.N. Pugh and J.S. Jahera Jr, 'State antitakeover legislation and firm financial policy' (1997) 18 *Managerial and Decision Economics* 681; B.H. Hall, 'The effect of takeover activity on corporate research and development', in A.J. Auerbach (ed.), *Corporate Takeovers: Causes and Consequences* (University of Chicago Press, 1988), 69 at n. 113; see also L. Stout, 'The problem of corporate purpose' (June 2012) 42 *Issues in Governance Studies* 1 at 11.

Many regard the singular pursuit of shareholder wealth maximisation as necessary for the efficient management of the corporation. Michael Jensen declares: '[I]t is logically impossible to maximise in more than one dimension at the same time... The result will be confusion and a lack of purpose that will handicap the firm in its competition for survival.'[10] He echoes Smith's concept, insisting that '200 years' worth of work in economics and finance indicate that social welfare is maximised when all firms in an economy attempt to maximise their own total firm value.'[11] Others, such as Henry Hansmann and Reinier Kraakman, believe stakeholders are sufficiently protected by contract law and regulation, thus 'the maximization of the firm's value by its shareholders complements the interests of those other participants rather than competing with them'.[12]

The underlying force behind the presumption is economic efficiency. Christopher Nicholls has observed that '[t]he shareholder primacy norm is much beloved by law and economics scholars, financial economists, and dogmatic conservatives generally'.[13] Hansmann and Kraakman identify profit maximisation, historical success, and international competitive advantage as factors that 'made the virtues of [the shareholder primacy] model increasingly salient'.[14] They have pointed to the standard model's many notable economic advantages, some of which they list as 'access to equity capital at lower cost (including, conspicuously, start-up capital), more aggressive development of new product markets... and more rapid abandonment of inefficient investments'.[15] Daniel Fischel notes that the public company 'is a type of firm that facilitates the organisation of production which is particularly effective when a large amount of capital is required'.[16] Common concerns surrounding efficiency and wealth maximisation typically relate to agency costs associated with divergent objectives between managers and shareholders and reducing those costs,

[10] M. Jensen, 'Value maximization, stakeholder theory, and the corporate objective function' (2001) 14 *Journal of Applied Corporate Finance* 8 at 10–11.

[11] Jensen, 'Value maximization', 11.

[12] H. Hansmann and R. Kraakman, 'The end of history for corporate law' (2001) 89(2) *Georgetown Law Journal* 439 at 449.

[13] C.C. Nicholls, 'Governance, mergers and acquisitions, and global capital markets', in J. Sarra (ed.), *Corporate Governance in Global Capital Markets* (UBC Press, 2003), 90.

[14] Hansmann and Kraakman, 'End of history', 449.

[15] Hansmann and Kraakman, 'End of history', 450–1.

[16] D.R. Fischel, 'The corporate governance movement' (1982) 35 *Vanderbilt Law Review* 1259 at 1262.

LIMITS TO CORPORATE REFORM AND ALTERNATIVE STRUCTURES 279

not whether the model itself is efficient.[17] Efficiency according to the shareholder primacy model is largely accepted as a norm within scholarly articles; improving efficiency according to the model has been the preferred focus. Consequently, the broader question about whether the ultimate purpose of such 'efficient' business activity is socially valuable and environmentally sustainable is hardly considered.

The convenience of calculating efficiency based on the normative view of shareholder wealth vis-à-vis share price is that it 'frequently externalizes particular costs of corporate activity such as environmental or consumer harms'.[18] Thus, corporations may choose to be unhampered by externalities such as social and environmental consequences, and allow others to bear the external costs that are not reflected in share or bond prices. Corporations are then only beholden to externalities that are regarded as serious enough to be protected (and adequately enforced) by external regulatory means, without having to comprehend the negative impact their collective actions have on the environment beyond those regulations.[19] The ability of corporations to ignore these negative effects simplifies questions of accountability and corporate purpose, providing a unified and measurable way to calculate success in the pursuit of corporate objectives without complicating factors of difficult-to-measure externalities, which perpetuate the continuance of the model.[20]

2.1.2 Stakeholder interests adequately protected by the law and through market forces

The singular objective of shareholder wealth maximisation does not necessarily mean that non-shareholder stakeholders are ignored in the

---

[17] See e.g. E.F. Fama and M.C. Jensen, 'Separation of ownership and control' (1983) 26 *Journal of Law and Economics* 301; M.C. Jensen and W.H. Meckling, 'Theory of the firm: managerial behavior, agency costs and ownership structure' (1976) 3 *Journal of Financial Economics* 305.

[18] J. Sarra, 'Oversight, hindsight, and foresight: Canadian corporate governance through the lens of global capital markets', in J. Sarra (ed.), *Corporate Governance in Global Capital Markets* (UBC Press, 2003), 41.

[19] In fact, the most severe environmental consequences are often regarded as a *force majeure* and are unprotected by the law. There have also been movements in EU law attempting to counteract negative externalities. See e.g. Directive 2002/96/EC, O.J. 2002 (L 27/24–39) (regarding waste electrical and electronic equipment).

[20] For a detailed discussion of the issues related to the internalisation of externalities, such as costs associated with negative environmental effects, see B. Sjåfjell, 'Internalizing externalities in EU law: why neither corporate governance nor corporate social responsibility provides the answers' (2008) 40 *George Washington International Law Review* 977 at 987–1007.

280   CAROL LIAO

process of corporate decision-making. Rather, for many proponents, it means that stakeholder interests are important to consider, but only in the context of pursuing increased shareholder wealth. A cognate perspective is that stakeholder interests are best protected through separate public regulation, such as pollution control legislation, labour regulation, and human rights standards, rather than through corporations that supposedly tend to lack the expertise, resources, or legitimacy to address such problems.

The rise of business models specifically addressing stakeholder interests came to the forefront in the mid 1980s, though some have attributed it to earlier beginnings.[21] The motivation behind stakeholder management was to build a framework that was responsive to the concerns of managers who were experiencing a business environment 'buffeted by unprecedented levels of environmental turbulence and change'.[22] A stakeholder approach sought to broaden the concept of strategic management beyond its traditional economic origins. The definition of a stakeholder includes 'any group or individual who is affected by or can affect the achievement of an organization's objectives', thus including any person or entity that can assist in or benefit from a corporation's success.[23] The theory encourages management to develop strategies that invest in all its relationships, including those with non-shareholder stakeholders, in order to ensure its long-term success. There is critical importance placed on developing an understanding of the actual stakeholders specific to the institution, since through this level of understanding, management can create strategies that have the support of all stakeholders to ensure the long-term survival of the institution.

Stakeholder theory has received broad, enthusiastic acceptance by corporate legal scholars on both sides of the shareholder versus stakeholder debate. For those believing corporations should have the singular objective of shareholder wealth maximisation, the theory supports that belief by its claim that incorporating stakeholder interests simply furthers that cause.[24] Where it does not, shareholder interests prevail. For those

---

[21] R.E. Freeman and J. McVea, 'A stakeholder approach to strategic management', in M. Hitt, R.E. Freeman, and J. Harrison (eds.), *The Blackwell Handbook for Strategic Management* (Blackwell Publishers Ltd, 2001), 190 (describing how its origins may have come from the Stanford Research Institute, now SRI International, in the 1960s).

[22] Freeman and McVea, 'A stakeholder approach', 189.

[23] R.E. Freeman, *Strategic Management: A Stakeholder Approach* (Pitman Publishing, 1984), 46.

[24] See Jensen, 'Value maximization'. Consider as well N. Gunningham, R.A. Kagan, and D. Thornton, 'Social license and environmental protection: why businesses go beyond

LIMITS TO CORPORATE REFORM AND ALTERNATIVE STRUCTURES   281

believing that managers should seek to serve the interests of other stakeholders – including ensuring sustainable practices within a corporation –
stakeholder theory also appeases on many fronts. While the economic
incentives propelling CSR are regarded by many as a drawback of the
movement, there is a question as to whether these arguments are more
academic in nature, rather than of practical concern. As more studies
show how long-term economic benefits are often realised from CSR practices, CSR advocates are motivated to trumpet those economic benefits
over environmental concerns in order to garner the attention of profit-
focused managers. Nevertheless, ensuring that a long-term perspective is
actualised by corporate boards and management is difficult, as market
forces and pressures tend to keep short-term interests as a high priority. Law and economics scholars have frequently pointed out that when
exposing the hidden agenda behind CSR, the shareholder primacy model
is ultimately revealed.[25] Since CSR is able to co-exist alongside shareholder primacy – despite significant temporal challenges that heavily
favour short-termism[26] – there tends to be little desire to reform the
model in order to incorporate stakeholder interests beyond what companies are already driven to do from the market.

2.1.3   Shareholder primacy viewed as superior to alternatives

Daniel Fischel states that the relevant comparison for alternative models
is not between 'the ideal and the real' but between different institutional
arrangements, and that it is a kind of nirvana fallacy to conclude that
the structure of corporate law should be changed because existing institutional arrangements are imperfect.[27] The proper comparison should
be between the costs and benefits of existing arrangements, and echo-
ing *laissez-faire* market principles, '[s]ince corporations are products of
voluntary contractual agreements, a strong presumption exists in favor
of the superiority of existing arrangements'.[28] Hansmann and Kraakman

---

compliance' (2004) 29 *Law and Social Inquiry* 308 (suggesting that corporations are limited
by a social licence that at times requires them to perform above regulatory compliance
standards).

[25] G. Becker and R. Posner, 'Do corporations have a social responsibility beyond stockholder
value?' *The Becker-Posner Blog* (24 July 2005), available at: www.becker-posner-blog.com.

[26] See e.g. F. Brochet, G. Serafeim, and M. Loumioti, 'Short-termism: don't blame the
investors' (June 2012) *Harvard Business Review* 1 (providing empirical research that suggests the issue of short-termism is not limited to investors, but is a fixation of management
as well, and is rooted in corporate culture).

[27] Fischel, 'Corporate governance movement', 1272.

[28] Fischel, 'Corporate governance movement'.

282 CAROL LIAO

have also argued that alternative governance models – identified by them as manager-oriented, labour-oriented, and state-oriented – have already been tried and have failed.[29] They describe the manager-oriented model as one that existed between the 1930s and the 1960s in the USA; the labour-oriented model as one that peaked in Germany in the 1970s; and the state-oriented model as one most extensively realised in France and Japan after World War II. They contend that '[a] simple comparison across countries adhering to different models – at least in very recent years – lends credence to the view that adherence to the standard model promotes better economic outcomes ... The main examples include, of course, the strong performance of the American economy in comparison with the weaker economic performance of the German, Japanese, and French economies.'[30]

Hansmann followed up his thoughts on shareholder primacy's superiority over other national models in 2006, noting that Japan and Germany have begun to adopt governance features that are similar to the US model, which 'is the most attractive social ideal for the organization of large-scale enterprise'.[31] Hansmann's comments were made prior to the 2008 Global Financial Crisis, and it is questionable how arguments of superiority hold up as national economies continue to reverberate in its wake. Nevertheless, the lack of a strong oppositional consensus on what a better alternative to the shareholder primacy model consists of only helps to bolster the belief that the existing model is superior. The most concerted reforms to date have focused on the relatively benign 'enlightened shareholder value' model, as found in the UK's Companies Act,[32] and recent jurisprudence of the Supreme Court of Canada.[33] Other than these modest countervailing pressures towards enlightened shareholder value, there is little to no collective contrary support pushing for the adoption of another nation's model.

In addition, while Fischel makes the fair point that it is premature to compare *theoretical* alternatives against the existing model, there is no consensus on a theoretical alternative to shareholder primacy in any case. Various alternative theoretical models and approaches have emerged in

---

[29] Hansmann and Kraakman, 'End of history', 443–7.
[30] Hansmann and Kraakman, 'End of history', 450.
[31] H. Hansmann, 'How close is the end of history?' (2006) 31 *Journal of Corporate Law* 745 at 746.
[32] Companies Act 2006, [UK Companies Act] at s. 172.
[33] *Peoples Department Stores Inc. (Trustee of) v. Wise*, [2004] 3 S.C.R. 461 and *BCE Inc. v. 1976 Debentureholders*, [2008] 3 S.C.R. 560.

legal scholarship in an attempt to highlight and counteract the problems associated with the modern corporation's focus on shareholder wealth maximisation. These works generally consider how to improve and potentially redesign the corporate institution so that it 'can assure that power is deployed in the service of individual and societal flourishing rather than against it'.[34] In addition to the enlightened shareholder value model noted above, alternative styles of governance have been classified in an assortment of approaches and models, such as the communitarian approach,[35] the progressive approach,[36] the team production theory,[37] systems theory (or 'enterprise corporatism'),[38] and the director primacy model,[39] to name but a few. Each theoretical model carries its own views on which corporate rules and structures should prevail, how value is measured, and whose rights should be protected, which may also cause problems if new theoretical models are introduced. Stakeholder theory, for example, is widely acknowledged among the alternative approaches, but there is considerable difficulty in conceptualizing a form of stakeholder theory within an alternative corporate legal framework, as its usage has become 'an umbrella for so many different theories and arguments, with so many express or implied foundations'.[40] Any attempts at countervailing models incorporating elements of the theory 'may unjustifiably be associated with [prior foundations] as soon as the term is employed'.[41] Nevertheless, while scholarly criticisms against the shareholder primacy model have been widely available, disagreements on the measure of success and the way forward have made concentrated attempts to reform the current model difficult to sustain. The shareholder primacy model will endure as

---

[34] K. Testy, 'Linking progressive corporate law and progressive social movements' (2002) 76 *Tulane Law Review* 1227 at 1228.

[35] See e.g. D. Millon, 'Communitarianism in corporate law: foundations and law reform strategies', in L.E. Mitchell (ed.), *Progressive Corporate Law: New Perspectives on Law, Culture and Society* (Westview Press, 1995).

[36] L.E. Mitchell (ed.), *Progressive Corporate Law: New Perspectives on Law, Culture and Society* (Westview Press, 1995).

[37] M. Blair and L. Stout, 'A team production theory of corporate law' (1999) 85 *Virginia Law Review* 248.

[38] G. Teubner, 'Enterprise corporatism: new industrial policy and the "essence" of the legal person' (1988) *American Journal of Comparative Law* 36.

[39] S. Bainbridge, 'Director primacy: the means and ends of corporate governance' (2003) 97 *Northwestern University Law Review* 547.

[40] T. Donaldson and L.E. Preston, 'The stakeholder theory of the corporation: concepts, evidence, and implications' (1995) 20 *Academy of Management Review* 73.

[41] Donaldson and Preston, 'Stakeholder theory of the corporation'.

284   CAROL LIAO

the superior model if there continues to be a lack of consensus or at least strong support for a better theoretical alternative.

2.2 Path dependence

While path dependence theory is generally used as an argument against the likelihood of wholesale global convergence, it also inversely explains why the shareholder primacy model will continue to have a dominant hold on norms and laws, despite its inefficiencies. Lucian Bebchuk and Mark Roe identify two sources of path dependence. The first is structure-driven path dependence, where corporate structures in an economy at any time are influenced by the corporate structures it previously had.[42] The second is rules-driven path dependence, which arises from the effect that initial structures have on subsequent structures through their effect on the legal rules governing corporations.[43] Exploring the efficiency analysis behind these two sources of path dependence, Bebchuk and Roe point out how the measure of a model's efficiency relative to alternatives is subject to 'sunk adaptive costs, complementarities, negative externalities, endow-ment effects, or multiple optima'.[44] A movement away from shareholder primacy to another model of governance would incorporate several costs. A helpful example is imagining costs associated for a country with no public subway system adopting the Vancouver SkyTrain as opposed to the city of London changing its existing Tube system. Adaptations may be more costly than starting from scratch. Complementarities and network externalities also mean that shifting from the shareholder primacy model to an alternative would have ripple effects on those most familiar with the existing model – requiring investment from those players to acquire new techniques in anticipation of a new model. Complex regulation has already been set up to address the needs of the model; new structures would require modifications that are costly and inefficient. Achieving an efficient control structure may also be difficult because of the endowment effect in human behaviour. An example given by Bebchuk and Roe is a sup-posed shift of control from those governed by American-style managers to European-style concentrated family-owners. Sellers may not agree with

---

[42] L. Bebchuk and M.J. Roe, 'A theory of path dependence in corporate ownership and governance' (1999) 52 *Stanford Law Review* 127 at 139.

[43] Bebchuk and Roe, 'Theory of path dependence', 153.

[44] Bebchuk and Roe, 'Theory of path dependence', 139.

those willing to buy due to their overvaluation of the asset's prior value given existing control structures, thereby creating inefficiencies.[45]

Thus, shareholder primacy may persist because of players who have the motivation and power to prevent any changes to the existing power arrangements. Holders of power are not motivated to relinquish their power (whether under the guise of ownership or control), even in scenarios where doing so would increase the total value of the corporation. Corporate insiders have the power to prevent the loss of their economic power since their position as controlling shareholders permits them to block changes in the firm's control structure simply by refusing to sell their shares. Their position also permits them to block changes in governance by selecting the firm's directors. This concentration of power also extends to aspects of rules-driven path dependence. Bebchuk and Roe note: '[L]egal rules are often the product of political processes, which combine public-regarding features with interest group politics . . . [t]hus, the corporate rules that actually will be chosen and maintained might depend on the relative strength of the relevant interest group'.[46] In particular, the concept of 'regulatory capture' exposes how power dynamics are intimately intertwined with rules-driven path dependence.[47] Regulatory agencies come to be dominated by the very industries they were charged with regulating, and eventually act in ways that benefit the industries they are to regulate, rather than the public.[48] Those holding economic and/or political power can and likely will obstruct attempts to establish rules that may compromise their position, preventing the development of efficient regulation.

Politically, Roe has documented the relevance of political determinants to corporate governance. He finds that there is considerably more to governance reform than creating proper legal institutions, as 'technical reforms have sometimes had little effect unless and until the underlying

---

[45] Bebchuk and Roe, 'Theory of path dependence', 141.

[46] Bebchuk and Roe, 'Theory of path dependence', 157.

[47] George Stigler is often cited as one of the main developers of capture theory. See G. Stigler, 'The theory of economic regulation' (1971) 2 *Bell Journal of Economics and Management Science* 3 at 3 ('as a rule, regulation is acquired by the industry and is designed and operated primarily for its benefits'); G. Stigler, 'Can regulatory agencies protect the consumer?' in G. Stigler, *The Citizen and the State: Essays on Regulation* (University of Chicago Press, 1975), 183.

[48] An often cited example of regulatory capture is regarding the catastrophic 2010 Deepwater Horizon Oil Spill, and the regulatory agency responsible for off-shore drilling, the Minerals Management Service. See G. O'Driscoll, 'The Gulf spill, the financial crisis, and government failure', *Wall Street Journal*, 14 June 2010, A17.

political reality changed'.[49] Culturally, the creation of property rights and the norms that accompany it mean that Anglo-American governance theory seeks to 'protect a particular hierarchy of property'.[50] Empirical research has suggested that traditional notions of property rights have influenced most private law.[51] These norms run parallel to those found within the shareholder primacy model, and it is likely that a serious destabilising effect might be required to upset any of those pre-existing norms. As well, Hansmann has noted that, globally, the 'most serious argument ... against the efficiency claim is that the [model] involves too steep a trade-off between material prosperity and social order'.[52] Nevertheless, while there may be a 'broad disquiet' among several nations, Hansmann taps into cultural reasoning for support, noting that 'it may be fine for Americans, who are intensely individualistic and place an exceptionally strong value on personal liberty'.[53] The cultural context may also hold true with regard to the belief that the shareholder primacy model is superior to alternative models. It is difficult to gauge the tenacity of this belief in international culture, but ethnocentrism may play a significant role in perpetuating the shareholder wealth maximisation norm in nations who possess this cultural mentality.

In summary, it seems the likelihood of shareholder primacy's continued dominance depends very much on path dependence and the resilience of all of the reasons provided above. Support for Adam Smith's invisible hand is on safe ground. The force of competition motivates efficient positions, and the Anglo-American cultural emphasis on free market capitalism in an era of multinational enterprises and global markets supports the endurance of shareholder primacy for the foreseeable future despite occasional unpleasant challenges such as from the Occupy Movement.[54]

How, then, do reformers champion progressive ideals when beliefs supporting the mainstream model are so ingrained in the psyche of corporate power? Reformation through CSR and other initiatives explored in this book must continue, but there are other avenues that should not be ignored. Section 3 and Section 4 of this chapter address several

---

[49] M. Roe, *Political Determinants of Corporate Governance* (Oxford University Press, 2003), 202.

[50] Sarra, 'Oversight, hindsight, and foresight', p. 41.

[51] J. Braithwaite and P. Drahos, *Global Business Regulation* (Cambridge University Press, 2000).

[52] Hansmann, 'How close is the end?', 747.   [53] Hansmann, 'How close is the end?'

[54] 'Occupy Movement', *The Guardian*, available at: www.theguardian.com/world/occupy.

LIMITS TO CORPORATE REFORM AND ALTERNATIVE STRUCTURES   287

alternative models that have, or are in the process of doing so, recalibrated efficiency within their design and integrated sustainable practices into corporate governance. These models are the cooperative model and five other alternative legal structures that have appeared in the UK, Canada, and the USA within the last decade.

3 An existing alternative legal model: the cooperative

As one of the oldest corporate structures in the world, the cooperative model allows its members the flexibility to pursue social, environmental, and/or economic mandates in a particularly collaborative manner. The International Cooperative Alliance (ICA), described as 'the voice of the cooperative movement', defines the cooperative as 'an autonomous association of people united voluntarily to meet their common economic, social and cultural needs through a jointly owned and democratically controlled enterprise'.[55] The roles of member and stakeholder are closely connected in a cooperative. A member is an individual who shares control of the cooperative and who is also a user of the cooperative in some way. This arrangement is distinct from that of a shareholder in a corporation. While the shareholder holds shares in the business – and thereby has the possibility of control – the shareholder is not by definition a user of the business.[56] Cooperatives, then, may be regarded as 'associations of people' whereas standard, for-profit corporations are 'associations of capital'.[57] By pooling their resources and working together, members can satisfy a common need through the cooperative. Joint membership means that all members are at least notionally equal decision-makers, using a democratic system of one member, one vote. Members share the benefits of the cooperative, based on how much they use its services.

The ICA has outlined the hallmarks of the cooperative model as follows: (1) voluntary and open membership; (2) democratic member control; (3) member in economic participation; (4) autonomy and independence; (5) education, training, and information; (6) cooperation among cooperatives; and (7) concern for community.[58] Because of its

---

[55] International Co-operative Alliance, 'Co-operative identity, values and principles', available at: http://ica.coop/en, under 'What's a co-op?'.
[56] To the contrary: transactions between the corporation and the shareholder are subject to company law rules intended to discourage tunnelling and other forms of self-dealing.
[57] British Columbia Co-operative Association, 'The co-op advantage', available at: http://www.bcca.coop/content/advantage.
[58] International Co-operative Alliance, 'Co-operative identity, values and principles'.

institutional flexibility, the cooperative is highly adaptable to meet a variety of community development needs. Cooperatives can be created for a wide range of purposes and activities – from purely commercial to charitable. While primarily driven to achieve benefits for their members, cooperatives can make community benefit their first priority, or they can combine member and community benefits as they choose. Success is not only defined as profitability, but by other yardsticks as well – such as the improved well-being of the members and the communities they belong to. The ability to quantify value beyond simply economic return in response to members' needs is one of the strengths of the cooperative model.[59]

Due to its ability to encompass multiple mandates, it is critical for the foundational objective of the cooperative to be consistently examined. While the values of a cooperative are the values of its members, scholars have pointed out that cooperatives likely house both individualistic- and collectivistic-minded members.[60] A section of the membership may expect the need for economic benefits to be top priority. Another may prefer cooperative management that considers other stakeholder interests as well. To satisfy the expectations of all the members, 'cooperatives must employ strategies that have their basis in individualistic view of ownership and business objectives, as well as in more collaborative and collectivistic views of ownership and business objectives'.[61] The cooperative's success will depend on how well these foundations are built within the enterprise.

Internationally, the UN has 'recognized and reaffirmed the role of cooperatives in economic, social, and cultural development and in the achievement of social policy objectives'.[62] The UN General Assembly declared 2012 to be the 'International Year of Co-operatives' in order to highlight the importance of cooperatives to economic development and

---

[59] For further discussion on the links between sustainability and the cooperative model, see H. Henrÿ, *Sustainable Development and Cooperative Law: Corporate Social Responsibility or Cooperative Social Responsibility?*, Research Paper No. 2012–23 (University of Oslo Faculty of Law, 2012).

[60] See e.g. I. Jussila, J.M. Saksa, and P. Tuominen, 'Distinctive features of co-operative ownership: implications for strategies of customer owned co-ops', paper presented at the 22nd International Cooperative Research Conference, Paris, October 2006.

[61] Jussila, *et al.*, 'Distinctive features of cooperative ownership', 4; see also P. Davis, 'The governance of co-operatives under competitive conditions: issues, processes and culture' (2001) 1(4) *Corporate Governance* 28.

[62] UN Department of Economic and Social Affairs, Division for Social Policy and Development, 'International day of cooperatives', available at: www.un.org/en/events/cooperativesday/.

social innovation around the world. Nevertheless, while for-profit corporations, charitable and non-profit organisations are commonly known and generally contemplated by many entrepreneurs looking to house their social businesses, it seems that outside of those situated in certain sectors such as agriculture and housing, entrepreneurs have either been unaware of or less inclined to adopt the cooperative form.[63] Entrepreneurs may cite a lack of control, complicated decision-making processes, or limited availability of additional capital as compelling reasons why the cooperative model is not suitable for their business. Equally so, mainstream corporate legal scholarship has paid comparatively little attention to the cooperative model. This omission is curious, given that the ICA reports that cooperatives have over 1 billion members worldwide and 'provide over one hundred million jobs around the world, 20 per cent more than multinational enterprises'.[64]

As corporate reformers desperately seek answers to the big sustainability question hanging over shareholder primacy, why is there such a huge gap between them and advocates of the cooperative form, who claim to hold the answers? The missing link between cooperative design and its widespread success is being addressed head-on by the ICA. Despite the cooperative's long history, the ICA contends that the model is being used well below its potential, and believes that 'with appropriate support and greater understanding and recognition, [cooperatives] could contribute much more'.[65] At the start of 2013, the organisation published a manifesto entitled 'Blueprint for a Co-operative Decade' with the 'unashamedly ambitious' vision for 2020 to be the year when the cooperative form of business 'is an acknowledged leader in economic, social and environmental sustainability, the model preferred by people, and the fastest growing form of enterprise'.[66] The ICA aims to elevate member participation and

---

[63] For example, the cooperative structure is not a prevalent one in Canada, where there were reported in 2010 to be only 8,400 cooperatives, compared to approximately 85,000 charities, 65,000 non-profit organisations, and over 2.4 million for-profit corporations. *Key Small Business Statistics*, July 2010, available at: www.ic.gc.ca/sbstatistics. This is similar to the findings in the UK and the USA, which report in 2012 some 5,933 and 29,000 cooperatives, respectively, which constitute a small fraction when compared to other structures in each country. See Co-operatives UK, 'About co-operatives', available at: http://uk.coop/what-co-operative; 2012 International Year of the Co-operative, 'About NCBA', available at: www.ncba.coop/add-value.

[64] International Co-operative Alliance, 'Co-operative identity, values and principles'.

[65] International Co-operative Alliance, 'Blueprint for a co-operative decade' (January 2013), 3.

[66] International Co-operative Alliance, 'Blueprint', 39.

governance while positioning cooperatives as 'builders of sustainability'.[67] It points out the main stumbling block in the cooperative movement is a lack of clarity as to how cooperatives are defined and distinguished, and cites a particular need to 'establish an "irreducible core" of what it means to be a cooperative'.[68] The blueprint outlines a multifaceted plan to secure the cooperative identity and increase its awareness, such as through cooperative education,[69] the engagement of young people,[70] and tapping into social media,[71] among other mechanisms. The blueprint hones in on two important areas for further improvement: (1) 'ensur[ing] there are supportive legal frameworks for cooperative growth';[72] and (2) 'secur[ing] reliable cooperative capital while guaranteeing member control'.[73]

The particular challenge facing the ICA with regard to cooperative legal frameworks is that legal issues are very jurisdiction-specific, particularly as to how cooperatives within jurisdictions are treated in comparison to other available corporate structures.[74] Recognising the difficulty in addressing these issues, the ICA has elected instead to provide high-level possible or indicative actions, such as: (1) creating an international network of registrars and regulators; (2) developing guidelines on how to apply the ICA Cooperative Principles; (3) providing assistance to national parliamentarians, legislators, and policy-makers through a comparative study on the ways laws apply to cooperatives in different jurisdictions; and (4) integrating the cooperative agenda into global development organisations;[75] among other tasks. The ICA would also be well served by employing its 268 member organisations in 93 countries[76] to garner greater support in identifying and addressing these jurisdiction-specific legal challenges. Issues may include cooperative treatment under tax laws, competition and antitrust laws, and other regulations.[77]

Securing reliable capital to finance the initiation of a cooperative business has historically been a stumbling block for entrepreneurs.

---

[67] International Co-operative Alliance, 'Blueprint', 6.
[68] International Co-operative Alliance, 'Blueprint', 30.
[69] International Co-operative Alliance, 'Blueprint', 24.
[70] International Co-operative Alliance, 'Blueprint', 11, 12, 23.
[71] International Co-operative Alliance, 'Blueprint'.
[72] International Co-operative Alliance, 'Blueprint', 26.
[73] International Co-operative Alliance, 'Blueprint', 32.
[74] International Co-operative Alliance, 'Blueprint', 26.
[75] International Co-operative Alliance, 'Blueprint', 30.
[76] As of May 2014: International Co-operative Alliance, 'Alliance members', available at: http://ica.coop/.
[77] International Co-operative Alliance, 'Blueprint', 29.

LIMITS TO CORPORATE REFORM AND ALTERNATIVE STRUCTURES   291

Cooperative capital may come from several sources, including members' and non-members' investment, and loans from banks, non-profits, and government sources.[78] However, cooperatives have limited access to most traditional sources of capital.[79] Lending institutions tend to (formally or informally) impose a set of conditions on those seeking financing to ensure they are a desirable investment. Generally, these institutions seek applicants that are low risk and high return, with minimal consideration for any value created beyond the economic level. These requirements make it difficult for cooperatives, whose capital has been described as 'more patient',[80] and, with regard to the high return, while cooperatives can pay interest on capital, under the ICA's third Cooperative Principle, members receive 'limited compensation, if any, on capital subscribed as a condition of membership'.[81] The ICA acknowledges that '[w]hen compared with company equity capital, cooperative capital does not offer to investors comparable economic benefits', thus putting cooperatives at a notable disadvantage.[82]

In response, the ICA has offered several ways in which access to cooperative capital may be improved. In addition to increasing access to existing funding sources, the ICA suggests creating a modern generic financial instrument designed specifically to address cooperative needs, using group structure arrangements as a way to address cooperative capital accumulation, and creating a cooperative-specific index to measure growth and performance.[83] These ideas are both innovative and ambitious, and it is unclear from the ICA 'blueprint' how they may be put into effect.

The cooperative model has been given new impetus by the UN's support and the ICA's aggressive plans for growth. The fusion of member and

---

[78] J.R. Baarda, 'Current issues in co-operative finance and governance: background and discussion paper' (University of Wisconsin-Madison, April 2006), available at: http://uwcc. wisc.edu/info/governance/baard.pdf.

[79] Nevertheless, there are new sources of capital being provided through the emergence of microfinance and private equity financing instruments devised from within the socially responsible investing (SRI) movement. International Co-operative Alliance, 'The cooperative model in microfinance: more current and pertinent than ever', available at: http://ica.coop.

[80] J. Katz and M. Boland, 'One for all and all for one? A new generation of co-operatives emerges' (2002) 35 *Long Range Planning* 73; J. Nilsson, 'Organizational principles for co-operative firms' (2001) 17 *Scandinavian Journal of Management* 329.

[81] International Co-operative Alliance, 'Co-operative identity, values and principles'.

[82] International Co-operative Alliance, 'Blueprint', 32. See also A. Wilson, 'Financing the co-operative movement: for better or for worse?' *The Dominion* (5 April 2010), available at: www.dominionpaper.ca/articles/3270; Baarda, 'Current issues', 62.

[83] Baarda, 'Current issues'.

user roles in the cooperative enforces an unassailable stakeholder-based style of governance that cannot be replicated in for-profit companies. Cooperatives provide a legal structure that is ideal for communities wishing to achieve economic self-determination and regain control of local economies. Furthermore, research indicates that the survival rate of cooperatives is significantly higher than that of traditional businesses.[84] As advocates mobilise in hopes of generating significant momentum behind the cooperative movement, it is likely there will be much more to be seen from this model and its contributions to sustainability in the years to come.

4   Emerging hybrid corporate models

Corporate hybrids are legal innovations that have received little scrutiny from scholars to date. This omission is largely because they are very new institutional phenomena. In the corporate context, a hybrid can be defined as a corporate legal structure that combines both for-profit and non-profit legal characteristics in its design to enable the dual pursuit of economic and social interests. Through the use of hybrids, traditional charitable and non-profit organisations are able to generate equity capital and make a profit. In theory, it enables profit-conscious businesses to integrate stakeholder interests and sustainability into their business practices well beyond what is normal under the shareholder primacy model. The emergence and development of corporate hybrids signify the beginning of a new institutional tool for the CSR movement. Hybrids provide opportunities for entrepreneurs seeking to house social enterprises while also attempting to counterbalance private sector negative externalities, affirming that 'the independence of social value and commercial revenue creation is a myth'.[85] The following hybrids will be explored in this section, offering a peek at the potential future of CSR and sustainability and how

---

[84] J. Birchall and L.H. Ketilson, 'Resilience of the co-operative business model in times of crisis' (International Labour Organization, 19 June 2009), available at: www.ilo.org. According to Co-operatives UK, between 2008 and 2011, while the UK economy as a whole shrank by 1.7 per cent, the cooperative economy grew by 19.6 per cent. In the same period, the number of cooperatives increased from 4,820 to 5,933. See also, for example, a 2008 Quebec study found that 62 per cent of new cooperatives were still operating after five years, compared with 35 per cent of other new businesses. After 10 years, the figures were 44 per cent and 20 per cent respectively. Canadian Co-operative Association, 'Co-op facts and figures', available at: www.coopscanada.coop.

[85] J. Battilana, et al., 'In search of the hybrid ideal', Summer (2012) *Stanford Social Innovation Review* 51 at 52.

LIMITS TO CORPORATE REFORM AND ALTERNATIVE STRUCTURES   293

these concepts can be built into a corporation's governing infrastructure, while also pointing out some potential challenges: the community interest company, the community contribution company, the low-profit limited liability company, the B Corporation (privately regulated), and the benefit corporation. None of these hybrids receive special tax treatment.

4.1   *The United Kingdom: the community interest company (CIC)*

The community interest company (CIC) was the very first of the new generation of hybrids. Implemented in the UK in 2005, CICs are established to trade goods or services for the community interest.[86] The particular novelty of CICs is that they are able to do what charitable and non-profit organisations cannot, which is raise equity capital in exchange for shares. CICs are designed to enable and encourage the investment of private wealth in community projects.

To qualify for CIC status, interested parties must first pass a 'community interest test' administered by the CIC Regulator, a public official who has 'a continuing monitoring and enforcement role' over CICs.[87] An interested party submits to the CIC Regulator a declaration that it is not an excluded company engaged in political activity[88] and presents a 'community interest statement' indicating that the company will carry on its activities for the benefit of the community and details how those activities will indeed create a benefit.[89] The CIC Regulator may elect not to allow a party to become a CIC if a reasonable person might consider that the activities only benefit 'the members of a particular body or the employees of a particular employer'.[90] The stated community purpose of the CIC is the primary focus for CIC directors.

The most noteworthy features in the CIC are its asset lock and dividend cap. The asset lock prevents CIC assets and profits from being transferred for full fair market value (to ensure the CIC continues to retain the value of the assets transferred), transferred to another CIC subject to an asset lock or a charity, or otherwise done for a community benefit.[91] This simple feature helps to ensure that assets that are intended for community benefit remain in that realm. Entrepreneurs interested in establishing a CIC need

---

[86] UK Companies Act; The Community Interest Company Regulations 2005, No. 1788 [CIC Regulations].

[87] UK Companies Act, s. 27, s. 35, and Sch. 3; see also Department for Business, Innovation and Skills, 'Community interest companies', available at: www.bis.gov.uk/cicregulator.

[88] UK Companies Act, s. 35(6); CIC Regulations, reg. 6.   [89] CIC Regulations, reg. 2.

[90] CIC Regulations, reg. 4.   [91] UK Companies Act, s. 30, 31; CIC Regulations, Part 6.

to pay particular attention to this feature. Once a business is established as a CIC, there are permanent, long-term consequences. Dividends on CIC shares and interest on bonds are capped to ensure that profits are either retained by the CIC or used for a community benefit purpose; cap amounts are set by the Regulator.[92] The dividend cap purports to ensure a reasonable balance between the interests of the shareholders and the community interest.

In addition to the asset lock and dividend cap, CICs have annual reporting requirements whereby they must account for how their hybrid has benefited the community and engaged stakeholders.[93] Stakeholder interests are prominent in the CIC model. CICs are recommended to form stakeholder advisory groups for the CIC's benefit and each CIC crafts its own individualised stakeholder process. The CIC is required to describe its stakeholder efforts in an annual report, which is placed on a public register at Companies House[94] and reviewed by the CIC Regulator.[95] The latter can reject a CIC's report or require revisions before it is accepted.[96]

The CIC Regulator plays a seminal role in administering and maintaining CICs in the UK. The Regulator's role is seen as one with 'a light touch regulation and an emphasis on proportionality'.[97] In addition to having the power to investigate complaints, the Regulator may also act if a CIC is found to be violating its community purpose or asset lock provisions, may change the make-up of the board, or even terminate a CIC, if necessary.[98] Along with ensuring proper registration and regulation of CICs, the Regulator has also been important in addressing big picture issues. In the CIC 2011/2012 annual report, the Regulator identified public concerns that CICs were taking away resources and business from the charitable sector, noting fears in these early years of 'private sector intrusion into public service delivery'.[99] This trend is a challenge that many hybrids catering to the non-profit sector will have to address in the early years.

Research on the CIC model is limited. Hybrids are faced with attempting to balance financial interests and enforceable rules to integrate social mandates, but each frequently seem to trade off against the other.[100]

---

[92] UK Companies Act, s. 51.94.   [93] UK Companies Act. s. 8.1.1.

[94] Companies House, available at: www.companieshouse.gov.uk.

[95] CIC Regulations, Part 7.   [96] CIC Regulations, Part 7.

[97] Regulator of Community Interest Companies, *Annual Report 2011/2012* (Office of the Regulator of Community Interest Companies, 2012), 15.

[98] UK Companies Act 2006.

[99] Regulator of Community Interest Companies, *Annual Report 2011/2012*, p. 7.

[100] Brakman Reiser, 'Governing and financing', 654.

One scholar notes that the CIC form 'faces the most serious obstacles to enhancing financing, by virtue of the dividend cap and asset lock... Yet, the very same... mechanisms endow the CIC with the staunchest commitments to social good of all the forms'.[101] Besides these mechanisms, 'the possibility of private enforcement by shareholders and public enforcement by the CIC Regulator' makes the CIC a particularly unique corporate form encapsulating dual mandates.[102]

The legal characteristics of the CIC may appear too limiting for many actors currently situated in the for-profit sector. The market for corporate control is disrupted by the asset lock and dividend cap, and entrepreneurs who envision broader market dissemination through acquisition by larger corporations will not clamour for this model. The CIC, therefore, tends to be more attractive for those in the non-profit sector. Since a CIC structure allows capital to be raised through the issuance of shares, it creates economic opportunities that have traditionally been closed off to charitable and non-profit organisations. As well, a CIC structure may be more attractive to individuals or groups wanting to start community projects or programmes but have little interest in relationships based on membership such as those found in a cooperative.

The number of CICs in the UK reached over 9,200 as of April 2014.[103] There were over 2,000 CICs created in 2012 alone.[104] It is reported that over 100 new CICs are registered every month,[105] and a considerable number of CICs have passed the three-year mark. With respect to cooperatives, sources indicate there are presently over 5,933 independent cooperatives in the UK, with the UK cooperative economy estimated at £35.6 billion and with approximately 13.5 million members.[106] There are no equivalent statistics available on CICs' monetary contributions to the UK economy, the average size of CICs, or total members. But if it is simply a numbers game, do 9,200 CICs spell success after nine years in existence? Compared to the number of cooperatives, the answer seems to be yes.

---

[101] Brakman Reiser, 'Governing and financing', 654.

[102] Brakman Reiser, 'Governing and financing', 630–6.

[103] Twitter account of the Office of the Regulator of Community Interest Companies (@Team-CIC) reports 9,276 registered CICs as of 24 April 2014, available at: https://twitter.com/TeamCIC.

[104] Regulator of Community Interest Companies, *Annual Report 2011/2012*, p. 13. Interestingly, the Regulator reports that 590 CICs were also dissolved, with key reasons for dissolution being 'lack of funding, no trading activity, and poor corporate governance'.

[105] CIC Association, 'What is a CIC?', available at: www.cicassociation.org.uk.

[106] Co-operatives UK, 'About co-operatives', available at: www.uk.coop/co-operatives.

4.2   Canada: the community contribution company (C3)

In March 2012, the British Columbia (BC) provincial government announced the creation of a hybrid model, the community contribution company (C3).[107] The regulations for this hybrid were completed in February 2013, and the hybrid became available to the public in July 2013.[108] As well, in November 2012, the Nova Scotia provincial government announced the creation of its own hybrid community interest company (NS CIC); no date has yet been provided as to when the accompanying regulations will be drafted and this entity will be made available to the public.[109] The proposed NS CIC has identical features to the C3, so for ease of reading, subsequent C3 references include the NS CIC in its meaning.

The C3 hybrid contains governing features that are largely modelled on the UK CIC, with the most noteworthy similarities being the asset lock, dividend cap, and the annual reporting requirements.[110] Like the UK CIC, the legal characteristics of the C3 make it particularly attractive for those in the non-profit sector who need to raise capital – which may be a significant number.[111] The C3 allows those in the non-profit sector to capitalise on the market to disseminate goods and services while ensuring social mandates remain intact.

The differences thus far in the BC and Nova Scotia version of the CIC are mainly administrative. Neither adopts the accountability mechanism of a CIC Regulator, as found in the UK. Rather than passing a community interest test with regulatory approval, interested parties are able to become a C3 through unanimous shareholder approval.[112] A C3 is required to indicate in its articles of incorporation that it is a C3 'and, as such, has purposes beneficial to society'.[113] Because of the restrictive nature of the

---

[107]   BC Ministry of Finance, 'BC introduces Act allowing social enterprise companies' (5 March 2012), available at: www2.news.gov.bc.ca.

[108]   BC Government Online News Source, 'Legislative changes encourage investment in social capital' (2 March 2013), available at: www.newsroom.gov.bc.ca.

[109]   Nova Scotia Canada, Service Nova Scotia and Municipal Relations, 'New opportunities for social entrepreneurs' (28 November 2012), available at: http://novascotia.ca.

[110]   Bill 23–2012, Finance Statutes Amendment Act [BC C3 Bill]; Bill No. 135, Community Interest Company Act [NS CIC Bill].

[111]   J. Wingrove, 'Marc and Craig Kielburger's do-gooding social enterprise', *Globe and Mail*, 19 March 2010, 2 (reporting on how there is a need for this type of structure in Canada). Paul Martin, Canada's former prime minister, has remarked, 'Government policy hasn't caught up . . . I think Canada is ready for it. I think Canada is looking for it', in Wingrove, 'Marc and Craig Kielburger's do-gooding'.

[112]   BC C3 Bill; NS CIC Bill.   [113]   BC C3 Bill, s. 51.911.

asset lock, legislators want to ensure all shareholders (including non-voting shareholders) are aware of the change and approve of them – no minority shareholder can be forced into a C3 model.

There is a question as to whether the lack of a regulator to monitor C3 compliance will become problematic. The C3 is only required to publish its annual report in the same manner that companies are required to publish financial statements and auditors' reports under the applicable provincial acts for standard corporations.[114] It remains to be seen how the BC and Nova Scotia versions will stand up to the UK CIC, and how each province's social sector will adapt, despite having less regulatory infrastructure and governmental oversight, and no direct official to contact. In comparison, the UK CIC Regulator's office has three full-time and four part-time staff members, and reported that in 2012 there were over 7,000 emails and 3,000 phone calls to their office.[115] Canadian C3s do not have this support; administering and governing C3s is entirely through self-regulation. On the other hand, some of the regulatory void has been filled by other sources. For example, in anticipation of the C3, the BC Centre for Social Enterprise provided a small number of free workshops to educate interested parties on the details of the C3 model.[116] Another example is Accelerating Social Impact CCC, a newly formed C3 in BC whose aim is to assist and advise social impact businesses on a variety of matters, including legal options.[117] Other organisations may also come on board to assist.

It is still early in the process. UK CICs have been in existence for only a handful of years, and research on the CIC model is limited. The Canadian hybrid is in its embryonic stage in BC, with only a handful of C3s created to date, and is yet to be made available to Nova Scotia businesses (as of July 2014), thus information is limited to projections. In the early years of the UK CIC's development, one scholar noted that the model 'assumes [there is] a pool of investors with an appetite for wedding financial and social return and sufficient brand awareness and confidence to appeal to them . . . [It also], however, requires these investors to be especially devoted to the blended enterprise concept by substantially limiting the upside of their investments'.[118] While it seems that this has not been a

---

[114] BC C3 Bill, s. 51.96.
[115] Regulator of Community Interest Companies, *Annual Report 2011/2012*, p. 13.
[116] BC Centre for Social Enterprise, 'Community contribution companies are coming' (2013), available at: www.centreforsocialenterprise.com/C3_BC.html.
[117] Accelerating Social Impact CCC, available at: http://asiccc.ca.
[118] Brakman Reiser, 'Governing and financing', 649.

problem for the UK CIC, given its numbers, the note of caution is also warranted for the C3, as the availability of these types of investors is likely to be location-specific in the embryonic years of a hybrid's development. The creation of the C3 again assumes there is a pool of investors willing to limit the upside of their investments for the sake of the wider social good. The growth of impact investing in BC and Nova Scotia suggests there are social investors who can balance these economic and social interests in order to sustain the C3 model, and presumably legislators would not have pursued hybrid legislation without some assurances of a means to support it, but one can only surmise.

With those cautionary notes in mind, it is important to emphasise that the creation of the C3 seems to be a positive development for Canada. There may also be hidden benefits from BC and Nova Scotia's secondary start. Canadian legislators and regulators may be wise to translate the eight- to nine-year lead of UK CICs into a latecomer advantage,[119] where lessons on how to successfully implement the hybrid may be learned from the UK's experience. Further research will be crucial for optimal results in the implementation of hybrids in Canada (if, indeed, other provinces follow suit). Governmental support is necessary in terms of education, administration, and regulation, as well as ongoing support from both corporate and individual leaders in the for-profit and non-profit sectors.

4.3   The United States

4.3.1   Low-profit limited liability company (L3C)

Difficulties in accommodating particular federal tax laws were the main motivator behind the development of the first US hybrid, the low-profit limited liability company (L3C), which began in the state of Vermont in April 2008.[120] The L3C model is designed to house program-related investments (PRIs) under existing Internal Revenue System (IRS) rules to enable foundations to better invest in PRIs without the fear of compromising their tax-exempt status. Robert Lang, identified as 'the creator of the L3C',[121] along with Carol Coren, describes the L3C as 'the for-profit with the non-profit soul' because '[b]y law, the "DNA" of the L3C brand

---

[119] T. Veblen, 'Economic theory in a calculable future' (1925) 15 *American Economic Review* 1.

[120] Vt. Stat. Ann. tit. 21, s. 3001(27) (2009); Vermont Secretary of State: Corporations Division, 'Low-profit limited liability company', available at: www.sec.state.vt.us.

[121] R. Lang, 'Letter from the creator of the L3C', available at: www.americansforcommunity development.org. Lang is the CEO of the Mary Elizabeth and Gordon B. Mannweiler Foundation.

LIMITS TO CORPORATE REFORM AND ALTERNATIVE STRUCTURES 299

ensures that profit is second to its social mission'.[122] As of mid 2014, L3C legislation was in place in eight states and two federally recognised Native American tribes.[123] Unusually, North Carolina repealed its L3C legislation in January 2014, apparently because the model was seen as unnecessary or redundant.[124]

The problem that the L3C hybrid has been designed to address is as follows. First, in the USA, foundations are non-profit organisations or charitable trusts that provide grants to unrelated organisations or individuals for charitable purposes. Under IRS rules, private foundations are required to pay out a 'distributable amount' (which equates to at least 5 per cent) of their assets each fiscal year in order to maintain their tax-exempt status.[125] They may elect to spend their funds in two ways: through grants, where there is no financial return on their investment, or through PRIs, which may provide a potential return.[126] To qualify as a PRI, the investment 'must be related to the foundation's mission and the risk-to-reward ratio must exceed that of a standard market-driven investment', meaning the risk must be higher and the return lower.[127] 'Jeopardizing investments' under IRS rules can subject private foundations to considerably high excise taxes.[128] A PRI is sheltered from designation as a jeopardizing investment if its primary purpose 'is to accomplish one or more of

---

[122] C. Coren and R. Lang, 'The L3C: the for-profit with the non-profit soul' (Winter 2009–2010) *Bridges*, Federal Reserve Bank of St. Louis, available at: www.stlouisfed.org.

[123] In addition to Vermont, legislation has been passed in Illinois, Louisiana, Maine, Michigan, North Carolina, Rhode Island, Utah, Wyoming, and the federal jurisdictions of the Crow Indian Nation of Montana and the Oglala Sioux Tribe. For more details on state legislation, see Americans for Community Development, 'Laws', available at: www.americansforcommunitydevelopment.org; see also J.W. Callison and A.W. Vestal, 'The L3C illusion: why low-profit limited liability companies will not stimulate socially optimal private foundation investment in entrepreneurial ventures' (2010) 35 *Vermont Law Review* 273 at n 3 (which lists all L3C legislation by state).

[124] 'North Carolina officially abolishes the L3C', *Forbes*, 11 January 2014, available at: www.forbes.com.

[125] The distributable amount is determined by Internal Revenue Code 4942 and the applicable regulations; see also IRS, s.16, 'General rules governing required distributions', in *Internal Revenue Manual* (at 7.27.16.1.1. and 7.27.16.2), available at: www.irs.gov. The *Internal Revenue Manual* notes that s. 823 of Public Law 97–34 reduced the required payout for private foundations so that they must distribute only their minimum investment return, statutorily defined as 5 per cent.

[126] IRS, 'General rules'.

[127] J. Witkin, 'The L3C: a more creative capitalism' (15 January 2009), available at: www.triplepundit.com; Internal Revenue Code 170(c)(2)(B).

[128] IRS, 'Taxes on investments which jeopardize charitable purposes', in *Internal Revenue Manual*, C. 27, s. 18, available at: www.irs.gov; see also Internal Revenue Service, 'Private foundation excise taxes', available at: www.irs.gov.

the [organisation's exempt] purposes... and no significant purpose... is [for] the production of income or the appreciation of property'[129] or expenditures for political purposes.[130] Many foundations are reluctant to invest in for-profit entities due to the uncertainty of whether they would qualify as PRIs, despite the potential return. The 'burdensome and costly' IRS requirements to verify PRIs mean that '[o]f the many thousands of grant making foundations in the US, only a few hundred make PRIs'.[131] For the fiscal years 2000 and 2001, PRIs were estimated as constituting approximately 0.45 per cent of the total grant and PRI output by private foundations.[132]

Enter the L3C, which has been designed to make it easier for foundations to make PRIs by bridging the gap between for-profit and non-profit agendas. The limited liability company (LLC) choice of entity is particularly favourable because of its flexibility,[133] and the LLC state laws provide the base for L3C laws to build upon. It is clear from the wording of the L3C laws that the entity was created solely to meet PRI criteria.[134] Lang notes that 'since the L3C is a legal business form with specific requirements... members are constrained to write the operating agreement in a manner consistent with L3C law', which then specifies its PRI-qualified purpose.[135] All the limitations accompanying an L3C essentially mirror the language set out in the IRS rules, including that the L3C would not have been formed but for its charitable or educational purpose, which is meant to assure foundations that their tax-exempt status will remain secure if they make a PRI in an L3C model.

Foundations, nevertheless, have sought further assurances from the IRS. While IRS private letter rulings (PLRs) are not required prior to a foundation making a PRI, many prefer the comfort of one, given the risks. In the early years of its development, many advocates of the L3C model sought legislative support and/or a blanket PLR from the IRS specifically identifying L3Cs as entities that automatically qualified for PRIs. The proposed 'Program-Related Investment Promotion Act of 2008' attempted to have L3C entitled to a rebuttable presumption that below-market

---

[129] Internal Revenue Code, s. 4944(c).   [130] Internal Revenue Code, at s. 4945.

[131] GrantSpace, a service of the Foundation Center, 'What is a program-related investment?', available at: http://grantspace.org.

[132] Callison and Vestal, 'The L3C illusion', at n 4.

[133] Callison and Vestal, 'The L3C illusion', 625.

[134] Brakman Reiser, 'Governing and financing', 622.

[135] R. Lang, 'The L3C: background and legislative issues', at 5, available at: www.americansforcommunitydevelopment.org.

LIMITS TO CORPORATE REFORM AND ALTERNATIVE STRUCTURES   301

investments from foundations qualified as PRIs.[136] The proposal did not end up being introduced to US Congress and thus was not successful in producing new federal legislation or IRS rulings. Similarly, a subsequent attempt under the proposed 'Philanthropic Facilitation Act of 2011'[137] was tabled before Congress. It attempted to provide a simple IRS registration and approval process to prevent foundations from spending considerable time and money obtaining PLRs each time a PRI was sought by an L3C. The proposed legislation also did not result in any federal action.

In May 2012, the IRS released proposed regulations that provided nine additional examples of investments that qualify as PRIs.[138] These regulations make no mention of the L3C but serve to better illustrate the application of the existing regulations, which may or may not help justify the existence of the L3C. Critics of the L3C model have argued that the L3C has 'little to no value' without accompanying federal legislation or an IRS ruling.[139] Furthermore, opponents have questioned whether L3Cs 'could divert charitable assets from non-profit organizations', as well as how L3Cs will be monitored 'to ensure that profit remains secondary to the charitable purpose and investors do not receive an improper benefit', among other things.[140] Lang and the organisation behind the L3C, Americans for Community Development, have often found themselves on the defensive regarding the viability of the model.[141] Lang has since conceded that 'the IRS is not going to ever rule on the blanket acceptability of the L3C as an entity... The IRS has no preference positive or negative, as to business organisational structure. They are interested only in that the resulting structure uses the charitable invested dollars to further an allowable exempt purpose.'[142]

It is unlikely the L3C will have global reach given its specificity and close adherence to jurisdiction-specific US federal tax rules. It remains to

---

[136] Mannweiler Foundation Inc., 'The Program-Related Investment Promotion Act of 2008: a proposal for encouraging charitable investments', available at: www.cof.org.

[137] Philanthropic Facilitation Act of 2011 (H.R.3420); Americans for Community Development, 'Proposed federal legislation' (15 November 2011), available at: www.americansforcommunitydevelopment.org; GovTrack, 'H.R. 3420 (112th) Philanthropic Facilitation Act', available at: www.govtrack.us.

[138] IRS, 'Notice of proposed rulemaking examples of program-related investments', *Internal Revenue Bulletin* 2012-21, Reg.-144267–11 (21 May 2012), available at: www.irs.gov.

[139] Callison and Vestal, 'The L3C illusion', 274.

[140] C. Reinhart, 'Low-profit limited liability companies or L3Cs' (7 October 2011) Connecticut General Assembly, Office of Legislative Research, available at: www.cga.ct.gov.

[141] Lang, 'Background and legislative issues', 23.

[142] R. Lang, 'L3Cs and the IRS', available at: www.americansforcommunitydevelopment.org.

302　　　CAROL LIAO

be seen how the L3C hybrid will fare in the USA, given the deliberate omission by the IRS in recognising the role of, or even the existence of, L3Cs in regard to PRIs. It is unclear if foundations have been particularly drawn to L3Cs – certainly the hybrid provides greater assurance in regard to PRIs than for-profit entities, but the IRS's silence on the matter has been deafening. As of June 2014, there were 1,037 L3Cs in operation, and it is inconclusive whether to date L3Cs have helped increase the percentage of PRIs relative to total grant and PRI output from foundations.[143]

4.3.2　B Corporation (privately regulated)

Consideration of stakeholder interests has generally been allowed in for-profit corporations under several US state laws since as far back as the 1980s, when the corporate takeover boom saw several states implement 'other constituency' (also known as 'nonshareholder constituency'[144] or 'corporate constituency'[145]) legislation. Such laws expressly permit (and in at least one state, require[146]) directors to consider the interests of groups in addition to shareholders in decision-making, often in particular when contemplating takeover situations.[147] The large majority of US states are now other constituency states[148] – only about a dozen states as of mid 2014 have not implemented such legislation.[149]

B Lab is a Philadelphia-based non-profit organisation that began in 2008 and has capitalised on the other constituency statutes. B Lab has created a certification system that builds upon those statutes by requiring corporations to enshrine stakeholder interests in their governing documents. The 'B Corporation' certification is unique in this regard; B Lab has elected to address governance issues in a way that is unrivalled by other CSR certifications in the market. Self-imposed and privately regulated,

---

[143] InterSector Partners L3C, 'Here's the latest L3C tally' (8 March 2013), available at: www .intersectorl3c.com (numbers based on active L3Cs reported by Secretaries of State).

[144] S. Bainbridge, 'Interpreting nonshareholder constituency statutes' (1992) 19 *Pepperdine Law Review* 991.

[145] L. Mitchell, 'A theoretical framework for enforcing corporate constituency statutes' (1992) 70 *Texas Law Review* 579.

[146] Connecticut Business Corporations Act, s. 33–600.

[147] For more on this, see A. Keay, 'Moving towards stakeholderism? Constituency statutes, enlightened shareholder value and all that: much ado about little?' (2010), available at: http://ssrn.com/abstract=1530990; Bainbridge, 'Interpreting'; Mitchell, 'Theoretical framework'.

[148] K. Hale, 'Corporate law and stakeholders: moving beyond stakeholder statutes' (2003) 45 *Arizona Law Review* 823 at 833 and n. 78.

[149] B Corporation, 'Corporation legal roadmap', available at: www.bcorporation.net.

LIMITS TO CORPORATE REFORM AND ALTERNATIVE STRUCTURES 303

B Lab is attempting to establish a new kind of company, one that 'harnesses the power of business to solve social and environmental problems'.[150] The founders of B Corporation have also been influential in persuading state legislators to create 'benefit corporations' in several US states (examined in Section 4.3.3), so there is particular value in understanding the motivations behind the creation of that hybrid through an examination of the B Corporation. The B Lab is actively marketing its branding internationally, and as of July 2014 there were 1,045 B Corporations in 34 countries, but overwhelmingly these are found in the USA.[151]

In order to become a B Corporation, a company is first required to take a 'B Impact Assessment' that surveys issues relating to accountability, employees, consumers, the community, and the environment. A corporation is certified by B Lab once an acceptable score is obtained according to their rating system (80 out of 200), and the company is required to submit supporting documents for a portion of the answers.[152] B Lab relies on the assessment and a separate auditing system to ensure B Corporations are pursuing and achieving their social mandates. Within an allotted time following certification, B Corporations must amend their articles of incorporation requiring directors to consider more than just shareholder interests when carrying out their duties.[153] In the past, a company must already be incorporated in an other constituency state, or must re-incorporate in one in order to make such amendments and be a certified B Corporation. B Lab is now allowing companies that are incorporated in states without this legislation to simply build stakeholder interests into a signed term sheet, with an understanding that if the company's resident state eventually creates a benefit corporation, the company will adopt benefit corporation status by the end of their two-year certification term.[154]

American B Corporations are directly carved out of the findings in the well-known US judicial case of *Revlon Inc. v. MacAndrews v. Forbes Holdings, Inc.* (*Revlon*).[155] In the case, the Supreme Court of Delaware held that directors owe a fiduciary duty to maximise shareholder value in takeover contexts, regardless of non-shareholder stakeholder interests. The *Revlon*

---

[150] B Corporation, available at: www.bcorporation.net.
[151] B Corporation, 'B corp community', available at: www.bcorporation.net/community.
[152] B Corporation, 'Become a B corporation', available at: www.bcorporation.net/become-a-b-Corp.
[153] B Corporation, 'Become a B corporation'.
[154] B Corporation, 'Corporation legal roadmap'.
[155] 506 A2d 173, ALR 4th 157 (Del Sup Ct 1985).

304   CAROL LIAO

decision is generally regarded as the leading judicial precedent in support of shareholder primacy in corporate America, and B Lab has elected to address the matter directly. The requirement by B Lab that a director 'shall' consider various stakeholder interests is an interesting one. Obligating directors to consider non-shareholder stakeholders, rather than simply permitting them to do so, is a significant legal difference. Such duties hold directors to a much higher standard, though B Lab's language includes the insertion of 'as the Director deems relevant', a subjective standard that softens the obligation considerably, and echoes the common law position. US courts have validated the business judgement rule, meaning that the courts will defer to the board's judgement as long as the directors have brought an appropriate degree of diligence in reaching a reasonable business decision at the particular time that it was made.[156] So, provided that the board's decision is within a range of reasonable alternatives, a court will always defer to that judgement.

While the numbers are sizable given the grassroots nature of the B Corporation, the number in existence is of course infinitesimally small when compared to the number of corporations in the USA, which, according to the US Census Bureau, totals over twenty-seven million businesses.[157] The growth of the B Corporation has been slow and steady since its inception in 2008, much like the L3C. Dana Brakman Reiser cautions that 'it remains to be seen whether this system will have strong teeth'.[158] She comments:

> [T]he B corporation form realistically offers only moral, rather than legal, assurances to non-shareholder constituencies and social interests. Stakeholders have no structural rights in governance, and no additional parties are granted standing to litigate. B corporation directors are empowered to act in the interests of other constituencies; whether they do so will depend on their own desires or feelings of moral obligation.[159]

Given that B Lab is a private organisation, it does not have the authority to manipulate existing legal structures. Instead, it works with existing laws to guide corporations to change their framework. The B Impact Assessment goes to the core of the business purpose and mission, and addresses

---

[156] *Grobow v. Perot*, 539 A.2d 180 (Del. 1988) (which outlines the business judgement test).
[157] US Census Bureau, 'statistics about business size (including small business) from the US Census Bureau', available at: www.census.gov/econ/smallbus.html (this number is as of 2009; more recent statistics are unavailable).
[158] Brakman Reiser, 'Governing and financing', 643.
[159] Brakman Reiser, 'Governing and financing', 642.

LIMITS TO CORPORATE REFORM AND ALTERNATIVE STRUCTURES   305

stakeholder and sustainability concerns. Corporations may choose to become B Corporations so they can align themselves with like-minded companies. The B Corporation branding may 'draw in directors committed to a blended mission and investors willing to enforce it'.[160] It could one day be a certification popularly recognisable to consumers. As a strategic movement that has tapped on the shoulders of business leaders and politicians for support, the B Corporation may become meaningful in educating companies how to integrate CSR principles into their governance practices.

Admittedly, B Corporations are loosely regulated, if at all. B Lab is a small organisation that is not equipped to regulate numerous companies effectively, particularly given its additional involvement in legislative policy-making and sharp focus on marketing its brand. B Lab's motivation has tended to lean towards attracting mass participation, not ensuring proper regulation. B Lab's standards are considerably weaker in comparison to other marketed CSR certifications.[161] It thus becomes a question of balance. There is some value to be had in generating a buzz and creating the impression of momentum, but the trade-off with mass inclusion is usually a lowering of standards. There may be a backlash from genuine 'good' companies that are reluctant to sign on due to seemingly lowered standards; one executive commented that joining the B Corporation movement would be like 'sprinkling holy water on the process', as the standards they have set for themselves and expect from their competitors are markedly higher than B Lab's offerings.[162] So the question is, is B Corporation a mass movement for change, or does it simply allow companies to market themselves better – and, if so, is this sufficient? Is there any meaning underneath the branding? There is certainly value in garnering collective strength from numbers, and legitimised advertising. Perhaps the value of aligning businesses with common interests through the B Corporation branding outweighs the need for high-quality standards and adequate regulation. While B Lab's focus has understandably been on establishing the B Corporation name, B Lab will have to be careful that its ongoing effort to gain mass participation does not dilute its branding to the point where it carries little meaning.

[160] Brakman Reiser, 'Governing and financing', 643.

[161] Some examples include the Global Initiative for Sustainable Ratings (GIRS), and standards provided by the Sustainable Accounting Standard Board and International Integrated Reporting Council.

[162] Comments made in a private interview by executives at Innate, an active gear company committed to clean design, www.innate-gear.com.

4.3.3 Benefit corporation

Following intensive lobbying by B Lab and their supporters in several US states, the states of Maryland and Vermont became the first to pass benefit corporation legislation in 2010, facilitating new corporate structures designed to create both social benefits and shareholder value.[163] Maryland's benefit corporation laws came into effect in October 2010[164] and Vermont's in July 2011.[165] In addition to Maryland and Vermont, benefit corporation legislation as of July 2014 has been enacted in 25 states, and 14 other states are reportedly developing or considering such legislation.[166] The governing features in benefit corporations vary somewhat from state to state, but the main common features across several of the states echo those that were first enacted in Maryland and Vermont, thus these two states are used as the example.

The ostensible purpose of a benefit corporation is to create a general public benefit, which is defined as 'a material positive impact on society and the environment, as measured by a third-party standard, through activities that promote [some] combination of specific public benefits'.[167] A corporation seeking benefit corporation status must include or make a clear and prominent statement in its articles that it is a benefit corporation.[168] There are no specific criteria to qualify as a benefit corporation so long as proper company approvals have been met, and that also applies if a company wishes to withdraw from being a benefit corporation. Existing state corporate laws are to fill any holes left in the benefit corporation laws.

A significant aspect of the benefit corporation laws is the codification of stakeholder interests in directorial decision-making. In Maryland, a director is required to consider the effects of any action or decision not to act on stockholders,[169] employees, subsidiaries, suppliers, customers, community and societal considerations, and the local and global

---

[163] *Corporate Social Responsibility Newswire*, 'Maryland first state in union to pass benefit corporation legislation' (14 April 2010), available at: www.csrwire.com; Outdoor Industry Association, 'Vermont becomes second state to pass B Corporation legislation' (2 June 2010), available at: www.outdoorindustry.org.

[164] Corporations and Associations, Md. Code Ann. tit. 5; s. 5–6C-01 (2010) [Maryland Act].

[165] Vermont Benefit Corporations Act, Vt. Stat. tit. 11A s. 21 (2011) [Vermont Act].

[166] Benefit Corp Information Center, 'state by state legislative status', available at: www.benefitcorp.net.

[167] Maryland Act, s. 5–6C-01(c); Vermont Act, s. 21.03(4).

[168] Maryland Act, s. 5–6C-03, s. 5–6C-05; Vermont Act, s. 21.05.

[169] In Maryland and certain other states, the term 'stockholder' is used instead of 'shareholder'.

LIMITS TO CORPORATE REFORM AND ALTERNATIVE STRUCTURES   307

environment.[170] Vermont has an additional sixth factor, encompassing 'the long-term and short-term interests of the benefit corporation, including the possibility that those interests may be best served by the continued independence of the benefit corporation'.[171] In contrast to the standard articulated in *Revlon*, this addition provides substantially the same protection as the similar provision offered by the B Corporation model by relieving directors of the duties to maximise shareholder value in a takeover situation.

In Maryland, the director has no duty (fiduciary or otherwise) to a person who is a general public beneficiary of the benefit corporation. Vermont, however, has actually gone a step further in expanding the definition of fiduciary duties for their directors.[172] Vermont directors have fiduciary responsibility only to those persons entitled to bring about a proceeding against the benefit corporation. A 'benefit enforcement proceeding' means a claim or action against a director or officer for failing to pursue the public benefit purpose set forth in its articles, or for violating any duty in the statute. These persons have been identified as shareholders, directors, persons, or group of persons who hold 10 per cent or more of the equity interests in an entity where the benefit corporation is a subsidiary, or any other persons specified in the articles of the benefit corporation.[173] While the expansion may seem slight, it is important. Shareholders, and shareholders of any parent company, can bring proceedings against the benefit corporation for violating the broader, codified stakeholder interests.[174] However, directors have the same immunity from

---

[170] Maryland Act, s. 5–6C-07(a)(1). Vermont has some *de minimis* differences in wording. See Vermont Act, s. 21.09(a).

[171] Vermont Act, s. 21.09(a)(1)(F). The explicit inclusion offers symbolic vindication for Vermont, home of the socially-minded ice cream business, Ben & Jerry's Homemade, Inc., whose board in 2000 had multiple offers to purchase the company but had no choice but to sell to the highest offer or risk a shareholder lawsuit. Ben & Jerry's Homemade, Inc., News Release, 'Ben & Jerry's and Unilever to join forces' (12 April 2000), available at: www.benjerry.com. But see A. Page and R.A Katz, 'Freezing out Ben & Jerry: corporate law and the sale of a social enterprise icon' (2010) 35 *Vermont Law Review* 211, which argues that Ben & Jerry's had strict anti-takeover defenses that their board declined to test, and that negative reactions to the sale of social enterprises may be misguided as such sales may create more opportunities for social enterprises to do good work. Ben & Jerry's have since become the first wholly-owned subsidiary to be a B Corporation. CSRWire, 'Ben & Jerry's joins the growing B corporation movement' (22 October 2012), available at: www.csrwire.com.

[172] Vermont Act, s. 21.09(e).   [173] Vermont Act, s. 21.13(b).

[174] Vermont's expansion of duties thus has required setting out proper parameters of the directors' duties. See Vermont Act, s. 21.09(a)(3). Directors are not subject to a different or

liability as directors of regular for-profit corporations. So unless they did not act diligently, or their acts constitute fraud or negligence, the courts are unlikely to intrude upon a director's business judgement.

A benefit corporation is responsible for creating an annual benefit report, with Vermont requiring board approval prior to the report being sent out to shareholders.[175] The report is required to include: (1) a description of how the benefit corporation pursued a public benefit during the year and the extent to which the public benefit was created; (2) any circumstances that hindered the creation of the public benefit; and (3) an assessment of the societal and environmental performance of the benefit corporation, prepared in accordance with a third-party standard.[176] Vermont includes more explicit instructions on how the report must be constructed, such as outlining specific goals or outcomes, disclosing the amount of compensation paid to each director and the name of each shareholder holding 5 per cent or more of the shares.[177] These additions add a heightened level of transparency and accountability that echoes some of the disclosure requirements of public companies.[178] Vermont also has created the requirement for one director of the board to be designated as a 'benefit director', who is required to be independent, and prepare an annual statement detailing whether, in the opinion of that director, the company acted in accordance with its benefit purpose, and if not, why not.[179] This statement and the annual benefit report are to be delivered and approved by the shareholders and also posted on the company website.

A potential alternative to shareholder primacy has been created to combat negative corporate behaviour that may be damaging to broader community, environmental, or other stakeholder interests. The question is whether social entrepreneurs, particularly those currently situated in the for-profit sector, will be attracted to the benefit corporation model. Along with the relative novelty of the entity, several states do not track

> higher standard of care when decisions may affect the control of the benefit corporation. Vermont Act, s. 21.09(a)(4). As well, a director is not liable for the failure of a benefit corporation to create general or specific public benefit. Directors have the same immunity from liability as directors of those state's corporations generally.

[175] Maryland Act, s. 5–6C-08(a).

[176] Vermont has also required a statement of the specific goals or outcomes, and actions that can be taken to attain them while improving its social and environmental performance. See Vermont Act, s. 21.14(a)(1)(D).

[177] Vermont Act, s.21.14(a)(4)–(7).

[178] Vermont Act, s. 21.14(b) and s. 21.14(d); Maryland Act, s. 5–6C-08(b), (c).

[179] See e.g. Vermont Act, s. 21.10.

the names and number of benefit corporations, so it is difficult to determine how many are currently in operation.[180] Nevertheless, the benefit corporation seems to be a very positive development for US corporate governance reform, as it is designed to address American corporate governance needs for social progress. The development of benefit corporation laws promotes a more stakeholder-based model with supporting infrastructure to encourage an active level of social responsibility, and it will be interesting to see how it fares in its critical nascent years of development. An important research enquiry will be to measure and quantify the contribution that benefit corporations ultimately make towards sustainable development and other stakeholder concerns.

5   Conclusion

The CSR movement has been effective in reducing some of the negative externalities from the private sector, but thus far CSR has not proven to be a successful change agent against the shareholder primacy model. Along with path dependence, several entrenched ideological beliefs supporting the model almost ensure its continued dominance into the foreseeable future. Nevertheless, while there seems to be a lack of cohesive theory on counter-hegemonic discourses in corporate law, and potentially divergent language between corporate scholarship and practice, it is still critical for there to be ongoing dialogue addressing the structural problems of the shareholder primacy model, and how to institutionalise alternative regimes. More importantly, this dialogue must consider the development of innovative alternatives that can meet the demands of a growing CSR trend towards social enterprises.

There is now a movement underway which has attempted to sidestep the shareholder primacy model, allowing businesses to pursue both economic and social mandates in their corporate decision-making through alternative legal structures. An emerging generation of hybrid corporate legal structures is finally coming into focus on the global stage. There are big picture issues to consider in future research, such as how these models are situated in local and global social economies, how they balance alongside other alternatives, how they are to be treated as subsidiaries in corporate groups, and if they indeed take away from resources that are more needed elsewhere or if instead they create an influx of private cash

---

[180] Benefit Corp Information Center, 'Find a benefit corp', available at: www.benefitcorp .net/find-a-benefit-corp.

into the social sector. There is also an important question as to whether tax and other laws should be adjusted to accommodate these models, and if so, exactly how. In addition to the models that have been described in this chapter, there is considerable space for nations to contemplate establishing new yet-to-be-seen forms of hybrid structures to better address growing demands from both for-profit and non-profit sectors. Ideas for innovative new models are being circulated. For example, a group of Canadian professionals and academics have put together a proposal urging their provincial governments to adopt a 'deliberate corporation' model, where the disbursement of dividends is made dependent upon the achievement of measurable, non-monetary goals.[181] Opportunities are available to seriously push for redesigning corporate legal models, whether from a grassroots level or as a result of legislative reforms in reaction to the market.

The next few decades will be very telling as to the success of hybrid legal structures, and whether they gain any traction in corporate practice. While there is always the potential for a particular hybrid to become a disruptive innovation[182] in a nation's corporate sector, working its way up the market and eventually displacing the mainstream model, in reality, the likelihood of this occurring is slim. As discussed in Section 2, entrenched ideological beliefs and path dependence will make it very difficult to uproot the established power structure, and pragmatically, it is questionable how hybrids would infiltrate global multinational enterprises and similar well-established forms of industry. Instead, it is likely that hybrids will become a niche sector of the market, operating more as a small supplement relative to the mainstream corporate model rather than as one that may overtake it. Nevertheless, hybrids are beginning to play a seminal role in challenging the mainstream model and forcing legislators to contemplate the legal limitations within that model. They

---

[181] J. Dudek and A. Zieba, 'The deliberate corporation: moving beyond social business', *Deliberate Economics*, April 2012, available at: http://deliberateeconomics.com. A UK team is also exploring the establishment of a Social Enterprise Limited Liability Company (SE LLC), where investor returns would be capped at 10 per cent, among other governing features. See C. Calahane, 'What is the perfect legal structure of a community interest company?' (4 April 2011), available at: http://socialenterprise.guardian.co.uk; see also A. Wood, 'New legal structures to address the social capital famine' (2010) 35 *Vermont Law Review* 45.

[182] I use the term 'disruptive innovation' liberally here, as it is often used to refer to technological advances. For more on disruptive innovation, see C. Christensen, *et al.*, 'Disruptive innovation for social change' (December 2006) 84 *Harvard Business Review* 12.

are 'a reminder to the international community that it is possible to pursue both economic viability and social responsibility'.[183] Hybrids may be integral in growing the social economy and significantly enhancing sustainable practices. There is untapped potential to be had in the correct implementation of hybrids in a nation's corporate landscape.

The ICA has noted: '[w]e are living in a time of great change, where popular attitudes and motivation are changing'.[184] They believe concerted action is needed, otherwise 'the moment will be lost'.[185] Indeed, it seems that the topic of sustainability has come to the forefront at present. Now is the opportunity for paradigm-busting, well-researched, and well-planned models to come into being. Leaders must begin to turn their focus to this emergent field of corporate law. Legislators will need to work quickly, but they should also be smart. It is therefore critical for a stream of intelligent and thoughtful commentary to develop that can address the possible elevation of sustainable practices through these innovative new hybrid legal structures.

---

[183] UN Department of Economics and Social Affairs, 'Co-operative enterprises build a better world' (26 October 2011), available at: http://undesadspd.org.

[184] International Co-operative Alliance, 'Blueprint', 33.

[185] International Co-operative Alliance, 'Blueprint', 2.

8

The future of company law and sustainability

BEATE SJÅFJELL AND BENJAMIN J. RICHARDSON

1 From incremental to fundamental reform

In spite of apparently earnest reform efforts on many levels and in many jurisdictions, including, for example, the adoption in April 2014 of new non-financial reporting requirements for the largest companies in the EU,[1] there are few signs that current governance regimes are or will be capable of producing more than just incremental improvements. Incrementalism is not even close to the fundamental shift we need to change from 'business as usual' to an environmentally sustainable path.

While politicians and business magnates emphasise solutions that are within the realms of what is perceived as politically or financially realistic, the fact that nature has its own realism is not well recognised outside of scientific and academic communities. In fact, some business and political elites conspire to retard progress by strenuously doubting the basic science of climate change. Australia, one of the world's worst climate polluters, as measured by per capita GHG emissions, provides such grim evidence when in July 2014 the federal government sensationally repealed its national carbon tax.[2] The speed at which we transgress the planetary boundaries[3] is unaffected by the limits of what is possible to win political consensus for, or to what the 'markets' at any time are perceived to be willing to accept. The celebration of these politically feasible incremental changes, mere nods towards sustainability, may in themselves hinder real

---

[1] See http://ec.europa.eu/finance/accounting/non-financial_reporting/index_en.htm.

[2] E. Griffiths, 'Carbon tax scrapped,' *ABC News*, 17 July 2014, available at: http://www.abc.net.au/news.

[3] See J. Rockström, *et al.*, 'Planetary boundaries: exploring the safe operating space for humanity' (2009) 14(2) *Ecology and Society*, available at: www.ecologyandsociety.org/vol14/iss2/art32/. The planetary boundaries under stress include climate change and biodiversity loss, global freshwater and land use, chemical pollution, ocean acidification, atmospheric aerosol loading, stratospheric ozone depletion, and cycling of phosphorus and nitrogen.

THE FUTURE OF COMPANY LAW AND SUSTAINABILITY 313

change. Incremental improvements may lull us into a dangerous complacency.

Recent scientific research in 2014 suggests humankind is perched on the precipice of a crisis in the biosphere, with climate change the gravest threat. Current GHG emissions from industrialisation and deforestation are likely to result in breaching the safe warming threshold of two degrees Celsius, and thus the danger of runaway climate change is looming.[4] The fifth Assessment Report on climate change by the Intergovernmental Panel on Climate Change (IPCC), published in April 2014, reiterates its message from its 2007 assessment, namely, that we must urgently begin massively reducing emissions if humankind is to avoid dangerous anthropogenic global warming.[5] The fifth Assessment Report also tells us that despite more climate change mitigation policies, total anthropogenic GHG emissions have continued to soar in recent years, especially since 1970 as emerging economies ramped up their growth agenda.[6] While voluntary business efforts such as the World Business Council for Sustainable Development's 'Action2020', on the face of it, are laudable,[7] science tells us that we do not even seem to have substantively slowed down the speed at which we are approaching a highly unsustainable future.[8] And our window of opportunity for preventive or restorative action is quickly closing.[9]

While the focus of this book is on the environmental dimensions of sustainability, for reasons explained in our introductory chapter, we recognise the inextricable interrelatedness of the environmental, social, and economic facets of sustainability and that climate change deeply affects the social dimension. We must not only seek a safe and prosperous space for humanity within the biosphere's boundaries, it must be a *just* living space for humanity – what Kate Raworth calls 'living within the doughnut'.[10] However, even with our more limited focus on the environmental dimensions of sustainability, it is clear that profound change is

[4] C.B. Field, *et al.*, *Approved Summary for Policy Makers* (IPCC, 2014), 11 et seq.
[5] O. Edenhofer, *et al.*, *Final Draft Summary for Policymakers* (IPCC, 2014), 8.
[6] Edenhofer, *et al.*, *Final Draft Summary*, 5.   [7] Action2020.org.
[8] Similarly, political efforts are far from sufficient: Edenhofer, *et al.*, *Final Draft Summary*, 16.
[9] The IPCC reports that delaying mitigation efforts beyond those in place today through 2030 is estimated to substantially increase the difficulty of the transition to low longer-term emissions levels; Edenhofer *et al.*, *Final Draft Summary*.
[10] See K. Raworth, 'A safe and just space for humanity: can we live within the doughnut?' (Oxfam International, 2012).

needed to recalibrate humanity onto a sustainable path.[11] The question is: how can we achieve a timely and orderly transition? Operationalised, the question is essentially this: what are the key pieces of the governance formula for sustainability – such as regulatory reforms, voluntary efforts, social movements, and international political agreements – and can these pieces be put into effect in good time?[12] This book discusses one of the required pieces of the formula: a legal infrastructure for companies that sets them on an environmentally sustainable path.

In a legal context, sustainability is increasingly proclaimed as an overarching goal, expressed with varying firmness or specificity across regions and nations. In the EU, sustainability has evolved through treaty reforms from an implicit goal of the Union[13] to become its explicit meta-norm.[14] In parallel, EU treaty reforms have seen a successive strengthening of what may be perceived as a codification of the most easily implemented facet of the sustainable development agenda: the environmental integration principle. Set out now in Article 11 of the Treaty on the functioning of the European Union (TFEU),[15] this codification obliges EU institutions (significant indirectly for the EU Member States) to integrate environmental protection requirements in all their policies and activities with the aim of furthering sustainable development. As Christina Voigt and Beate Sjåfjell have shown, the general principle of sustainable development and the codified EU rule require a prioritisation of the environmental dimension to the extent necessary to be able to achieve sustainability.[16] That this obligation is not followed routinely in practice

---

[11] See e.g. T. Jackson, *Prosperity Without Growth: Economics for a Finite Planet* (Earthscan, 2011).

[12] The alternative being that we, or our children and their children, will witness the breakdown of societies, and such fundamental threats to the very basis of human existence that rebuilding any type of civilisation may not be possible.

[13] See B. Sjåfjell, *Towards a Sustainable European Company Law* (Kluwer Law International, 2009), Part III.

[14] Art. 3(3): 'The Union shall . . . work for the sustainable development of Europe' and art. 3(5): 'The Union shall [. . . contribute to . . .] the sustainable development of the Earth' of the Treaty on European Union (1992), last amended by the Treaty of Lisbon, OJ 2008 C115 (consolidated version).

[15] The Treaty on the Functioning of the European Union, last amended by the Treaty of Lisbon, OJ 2008 C115 (consolidated version).

[16] See C. Voigt, *Sustainable Development as a Principle of International Law: Resolving Conflicts between Climate Measures and WTO Law* (Martinus Nijhoff Publishers, 2009); B. Sjåfjell, 'Quo vadis, Europe? The significance of sustainable development as objective, principle and rule of EU law', in C. Bailliet (ed.), *Non State Actors, Soft Law and Protective Regimes* (Cambridge University Press, 2012), 254.

THE FUTURE OF COMPANY LAW AND SUSTAINABILITY 315

by EU institutions does not in itself diminish the legal nature of the duty in question.[17]

The environmental integration principle embodies what working towards sustainability entails for business as well: internalising environmental (and social) externalities so as to create long-term value for the company and its stakeholders within the planetary boundaries.[18] Sadly, however, this is not what we commonly see in practice. Rather, business lobbyists have often captured the debate about how business should contribute to sustainability, with CSR predominantly defined as businesses' voluntary contribution, i.e. something that business can choose to do based on an implicit deal that legislators will refrain from regulating standards.[19] CSR has been portrayed as anything benign a company chooses to do, with corporate charity work used as a sleight of hand to shift attention from how the company is conducting its business and who or what it affects.[20]

If CSR is to be a useful concept in our context,[21] this would require first of all that CSR must encompass both the level of legal compliance and action beyond minimal legal standards.[22] Second, CSR must go beyond community and charitable contributions to deal with the core business of the company, how that is conducted, and the social and environmental impacts of that business. Furthermore, CSR must entail an integration of environmental (and social) concerns in the decision-making of the company in such a way as to lead to an internalisation of costly externalities.[23]

---

[17] Rather, it shows the necessity of spelling out the legal significance clearly and repeating the message until it gets through, see Sjåfjell, 'Quo vadis', s. 4.2, and s. 3.1 about the concept of duty in this context.

[18] B. Sjåfjell and J. Mähönen, 'Upgrading the Nordic corporate governance model for sustainable companies' (2014) 11 *European Company Law* 58.

[19] As discussed in more detail in this book's introductory chapter.

[20] The problematic nature of CSR in its voluntary form and the 'greenwashing' that is done under its guise are some of the reasons that one may be reticent about using the concept at all. See further Millon's Chapter 2 in this book, and B. Sjåfjell, 'Internalizing externalities in EU law: why neither corporate governance nor corporate social responsibility provides the answers' (2008) 40 *George Washington International Law Review* 977.

[21] Which the EU seems to be believe it can be: 'Through CSR, enterprises can significantly contribute to the European Union's treaty objectives of sustainable development and a highly competitive social market economy', COM (2011) 681 final, s. 1.2.

[22] Defining CSR as voluntary tends to lead to delimitation against legal obligations and an unwarranted corporate governance/CSR dichotomy: B. Sjåfjell, 'Why law matters: corporate social irresponsibility and the futility of voluntary climate change mitigation' (2011) 8 *European Company Law* 56.

[23] Sjåfjell, 'Internalizing externalities in EU law'.

While we have seen an increasing tendency towards a broader recognition of the social impact of companies and, notably on the EU level, a paradigm shift in the way CSR is defined, in the business law context, legislators, including the EU and its members, still hesitate to actually mandate that companies change their behaviour fundamentally. At the regulatory level, the reflexive theory inspired the hope of changing how companies act through requiring them to report on their external impacts, a theory that appeals to governments in favour of lighter regulation.[24] In spite of complaints about the ostensible bureaucratic burden of reporting, this method seems to be the preferred compromise, giving NGOs and earnest politicians a sanguine feeling of progress while leaving the way business earns its money and shares that wealth with shareholders generally untouched.[25] If indeed regulators had been serious about actually altering how companies operate through reporting, one would have assumed that robust assurance and enforcement mechanisms would have been put in place, which they have not. In the broader regulatory context, these light-touch controls on business have their lenient-approach cousins in the economic policy instruments of carbon cap-and-trade schemes and carbon taxes. They have generally not been as effective as they could be, again because of regulatory capture by business lobbyists that dilute the goals through concessions and loopholes such as grandfather clauses, tax holidays, and offsetting compensatory payments.[26]

We thus see two divergent trends in the areas of sustainability and company law. First, the growing societal awareness that companies have a deleterious impact on important public goods, such as the global climate, as well as other 'social' interests, as epitomised by the recent shift in the EU's definition of CSR, focusing on the responsibility of companies for their 'impact on society' and requiring an integration of 'social, environmental, ethical, human rights, and consumer concerns into their

---

[24] See G. Teubner, 'Social order from legislative noise? Autopoietic closure as a problem for legal regulation', in G. Teubner and A. Febbrajo (eds.), *State, Law, Economy as Autopoietic Systems: Regulation and Autonomy in a New Perspective* (Giuffrè, 1992), 631; G. Teubner, 'After legal instrumentalism?' in G. Teubner (ed.), *Dilemmas of Law in the Welfare State* (Walter de Gruyter, 1986), 229.

[25] R. Howitt, 'The EU law on non-financial reporting – how we got there', *Guardian*, 16 April 2014, available at: www.theguardian.com/sustainable-business/eu-non-financial-reporting-how-richard-howitt. Howitt is a long-standing member of the European Parliament and the Rapporteur for the Parliament on Corporate Social Responsibility.

[26] D. Driesen, 'Economic instruments for sustainable development', in B.J. Richardson and S. Wood (eds.), *Environmental Law for Sustainability* (Hart Publishing, 2006), 277.

THE FUTURE OF COMPANY LAW AND SUSTAINABILITY   317

business operations and core strategy'.[27] This impetus is also evident in the emerging tendency to include consideration of such interests in business legislation,[28] and is supported in some jurisdictions by soft-law instruments such as the OECD Guidelines for Multinational Enterprises[29] and the UN Guiding Principles on Business and Human Rights.[30]

An antagonistic development is the corporate governance trend solidifying the shareholder primacy drive, with the privileging of short-term returns to shareholders. This orientation is supported by the enduring belief in simplistic postulates derived from mainstream legal-economic theories combined with the interlinked belief in economic incentives as the ultimate solution. It is further strengthened by being firmly embedded in the larger economic system of capitalism, where companies in the models of mainstream economic theory are perceived as vehicles for optimising societal welfare through the maximisation of returns to shareholders. Over time, the starting premise that shareholder value is only a means to an end seems to have disappeared, along with the caveat concerning externalities. Only the conclusions drawn from those models remain, and cut off from their theoretical origins, they have become postulates and conventional wisdom, with a strong influence on legislative discussions.

The dominance of these economic theories and their influence on the understanding of how our societies function are illustrated by the tenacity of the singular logic of the economic thinking where the fact that a finite planet cannot hold infinite growth is blatantly ignored. The concurrent simplistic thinking with its faith in economic incentives and giving predominance to that which can easily be measured carries with it the 'functional fallacy' of encouraging people to act for

---

[27] B. Sjåfjell and L. Anker-Sørensen, 'Directors' duties and corporate social responsibility (CSR)', in H.S. Birkmose, M. Neville, and K.E. Sørensen (eds.), *Boards of Directors in European Companies: Reshaping and Harmonising Their Organisation and Duties* (Kluwer, 2013), 153.

[28] Typically in new reporting requirements, which on their own are insufficient, see Villiers and Mähönen's Chapter 5 in this book, and corporate governance codes, the hallmark of shareholder primacy, D.G. Szabó and K. Engsig Sørensen, *Integrating Corporate Social Responsibility in Corporate Governance Codes in the EU* (Nordic and European Company Law, LSN Research Paper Series, 2013), 4.

[29] OECD Guidelines for Multinational Enterprises, last revised in 2011, see www.oecd.org/corporate/mne. See especially its Chapter VI, Environment.

[30] See UN Guiding Principles for Business and Human Rights, available at: www.business-humanrights.org/Documents/UNNorms, and e.g. M.B. Taylor, 'Beyond "beyond compliance": how human rights is transforming CSR', in A. Midtun (ed.), *CSR and Beyond: A Nordic Perspective* (Cappelen Damm Akademisk, 2013), 253.

financial reward rather than working for less easily defined, social and environmental values.[31] It is difficult to overestimate the negative consequences of the naïve thinking that has led many policy-makers worldwide to believe that the right mix of economic incentives is all that is needed to create prosperity and minimise any collateral environmental damage.

While the Sustainable Companies Project from which this book is derived began with a narrower focus on analysing the barriers to and possibilities of company law in promoting sustainability, the importance of addressing other interrelated areas of policy and governance has become clearer. We acknowledge the significance of the evolving alternative models of organising business through corporate hybrids,[32] the importance of financiers in influencing business,[33] and the broader context of market capitalism. These insights should be borne in mind as we discuss future directions in corporate law and an agenda for future legal reform and academic research.

2 Barriers and possibilities in current corporate law

A seminal finding of the Sustainable Companies Project is that there is much unexplored potential within current company law regimes for businesses to move towards sustainability. Boards of directors, these strategy-setting, monitoring organs with their duty to promote the interests of the company, are key to this shift. As we have seen in the comparative company law analysis in Chapter 3 by Sjåfjell and others, boards have, as a matter of law, a perhaps surprisingly broad scope to integrate environmental concerns into their decision-making. Besides the obvious, that boards across jurisdictions are duty-bound to ensure that companies comply with environmental law, company law confers upon governing boards the discretion to further internalise environmental externalities, at least where there is a defensible business case. The business judgement rule leverages this discretion. In some jurisdictions, as shown in this book, the internalisation of environmental externalities beyond the business case is permitted or – exceptionally – mandated.

---

[31] This is not only bad social science; it also carries the seeds of eventual catastrophe. For once every relationship is monetised into a 'nexus of contracts', people indeed do optimise and game the system, see P. Cornelius and B. Kogut, 'Introduction', in P. Cornelius and B. Kogut (eds.), *Corporate Governance and Capital Flows in a Global Economy* (Oxford University Press, 2003), 21.

[32] See Chapter 7 by Liao in this book.   [33] See Chapter 6 by Richardson in this book.

According to Blanaid Clarke, this potential for environmentally sustainable companies is strengthened through the possibilities provided by the rise of non-executive and independent board directors, on whom corporate governance codes bestow a role, both in strategic decision-making and in monitoring management, which includes monitoring compliance with environmental regulations and the management of environmental risks. Although the promotion of independent/non-executive directors springs out of debate focused on enhancing shareholders' interests, they could nevertheless play a valuable role in ensuring that companies adopt high environmental standards.

Given that the IPCC already in 2007 stated that there is enormous potential for reducing GHG emissions with existing technologies, and that company law to a large extent allows for environmentally responsibly practices, why then do companies often fail to realise this potential? Why do boards rarely mandate the environmentally friendly, low-carbon option where there is an arguable business case, let alone push the outer boundaries of corporate governance rules by pursuing sustainability where the legal risks of being challenged are probably remote? As Chapter 3 by Sjåfjell and others shows, the social norm of shareholder primacy is a formidable barrier. While no company law system requires boards to maximise returns to shareholders at all costs, the social norm of shareholder primacy provides incentives and pressures to do so. This norm springs from the historically contingent focus of company law on the position of shareholders (albeit one that varies across jurisdictions). Shareholder primacy has been allowed to develop because the law contains neither an explicit statement of what the societal purpose of companies is, nor of what the interests of the company are. Company law provides shareholders with tools for monitoring and sanctioning boards, which entails that boards may promote what they believe is the shareholder interest for fear of being replaced (as is generally within the competence of the annual general meeting to do without cause) or because they themselves believe that focusing on (short-term) returns for shareholders is their legal duty. Shareholder rights, which the corporate governance movement has worked hard to strengthen, tend to perpetuate the misconception that companies are vehicles for the maximisation of returns to shareholders only, and that the duty of the boards is to ensure this maximisation. In the context of corporate groups, shareholder primacy is even more prominent, with the parent company's tight control of the group in practice perversely matched by limited legal possibilities for holding the parent company liable for subsidiaries' environmental transgressions.

Shareholders, including parent companies in corporate groups, *could* use their power and influence to demand a shift towards more ethical and socially responsible business. Many jurisdictions give broad powers to the participants in the company's annual general meeting that could facilitate this shift. However, as Richardson has shown in Chapter 6, SRI in the absence of legal reforms is likely to remain a small, niche sector of the financial economy, unable to greatly influence the environmental practices of companies. Conversely, the general influence of shareholders tends to be an uncritical push to maximise returns for themselves.

Although company law does erect some barriers to the pursuit of sustainability, these are modest compared to the impact of the social norm of shareholder primacy and the market system that nurtures it and associated pressures to externalise environmental harm. The fact that non-listed public companies as well as private companies are often similarly beholden to the competitive market pressures that precipitate environmental costs should remind us that there are broader structural barriers within the market economy to be reckoned with beyond the institutional and legal structure of public, and especially public listed, companies that are the focus of this book. Combating this powerful norm with its economic incentives and support in the market economies is crucial, and will require an equally powerful transition in the reform of company law and other legal arrangements for private enterprise. An important factor to consider in future reform work is the wide-ranging spectrum from, at the one end, the gigantic listed public companies and the multinational corporate groups they are involved in, to, at the opposite end, the smallest private companies consisting perhaps of only one person as shareholder, director, and only employee.

We have found some glimmers of hope and positive tendencies in some jurisdictions. The bastion of shareholder primacy, the UK, expressly included in its Companies Act 2006 the impact on the environment in its list of issues the board of directors should consider. However, as the UK expressly subordinates all other interests to that of the shareholders, this reform has not been the breakthrough that some scholars hoped. While the shareholder primacy drive is strong and influences legal scholars and law-makers in traditionally pluralistic countries, there are some places, like the Netherlands, that stand firm in their insistence that companies have a broader societal purpose. And in some common law jurisdictions such as Canada and India, we see a broadening of the scope of interests that the board should consider through case law or legislative reform, respectively. Some of the most interesting developments are in emerging

THE FUTURE OF COMPANY LAW AND SUSTAINABILITY   321

economies, where, in addition to India, for example, Indonesia, China, Turkey, South Africa, and Albania show tentative, promising tendencies towards internalising environmental (and social) externalities.[34] There are also positive international developments. The EU's new non-financial reporting requirements are seen as a step forward by many, while CSR reporting is becoming a trend among national legislators (as a way to show that they take environmental and social issues seriously) and among companies (as a way to at least be perceived as meeting societal expectations), who also increasingly pledge to voluntary sustainability reporting codes.[35] Particularly interesting is South Africa's integrated reporting system and Australia's internalising of the objectives of more comprehensive reporting into company law itself rather than relying on external legislation.

With regard to corporate reporting, Charlotte Villiers and Jukka Mähönen have shown in Chapter 5 that accounting techniques for so-called non-financial issues are still at an early and rather primitive developmental stage and that further enunciation of the responsibilities of accountants and auditors and their professional bodies nationally and internationally is very important. Much CSR reporting remains left to voluntary and discretionary measures, leading to risks of corporate capture, lack of comparability, and lack of consistency and uncertainty in benchmarking. Proper environmental reporting should be an indelible part of any new accountability regime. Reporting requirements could offer possibilities also in their own right in the sense that if accounting is revolutionised, this could in itself lead to an internalisation of externalities. However, that would require a fundamentally different approach than that illustrated by the much-lauded non-financial reporting requirements recently adopted in the EU. The EU reform does not cover large, non-listed firms at all, only public-interest entities (listed companies, including banks and insurance companies) with more than 500 employees are subject to the reporting rules. The concentration on listed companies creates a new incentive to delist in order to avoid the new reporting requirements. And the EU reform lacks mechanisms to provide effective compliance and enforcement. As the reported information is expected to be included in the management report rather than the financial

---

[34] See Sjåfjell, et al., Chapter 3 in this book.

[35] See Chapter 5 by Villiers and Mähönen in this book, and C. Villiers, 'Integrated reporting for sustainable companies: what to encourage and what to avoid' (2014) 11 *European Company Law* 117, where Villiers warns against the capture by market actors and urges greater involvement of NGOs and civil society in the development of integrated reporting standards.

report, it may fail to be audited unless an implementing state decides otherwise. The resulting discretion given to corporate management leads to greater reliance on unreliable market-based pressures to discipline firms.[36]

Steadily gaining academic and policy-makers' interest are the alternative business models discussed in Chapter 7 by Carol Liao. As she explains, entrenched ideological beliefs and path dependence make it difficult to uproot the established power structures, and these alternative models will most likely remain a niche sector of the market for the foreseeable future. Cooperatives, B Corporations, corporate hybrids, and related alternative business models are interesting developments that she believes have the potential to contribute as a bottom-up trend in the transition towards greater sustainable development. However, they are insufficient today to change the practices of the mainstream for-profit corporations or to engender more widespread reform of their legal infrastructure. Some of the innovative solutions of these new initiatives, such as tying the payment of dividends to non-financial performance, could serve as inspiration for how the legal infrastructure for the dominant company model could be transformed. On the other hand, the success of corporate hybrids may foster a 'ghetto' sector of socially responsible businesses that deflects attention away from the need to rehabilitate mainstream business.

In summary, the positive tendencies that we have identified are largely incremental and insufficient to foster comprehensive and urgent transition towards sustainable prosperity. All these glimmers of hope tend to be negated by the hegemony of the shareholder primacy norm as an integral part of an economic system geared towards infinite growth. The positive tendencies bring with them their own danger as well. If these are seen as sufficient steps forward, they may serve to take the pressure off legislators to undertake proper reform, due to the misconception that progress is being made in terms of internalising externalities in business decision-making, when the truth seems to be that nothing has changed at all – at least not for the better. We are still seeing business as usual – or, with the current financial unrest following the financial crisis of 2008,

---

[36] Such as the international integrated reporting initiative (www.theiirc.org) and the reporting and CSR standards advocated by Ceres, in collaboration with BlackRock and other major institutional investors, to engage global stock exchanges on a possible uniform reporting standard for sustainability reporting by all exchange members. See further: www.ceres.org/press/press-releases/world2019s-largest-investors-launch-effort-to-engage-global-stock-exchanges-on-sustainability-reporting-standard-for-companies.

THE FUTURE OF COMPANY LAW AND SUSTAINABILITY   323

desperate attempts to keep business going as usual.[37] But the status quo is not and cannot be an alternative for humanity desiring to ensure viable ecosystems for future generations.[38] More ambitious reforms may, as Benjamin Richardson writes in Chapter 6 about financial institutions, seem impossible, but with a looming planetary environmental crisis, more radical and bitter alternatives may one day be contemplated if the necessary transition is not achieved now. Legal reform is a necessary, albeit not sufficient, prerequisite for a transition to truly sustainable societies.

3 The *lex ferenda* of sustainable companies

The reopening of the debate on the purpose of the company and a new questioning of conventional wisdom give hope for a better era.[39] Even within the current legal regime, some progress could be possible merely through proper enforcement, which is often lacking when it comes to violations of environmental law generally,[40] and in the business law context the environmental reporting requirements for companies are similarly often haphazardly or perfunctorily implemented.[41] While the current regime has limitations regardless, this also serves as a reminder that jurisdictions that favour a new legal infrastructure for business would need to ensure that enforcement mechanisms are in place and properly deployed,

---

[37] M. Wolf, 'Britain must escape its longest depression', *Financial Times*, 1 September 2011, available at: www.ft.com/.

[38] '[A]n acceptable environment is not the product of social development, but a prerequisite for it to exist, and is a right bound up with human life, without which there is neither mankind nor society nor law': Case C-176/03, *Comm'n v. Council*, 2005 E.C.R. I-7879, I-7896 n.51 (citing D.L. Rota, 'Los derechos al Medio Ambiente adecuado y a su protección' (1999) 3 *Revista Electrónica de Derecho Ambiental* 87.

[39] For example, G. Serafeim, *The Role of the Corporation in Society: An Alternative View and Opportunities for Future Research*, Working Paper 14–110, (Harvard Business School, 2013).

[40] See e.g. the Commission Staff Working Paper on the Implementation and Enforcement of Community Environmental Law. Despite increasing EU incentives on regulating CSR matters as environment and human rights, the implementation and enforcement of these laws are lagging. Indeed, there is a greater lack of implementation and enforcement of EU environmental requirements than of any other area of EU regulation, see Commission Staff Working Paper, *Sixth and Seventh Annual Survey on the Implementation and Enforcement of Community Environmental Law* (August 2005 and September 2006), available at: http://ec.europa.eu/environment/legal/law/implementation.htm.

[41] See further, Chapter 5 by Villiers and Mähönen in this book.

otherwise the new legal edifice could become just the emperor's new clothes.

In these closing sections of this book, we canvass the reform ideas springing out of or related to the Sustainable Companies Project, indicating the potential for law to stimulate environmentally sustainable companies. The menu of desirable reforms to corporate law and associated areas of business governance is conceivably vast, and a fulsome discussion of them would necessitate a separate, lengthy treatise. Already, the contributors to this volume have canvassed a variety of ideas and proposals for furthering sustainable companies. The following discussion only samples a few particularly salient components of our reform agenda.

Research shows that the main company law barrier to sustainable companies, the shareholder primacy norm, has been allowed to flourish because the law has not specified what the societal purpose of companies is, thus leaving a vacuum that has been filled with this social norm. This also indicates a way forward. A reform that clearly spells out the societal purpose in a principle-based manner could dramatically enable forward-looking sustainable business. The following sections outline two, not mutually exclusive, options for such a reform: a duty on key corporate decision-makers to manage their business for the long term, thereby incorporating the core temporal dimension of sustainability; and a duty of environmental care, which focuses more explicitly on environmental performance.

3.1 Acting for the long term

We need to get corporations and other economic actors to think and act for the *long term*. Sustainability is a temporal concept that seeks to guide humankind towards a new time frame for decision-making that moves us from the frenzied, myopic, and standardised industrial clock time of capitalism to a patient, slower, and extended time horizon that dovetails with nature's rhythms. Because ecological systems function over indefinite time horizons, valuing the future is essential for sustainable companies. We need to modernise corporate and business laws to reflect this temporal orientation, as the basis for sustainable enterprise.

The prevailing ethos of shareholder primacy takes its cues from the market where the destructive pressure to focus excessively on the short-term return is so potent. Conventional 'wisdom' has egregiously herded business managers and investors towards a limited range of unimaginative practices, which become shielded from challenge by legal concepts

THE FUTURE OF COMPANY LAW AND SUSTAINABILITY   325

such as the business judgement rule (for company managers) or fiduciary responsibility (for investment fund trustees) that give decision-makers considerable latitude. The fetishistic focus on short-term business performance may involve inflating current profits at the expense of the long-term health of a firm, for example, by buying assets with concealed risks or borrowing excessive debt to deceptively boost short-term profits.[42] Consequently, market prices may fail to reflect the enduring value of companies' (un)sustainability performance. One disturbing indicator of the excessive short-termism is the soaring turnover of corporate securities. The average holding period for shares listed on the New York Stock Exchange plunged from about seven years in the 1940s to just over five years in 1970 and down to six months in 2009.[43] The average holding period for UK corporate shares has reportedly dropped from five years in the mid-1960s to 7.5 months in 2007.[44] When shareholders thus have such a fleeting commitment to their companies, it encourages those who manage them to likewise focus on near-term market performance.

The extreme fixation on short-term performance is not only environmentally reckless; it also can precipitate great economic distress, as epitomised by the Global Financial Crisis (GFC) in 2008. A study by the CFA Centre for Financial Market Integrity and Business Roundtable Institute for Corporate Ethics concluded, 'The obsession with short-term results by investors, asset management firms, and corporate managers collectively leads to the unintended consequences of destroying long-term value, decreasing market efficiency, reducing investment returns, and impeding efforts to strengthen corporate governance.'[45] The 2012 *Kay Review of UK Equity Markets and Long-Term Decision-Making*, a study commissioned as part of the UK's evaluation of the governance failures that contributed to the GFC, found the problems of short-termism rooted in:

> [a] tendency to under-invest, whether in physical assets or in intangibles such as product development, employee skills and reputation with customers, and . . . hyperactive behaviour by executives whose corporate strategy focuses on restructuring, financial re-engineering or mergers and

---

[42] L.L. Dallas, 'Short-termism, the financial crisis, and corporate governance', (2012) 37(2) *Journal of Corporation Law* 266, at 267.

[43] H. Blodget, 'You're an investor? How quaint', *Business Insider*, 8 August 2009, available at: www.businessinsider.com/henry-blodget-youre-an-investor-how-quaint-2009-8.

[44] A. Haldane, 'Patience and finance', *Oxford China Business Forum*, September (2010), 6.

[45] CFA Centre for Financial Market Integrity and Business Roundtable Institute for Corporate Ethics, *Breaking the Short-Term Cycle* (CFA, 2006), 1.

326 BEATE SJÅFJELL AND BENJAMIN J. RICHARDSON

acquisitions at the expense of developing the fundamental operational capabilities of the business.[46]

Such myopic corporate behaviours, found the Kay Report, 'have been supported or even encouraged by a majority of the company's shareholders'.[47] Any shareholder dissatisfaction in corporate performance is usually addressed by exit (selling shares) rather than voice (exchanging views with the company).

Encouragingly, some more enlightened thinking is gradually percolating into some business circles, at least in espoused rhetoric.[48] The World Economic Forum has cautioned that economic activity 'requires an orientation towards strategies that optimize long-term returns, both because this delivers better financial returns over the time profile that interests intended beneficiaries, and because over these periods social and environmental issues become more material and so can be better considered'.[49] Interestingly, Andrew Haldane, Executive Director of the Bank of England, in 2010 recommended robust public policy intervention 'to provide incentives for longer-duration asset holdings'.[50] This message has also been picked up increasing by some institutional funds interested in SRI, as evident in the UK-based Marathon Club,[51] formed in 2004 by a cohort of pension funds to draft practical guidance for trustees on long-term investment management, and the Long-Term Investors Club, established in 2008 by the French state-owned bank Caisse des Dépôts et Consignations.[52] The hope that institutional shareholders will become more active in promoting social and environmental goals also informs the EU Commission's reform package of April 2014, including a proposal to reform the Shareholder Rights' Directive with the explicit aim of encouraging especially institutional shareholders to have more long-term and transparent strategies.[53]

---

[46] J. Kay, *Kay Review of UK Equity Markets and Long-Term Decision-Making* (Department of Business Innovation and Skills, 2012), 10.

[47] Kay, *Kay Review*, 21.

[48] N. Grossman, 'Turning a short-term fling into a long-term commitment: board duties in a new era' (2010) 43 *University of Michigan Journal of Law Reform* 905.

[49] World Economic Forum (WEF), *Mainstreaming Responsible Investment* (WEF and AccountAbility, 2005), 10.

[50] Haldane, 'Patience and finance', 22.

[51] See www.uss.co.uk/UssInvestments/Responsibleinvestment/marathonclub/.

[52] See www.ltic.org.

[53] European Commission, *Proposal for a Directive Amending Directive 2007/36/EC as Regards the Encouragement of Long-Term Shareholder Engagement and Directive 2013/34/EU as*

THE FUTURE OF COMPANY LAW AND SUSTAINABILITY 327

A more visionary path to disseminate such thinking across the business world would be to enshrine an explicit legal duty on corporate managers and boards, as well as the custodians of funds that invest in these companies, to undertake *long-term stewardship* of their business in a manner that respects the environmental conditions for economic prosperity. Such a duty could also be imposed directly on companies, banks and other legal entities, to reinforce the responsibility of those who manage them, as well as to provide deeper financial pockets to meet any liability claims for derelict behaviour. A new legislated benchmark of business success would affirm the long-term, inter-generational dimension and impact of business activity. A duty to act for the long term would go beyond current permissive approaches, such as the scope of action company law gives corporate boards today or that encompassed by the introduction of corporate hybrids.[54] Both regimes problematically leave room for business laggards. Such an obligation could develop into a new fundamental business norm internalised in the organisational culture of corporations.

A workable legal duty would require providing some parameters to such a potentially expansive temporal concept, and meaningful sanctions for any transgressions. Defining 'long term' as encompassing time ad infinitum does not appear to create a workable and accountable legal standard. Conceptions of inter-generational equity found in modern environmental law and policy typically have an upper limit of approximately 50 years, such as the long-term carbon emission targets adopted by some countries.[55] In recent US climate change litigation of *Massachusetts v. EPA*,[56] the Supreme Court considered future harm that the state would experience through to the year 2100.[57] Definitions of 'long term' or 'future generations' thus raise the intangible issues found in the debates about sustainability, whose analysis depends heavily on the specific context. Whether a company is in fact successfully managed for such a time-frame might be known only with the benefit of hindsight, many decades from now, at which point any legal remedy offered might be redundant.

Regards Certain Elements of the Corporate Governance Statement, COM(2014) 213 final, 9 April 2014.

[54] See Chapter 7 by Liao in this book.

[55] The UK's Climate Change Act of 2007 has a goal of an 80 per cent reduction in GHGs from 1990 emissions by the year 2050.

[56] (2007) 549 US 497, 127 S. Ct. 1438.

[57] B.C. Mank, 'Standing and future generations: does *Massachusetts v. EPA* open standing for generations to come?' (2009) 34 *Columbia Journal of Environmental Law* 102.

Therefore, a workable duty of long-term investing would need to be embellished with prophylactic rules that set performance standards for business managers today. Markets have yet to devise incentives to overcome the mismatch between the long-term horizons over which environmental issues such as climate change become financially material and the short-term performance benchmarks against which investment and corporate managers measure success. A range of collateral measures therefore would need to be adopted. An excise tax on securities transactions and modification of capital gains tax rules, for instance, could help incentivise lasting performance. Short-termism might also be combated by restructuring the exercise of voting rights of investors, which are sometimes used to pressure firms to engage in expedient decisions. Company law could reward patient shareholders with weighted voting rights, while excluding from voting the shares acquired through opportunistic borrowing or equity swaps. Such reform would need to be designed cautiously to avoid the entrenchment of reactionary shareholders and the posing of barriers to progressive new investors with environmental business reform agendas.

To address informational deficits or deficiencies that foster short-termism, such as lack of knowledge about climate change risks in a business practice, a reassessment of financial reporting obligations would be necessary to mitigate the myopic culture of business and reorient companies to long-term value. Companies and financial institutions should be required to report periodically on their progress in acting for the long term. This should include environmental impacts and performance, including active steps to reduce the risk of harm. Properly enforced, such information requirements could have the potential of not only helping regulators to supervise compliance; it could enable more informed dialogue on sustainability within companies and between companies and their stakeholders. This approach could involve conducting environmental risk and impact studies, and incorporating such information into business models and company plans. Decision-makers violating such legal process standards would then be subject to remedies available to aggrieved persons, such as specific performance, monetary damages, and injunctions.[58] Because beneficiaries such as shareholders may be unwilling to sue for breach of such obligations if their company or fund is

---

[58] G. Moffat, G. Bean, and J. Dewar, *Trusts Law: Text and Materials* (Cambridge University Press, 2005), Chapter 14.

THE FUTURE OF COMPANY LAW AND SUSTAINABILITY 329

presently prosperous, state regulators and even NGOs could concurrently be empowered to act as compliance watchdogs.

3.2 Caring for the environment

A related option for inculcating a new business culture to act for the long term would be to impose on companies and their managers a cognate duty of environmental care. Whereas an obligation of long-term stewardship of business implies a duty to consider the environmental preconditions to such long-term performance, it still risks being viewed as focusing on the *company's* long-term fortunes. It might be difficult to ensure accountability directly to the environment and its stakeholders if managers, in their legally shielded 'business judgement', decide to ignore these interests.

Such a proposed duty builds on the ancient ethical norm of nonmaleficence – the obligation to avoid harm to others. Extension of this basic duty of care to require every person to mitigate their risks to the environment and take all reasonable steps and practical measures to prevent foreseeable harm to it has been accomplished statutorily in several jurisdictions.[59] The approach is inspired by the common law tort of negligence, encapsulating the ethical responsibility of every person to take reasonable and practical measures in their activities to avoid foreseeable harm to another person or their property.[60] The common law doctrine, however, has several attributes that render it somewhat unsuitable in its current formula to reorient companies towards sustainability, as evident in recent attempts in the USA to impose tortious liability on power companies for climate change damage.[61] These deficiencies include that the duty of care aims to correct negligent conduct that harms private interests, such as property or personal health (the natural environment and the interests of posterity in its protection are addressed only indirectly). Causation of environmental impacts stemming from numerous business and other sources over long periods is also hard to prove. And enforcement through courts carries onerous transaction costs, which may deter plaintiffs.

---

[59] M. Shepheard and P. Martin, 'The political discourse of land stewardship reframed as a statutory duty', in B. Jessup and K. Rubenstein (eds.), *Environmental Discourses in Public and International Law* (Cambridge University Press, 2012), 71.

[60] *Donoghue v. Stevenson*, [1932] AC 562, at 580.

[61] See J. Salzman and D. Hunter, 'Negligence in the air: the duty of care in climate change litigation' (2007) 156 *University of Pennsylvania Law Review* 101; J. Lin, 'Climate change and the courts' (2012) 32(1) *Legal Studies* 35.

330   BEATE SJÅFJELL AND BENJAMIN J. RICHARDSON

Moreover, in civil law systems, such a judicial-based legal standard would be unorthodox.[62]

A duty of environmental care would therefore need a legislative basis within company law with provisions to ameliorate the above factors. It could be drafted in light of the experience of precedents adopted in several jurisdictions, albeit outside of business law. Examples include the UK's Environmental Protection Act of 1990, South Africa's National Environmental Management Act (NEMA) of 1998, and legislation adopted in several Australian state jurisdictions such as South Australia (1993), Queensland (1994), and Victoria (1994). To illustrate, under the South African law, 'Every person who causes, has caused or may cause significant pollution or degradation of the environment must take reasonable measures to prevent [it] or... minimise and rectify such pollution or degradation of the environment.'[63]

Embedding such a duty within the legal architecture of corporate governance is starting to gain scholarly attention.[64] Sjåfjell and Mähönen have tentatively indicated how this could be done, in their proposal to Nordic company law. Their proposal centres on the concept of 'planetary boundaries'[65] that should be included in the law, as a key concept in a redefined purpose of the company, setting out a framework within which value-creation can take place and profit be sought.[66] Although a concept foreign to company law, the 'planetary boundaries' norm builds on state-of-the-art science of the biosphere and our impacts on it.[67] If we are to achieve a safe operating space for humanity, we cannot

---

[62] About such an approach in a civil law country, see R. Cox, 'The liability of European states for climate change' (2014) 30(78) *Utrecht Journal of International and European Law* 125.

[63] NEMA, s. 28(1).

[64] D. Saxe, 'The fiduciary duty corporate directors to protect the environment for future generations' (1992) 1(3) *Environmental Values* 243; J. McConvill and M. Joy, 'The interaction of directors' duties and sustainable development in Australia: setting off on the uncharted road' (2003) 27(1) *Melbourne University Law Review* 116.

[65] See Rockström, *et al.*, 'Planetary boundaries: exploring the safe operating space for humanity'.

[66] See B. Sjåfjell and J. Mähönen, 'Upgrading the Nordic model for sustainable companies' (2014) 11(2) *European Company Law* 2, where they tentatively suggest the following wording: 'The purpose of a company is to create sustainable value through the balancing of the interests of its investors and other involved parties within the planetary boundaries.' Through the norm of 'sustainable value', these authors seek to codify the Nordic long-term perspective.

[67] Employed in practice, for example, in Sweden: B. Nykvist, *et al.*, *National Environmental Performance on Planetary Boundaries: A Study for the Swedish Environmental Protection Agency*, Report 6576 (Swedish Environmental Protection Agency, 2013).

THE FUTURE OF COMPANY LAW AND SUSTAINABILITY   331

continue with incremental improvements; neither can we focus on whichever environmental challenge garners the most attention at any given time.

Reforming company law to expressly set out the role and the duties of the board and senior managers consistent with this proposed redefined purpose of the company would expand the competence and the duty of these agents to pursue sustainable value within the non-negotiable planetary boundaries. Sjåfjell and Mähönen suggest that a specification of the redefined role of the board should be integrated into the description of the duties of the board as set out in the companies' statutes, to stipulate a clear duty to promote the purpose of the company.[68] The duty would clarify the business judgement rule, emphasising notably that the due care includes a duty to implement a life-cycle analysis of the business of the company and an integrated internal control and risk management system. This would contribute to establishing a duty of environmental care as a meta-duty, prevailing over any other corporate fiduciary or other responsibilities, and resonates with McConvill's and Joy's proposal for an 'environmental judgement rule'.[69] It would relieve corporate managers of liability under general law or statute for failure to promote the best financial interests of shareholders, if they make rational investment decisions to comply with the duty of environmental care.

This proposed legal duty is not so radical once we appreciate that there has never been a legal *carte blanche* for market participants to act outside the legal norms of a civilised society. To illustrate, if deforestation were illegal but still profitable for a business given the foreseeable legal penalties, corporate managers would clearly not be obliged to violate the environmental law to obtain the extra financial returns. Indeed, they would affirmatively violate one dimension of fiduciary accountability if they chose to act unlawfully.[70] The ultra vires doctrine, explains Greenfield, sets off illegal activities as 'beyond the power' of corporations.[71]

---

[68] Sjåfjell and Mähönen, 'Upgrading the Nordic model'. See also Clarke's Chapter 4 in this book on the role of independent, non-executive board members in promoting sustainable companies.

[69] McConvill and Joy, 'The interaction of directors' duties and sustainable development in Australia'.

[70] American Law Institute (ALI), *Principles of Corporate Governance: Analysis and Recommendations* (ALI, 1994), s. 2.01(B)(1) and s. 4.01.

[71] K. Greenfield, *The Failure of Corporate Law: Fundamental Flaws and Progressive Possibilities* (University of Chicago Press, 2007).

Sjåfjell and Mähönen's proposal arguably casts the duty as a positive one, akin to a duty to promote sustainable development, in contrast to a conceivably more narrowly framed duty to merely *avoid* environmental harm or material risks. A positive duty would obviously require a greater commitment by companies and their investors and be more legally challenging to enforce. An open-ended responsibility to 'promote sustainability' or 'respect planetary boundaries' could be too indeterminate and potentially usurped by discretionary interpretations to which managers and boards could not easily be held accountable. Indeed, Sjåfjell and Mähönen have carefully worded their proposal to state that value is to be created '*within* the planetary boundaries', to signal that these are non-negotiable boundaries, where the room for trade-offs is limited. As a matter of principle, there can be no trade-offs threatening the planetary boundaries that are essential for sustaining life, as opposed to balancing social and economic aspects.[72]

Conversely, such a duty might also be unworkable if it were rigidly prescriptive, absolute, and unconditional, as the parameters of sustainable development often depend heavily on local contexts and specific circumstances. Judicial case law would gradually help to 'settle' the law, but it would be unlikely to settle all situations and thus leave a penumbra of uncertainty outside the core examples.

Ex ante standards that can comprehensively determine the constituent elements of a duty to promote sustainability would therefore, at least in the initial stage, need to be supplemented through subsidiary regulations and administrative guidance. Sustainability performance indicators and CSR performance standards have already been designed, which could help inform this task.[73] Sjåfjell herself has suggested some ways to meet this challenge of operationalising the duty, recommending that the company board be responsible for ensuring that the company draws up a long-term, life-cycle-based business plan.[74] To use the typical manufacturing

---

[72] While recognising that the ultimate goal is to achieve not only a safe operating space for humanity, but also a safe and *just* space for humanity: Raworth, 'A safe and just space for humanity: can we live within the doughnut?'.

[73] J. Keeble, S. Topiol, and S. Berkeley, 'Using indicators to measure sustainability performance at a corporate and project level' (2003) 44(2–3) *Journal of Business Ethics* 149; H. Schäfer, *et al.*, *Who Is Who in Corporate Social Responsibility Rating? A Survey of Internationally Established Rating Systems that Measure Corporate Responsibility* (Bertelsmann Foundation, 2006); S. Fowler and C. Hope, 'A critical review of sustainable business indices and their impact' (2007) 76 *Journal of Business Ethics* 243.

[74] B. Sjåfjell, 'Corporate governance for sustainability: the necessary reform of EU company law', in B. Sjåfjell and A. Wiesbrock (eds.), *The Greening of European Business under EU Law* (Routledge, 2015), Chapter 6.

THE FUTURE OF COMPANY LAW AND SUSTAINABILITY   333

business as an example, the life-cycle analysis would bring a cradle-to-cradle perspective that spans the very design of new products, the choice of raw materials used, the production process, the marketing and selling of the products, the service offered during the lifetime of the product, and the final recycling or discharge of the product.[75]

As with the proposed duty of long-term business stewardship, the focus of the duty would have to be on compliance with subsidiary, pro-phylactic rules that require companies to adhere to specific procedures, including environmental assessment and reporting on the sustainability performance. To ensure that market forces support this reform rather than work against it, the corporate duty to draw up a long-term, life-cycle-based business plan should be included as a key concept in complementary reform of financial market law such as regulation of entry into the stock market for public companies and rules concerning bids for taking over control of listed companies.[76]

To facilitate both the internal operations of the board and the management and the public supervision of the duties of the company, including the board, we need – as has been repeatedly emphasised – better reporting requirements.[77] A general criticism against the preferred compromise solution of reporting requirements for encouraging companies to become responsible has been that it is reporting without a core duty to report on, combined with a lack of proper enforcement.[78] The proposal for a sustainability business plan requirement would bridge the gap between the internal decision-making in the company and reporting, in that it would stipulate a substantive duty for the board to discharge, and on which to report. This would give content to and make mandatory the recently adopted non-financial reporting requirements that the European Parliament adopted in April 2014 (where only a 'comply-or-explain' mode of compliance is required).[79] By requiring companies to report annually on

---

[75] See e.g. P. Dauvergne and J. Lister, *Eco-business: A Big-brand Takeover of Sustainability* (MIT Press, 2013); E. Maitre Ekern, 'Creating a coherent environmental protection in European Union law? An analysis of life cycle thinking in product regulation', in B. Sjåfjell and A. Wiesbrock (eds.), *The Greening of European Business* (Routledge, 2015), Chapter 8.

[76] Sjåfjell, 'Corporate governance for sustainability: the necessary reform of EU company law', s. 3.5.

[77] Y. Biondi, 'Accounting for corporate shareholding and beyond: implications for corporate governance and social responsibility'; and D. Monciardini, 'Accounting for sustainable companies: preliminary considerations on the forthcoming EU Directive' (2014) 11(2) *European Company Law* 121.

[78] Sjåfjell, 'Why law matters: corporate social irresponsibility and the futility of voluntary climate change mitigation'.

[79] See Chapter 5 by Villiers and Mähönen in this book.

the key performance indicators identified in the business plan, this would also make best practice mandatory. Financial reporting needs generally to take more seriously the environmental impacts of corporate activities,[80] and a proper periodic integrated annual reporting according to internationally recognised standards should be required.[81] All public reports should be properly audited (with assistance, if necessary, by external environmental verifiers) at least annually,[82] and a full environmental audit by accredited controllers might also be required.[83]

Enforcement through liability claims, which may be necessary to ensure proper compliance, gives rise to difficult issues here as it does in other contexts. Indeed, a narrower duty to avoid environmental harm would arguably be more difficult to enforce, because the harm is 'essentially aggregative: there is nothing intrinsically harmful to the environment or other people in burning fossil fuels; the harms depend on the joint effects of many people's action'.[84] Negative environmental duties require two elements to be present in order to function effectively: the individual entity's conduct is sufficient, without other entities' acts or involvement, to cause harm; and the harmful effects of an entity's behaviour generally manifest nearby and immediately. Only in limited circumstances, such as major infrastructure like a pipeline, power station, or dam, could we easily identify an individual corporate actor and proximate environmental consequences. Even relying on collective attribution of responsibility, as proposed by Teubner[85] – suggesting that liability could be assigned to a specific economic sector and then reassigned among its members in accordance with their economic significance, size, or other indicator – problems would remain in the context of corporate groups, international subsidiaries, the presence of institutional shareholders, and other permutations.

---

[80] R.J. Heffron, 'Energy subsidy reporting: its creation and enforcement through International Financial Reporting Standards (IFRS)' (2014) 11(2) *European Company Law* 133.

[81] C. Villiers, 'Integrated reporting for sustainable companies' (2014) 11(2) *European Company Law* 117.

[82] See A. Sonnerfeldt, 'Regulating third party assurance engagements on sustainability reports: insights from the Swedish case' (2014) 11(2) *European Company Law* 137.

[83] Sector guidelines as well as a revised and mandatory version of EMAS may be useful here, see C. Bradshaw, *Corporations, Responsibility and the Environment* (Hart Publishing, forthcoming).

[84] J. Lichtenberg, 'Duties, positive duties and the "new harms"' (2010) 20(3) *Ethics* 557.

[85] G. Teubner, 'The invisible cupola: from causal to collective attribution in environmental liability', in G. Teubner, L. Farmer, and D. Murphy (eds.), *Environmental Law and Ecological Responsibility: The Concept and Practice of Ecological Self-Organization* (John Wiley & Sons, Ltd, 1994), 17.

THE FUTURE OF COMPANY LAW AND SUSTAINABILITY   335

Liability for the proposed business plan requirement could arise for procedural failures, in addition to any specific environmental impacts that might flow from such failures. The statutory duty of care would arguably also need to be owed to the environment and community at large, so that anyone, including the government, would have standing to uphold it. Shareholders or bondholders in a company could not be relied on to undertake enforcement when their own financial interests might be at stake. Charity law offers a useful precedent here, in its guardianship duty of the state attorney-general to uphold the legal (philanthropic) responsibilities of the charity. Enforcement might involve issuance of an administrative order or notice for which non-compliance is a statutory offence.

The considerable challenges to operationalising effective duties of environmental care and long-term stewardship, whether they are framed as positive or negatives obligations, must also address how corporate compliance with traditional environmental regulation is taken into account. If a company were meeting regulators' expectations regarding pollution licensing, for example, what residue of legal responsibility would be left to meet under any additional environmental performance duties within corporate law?

A variety of considerations must be noted here. First, as explained in Chapter 1 of this book, existing environmental law has a rather mediocre record of success, partly because its structural placement outside of corporate governance undermines its efficacy when companies function under legal and market norms that can convey contrary signals to ignore environmental externalities. Such dichotomous messages from separate legal silos increase legal complexity, and perversely incentivise businesses to engage in 'creative compliance' in an effort to shirk responsibilities. Second, owing to deficiencies in the robustness or scope of environmental regulation, it cannot be deemed to fulfil all the environmental responsibilities of companies. Courts in a variety of jurisdictions have affirmed that environmental regulation itself does not necessarily exhaust the legal claims that may be brought against a business; for example, development permissions issued by authorities may not shield a defendant from a common law action in nuisance that affects a third party.[86] Third, environmental regulation cannot easily adjust quickly to new and dynamic circumstances such as emerging environmental risks associated with new

---

[86] From Canada, see *Portage La Prairie v. (B.C.) Pea Growers Ltd.* [1966] SCR 150; from the UK, *Wheeler v. Saunders*, [1994] EWCA Civ 32; from New Zealand, *Ports of Auckland v. Auckland City Council*, [2000] NZCA 190.

technologies, chemicals, or other sources of potential harm to nature. Thus, placing a general environmental duty on companies can motivate them to be responsive to such emerging and new risks and impacts before legislatures have time to intervene. Fourth, for businesses operating transnationally and in jurisdictions where local environmental laws are lax, the additional reforms proposed in this chapter would provide a legal safeguard.

In such circumstances, having a catch-all standard of environmental responsibility for companies can help close a variety of regulatory lacuna. Redefining the purpose of companies to accommodate long-term environmental stewardship would conceivably behove companies to go beyond the basic requirements of external regulation to apply the best available and feasible means to continually improve their environmental performance, both for their own long-term business success and also for the well-being of the biosphere and society that depend on it. A company would need on an ongoing basis to assess, report, and monitor its environmental performance, to consult with potentially affected stakeholders, and seek out technologies and methods to lower its burden on nature.

In designing such a company law reform, careful consideration would need to be made of the vast range of companies in term of size, capacity, and impact. The focus of this book is on the large, public companies, with emphasis on the listed companies, as they are especially dominant, perceived particularly difficult to regulate for national legislators because of their transnational nature, and because they notably are most affected by the social norm of shareholder primacy. This is not to ignore the fact that small and medium-sized enterprises (SMEs), many of which are non-listed, private companies, are the backbone of our economies.[87]

Company law reform would need to consider encompassing all types of companies, listed and non-listed, from the largest public companies to the smallest private companies. A reform proposal modulated on large companies cannot, however, be superimposed on SMEs without further analysis. On the other hand, exempting all non-listed companies, all private companies, or companies below a certain size would run the risk, first of all, of not covering enough of business and, second, of encouraging de-listing, re-registration (from public to private), and of exacerbating the

---

[87] Of all European businesses, 99 per cent are SMEs. Nine out of ten SMEs are micro-enterprises with less than 10 employees; the mainstays of Europe's economy are micro-firms, each providing work for two persons, on average: see http://ec.europa.eu/growth/smes/index_en.htm.

THE FUTURE OF COMPANY LAW AND SUSTAINABILITY 337

already problematic tendency of pulverisation of responsibility through the fragmentation of businesses into smaller enterprises. Also, while the difference between the largest public and the smallest private companies is vast, so is the difference between the smallest and the largest private companies, where the latter may have much more in common with the public companies. Nor must we ignore that many SMEs may be subsidiaries of larger companies or be a part of their supply chains.

Designed carefully, the proposal for integrating planetary boundaries into the corporate purpose and directors' duties, initially aimed at the largest, multinational enterprises, could easily encompass many SMEs while supporting the trend towards enabling regulation for small businesses. The requirement for drawing up a life-cycle-based business should contain exemptions for subsidiaries where the parent company had drawn up such a business plan for the group (as it is meant to), as well as for suppliers that are covered by the larger customer. For independent small companies, a simplified version could be envisaged. Interestingly, empirical studies indicate that managers of small companies are more concerned with sustaining their business and work places for their employees than growth.[88]

Reform would also need to consider other legal forms for business, including the alternative structures discussed by Liao, both as a source for inspiration (for example, tying dividend payments to non-financial performance) and to critically assess whether also the legal infrastructure of these forms require refinement.

4 Sustainable companies in sustainable societies

Clearly, the foregoing proposals are ambitious, and given the reticence of most governments worldwide to enact or enforce robust environmental law, we can similarly expect serious political obstacles to proposals to extend environmental responsibility into the nucleus of business decision-making. But Realpolitik must not be used to surrender to the status quo and stifle academic debate. Indeed, revolutionary societal shifts through law and the political process are not unprecedented. The historical record

---

[88] For example, M. Neville, 'The role of boards in small and medium sized firms' (2011) 11(5) *Corporate Governance* 527. Note that boards here seem to 'help' managers focus on growth, which indicates that a (simplified) duty also for boards of the smallest companies to envisage a long-term business plan for sustainable value creation would be helpful, both for businesses and to improve their environmental performance.

shows that some societies have occasionally dramatically shifted their moral sensibility, for example, through the abolition of slavery,[89] and, more recently, the rise of the animal welfare movement,[90] and the greatly improved status of women in many countries.[91]

What makes the environmental sustainability particularly challenging for humanity is that it requires profound changes in so many spheres of human endeavour. Business corporations are a significant part of this sphere, but the agenda for reform is much wider. The subject matter of this book must thus be placed in the broader academic and policy debates about sustainability that engage with a wider variety of social, economic, and political phenomena. Even in the world of business law, there is much more than just company law reform at stake; complementary reforms are necessary in a number of other areas of governance, including insolvency,[92] financial markets (especially for listed companies),[93] taxation, public procurement,[94] and market competition and state aid, including shifting financial subsidies from non-sustainable to sustainable industries.[95]

Thus, much further research is required both with regard to the ideas canvassed in this book and the host of collateral reforms needed for sustainable societies. Broader issues of capitalism, industrialisation, the consumption ethic, and the human condition need attention. Drawing on the insights of pioneering ecological economists, deep ecologists, and social economy theorists,[96] future research should situate the reform of companies and financial investors in the larger context that is required in

[89] S. Drescher, *Abolition: A History of Slavery and Anti-Slavery* (Cambridge University Press, 2009).

[90] K. Shevelow, *For the Love of Animals: The Rise of the Animal Protection Movement* (Henry Holt and Co., 2008).

[91] K.C. Berkeley, *The Women's Liberation Movement in America* (Greenwood Press, 1999).

[92] See J. Lou, 'Introducing environmental auditing at the closure of business in China' (2014) 11(2) *European Company Law* 125.

[93] See e.g. A.M. Halvorssen and C. Eldredge, 'Investing in sustainability: reform proposals for the ethics guidelines of the Norwegian sovereign wealth fund' (2014) 11(2) *European Company Law* 107.

[94] See A. Wiesbrock, 'An obligation for sustainable procurement? Gauging the potential impact of article 11 TFEU on public contracting in the EU' (2013) 2 *Legal Issues of Economic Integration* 105.

[95] For example, A. Wiesbrock, 'Sustainable state aid: a full environmental integration into state aid rules?' in B. Sjåfjell and A. Wiesbrock (eds.), *The Greening of European Business under EU Law* (Routledge, 2015), Chapter 5.

[96] Including contributions like J. Porrit, *Capitalism as if the World Matters* (Routledge, 2005) and T. Jackson, *Prosperity Without Growth*.

THE FUTURE OF COMPANY LAW AND SUSTAINABILITY   339

order to build a more socially compassionate and ecologically sustainable economy.

Future research should contribute to a new understanding of capitalism's successes and failures, both at the macro-economic level and at the micro-level, by focusing on the interactions and activities between two key groups of actors: market actors (companies, investors, and consumers) and social actors (e.g. community groups and social movements). Such an approach would open up a reimagining of the institutional structure and governance of our current market economies, and contribute to a new model of the 'social economy' that supports a climate-safe future and other dimensions of sustainability.[97] The potential for changes to the governance of the market should be considered that would take account of the interactions between companies, investors, consumers, and civil society actors. This could promote a shift towards a social economy by utilising existing creative potential within markets and civil society (e.g. voluntary codes, civil society networks, social investor groups) and facilitate a better basis for and responsiveness to regulatory intervention. A further necessary piece of the jigsaw puzzle of sustainability would be social mobilisation to influence high-level policy-makers and decision-makers and a shift in attitudes among social and economic actors, including consumers, entrepreneurs, and investors.

A number of promising initiatives and interesting tendencies in the recent questioning of conventional wisdom and a renewed discussion of age-old issues lend hope to the idea that underpins the Sustainable Companies Project and this book: fundamental change is possible. Not only do we see the continuation of academic initiatives such as Daly's *Steady State Economics*[98] and newer initiatives both specific to business law such as the Corporation 20/20[99] and broader such as the Sustainable Economy

---

[97] This may be said to be supported by the Lisbon reform of the EU Treaty, where the word 'social' was added to the 'market economy' that forms the basis for the collaboration between a majority of European states.

[98] H. Daly, *Steady-State Economics*, 2nd edn (Island Press, 1991); Center for Advancement of Steady State Economy, available at: http://steadystate.org. See also e.g. R. Dietz and D. O'Neill, *Enough Is Enough: Building a Sustainable Economy in a World of Finite Resources* (Berrett-Koehler, 2013).

[99] See www.corporation2020.org; see also e.g. B Team, available at: http://bteam.org/; the Globally Responsible Leadership Initiative's 50+20 project: Management Education for the World, www.grli.org/projects/50+20/; The Purpose of the Corporation Project, www.purposeofcorporation.org/cs.

Project,[100] the EU Commission has in 2014 notably adopted its own Circular Economy 'package' with the aim of establishing 'a common and coherent EU framework to promote the circular economy'.[101] Although the EU Commission does not yet seem to fully acknowledge the incompatibility of the goals to its Europe 2020 strategy of (infinite) growth and a 'smart, sustainable and inclusive economy',[102] the way the circular economy idea is gaining traction at the EU level inspires a belief that also high-level policy-makers may be starting to recognise that fundamental reform must take place. We owe it to our fellow human beings, now and future generations, and to the other life forms with which we share this planet, to continue the work of completing the programme of reform for sustainability.

[100] See www.the-sustainable-economy.org; see also the Circle Economy, http://www.circle-economy.com/.

[101] Communication from the Commission, 'Towards a circular economy: a zero waste programme for Europe', COM/2014/0398 final; available at: http://ec.europa.eu/environment/circular-economy.

[102] See http://ec.europa.eu/europe2020.

INDEX

AA 1000 AS standard, 207, 219–20
ACCA. *See* Association of Chartered
    Certified Accountants (ACCA)
Accelerating Social Impact CCC, 297,
    298–309
Accountability Organisation, 207
AccountAbility Principles Standard,
    218
Accountants for Sustainability, 214
accounting, 176
    Accounts Modernisation Directive,
        186–9
    as challenge to sustainability, 179–81
    contribution to sustainability, 181–3
    Generally Accepted Accounting
        Principles, 184–6
    International Financial Reporting
        Standards, 184–6
    negative role of accountants, 178–9
    positive role of accountants, 176–8
    regulation of, 183–4
    requirements and practices, 183–9
Accounting Standards Board (United
    Kingdom), 184, 193
Accounts Modernisation Directive,
    186–9, 190–1, 210, 222
Action 2020, 313
Action Plan on European Company
    Law and Corporate
    Governance, 52, 148, 152–3
agency theory, 83
agenda, 233
Agenda 21 action plan, 27, 212
Albania, 142, 321
Allen, William, 98
American Fund, 253
Amnesty International, 249

annual general meeting (AGM),
    202–3
anthropogenic collapse, 12
anti-globalism movement, 23
apartheid, 233
arbitrage pricing theory, 10
Argentina
    disclosure requirements on listed
        companies, 199
    duty of vigilance in, 117
    environmental management
        schemes, 204
    Equator Principles, 266
    shareholder value in, 97
Argentine Corporation Law, 200
Argentine Securities Exchange
    Commission, 199
Armour, John, 84
Association of Chartered Certified
    Accountants (ACCA), 62, 179,
    214
atmospheric carbon dioxide, 12
Auditing Directive of 2006, 207–8
Australia
    appointment and dismissal of board
        in, 128
    carbon emission trading, 269
    carbon tax, 312
    common law doctrine, 98
    directors' liability in, 116, 117
    disclosure requirements on listed
        companies, 198–9
    recipients of information, 202
    reporting requirements, 196, 321
    shareholder primacy in, 128
    soft disclosure in, 205
    statutory auditing in, 208

341

INDEX

Australia (*cont.*)
  transparency reforms in, 230
  two-tier board system in, 150
Australian and New Zealand Bank, 235, 247, 266
Australian Business Roundtable on Climate Change, 255
Australian Securities and Investments Commission (ASIC), 198–9
Austria, 48

B Corporation, 302–5. *See also* corporate hybrids
B Lab, 302–5
Baku–Tbilisi–Ceyhan pipeline, 266
Banca Etica, 240
bank assets, 6, 248
BankTrack, 266
Bebchuk, Lucian, 284
Belgium, 117
benefit corporations, 306–9. *See also* corporate hybrids
benefit enforcement proceeding, 307
biodiversity conservation, 18
biosphere, 7
Blueprint for Co-operative Decade, 289–309
Blumberg, Philip, 82, 137–8
board of directors, 148–74. *See also* companies; corporate boards
  appointing and dismissing, 128–30
  character, 172–3
  diversity in, 165–9
  duty/discretion to promote company interest, 97–112
    convergence, 110–12
    group interest, 107–10
    pluralist approach, 101–7
    shareholder value, 97–101
  independence of, 161–5
  knowledge of company, 169–72
  non-executive directors, role of, 153–61
  obstacles to, 148–74
  regulation of corporate boards, 150–3
  as shareholders' agents, 83

special interest directors, 170–2
women in, 166–7
BP Blackwater oil spill, 35
Brazil, 97, 116, 138, 142
British Columbia, 296
British Petroleum (BP), 164, 261
'business as usual', 79–80
business judgment rule, 112–20, 325
business managers, 5
business review, 191
Business Roundtable Institute for Corporate Ethics, 325

C3. *See* community contribution company (C3)
Cadbury, Adrian, 150
Cadbury Code, 150–1, 154, 161, 162, 172
Cadbury Committee, 161, 162
Cadbury PLC, 64
Caisse des Dépôts et Consignations, 326
California Public Employees Retirement System (CalPERS), 57, 250, 251, 270, 271
Calyon, 266
Canada
  common law, 100
  community contribution company (C3), 296–8
  disclosure requirements on listed companies, 197–8
  instructions to board in, 133
  mutual fund regulation in, 231
  shareholder primacy in, 320
  shareholder proposals in, 257
  socially responsible investments in, 239
  soft disclosure in, 205
  statutory auditing in, 208
Canada Pension Plan, 254
Canadian Business Corporations Act (CBCA), 257, 269
Canadian Securities Administrators, 197, 205
Cancer Stage of Capitalism (McCurtry), 6
cap-and-trade, 269

INDEX

343

capital
  cost, alteration of, 244–8
  social responsibility and, 9–10
capital asset pricing model, 10
capitalism, as challenge to
  sustainability, 179–81
Carbon Disclosure Project (CDP), 204,
  254, 261
carbon markets, 227
carbon tax, 269, 312
Cardozo, Benjamin, 110
CBCA. *See* Canadian Business
  Corporations Act (CBCA)
CDP. *See* Carbon Disclosure Project
  (CDP)
Ceres (Coalition for Environmentally
  Responsible Economies), 270–1
CERES Principles, 259
CFA Centre for Financial Market
  Integrity, 325
Chandler v. Cape plc, 140
charitable trusts, 299
chemical industry, 231
chief executive officers (CEO),
  compensation packages, 57–8
China, 321
  disclosure requirements on listed
    companies, 196
  global environmental burden and, 7
  group interest in, 108
  judicial liability approach in, 139
  publication of information in, 203
  shareholder value in, 97, 100
  soft disclosure in, 205
  sustainability, 36
Chinese Securities Law, 196
Circular Economy package, 340
Cisco Systems, 68
City Code of Takeovers and Mergers, 64
Clark, Gordon, 11
Clarke, Blanaid, 319
Climate Bonds Standards and
  Certification Scheme, 242
climate change, 6, 25–6, 36, 72
climate risk, 247
Clorox, 68
Code of Best Practice, 150–1
codes of conduct, 258–72

Collevechio Declaration on Financial
  Institutions, 259, 262
command and control regulation, 15
Committee on Corporate Governance,
  151
Committee on the Financial Aspects of
  Corporate Governance (UK),
  150–1
common law, 329
  fiduciary duties and, 136–7
  monistic approach in, 98
  shareholder-centricity of, 124
communications practices, in
  environmental sustainability, 68
community contribution company
  (C3), 296–8. *See also* corporate
  hybrids
community interest company (CIC),
  293–5. *See also* corporate
  hybrids
  asset lock, 293–4
  dividend cap, 293–4
  qualifications for, 293
  regulation of, 294
  reporting requirements, 294
  statistics, 295
companies. *See also* board of directors
  'business as usual', 79–80
  constitution, 128
  corporate group and, 80–2
  interlinked issues of purpose and
    interests of, 88–90
  listing of shares, 81–2
  organising, 80–1
  purpose of, 90–4
  significance of, 79–88
  sustainable. *See* sustainable
    companies
Companies Act 2006 (United
  Kingdom), 59–62, 99–100, 115,
  133, 152, 160–1, 173, 190, 193,
  220, 282, 320
company interests
  board of directors and, 97–112
  conception of, 110
  convergence, 110–12
  group interest, 107–10
  pluralist approach, 101–7

INDEX

company interests (*cont.*)
  pluralistic approach to, 95–6
  shareholder value, 97–101
company law, 79–88
  barriers and possibilities in, 318–23
  'business as usual', 79–80
  business judgment rule, 112–20
  company and corporate group, 80–2
  corporate legal structure and, 80–1
  directors' liability, 112–20
  environmental care duty and, 330
  environmental performance and,
    86–8
  EU's sustainability policy and, 51
  fiduciary duties and, 136–7
  future of, 312–40
  group interest, 107–10
  lex ferenda of sustainable companies,
    323–37
  national law and, 86–8
  planetary boundaries and, 330–1
  pluralist, 101–7
  purpose of company and, 90–4
  reforming, 331
  reforms, 312–18
  shareholder control and, 143–4
  shareholder influence and, 133–5
  shareholder primacy and, 53–8,
    82–6, 120–5, 145–6
  shareholder value and, 59–64,
    97–101
  sources of, 86–8
  stakeholder interests and, 49
  sustainability and, 41, 316–17
  Sustainable Companies Project and,
    29
  trends, 146–7, 316–17
  unexplored potential in, 144–5
Company Law Review, 115
Company Law Review Steering
    Committee, 160
Company Law Steering Group, 61
compensation, for CEOs, 57–8
comply-or-explain principle, 151,
    152–3, 204
Conley, John, 263
constitution, 128–37
consumer expenditures, 5

Continental Europe, 47–53
control groups, 127
cooperatives, 287–8, 292
Core, Carol, 298
corporate boards. *See also* board of
    directors
  one-tier system, 150
  regulation of, 150–3
  two-tier system, 150
corporate constituency, 302
corporate engagement, 233, 248–58
  current engagement practices, 250–5
  legal milieu of, 256–8
  shift from exit to voice, 248–50
corporate enterprises, 54
corporate finance theory, 244
corporate governance, 45–7, 210,
    285–6, 317
  Code of Best Practice, 150–1
  Companies Act 2006 and, 59–62
  comply-or-explain principle, 151,
    152–3, 204
  debate, 27–8
  diversity of boards, 167
  Dutch, 50
  European Commission's policy on,
    51–2
  independence, 162, 163
  knowledge of company, 169
  main principle, 155
  non-executive directors, 157
  outsourcing to proxy advisors, 253
  political determinants, 285–6
  recommendations/guidance
    documents, 204
  regulation of corporate boards and,
    150–3
  shareholder involvement in, 134–5
  shareholder primacy and, 102,
    110–11, 121, 317
corporate governance code, 49, 210,
    257–8
  appointment/dismissal of board
    and, 129
  listing of stocks and, 81–2
  national, 257–8
Corporate Governance Green Paper,
    153, 157

INDEX

corporate groups, 80–2
  categories, 126–7
  components of, 82
  control groups, 127
  equity groups, 126
corporate hybrids, 275, 292
  B Corporation, 302–5
  benefit corporation, 306–9
  community contribution company, 296–8
  community interest company, 293–5
  corporate law and, 322
  low-profit limited liability company, 298–302
  in the United States, 297, 298–309
corporate law, 195–6. *See also* company law
corporate purpose, 45–7
corporate reform, 276–87
  ideological beliefs and, 277–84
  limitations to, 276–87
  path dependence and, 284–7
  protection of shareholder interests and, 279–81
  shareholder primacy and, 281–4
  shareholder wealth maximisation and, 277–9
corporate responsibility, 212, 213
corporate social responsibility (CSR)
  corporate governance and, 18, 45–7
  corporate purpose and, 45–7
  definition of, 148
  ethical model, 37, 41–7
  financial benefits of, 70
  importance of, 38–41
  institutional context and, 47–65
    shareholder primacy in USA, 53–8
    shareholder value in UK, 59–64
    stakeholder-oriented traditions in Europe, 47–53
  obligations, 39–40
  overview, 2–4
  philanthropic model, 44
  problem of time in, 65–6
  prospects for, 45–7
  reforms and, 315
  strategic, 37–8, 65–71

Sustainable Companies Project and, 27–8
  voluntariness in, 40–1
corporate veil piercing, 137
Corporation 20/20, 339
corporations
  aggregate theory of, 42
  citizenship of, 42
  obligations, 39–40
  regulation of, 36–7
  role in sustainability, 35–6
  stakeholder theory of, 42–3
Corporations Act, 256
Council of Institutional Investors, 254
CSR. *See* corporate social responsibility
Czech Republic, 48

Daly, Herman, 339
Danish Financial Statements Act, 195
Danish Financial Supervisory Authority, 195
Davies, Lord, 165, 166–7
debt financing, 247–8
decision-making, 25–6
Deepwater Horizon oil rig explosion, 164, 261
Delaware, 96
Delaware case law, business judgement rule, 114–15
Delaware company law, 54–5
Delaware Court of Chancery, 98
Delaware Supreme Court, 55
Denmark
  audit checks in, 206
  board election in, 48
  CSR reports in, 209
  disclosure requirements, 188
  environmental management schemes, 204
  EU Directives' requirements and, 216
  Financial Statements Act, 262
  group interest in, 108
  judicial liability approach in, 139
  pluralist approach in, 105–6
  publication of information in, 203
  reporting requirements, 194–5

346 INDEX

Department for Business, Innovation and Skills, 62
developed countries, environmental law in, 13–14
developing countries, 36
　disclosure requirements on listed companies, 199
direct liability schemes, 139, 141–2
directors' liability, 112–20
Dodd-Frank Wall Street Reform and Consumer Protection Act, 197
Dow Jones Sustainability Index, 245, 261
Dutch Corporate Governance Code, 50
duty of loyalty, 112

Earth Summit, 27, 28
eco-friendly products, 72–3
ecological crisis, 5–12
ecological modernisation, 22–3
economic agency theory, 83
economic decision-makers, 5
economic efficiency, 278–9
economic trends, 5–6
ECOSENSE, 205
EEA. *See* European Economic Area
efficient market hypothesis, 10, 121
EFTA. *See* European Free Trade Association
Ekobanken, 240
elasticity, 244–5
Elkington, John, 213
emerging economies, 7
Enbridge Northern Gateway Project, 251
English Law Commission, 232
enlightened shareholder value, 59–64, 95–6
enterprise corporatism, 283
environment, strategic CSR and, 67–9
environmental care, 329–37
　common law doctrine and, 329
　legislative basis for, 330
　liability claims, 334–5
　long-term stewardship and, 335–6
　planetary boundaries and, 330–1
　sustainability and, 332–3

Environmental Goals and Sustainable Prosperity Act (Nova Scotia), 21
environmental integration principle, 315
environmental judgement rule, 331
environmental law, 12–20. *See also* pollution
　anthropogenic collapse and, 12
　company compliance to, 318
　compliance, 86–8
　differences in design and impact, 13
　domestic laws, 36
　in dyadic state, 12–20
　effectiveness of, 15–16
　function of, 13
　inter-generational equity, 327
　mediocre record of success, 335
　negative factors undermining, 13–14
　outside the EU, 195–6
　reflexive law approaches, 16–18
　state and, 14–15
　statutory liability, 139
　sustainable companies and, 26, 337
　targets of, 14
　violations of, 323, 331
Environmental Protection Act of 199, 330
environmental sinks, 66
environmental, social and corporate governance (ESG), 267–8
environmental treaties, 18
Equator Principles, 235, 259, 263–7
Equator Principles Association, 264
equity financing, 247–8
equity groups, 126
Essay on Population (Malthus), 6
ethical CSR, 37, 41–7. *See also* corporate social responsibility (CSR); strategic CSR
　stakeholder interests and, 41–4
　standard objection to, 67
Ethical Funds, 270
ethical investing, 236
ethical investment, 233
EU Environmental Liability Directive, 141

INDEX

EU Market Abuse Regulations 2005, 192
EU Recommendation on Non Executive Directors, 152, 163
Europe 2020, 340
Europe, stakeholder-oriented traditions in, 47–53
European Commission
 Accounts Modernisation Directive, 187
 Action Plan, 148, 152–3
 Circular Economy package, 340
 policy on CSR/corporate governance, 51–2
 shareholder primacy and, 124–5
European Economic Area (EEA), 184
European Free Trade Association (EFTA), 187
European Union, 184
 Accounts Modernisation Directive, 186–9
 group interest in, 109–10
 Market Abuse Directive, 201
 New Accounting Directive, 197
 reporting requirements, 321–2
 sustainability, 20, 51
 treaty reforms, 314–15
 two-tier board system in, 150
evaluation, 210–22
Exxon Valdez, 35

factual groups, 127
Fédération des Experts Comptables Européens (FEE), 206–7, 215, 219
FedEx, 68
FEE. *See* Fédération des Experts Comptables Européens
Fidelity, 253
fiduciary duties, 59, 112, 116
 long-term investing and, 325
 for shareholders, 135–7
fiduciary law, 232
finance capitalism, 226–32
Financial Accounting Standards Board, 200
financial crises, 10

financial markets
 deregulation, 18
 socially responsible investing and, 226–58
financial reporting, 214
Financial Reporting Council (FRC), 151, 193, 220
Financial Reporting Review Panel, 220
Financial Services and Markets Act 2000 (UK), 270
Financial Services Authority, 256, 270
Financial Statements Act (Denmark), 262
Finland
 audit checks in, 206
 direct liability scheme in, 142
 directors' liability in, 116
 instructions to board in, 131
 reporting requirements, 106
 statutory auditing in, 207
 voluntary assurance in, 209
 women board directors in, 167
Finnish Accounting Board, 192–3
Fischel, Daniel, 278, 281, 282
Ford Motor Company, 69
for-profit corporations, limitations to reforming, 276–87
Forum for Sustainable and Responsible Investment (US-SIF), 239
Fossil Free, 246
fossil fuel industry, 243
foundations, 299
Fourth Directive, 186–7, 188, 206, 208
France
 directors' liability in, 116
 disclosure requirements, 188
 fiduciary duties in, 136
 Grenelle II Law, 202
 instructions to board in, 132
 reporting requirements, 107, 190
 Rozenblum doctrine, 109
 senior managers in, 48
 shareholder primacy in, 121
 two-tier board system in, 150
 women board directors in, 167
Freshfields Bruckhaus Deringer, 265, 266

348 INDEX

Friedman, Milton, 3, 40, 156
Frijns Code, 104
front-line companies, 14, 19
FTSE 100, 166–7
fund managers, 5

Generally Accepted Accounting
    Principles (GAAP), 183, 184–6
German Commercial Code, 189
German Corporate Governance Code,
    103
German Council for Sustainable
    Development, 49
German Stock Corporation Act
    (AktG), 192
German Sustainability Code, 21, 49, 50
Germany
    appointment and dismissal of board
        in, 129
    co-determination in, 48
    directors' liability in, 118
    disclosure requirements on listed
        companies, 192
    ECOSENSE, 205
    fiduciary duties in, 136
    group interest in, 108
    Hausbank phenomenon in, 255
    indirect liability schemes, 140
    instructions to board in, 131–2
    pluralist approach in, 102–3
    recipients of information, 202
    senior managers in, 48
    shareholder primacy in, 123–4,
        282
    statutory auditing in, 208–9
    two-tier board system in, 150
GFC. *See* global financial crisis
Ghana, 97, 133, 139, 201, 207
global economic crisis, 5–12
global financial crisis (GFC), 2, 227
    institutional investors and, 249
    risk-taking and, 9
    sustainability agenda and, 19
global financial economy, 6
Global Green New Deal, 19
Global Reporting Initiative (GRI), 50,
        184, 203, 214, 216–18, 219
Global South, 13–14, 23

Gordon, Jeffrey, 84
Gray, Rob, 211
Green movement, 274
Green Paper on EU Corporate
    Governance Network, 148
green products, 36, 72–3
Green Project Directive, 231
Greenbury, Richard, 151
greenhouse gases, 36, 72, 87, 176, 193,
        266, 313, 319
greenwashing, 41, 210, 274
Grenelle II Law, 190, 202
Grenelle II reforms, 107
GRI. *See* Global Reporting Initiative
    (GRI)
gross domestic product (GDP), 8
group interest, 107–10
Guidance on, 203
Gunns, 235

Haldane, Andrew, 326
Hampel, Ronald, 151
Hampel Report, 154
Hansmann, Henry, 83, 278, 281–2,
        286
Hapt, Klaus, 97
Hausbank phenomenon, 255
Hawken, Paul, 7
Heal, Geoffrey, 7
Hebb, Tessa, 11
hedge funds, 134–5
Hermes, 250
Heuschmid, Johannes, 99
Higgs, Derek, 151
Higgs Review, 162
High Level Group of Company Law
    Experts, 109
high sustainability group, 70
Hungary
    board election in, 48
    EU Directives' requirements and,
        216
    group interest in, 109
    reporting requirements, 188
    voluntary assurance in, 191, 209
hybrid car, 69
hybrids, 275, 292
    B Corporation, 302–5

INDEX   349

benefit corporation, 306–9
community contribution company, 296–8
community interest company, 293–5
corporate law and, 322
low-profit limited liability company, 298–302
in the United States, 297, 298–309

IAASB. *See* International Auditing and Assurance Standards Board
IASB. *See* International Accounting Standards Board
ICA. *See* International Cooperative Alliance
ICAEW. *See* Institute of Chartered Accountants in England and Wales
ICGN. *See* International Corporate Governance Network
Iesini v. Westrip Holdings, 62
IFAC. *See* International Federation of Accountants
IFC. *See* International Finance Corporation
IFRS. *See* International Financial Reporting Standards
IFRS Foundation, 184
IIRC. *See* International Integrated Reporting Council
index funds, 245
India, 7
  common law, 100, 320
  CSR reporting in, 204
  reporting requirements, 196
  veil piercing doctrine, 139
indigenous people, 24
indirect liability schemes, 139–41
Indonesia, 117, 321
informal channels, 133–5
insiders, 284
Institute of Chartered Accountants in England and Wales (ICAEW), 176–7, 179
institutional investors, 56–7
  activism of, 134–5
institutional shareholders, 126
intergenerational equity, 21

Intergovernmental Panel on Climate Change (IPCC), 313, 319
Internal Revenue System (IRS), 298
International Accounting Standards Board (IASB), 185
International Auditing and Assurance Standards Board (IAASB), 205, 207
International Cooperative Alliance (ICA), 287–92
International Corporate Governance Network (ICGN), 252, 254
International Federation of Accountants (IFAC), 205
International Finance Corporation (IFC), 263–4
International Financial Reporting Standards (IFRS), 183, 184–6, 215
International Integrated Reporting Council (IIRC), 185, 214
International Standards on Auditing (ISAs), 205, 207
International Standards on Review Engagements (ISREs), 206
international trade, 5
International Year of the Cooperatives, 288
intragenerational equity, 21, 24
investor activism, 252
investors
  institutional, 56–7
  social responsibility of, 9–10
  transient, 56
invisible hand, 277, 286
IPCC. *See* Intergovernmental Panel on Climate Change
Ireland, 116
  instructions to board in, 132
  reporting requirements, 192
Irish Stock Exchange Listing Rules, 192
ISAs. *See* International Standards on Auditing
ISO 26000 Guidance on Social Responsibility, 203
ISREs. *See* International Standards on Review Engagements
Italy, 109, 150

Index

Japan
  appointment and dismissal of board in, 129
  audit checks in, 206
  business judgment rule, 115
  CSR reporting in, 204
  pluralist approach, 102
  shareholder primacy in, 282
  specific legislation, 200
  voluntary assurance in, 209
Jensen, Michael, 278
Johnson & Johnson, 66–7
judicial liability, 139
juridification, 16

Kay Review of UK Equity Markets and Long-Term Decision-Making, 325
key performance indicators (KPIs), 212, 215
King Code III, 199, 202
Konzernrecht, 109, 138
KPIs. *See* key performance indicators
Kraakman, Reiner, 83, 278
Kraft Foods, 64

L3 C. *See* low-profit limited liability company
Lagarde, Christine, 166
Lang, Robert, 298
Latvia, 167
liability claims, 334–5
limited investor liability, 137–8
limited liability company, low-profit, 298–302
l'intérêt social, 107, 136
Lithuania, 97, 140
local GAAP, 183, 186
London Principles of Sustainable Finance, 262
London Stock Exchange, 151
Long-Term Investors Club, 326
long-term stewardship, 324–9, 334
low sustainability group, 70
low-profit limited liability company (L3 C), 298–302. *See also* corporate hybrids

Luxembourg, 48, 117

Macedonia, 190, 191, 194, 204, 207
Mähönen, Jukka, 106
majority shareholders, 128–37. *See also* shareholders
  appointing and dismissing board, 128–30
  categories of, 126
  control, 128–37
  influence through informal channels, 133–5
  instructions, 130–3
  power over company constitution, 128–37
Malthus, John, 6
Marathon Club, 326
Market Abuse Directive, 201
market governance, 234–9
market licence, 234
Maryland, 306, 307–8
Massachusetts v. EPA, 327
McCurtry, John, 6
microfinance, 227
Millennium Ecosystem Assessment, 7
minority shareholders, directors' liability and, 115
mission investment, 233
modern portfolio theory, 10
Monks, Robert, 11
mutual funds, 231, 248, 253, 271
mutual regulations, 16

National Association of Pension Funds, 254
National Environmental Management Act, 330
National Greenhouse and Energy Reporting Act (Australia), 199
National Instrument 51–102, 198
National Pollutant Inventory (Australia), 200
natural capitalism, 7
NEI Investments, 251, 270
Nestlé, 66
Netherlands, the
  board election in, 48

INDEX

corporate governance code, 50, 257
directors' liability in, 117
Green Project Directive, 231
group interest in, 109
pluralist approach, 104
shareholder primacy in, 121, 320
women board directors in, 167
New Accounting Directive, 187, 188,
   197–8, 223–4
New York Stock Exchange, 325
New Zealand, transparency reforms in,
   230
nexus of contracts theory, 84–5
Nichols, Christopher, 278
non-executive directors, 153–61
non-governmental organisations
   (NGOs), 24, 41, 255
nonmaleficence, 329
non-profit organisations, 299
nonshareholder constituency, 302
Nordic countries
   conception of company interests in,
      110
   fiduciary duties in, 136
   instructions to board in, 131
   national companies legislation, 92
   pluralist approach in, 105–7
   shareholder primacy in, 124
North Carolina, 299
Norway
   Accounting Act, 191
   appointment and dismissal of board
      in, 129
   enforcement mechanism in, 220
   EU Directives' requirements and,
      216
   group interest in, 108
   instructions to board in, 131
   judicial liability approach in, 139
   reporting requirements, 195
Norwegian Companies Act, 92
Norwegian Government Pension
   Fund – Global (NGPF-G), 254
Nova Scotia, 296

Occupy Movement, 23, 227, 286
OECD Guidelines for Multinational
   Enterprises, 51, 111, 317

oil sands, 243
one-tier board system, 150
Ontario Securities Act 1990, 198
operational practices, in environmental
   sustainability, 68
organisational shareholders, 126
Orts, Eric, 17
other constituency, 302
Oxfam, 230

parens patriae, 14
parent company, 126
   indirect liability of, 139–41
   limited liability of, 138
passive investors, 9, 228
path dependence, 284–7
Pennsylvania statute, 54
pension funds, 57, 122, 134, 230, 234,
   248
People & Planet v. HM Treasury, 62
Philanthropic Facilitation Act of 2011,
   301
planetary boundaries, 330–1
planning and organisational practices,
   in environmental sustainability,
   68
Plato, 172
PLRs. *See* private letter rulings
pluralism, 101–7
Poland, 101, 131
   shareholder value in, 97
'polluter pays' principle, 21
pollution, 39
   ecological modernisation and,
      22–3
   environmental law and, 13–14, 15
   environmental sinks for, 6
   transboundary, 18
population, 6
Porrit, Jonathon, 182
portfolio screening, 232–4
Portugal
   direct liability schemes, 141
   directors' liability in, 116
   group liability in, 138
   shareholder value in, 100
   two-tier board system in, 150
post-regulatory governance, 16

precautionary principle, 21
PRIs. *See* program-related investments
private equity funds, 248
private letter rulings (PLRs), 300
Procter & Gamble, 68
product design, 68
product disclosure statements, 198–9
program-related investments (PRIs),
   298, 299–300, 302
*Promoting a European Framework for
   Corporate Social Responsibility*,
   156
proposed Program-Related Investment
   Promotion Act of 2008, 300
proxy voting, 253
public interest directors, 170–2
Public-Interest Entities Auditing
   Regulation, 208
public sector funds, 254–5

Quakers, 233
Queensland, 330

Raworth, Kate, 313
Re Southern Counties Fresh Foods Ltd,
   62
Reflection Group on the Future of
   European Company Law, 109
reflexive law, 16–18, 183, 316
Regulation Fair Disclosure, 256
Regulation S-K, 197
regulatory capture, 285
*Renewed EU Strategy 2011–14 for
   Corporate Social Responsibility*,
   159
reporting requirements, 189, 192–5
   emerging themes in, 200–10
      auditing and assurance of reports,
         205–10
      issues covered, 201–2
      publication of information, 202–3
      recipients of information, 202
      soft measures, 203–5
   in EU and EEA Member States,
      189–95
      Accounts Modernisation
         Directive, 190–1
      primary legislation, 189–90

outside the EU, 195–200
   corporate law, 195–6
   environmental law, 195–6
   professional standards, principles
      and guidance, 200
   role of securities regulators,
      196–9
   specific legislation, 199–200
Republic, 172
Resource Management Act (New
   Zealand), 21
Responsible Care, 41
responsible investing, 212
Responsible Investment Association,
   269
responsive regulation, 16
*Revlon Inc. v. MacAndrews v. Forbes
   Holdings, Inc.*, 303, 307
Rio+ 20 Summit, 193
Risk Limitation Act of 2008
   (Germany), 257
Rivoli, Pietra, 245
Roe, Mark, 284
Rozenblum doctrine, 109
Ruggie Guiding Principles, 270
rules-driven path dependence, 284

Sakhalin-II oil and gas project, 266
Section 172 of Companies Act 2006
   (United Kingdom), 59–62,
   160–1, 173
Section 417 of Companies Act 2006
   (United Kingdom), 61, 193, 220
Securities and Exchange Commission
   (SEC), 196, 271
SEIA. *See* social and environmental
   impact assessment
self-organisation, 16
Seventh Directive, 187, 188
SHARE. *See* Shareholder Association of
   Research and Education
shareholder activism, 252
Shareholder Association of Research
   and Education (SHARE), 269
shareholder primacy, 79–147, 319
   vs. agency theory, 83–4
   business judgement rule and,
      112–20

INDEX

company interests and, 94
company law and, 79–88
continued dominance of, 120–5
conventional wisdom and, 82–6
directors' liability and, 112–20
methodology, 86–8
nexus of contracts theory, 84–5
social norm of, 95, 121–2, 145–6
sources of, 86–8
starting points, 86–8
in the United States, 53–8
Shareholder Rights' Directive, 326
shareholder value, 97–101
shareholders
  in benefit corporations, 307
  control, 143–4
  corporate social responsibility vs.
    interests of, 43–4
  fiduciary duties for, 135–7
  influence through informal
    channels, 133–5
  institutional, 56–7
  involvement in corporate
    governance, 134–5
  liabilities, 137–43
  majority, 126, 128–37
  power of, 126–47
  proxy votes, 230
  purpose of, 91
  as residual risk bearers, 84
  sanctions, 137–43
  in the United Kingdom, 59–64
  wealth maximisation, 277–9
shares, listing of, 81–2
short-termism, 71–3, 325–6
Sierra Club, 249
sin stocks, 233, 236
slave trade, 233
Slovenia
  auditing standards, 207
  board election in, 48
  directors' liability in, 116
  general meeting, 132
  group interest in, 109
  reporting requirements, 188
small and medium-sized enterprises
  (SMEs), 336–7
smart regulation, 16

Smith, Adam, 277
Social Accountability International,
  218
social accounting, alternate models of,
  221
social and environmental impact
  assessment (SEIA), 264, 265
social enterprise, 275
social entrepreneurs, 307
social investment, 233
Social Investment Organisation, 239,
  269
social investors, 245
social justice principle, 21, 24
social licence, 234
social returns, 236
social welfare, 83
socially responsible investing (SRI), 3,
  18, 232–4
  capital cost alteration and, 244–8
  corporate engagement and, 248–58
  financial markets and, 226–58
  financial rationale for, 239–44
  influences of, 236–7
  legal reforms, 269
  market size/value, 238–9
  as means of market governance,
    234–9
  methods, 233
  pioneers of, 233
  public policy, 269
  Sustainable Companies Project and,
    27–8
  terminology, 233
  voluntary codes of conduct, 258–72
societal awareness, 110–11
South Africa
  apartheid, 233
  business judgement rule, 115
  CSR reporting in, 321
  environmental law, 330
  King Code III, 199, 202
  voluntary assurance in, 209
South Australia, 330
Spain
  disclosure requirements, 188
  general meeting, 132
  liability of parent companies in, 141

354 INDEX

Spain (*cont.*)
  shareholder value in, 100
  Sustainable Economy Act, 192
  voluntary assurance in, 209
Spanish Company Capital Act, 190
special interest directors, 170–2
species extinction, 12, 25–6
SRI. *See* socially responsible investing
stakeholder theory, 280–1, 283
stakeholders, 24
  in continental Europe, 47–53
  definition of, 280
  ethical CSR and, 41–4
  financial returns for, 39
  interests, 41–4, 279–81
statutory auditing, 207–8
statutory liability, 139
Steady State Economy, 339
Stewardship Code, 134
Stock Corporation Act, 49, 103
stock index, 245
Strasser, Kurt, 137–8
strategic CSR, 37–8, 65–71. *See also*
    corporate social responsibility
    (CSR); ethical CSR
  benefits, 65–7
  business case for, 69–70
    limits of, 74–6
  environment and, 67–9
  high sustainability group, 70
  long-term perspective, 65–7
  low sustainability group, 70
  management's duty in, 66
  short-termism and, 71–3
strategic report, 191
strong sustainability, 213
structure-driven path dependence, 284
Study Group of Directors'
    Remuneration, 151
Sullivan Principles, 259
Superfund, 231, 271
suppliers, 91
sustainability, 1, 18, 20–6
  accounting as challenge to, 179–81
  accounting's contribution to, 181–3
  agendas, 20
  ambiguity/open-endedness of, 22

business case for, 69–70
  limits of, 74–6
capitalism as challenge to, 179–81
capitalism's contribution to, 181–3
challenges, 35–8
decision-making and, 25–6
definition of, 211–13
ecological modernisation and, 22–3
environmental governance/policy
    and, 21
environmental policy/law and, 20
future of, 312–40
key concepts, 212
policy principles, 21
reforms, 312–18
resistance to, 23
social justice and, 24
trends, 316–17
sustainability reporting
  alternate models of social
    accounting, 221
  audit/assurance, 219–20
  barriers/opportunities in, 211–22
  definition of sustainability, 213
  emphasis on financial reporting, 214
  enforcement and engagement, 220–1
  Global Reporting Initiative, 216–18
  lack of consistency, 214–16
sustainable companies, 23–4, 26,
    323–37. *See also* companies
  decision-making, 25–6
  lex ferenda of, 323–37
    acting for long term, 324–9
    environmental care, 329–37
  in sustainable societies, 337–40
Sustainable Companies Project, 26–30,
    183, 184, 188, 192, 318, 339
sustainable development. *See*
    sustainability
Sustainable Economy Act 2011 (Spain),
    192
sustainable finance, 233
Sweden, 167
  group interest in, 108
  reporting requirements, 189–90
  shareholder primacy in, 121
Switzerland, 116

INDEX

Taiwan, 97
Takeover Code, 64, 256
Takeovers Directive, 208
Tasmania, 266
Teubner, Gunther, 17, 334
Time/Warner case, 55
Toyota, 69
transient investors, 56
Treaty on the Functioning of the
    European Union (TFEU), 314
triple bottom line, 213
trust departments, 57
Turkey
    auditing standards, 207
    CSR reporting in, 321
    group interest in, 108
    group liability in, 138
    liability schemes in, 142
    reporting requirements, 191, 194
    shareholder value in, 97
two-tier board system, 150

UK Corporate Governance Code, 151
    diversity of boards, 167
    independence, 162, 163
    knowledge of company, 169
    main principle, 155
    non-executive directors, 157
UK Pensions Act 1996, 193
UK Social Investment Forum
    (UK-SIF), 270
ultra vires doctrine, 331
UN Guiding Principles on Business
    and Human Rights, 111
UNGC. *See* United Nations Global
    Compact
United Kingdom, 188
    community interest company, 293–5
    Companies Act 2006, 99–100
    corporate governance code, 257
    instructions to board in, 132–3
    senior managers in, 48
    shareholder primacy in, 121
    shareholder value in, 59–64
United Nations Environment
    Programme, 263
United Nations General Assembly, 288

United Nations Global Compact
    (UNGC), 4, 195, 209, 261
United Nations Guiding Principles on
    Business and Human Rights, 51
United Nations Norms on the
    Responsibilities of
    Transnational Corporations,
    19
United Nations Principles for
    Responsible Investment, 4, 195,
    209, 259, 262, 267–8
United States, 36, 98–9
    B Corporation, 302–5
    low-profit limited liability
    companies, 302
    mutual fund regulation in, 231
    shareholder primacy in, 53–8, 121
universal investors, 237, 249
universal owner, 237
Universities Superannuation Scheme
    (USS), 251
University of Oslo, 27
unseen polluters, 226–32
Unternehmensinteresse, 103, 123–4
Uruguay, 266
U.S. Supreme Court, 141
USS. *See* Universities Superannuation
    Scheme

Vanguard, 253
veil piercing, 137
Vermont, 298, 306, 308
Victoria, 330
virtue ethics, 172–3
voluntariness, 40–1
voluntary codes of conduct, 258–72
    Equator Principles, 263–7
    for systemic change, 258–63
    UN Principles for Responsible
    Investment, 263–7

Walker, David, 151
WBCSD. *See* World Business Council
    for Sustainable Development
weak sustainability, 213
wealth maximisation, 277–9
Wealth of Nations, The (Smith), 277

Werlauff, Erik, 105–6
Westpac, 247, 255, 269
Williams, Cynthia, 263
Winter, Jaap, 109
Wójcik, Dariusz, 11
Women on Boards (Davies), 165

World Bank, 263–4
World Business Council for Sustainable Development (WBCSD), 3, 313
World Economic Forum, 326

Yara International, 66

For EU product safety concerns, contact us at Calle de José Abascal, 56–1°,
28003 Madrid, Spain or eugpsr@cambridge.org.